THE NEW NATURALIST LIBRARY

A SURVEY OF BRITISH NATURAL HISTORY

BUMBLEBEES

The aim of this series is to interest the general reader in the wildlife
of Britain by recapturing the enquiring spirit of the old naturalists.
The editors believe that the natural pride of the British public
in the native flora, fauna and fungi, to which must be added
concern for their conservation, is best fostered
by maintaining a high standard of accuracy
combined with clarity of exposition
in presenting the results
of modern scientific
research.

THE NEW NATURALIST LIBRARY

BUMBLEBEES

THE NATURAL HISTORY & IDENTIFICATION OF THE SPECIES FOUND IN BRITAIN

TED BENTON

Collins

This edition published in 2006 by Collins,
an imprint of HarperCollins Publishers

HarperCollins Publishers
77–85 Fulham Palace Road
London w6 8jb

www.collins.co.uk

First published 2006

© Ted Benton, 2006

A cip catalogue record for this book is available
from the British Library

Set in ff Nexus by
Rowland Phototypesetting Ltd,
Bury St Edmunds, Suffolk

Printed in Singapore by Imago
Reprographics by Saxon Photolitho, Norwich

Hardback isbn 0 00 717450 0
Paperback isbn 0 00 717451 9

Contents

Editors' Preface

IN 1959 THE FIRST New Naturalist on bumblebees appeared. Written by John Free and Colin Butler, it was a godsend, giving us for the first time ready access to a group of insects of major importance both ecologically, as pollinators, and aesthetically, as contributors to the English summer scene. Since that beginning our understanding of bumblebee natural history has increased by leaps and bounds. Attracted by their ease of observation and their attractive appearance, many research workers in Europe and America have used bumblebees as models to help them explore ecological principles of more general application. Conservationists and commercial suppliers have examined the value of bumblebees as pollinators of wild flowers and crops, and explored ways of managing habitats to benefit them, and of rearing them in captivity. In this book Ted Benton draws on this treasure-trove of new information to present a comprehensive picture of the natural history of bumblebees, refreshed and illuminated by his background as a sociologist. He gives keys and descriptions of the British species, and highlights the diagnostic features and ecological idiosyncrasies of the different British species. We hope this book will enable many more people to embark on the study of bumblebee natural history, and, like its predecessor, will stimulate further advances in the subject.

Author's Foreword and Acknowledgements

THIS BOOK IS the outcome of over 20 years of field observation of bumblebees, but could not have been written without the help, support and inspiration of numerous friends, family and colleagues. My own passionate interest in natural history – and fascination with insects in particular – had its origins as far back into childhood as I can remember. No matter how hard up they were, my parents still bought me the Observer's and Wayside and Woodland series that were indispensable to me. A primary school teacher – Miss Todd – noticed the hobby I shared with several classmates and introduced us to the local natural history society, so, without knowing it, setting us up for a lifetime enhanced by an unendingly rewarding pursuit (some would say obsession!). The interest in field natural history has been maintained ever since, in tandem with 'day jobs', first as a science teacher and then as a sociology and philosophy lecturer. Only in recent years did I finally wake up to the obvious connections between my work as a sociologist and the environmental changes that all too often caused me distress as a lover of nature. The destruction of wild places – including, perhaps especially, the wild places in our towns and cities – has economic, social and political causes. These need to be understood and questioned, and who but social scientists are best placed to do that?

This background may help to explain some unusual features of this book. Chapters 10 and 11 place the patterns of bumblebee decline and the prospects for their conservation in the wider contexts of planning law, agricultural economics and the politics of social movements and pressure groups. Effective and lasting conservation strategy needs to understand these processes and how to intervene in them. Another feature is influenced by recent feminist and sociological approaches to understanding science. Rather than simply presenting known facts about bumblebees, I have tried to say something about the patterns of thinking that have shaped the questions researchers have addressed to their objects of study. I have tried, also, to give a sense of the 'dialogue' between research traditions and the elusive nature of the bees and their behaviour – how what we think we know is always provisional and open to revision in the light of further research, and how each new piece of research reveals further unknowns at the same time as it settles others. The discussions of bumblebee psychology and the role of chemical communication (Chapter 3), the discussion of optimal foraging theory (Chapter 6), pollination syndromes (Chapter 7), and parasites and predators (Chapter 5) illustrate all this.

The prospect of following after the brilliant earlier New Naturalist *Bumblebees*, by Free & Butler, was a truly daunting one. My family and closest friends have, of course, the first call on my gratitude. But two people, in particular, have been indispensable to the preparation of this book. Mike Edwards, co-ordinator of the Bumblebee Working Group, has unstintingly shared his great expertise, passionate concern for the bees and their conservation, and precious, limited time. My editor, Sally Corbet, has given me her expert advice, thorough and intelligent comment, and enthusiastic support through the whole process. Probably unknown to her she also inspired me in my early days as a 'bombologist' through my encounter with the book she coauthored with Oliver Prŷs-Jones. But many other people also gave time, expertise and other sorts of help: thanks to Paul Williams and George Else of the Natural History Museum for many helpful conversations, access to their collections, and comments on early drafts of the book. Thanks also to Dr Claire Carvell, Dr Juliet Osborne and Peter Harvey for letting me use some of their excellent photos, and for reading and commenting on parts of the book. John Kramer, Dr A. F. G. Bourke, Dr Chris Gibson, Peter Harvey, Bryan Pinchen, Dr Christine Müller, Dr Rick Fisher, Dr Roselle Chapman, Dr Dave Goulson, Gill Nisbett and Murdo Macdonald all read parts of the manuscript and gave valuable help and advice. Manfred and Mrs Intenthron offered both hospitality, and an opportunity to witness Manfred's extraordinary gift of persuading wild bumblebees to nest in his garden. Tony Hopkins very kindly agreed to allow me to use several of his excellent bumblebee paintings. Mike and Sue Edwards and Martin and Maria Jenner gave me convivial hospitality and indispensable help in locating some of the more elusive species for study and photography. Sean Nixon provided great companionship on a marvellous trip to the Inner Hebrides in search of *Bombus distinguendus*. Dr Stuart Roberts very kindly provided me with up-to-date distribution maps based on data submitted by members of the Bees, Wasps and Ants Recording Society, and collated by Mike Edwards. The maps were produced using DMAP software developed by Alan

Morton, and the following gave permission for me to use illustrations or tables: Dr S. A. Corbet, Dr O. Prŷs-Jones, Dr R. M. Fisher, Dr D. V. Alford, Mike Edwards, Dr Paul H. Williams, Harvard University Press, International Bee Research Association, Royal Entomological Society, Brill Academic Publishers, Dr B.-G. Svensson, Gem Publishing Company, *Entomologica Fennica*, University of Copenhagen Zoological Museum, Springer Verlag, Birkhaüser Verlag, Elsevier, Juliet Osborne/Rothamsted Research, Institute of Biology, Oxford University Press, British Wildlife Publishing. Martin Heywood, Don Down, Chris Gibson, Sue Burden, Jenny Rose, Shelley Pennington, Paul Talbot, Paul Mabbott, David and Adrienne Lee, Dr Bill Landells, John Dobson, Mary James and others contributed valuable observations or helped in many other ways. Finally, Helen Brocklehurst, Emily Pitcher and Isobel Smales, of HarperCollins, could not have been more helpful, and I am very grateful for their hard work and encouragement.

CHAPTER 1

Introducing Bumblebees

B UMBLEBEES have a firm place in public affection: they are relatively large, furry and rather 'cuddly' insects, and we associate their gentle buzzing with flowery meadows and summer gardens. This is an association literally cashed in on by numerous advertisers intent on identifying their product with the goodness and purity of nature. The seemingly purposeful and industrious activity of bumblebees when foraging for nectar or pollen endears them to the more economically minded, while their co-operative social life has made them a model for social and political thinkers of both left and right. The popular image is of a tubby, furry, black-and-yellow banded creature, often with a friendly, smiling face. Apart from the face, this will do quite well for a start! The rather rounded, densely furry body is typical of bumblebees, and many species share the black-and-yellow banded colour pattern. However, quite a few do not: ginger-brown and combinations of black and red are also common patterns. As we shall see, there are also other insects – most often flies and other bees – which mimic one or other of the bumblebee patterns. These are supposed to fool predators, and can fool us, too.

The 'friendly' image is also well founded for several reasons. Although female bumblebees can sting, they rarely do so unless severely provoked. Many of the familiar species have adapted to human-made environments such as parks and gardens, where they forage from flowers or make their nests showing little fear of human presence. Bumblebees are also 'friendly' in the sense that they are social animals with a highly developed division of labour and co-operation with each other in raising their offspring. However, this needs to be qualified a little: it is usually the offspring of the queen that are raised, not those of the workers, but there comes a time in the life cycle of the colony when the workers try to lay eggs and conflict breaks out. Also, there are some bumblebee species – the cuckoo bumblebees – that take over the nests of other species and persuade the workers to raise their own young.

Finally, bumblebees are 'friendly' in another respect: this time to humans. Unlike honey bees, bumblebees cannot be profitably domesticated for their honey stores. However, they are very effective pollinators of a wide variety of horticultural and agricultural crops as well as numerous wild flower species. They thus have considerable economic and ecological importance. Above all, however, their endlessly fascinating and astonishingly complex modes of life are a source of intrinsic wonder and respect for all who take the trouble to study them. It is for these last reasons, in particular, that the alarming rate of decline of many species has become an issue for policy makers.

DISTRIBUTION AND DECLINE – THE PLIGHT OF THE BUMBLEBEE

The great majority of bumblebee species live in northern temperate regions of the world (Fig. 1). The most fully studied are those of North America and Europe, but Central Asia probably has the richest bumblebee fauna. There is also a small number of species in Southeast Asia and tropical Central and South America, and several species were introduced into New Zealand from Britain at the end of the nineteenth century, where they still survive. Compared with other insect groups, which have far more species, it seems likely that most of the world's bumblebee species have been discovered. There has, however, been considerable confusion over their naming and description, but clarification is provided by Paul Williams's checklist of 239 species (Williams, 1998).

Aspects of their structure and physiology suggest that bumblebees have evolved as relatively cold-adapted species, and they certainly seem to suffer from overheating on very warm summer days, often not venturing out of the nest on the hottest days. Some species thrive in the Arctic far north (Fig. 2), and also on high mountain habitats. Climate change may be having significant effects on bumblebee populations and distributions, both directly and indirectly (Williams, 1986). There is evidence of a northward extension of the range of some more southern species in the last 10–20 years (see, for example, Macdonald (2001)), and a recent tendency for a few colonies of some species to continue through the winter months in favoured localities in southern Britain. At the same time, some species have been lost from the more southerly parts of their British range (notably *B. distinguendus*).

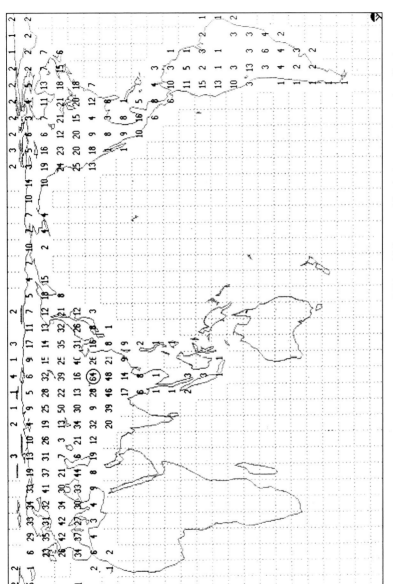

FIG. 1. Map of indigenous species richness for regional faunas of all bumblebees worldwide from specimens in collections, published and unpublished records shown as numbers of species (reproduced from Williams, 1994, with permission).

FIG 2. Arctic bumblebee habitat at Abisko, northern Sweden.

It seems likely that the greatest threat to bumblebee populations comes from habitat degradation and destruction. The twin pressures of the industrialisation of agriculture and the encroachment of human settlements constitute a growing threat to the populations of bumblebees, no less than to those of butterflies, farmland birds, wild flowers and other wildlife. Distribution maps published in 1980 (IBRA/ITE, 1980), despite significant limitations, provided evidence of very steep declines in the distribution of several bumblebee species across the two date categories used in compiling the maps: prior to 1960, and from 1960 onwards. Similar declines – often involving the same species – were also being observed in some parts of mainland Europe (Banaszak, 1995; Rasmont & Mersch, 1988 and Westrich, 1989).

In a series of publications through the 1980s (Williams, 1982, 1986, 1988, 1989b), Paul Williams combined this evidence with local field work in Kent and evidence from other surveys in mainland Europe in an attempt to provide a general model of the causes of decline. Dividing Britain into broad regions, and classifying bumblebee species in terms of their status in the various regions, he was able to distinguish three main groups of species: mainland ubiquitous, widespread local and southern local. The mainland ubiquitous species were, and remained, generally distributed throughout Britain. The widespread local species had been lost from large areas of southern and central lowland Britain, generally retreating northwards and westwards. The southern local species had retreated to the south, and both the latter two categories were increasingly localised within their reduced ranges (Fig. 3).

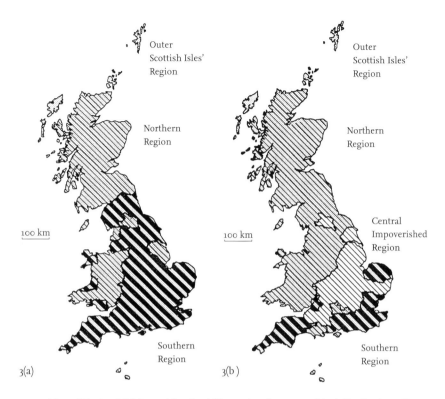

FIG 3. Map of England, Wales and Scotland illustrating the geographical distribution of British bumblebee species (a) pre-1960 and (b) 1960 onwards. Dots represent Widespread Local Species, narrow lines Mainland Ubiquitous Species and broad stripes Southern Local Species (reproduced from Williams, 1982, with permission).

Systematic recording work carried out since 1980 by members of the UK's Bees, Wasps and Ants Recording Society (BWARS) continued to indicate severe declines in populations of all except six widespread and common bumblebee species – declines probably more severe than was evident from the 1980 *Atlas*, and continuing since the mid-1970s, the latest data included in that document (see Table 1). An important report, collecting together available knowledge of the status and conservation requirements of scarce and threatened bees, wasps and ants, was published in 1991 (Falk, 1991). This provisionally placed five species in the 'Notable' category: that is, as scarce species, recorded from no more than 16 to 100 10-kilometre squares in Britain since 1970. These species were: *Bombus distinguendus*, *B. ruderatus*, *B. subterraneus*, *B. sylvarum* and *Psithyrus* (now *Bombus*)

TABLE 1. The British bumblebee species, their distribution and current status.

SPECIES	BRITISH DISTRIBUTION AND STATUS
Bombus lucorum	Widespread and common throughout. Stable.
Bombus terrestris	Widespread and common, more local in far north. Northward extension of range.
Bombus soroeensis	Widespread but very local in south and declining. More frequent in Scotland.
Bombus cullumanus	Formerly very local, southern, now presumed extinct.
Bombus jonellus	Widespread but local, more frequent in Scotland.
Bombus pratorum	Widespread and common throughout. Stable.
Bombus monticola	Widespread but very local in northern and western uplands. Declining.
Bombus hypnorum	A recent colonist of Britain.
Bombus hortorum	Widespread and common throughout. Probably declining.
Bombus ruderatus	Widespread but local in south-eastern England and east midlands. Possibly recovering after steep decline.
Bombus lapidarius	Widespread and common, but more local in far north. Northward extension of range.
Bombus ruderarius	Mainly southern and local. Declining.
Bombus pascuorum	Widespread and common throughout. Stable.
Bombus humilis	Southern and local. Recent steep decline, but may be stabilising.
Bombus muscorum	Widespread but very local, mainly coastal. Declining.
Bombus sylvarum	Southern and very local. Declining steeply.
Bombus distinguendus	Mainly northern and extremely local. Now retreated to north coast of Scotland and Isles.
Bombus subterraneus	Formerly southern and very local, now believed to be extinct.
Bombus pomorum	Extinct. Known in Britain only from a few nineteenth-century records from Kent.
Bombus vestalis	Cuckoo of *B. terrestris*. Common and widespread in south-east, more local to north and west.
Bombus bohemicus	Cuckoo of *B. lucorum*. Common and widespread, especially in north and west.
Bombus rupestris	Cuckoo of *B. lapidarius*. Mainly southern. Formerly very scarce, but becoming more common in some localities.
Bombus barbutellus	Cuckoo of *B. hortorum*. Widespread, more common in south. Probably stable.
Bombus campestris	Cuckoo of *B. pascuorum*. Widespread, more common in south. Declining in some areas.
Bombus sylvestris	Widespread and fairly common. Probably stable.

rupestris. A further two species, *B. pomorum* and *B. cullumanus,* were included in the report, but had not been seen for many decades, and were believed already extinct in Britain.

The following year, the Earth Summit held in Rio de Janeiro highlighted the issue of species loss as a matter of intense global concern. One of the key outcomes of this unprecedented conference was a Convention on Biological Diversity. Although much of the content of this was concerned with international issues arising from the commercial exploitation of biological resources, it did place national governments under an obligation to establish strategies for the conservation and sustainable use of biological diversity. Such a strategy would entail identifying and monitoring components of biological diversity, and taking appropriate conservation measures, including establishment of protected areas, restoring degraded ecosystems and protecting indigenous knowledge. As this last requirement suggests, the greatest priority was attached to those regions, mainly less 'developed' tropical countries, which held the richest diversity of species and ecosystems. Nevertheless, the convention did have implications for the richer countries, including the UK.

One of these implications was the production of a UK Biodiversity Action Plan (D.o.E., 1994) and the setting up of a steering group of scientists, conservationists and planners to develop a strategy for the selection and protection of key species and habitats in the UK (UK Biodiversity Steering Group, 1995, 1999). Including the cuckoo bumblebees, 12 species of bumblebee were thought still to occur throughout their pre-1960 range. A further seven species had suffered declines of up to 50 per cent of their previous range, and were designated 'local'. Five more species had declined by more than 50 per cent of their previous range, and were declared 'scarce'. Since there was strong evidence that the scarce and local species had continued to decline at an alarming rate since the data for the 1980 *Atlas* had been collected, four of the scarce (excluding the cuckoo, *B. rupestris*) and one of the local species were targeted for action under the UK Biodiversity Action Plan. These were: *B. distinguendus, B. humilis, B. subterraneus, B. sylvarum* and *B. ruderatus.* Under the leadership of the Worldwide Fund for Nature, a UK Bumblebee Working Group was established to develop and implement the plan for bumblebees. The group included representatives of the Countryside Council for Wales, English Nature, Scottish Natural Heritage and the Worldwide Fund for Nature, together with the specialist entomologists M. Edwards, G. R. Else, C. O'Toole and P. H. Williams.

Starting with a species action plan for *B. sylvarum,* the Group devoted itself to establishing the current distribution and status of the Biodiversity Action Plan (BAP) species, and researching the ecological requirements of each species. Since data to back up the distributions given in the *Atlas* proved to be incomplete, and in some cases of doubtful reliability, the importance of getting a clear picture of current distributions for the BAP species was clear and urgent. Expansion of the Working Group followed, and the efforts of many amateur entomologists, notably through the work of BWARS, were galvanised and co-ordinated to provide vital new knowledge of the distribution and ecology of the BAP species. Academic specialists, too, have supervised important research projects by graduate students, and involved a wider public in surveying bumblebee behaviour and distribution. Initial work on *B. sylvarum* and, in Scotland, on *B. distinguendus* has led to valuable insights into the status and conservation requirements of both species. However, systematic searches have led to the provisional conclusion that the action plan came too late for *B. subterraneus*, now believed extinct in the UK. Another of the BAP species, *B. ruderatus*, proved elusive for the first years of the Group's work: no viable breeding population could be located, and some doubts were expressed concerning its taxonomic status (given its close similarity to *B. hortorum*). However, in 2002, strong populations were identified in parts of East Anglia and the east Midlands, and research is under way.

The fifth species, *B. humilis*, proved to be in a somewhat stronger position than the other BAP species, and prospects for its conservation seemed relatively good. Also, the cuckoo bumblebee *B. rupestris*, which had not been included in the BAP list, now appeared to be regaining lost ground, particularly in the Southeast. However, the research effort was beginning to show that other species, not initially selected for BAP status, were also in trouble. *Bombus monticola* (formerly known as *lapponicus*), a species of upland moors, with a mainly northern and western distribution, appeared to be in steep decline. *Bombus muscorum*, too, a close relative of *B. humilis* and *B. sylvarum*, was giving rise to concern. Another species included in the 'local' category in the UK Action Plan, *B. ruderarius*, also appeared to be declining alarmingly. *Bombus monticola* was subsequently the target of a Species Recovery Plan, whilst *B. muscorum* and *B. ruderarius* have been added to the list of target species (Edwards, 1997, 1998, 1999, 2000, 2001, 2002).

This research effort is now providing some important insights, but many questions remain unanswered. In general, the evidence supports Williams's broad view that the twin pressures of urbanisation and the industrialisation of agriculture have been the most important causes of bumblebee decline, with the strongest emphasis on the latter. However, it is now clearer that very specific features of the ecology and life cycles of the declining species may be at work in each case. The patterns of decline have varied from species to species, and may not be explicable in terms of a single general model. We will return to a fuller discussion of the evidence on bumblebee decline, and the prospects for conservation, in Chapters 10 and 11.

WHAT IS A BUMBLEBEE?

Bumblebees form a distinct grouping – now accepted as a single genus – among the bees, and these, in turn, belong to the suborder Aculeata (bees, wasps and ants) of the insect order Hymenoptera. The order Hymenoptera also includes sawflies (Fig. 4) and a very large group of mainly parasitic insects (the Parasitica) of which the ichneumons are the best known. These are mainly parasitic on various life-history stages of other insect groups (Fig. 5). Many of us who have tried to rear butterflies and moths from caterpillars will have experienced the disappointment of witnessing the emergence of ichneumon larvae or adults from our carefully nurtured 'pets'. The ichneumons themselves are much neglected and well worthy of study.

Like other winged Hymenoptera, the bees have two pairs of fully developed, membranous wings (Fig. 6). The body is usually hairy, and the hind legs are often enlarged. The front segment of the thorax (the pronotum) does not reach as far back as the wing bases. The bumblebees are a subgrouping within the bees, but distinguishing them from other groups of bees is more difficult than it might seem. There are details of the facial structure and also the wing venation that can

FIG 4. The horntail, a large species of sawfly. Note the lack of a 'waist' between the thorax and abdomen.

FIG 5. *Rhyssa persuasoria*, a 'wasp' whose larvae parasitise those of the horntail.

FIG 6. A leafcutter bee (*Megachile*).

be used with dead specimens where there is doubt. However, for most purposes bumblebees can be recognised by their densely hairy bodies, relatively large size, flattened and widened hind tibiae (lower leg segments – see Fig. 7), and characteristic colour patterns. This leaves only a few other bee species that look similar, and these can be learned species-by-species. In Britain, the flower bees, *Anthophora* species, look very similar to bumblebees, and often visit the same range of flowers for nectar and pollen. The hairy-footed flower bee, *A. plumipes*, is quite common in gardens in southern Britain. The females are black, with the outer surface of the hind tibiae and first segment of the hind tarsi flattened and covered with yellow hairs (Figs 8 & 9). These are used for pollen collection and superficially resemble the full pollen baskets of bumblebee queens and workers. The males are ginger-brown in colour, with darker hairs on the abdomen, resembling workers of the common carder bumblebee (*Bombus pascuorum*), but, as their common name implies, they have long tufts of hair on the tarsal joints of the mid-legs (Fig. 10).

Some of the other bumblebee lookalikes are not bees at all, but flies. Several common species of hover fly are bumblebee mimics, with furry bodies, similar colour patterns, and even, in some cases, swellings on the hind legs. The two most common of these are *Volucella bombylans* and *Merodon equestris*. *Volucella bombylans* has several colour forms, each of which mimics a particular bumblebee colour pattern. The typical form is black with a ginger-red tail, resembling *Bombus lapidarius*, whilst another form closely resembles *B. hortorum*, and yet another

(a)

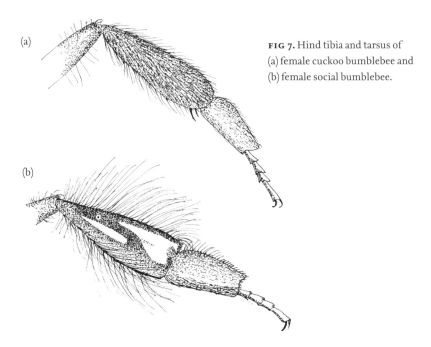

FIG 7. Hind tibia and tarsus of
(a) female cuckoo bumblebee and
(b) female social bumblebee.

(b)

FIG 8. A female of the hairy-footed flower bee (*Anthophora*), a bumblebee lookalike. Note the
yellow hairs on the outer surface of the hind tibia.

FIG 9. Hind tibia and tarsus of female flower bee (*Anthophora plumipes*).

FIG 10. A male flower bee, a lookalike of *Bombus pascuorum*.

B. pascuorum. *Volucella bombylans* not only resembles bumblebees in appearance, but also lays its eggs in their nests (as well as in those of wasps). The resulting larvae feed on detritus, but it is possible that they also consume some bumblebee larvae. *Merodon equestris* is another common hover fly, and, like *Volucella*, has several colour forms. These broadly resemble *Bombus lapidarius, B. pratorum, B. lucorum/terrestris* and the *B. pascuorum* group. Unlike *Volucella bombylans*, there appear to be no other links with the bumblebees, as the larvae live in plant tissue – especially bulbs of bluebells and daffodils. A third bumblebee mimic among the hover flies is *Eristalis intricarius*, which also has several colour forms, and there are other, less common mimics in other genera (Figs 11–16).

Other groups of flies also have their bumblebee mimics. The common bee fly (*Bombylius major*) is a familiar sight on woodland rides and edges and in gardens in spring (Fig. 17). Although it is usually smaller, it closely resembles workers of *B. pascuorum*. It even has a long proboscis projecting forwards, but

FIG 11. The tawny mining bee could be mistaken for a small bumblebee.

FIG 12. *Volucella bombylans*, a hover fly. This colour form is a mimic of *Bombus hortorum*.

FIG 13. Another colour form of *Volucella bombylans*, this one a *Bombus lapidarius* lookalike.

FIG 14. *Merodon equestris*, a hover fly mimic of *Bombus pascuorum*.

FIG 15. Another colour form of *Merodon equestris* that resembles the red-tailed bumblebee species.

FIG 16. *Eristalis intricarius*, another common hover fly mimic of several bumblebee species.

FIG 17. The common bee fly (*Bombylius major*), which resembles a small worker of *Bombus pascuorum* and often visits the same flower species (note the elongated proboscis).

this is not retractable as it is in the bumblebees. The warble fly (*Hypoderma bovis*), a cattle parasite, also resembles one or other of the red-tailed bumblebee species.

These convergent colour patterns, exhibited by quite distantly related species, may be genuine mimicry, in the sense of having been acquired because of the resemblance to bumblebees. We cannot, of course, assume that this is true in all cases, and some resemblances may be coincidental or the result of similar pressures acting independently. However, where there are structural features, or behaviours that go together with the colour patterns, it seems reasonable to guess that the species concerned acquired their resemblance to bumblebees because of some selective advantage derived from doing so.

It is conventional to distinguish two sorts of true mimicry. As you will discover when you start to learn how to distinguish the bumblebee species, many species bear a very close resemblance to one another in their colour patterns. It is generally believed that these convergent colour patterns have evolved because they give protection from predators, which quickly learn to associate the colour patterns with the bees' ability to deliver a painful sting. Members of each bee species would then benefit from the lessons delivered by those of similarly coloured species. This is called Müllerian mimicry. However, the flies that resemble bumblebees do not sting, and their similarity to bumblebees allows them to 'free-ride' on the protection from predators this gives them. This is known as Batesian mimicry.

Some of the hover flies are very impressive mimics and sometimes quite close inspection is needed to separate them. Often behaviour is a giveaway, but where it is not, there are clear structural differences. Flies have only one pair of developed wings, whereas bumblebees, like all bees, have two pairs. The flies also have antennae of various shapes, but bumblebees all have simple, thread-like antennae made up of 12 or 13 segments. Flies have a variety of differently shaped mouthparts, but none has the combination of strong mandibles and a long, retractable tongue characteristic of bumblebees. More details on how to identify bumblebees are given in Chapter 8.

BUMBLEBEE LIVES

Bumblebees are almost entirely dependent on the resources provided by flowering plants for their nutrition. All species feed primarily on a combination of pollen and nectar, and many have evolved close associations with particular groups of flowering plants, playing a significant part in their pollination in return for the 'reward' offered by the flowers. However, no bumblebees are entirely dependent on just one species of plant, and many are very wide ranging in the species they will visit, including many of the more exotic plant species grown in parks and gardens. These and other aspects of bumblebee foraging behaviour and interactions with plant species will be dealt with in Chapters 6 and 7.

Most bumblebee species are social (or, strictly, eusocial) animals. Unlike the honey bees, their colonies usually last for just one season – or sometimes less. Usually, only the fertilised queens survive the winter. They emerge from hibernation in spring, feed actively and begin to search for a suitable site to make their nest. Eggs are laid in a wax cell, and the resulting larvae are fed by the queens with a mixture of pollen and nectar. When the larvae are fully developed they enter a brief 'resting' stage as pupae, and eventually emerge as worker bumblebees. These are generally much smaller than the queen, and their role is to take over from the queen the role of foraging for food, and many 'household' duties, including tending subsequent broods of larvae (Fig. 18). Meanwhile the queen remains in the nest, and continues to lay eggs. In this way the colony grows until at a certain point the queen switches from laying fertilised eggs, which produce new workers, to laying unfertilised eggs which give rise to males. At around the same time some of the larvae from fertilised eggs go on to develop more fully to

FIG 18. The comb of *Bombus pratorum*. Note the honey stores below the cluster of cocoons.

produce fresh fertile females: sometimes called daughter queens or gynes. The males and daughter queens leave the nest, and thereafter live independent lives. The daughter queens mate, usually only once, and go into hibernation very soon afterwards. Back at the nest, workers will often attempt to lay eggs, and conflict among them, and between them and the old queen, ensues, leading to the demise of the colony. Remaining males and workers die before winter sets in, leaving the fertilised daughter queens to begin the cycle again the following year.

This is, of course a very simplified account. The mechanisms that trigger the various phases in the life of the colony are so far only partially understood, and also they vary greatly from species to species. The annual cycle is also subject to variation. In Britain and much of mainland Europe some species complete more than one colony cycle in a single season, and there is growing evidence of colonies continuing to be active through the winter months in some areas with mild winter climates. *Bombus terrestris*, one of the species introduced to New Zealand at the end of the nineteenth century, has perennial colonies there, and the colonies of some tropical species are also perennial.

Some of these puzzles and variations will be discussed in Chapter 2, but it is worth mentioning here that there is yet another major variation in life history among the bumblebees. Where there is a shortage of suitable nest sites, there may be conflict between would-be queens for possession, and the dead bodies of

FIG 19. A female cuckoo bumblebee (*Bombus sylvestris*). Note the lack of a pollen basket on the hind leg.

unsuccessful rivals can sometimes be found in or around established nests. Queens of a few species of social bumblebees will also under certain conditions take over nests already established by other queens. But there is also a subgroup of species that never make their own nests, and are fully dependent on their ability to successfully invade and take over the nests of one or other of the social species. These are the cuckoo bumblebees (Fig. 19). They share some structural features, as well as their parasitic mode of life, and used to be placed in a separate genus (Psithyrus) from the 'true' bumblebees. However, there are very strong taxonomic arguments for including them in the same genus as the social bumblebees, and this is now generally accepted practice (Williams, 1994). For field naturalists and students of behaviour and ecology, on the other hand, the cuckoo bumblebees form a very distinct group. There is no worker caste, and individual cuckoos forage for themselves only, so here the cuckoo bumblebees will be treated somewhat separately from the social bumblebees, whilst giving due respect to the new view on taxonomy. Chapter 4 gives more detail on the life history and behaviour of the cuckoos, to the extent that this is so far understood, and more detailed accounts of the British species are given in Chapter 9.

BUMBLEBEE FRIENDS AND ENEMIES

For many bumblebee species, humans – or, rather, some of their economic and agricultural practices – are by far their greatest enemy. But we are not alone. Bumblebee nests concentrate many individuals and resources, and this makes them a prime target for parasites and predators. Individual bumblebees out foraging are subject to attacks from insectivorous birds, some of which have developed ways of killing and eating them without getting stung. Hornets prey on them, crab spiders often lie in wait for them on flowerheads, and a group of flies – conopids – specialise in laying their eggs in bumblebees as the latter forage or fly between flowers. The resulting larvae develop in the body of the bees, eventually killing them.

Larger mammals – notably badgers and foxes – are fond of digging out bumblebee nests for their stores of honey and brood (Fig. 20). And there are

FIG 20. A nest of *Bombus lapidarius* that has been damaged by a large mammal. The workers have left the comb to repair the damage.

enemies on a much smaller scale – nematode worms, protozoan internal parasites, and various species of parasitic mites. Wax moth larvae, too, feed on the early stages of bumblebee brood, and can devastate colonies. Levels of nest parasitism by cuckoo bumblebees can also be very high, and destroy or seriously reduce the reproductive success of bumblebee colonies. But there are also species of mites, flies and other invertebrates that live in the bumblebee nest, gaining shelter and feeding mainly on detritus, and these seem to have little or no adverse effects on the colony – perhaps even benefiting it (Fig. 21).

Many fascinating questions surround the relationships between bumblebees and these other species. How far and in what ways have the evolution of the bumblebees and their patterns of social life been shaped by their past interactions with them? To what extent are the structure and dynamics of bumblebee populations affected by predation, parasitic infection and the like? How far might conservation measures to protect declining bumblebee species need to take into account these interactions? Of course, getting reliable information to begin answering these questions is a very tall order, but intriguing and imaginative research has been and is being done. Much of this will be reviewed in Chapter 5.

FIG 21. An overwintered queen *Bombus monticola* with mites attached to her body.

IDENTIFYING BUMBLEBEES

The majority of bumblebees can be identified with reasonable confidence on the basis of features that are visible when the bees are observed carefully while they rest or forage. Colour pattern is the most easily used characteristic, and once the distinctive patterns have been learned they are quite reliable guides for most purposes. Males and females of some species have different colour patterns, so these need to be taken into account for that part of the season when the males are present. Some groups of species, such as *B. muscorum, B. humilis* and *B. pascuorum*, have very similar colour patterns. Here, features such as behaviour, the evenness of the coat, or the shape of the head or abdomen, often provide clues that can be picked up with experience. Females of social and cuckoo bees can be distinguished by checking the hind legs for presence or absence of the pollen baskets (corbiculae). Cuckoos are often more slow moving and less irritable than workers of the social species, but this applies to male social bumblebees, too.

Where reliable identification is needed, it is important to remember that patterns and shades of colouring can be variable, and structural features must be studied. Often this can be done by enclosing a foraging bee in a glass tube. Movement can be stopped by gently pressing the captive against the side of the container with a wad of tissue or cotton wool. It can then be observed with a hand lens, and released without harm. Using this method, the shape of the head, patterns of sculpturing and pitting of the cuticle, shape and distribution of hairs on legs, and relative lengths of antennal segments can usually be picked out in good light. These are often useful external structural features to back up or resolve doubts about provisional identifications made on the basis of colour patterns and jizz.

Chapter 8 gives more detailed suggestions about how to begin learning to identify the common species, and then move on to recognising some of the similar, but often scarcer species. The aim of that chapter is to make it possible for you to identify the different British species, as well as distinguish males, queens and workers without killing and dissecting them. Unfortunately, some species can only be identified with certainty by microscopic examination of structural features such as the male genitalia or the sting sheaths of females. Details of these are given in both the keys and the 'similar species' sections of the accounts of each individual species in Chapter 9.

BUMBLEBEE STRUCTURE

External features

To use the identification key given later in this book it will be important to
be able to refer to details of the external structure of bumblebees, and so further
information will be given in the guide to the keys (Chapter 8). For now, it will be
enough to learn the basic features of the bumblebee and the parts they play in
its life.

Like that of other insects, the body of a bumblebee is divided into three main
parts: the head at the front, the thorax in the middle and the abdomen at the rear
(Fig. 22). The most prominent features of the head are the two large compound
eyes, which are sensitive to shape, colour and movement. Also on the head are the
antennae, which are important for the bee's senses of touch and scent, and the
mouthparts. These are made up of a pair of powerful mandibles and the tongue
(proboscis). The mandibles have a variety of uses, including manipulating wax
and other materials in nest building and maintenance, biting into plant tissue
in nectar robbing, and in grasping or nipping potential enemies. The proboscis
is an elongated structure that the bee uses to probe and suck up nectar from
flowers (Fig. 23). Bumblebees are all relatively long-tongued insects, but there are
considerable differences in average tongue lengths among the species. These
differences seem to be associated with preferences for variously structured flowers,
the longer-tongued species tending to forage more from deep flowers. However,
bumblebees are remarkably inventive in finding ways to exploit an extraordinary
range of flower structures. The tongue is articulated, and is tucked away under the
head and thorax when not in use.

The thorax carries the two pairs of wings and the six legs. The wings are folded
over the back of the bee when it is at rest or foraging, but in flight the hind and
forewings are attached together by tiny hooks on the leading edge of the
hindwings. The legs are composed of a series of jointed segments, and the front
pair have a tiny spine and groove, used to clean the antennae (Fig. 24). In females
of the social bumblebees, each of the hind legs has a wide, flattened segment
fringed with long hairs (the pollen basket, or corbicula, Fig. 7(b)). Foragers scrape
pollen grains from the body hairs and press them into this for transport back to
the nest (Fig. 25).

The abdomen is roughly ovoid in shape, and made up of six visible segments
in the females, seven in the males. There are tiny breathing holes (spiracles) at the
sides of these segments, and the genital organs are contained in the rear end of
the abdomen. Both queens and workers also have a sting, which is a modified egg-

laying tube and is kept concealed in a cavity at the rear end of the abdomen when not in use.

Most of the outer surface of the body is covered by a hard cuticle (the exoskeleton), composed of chitin, which is secreted by a single layer of epidermal cells. The cuticle remains flexible in some areas, such as the joints of the abdominal segments, to allow for flexibility and movement. The surface of the cuticle has tiny pits and sculptures. It may appear shiny if the puncturing is sparse or shallow, or dull if it is denser. In some cases, the pattern of sculpturing or pitting is important for identification of bumblebee species. A dense pile of hairs arises from the exoskeleton over most of the body. The hairs are variable in shape, but many are feathery, and they are important both in the collection of pollen and

FIG 22. Structure of a bumblebee, viewed from the side.

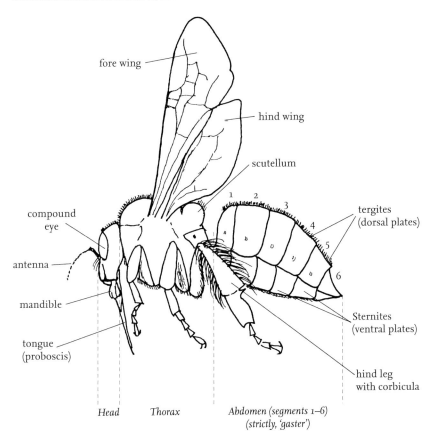

fore wing

hind wing

scutellum

1 2 3 4 5 6

compound eye

tergites (dorsal plates)

antenna

mandible

tongue (proboscis)

Sternites (ventral plates)

hind leg with corbicula

Head   Thorax   Abdomen (segments 1–6) (strictly, 'gaster')

FIG 23. View of the face and partially unfurled tongue of a long-tongued species.

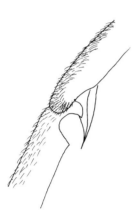

FIG 24. The antenna-cleaner on the front leg of a female bumblebee.

FIG 25. The pollen-press on the hind leg of a female bumblebee.

in temperature regulation. Some also act as sensory organs (see Chapter 3). Since the cuticle is for the most part uniformly black, the colour patterns of the bumblebees are the result of pigmentation of the body hairs.

Internal organs

Detailed treatment of these is beyond the scope of this book, but some general discussion is necessary for understanding aspects of bumblebee behaviour and ecology. The central nervous system is quite typical of insects, with a brain and a central nerve cord that runs the length of the bee, ventrally. It has a series of swellings, or ganglia, at intervals along it, and lateral nerves spreading out from these. The brain is the main centre for receiving and processing sensory information, and initiating motor activity, but there is a good deal of decentralisation of control to the ganglia. The thorax is packed with powerful flight muscles that are attached to moveable sections of the thoracic exoskeleton. The musculature operating the legs is also contained in the thorax (Fig. 26).

Glands in the abdominal wall secrete wax, which is exuded from the surface of the abdominal segments and used in nest construction. Also in the abdominal wall are muscles that are involved in expanding, contracting and flexing the abdomen, and irregular masses of cells known as the fat body. This is a nutritional store, expanded considerably by daughter queens prior to hibernation. The main body cavity is called the haemocoel and the organs in it are bathed in the bee's 'blood': the haemolymph. Circulation is maintained primarily by a muscular tube, the 'heart', which runs the length of the bee and pulsates regularly, driving the fluid in it forwards.

The digestive system consists of an elongated and coiled tube from the mouth to the anus. A narrow oesophagus leads back to an expanded 'crop' or honey-stomach in the abdomen. This is capable of receiving and storing large quantities of nectar, which can be regurgitated by returning foragers to feed the larvae and house-bees. The honey-stomach can expand to carry up to 90 per cent of the body weight of the bee. For the bee's own nutrition, a valve at the end of the honey-stomach can be opened to allow nectar and pollen to pass through into the rest of the alimentary tract where digestion and absorption of nutrients into the blood take place. A cluster of fine Malpighian tubules carries waste products from the haemolymph to the gut, to be discharged from the anus.

The male internal genital organs include two testes, each with a tube connecting it to a vesicle in which the sperms mature and are stored prior to mating. The tubes leading from these connect together and lead out into the penis. The female internal reproductive organs include two ovaries. Each of these consists of a series of tubes (four in the social bumblebees, more in the cuckoo

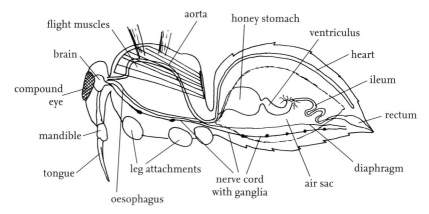

FIG 26. Diagrammatic representation of the internal organs of a bumblebee.

bees) in which the eggs are formed. When the ovaries are fully activated in the fertilised queen, and she begins to lay eggs, these are passed from the ovary along a tube (the oviduct), to join the vagina. There is a small container called the spermatheca attached by a narrow tube to the wall of the vagina. It contains sperm held in store since mating took place the previous year. Initially the queen releases sperm to fertilise eggs when they pass into the vagina, prior to being laid. These eggs eventually develop into worker bees. Somewhat later in the colony cycle, eggs are laid without fertilisation, and these go on to develop as males. Under certain conditions the ovaries of workers may develop, but the resulting eggs have not been fertilised and only males are produced.

Finally, a few words must be said about the system of glands that produce a variety of secretions essential to the internal development and functioning of the individual bees, and also play a crucial role in communication between them. The first group are the endocrine glands, which secrete their products within the bee's body; the second are the exocrine glands, which secrete to the outside. As structures, these glands have long been known, but their functions are only now becoming fully understood. Two pairs of endocrine glands, the corpora cardiaca and the corpora allata, are situated to the rear of the brain and close to the oesophagus. The hormones they secrete play important roles in the growth and development of the bees. The corpora allata, in particular, secrete a hormone that stimulates the development of the ovaries, and their functioning is suppressed in workers while the queen remains dominant in the nest. In the head are the labial, mandibular and hypopharyngial glands. Some of these secrete saliva, important for mixing and chemically altering nutrients, and also for softening nest materials.

The exocrine glands are responsible for secreting a variety of more-or-less volatile compounds – pheromones – which are important means of communication in such activities as mating, recognition and nest location, as well as in regulating the social life and development of the colony.

We will return to some of the recent work on the role of scents and tastes in the communication system of bumblebees in Chapter 3, but for the next chapter we turn to the life cycle of the bumblebee colony.

CHAPTER 2

The Bumblebee Life Cycle

T HE GREAT majority of the bumblebees with which we are familiar
are social insects (Fig. 27). They live in colonies, in which the dominant
individual, the queen or gyne, first establishes a nest and lays some
eggs. The larvae that hatch from these are fed by the queen till they form pupae
from which finally emerge smaller, usually infertile, females. These are a distinct
caste of female bees – the workers. Their main tasks are to collect food and help
tend the growing family in the nest as the queen continues to lay more eggs.
Finally, if the colony is successful, males and fertile females (daughter queens)
are reared. These emerge from their nest, find mates, and the resulting fertilised
females are ready, usually following winter hibernation, to start the cycle over
again. However, a smaller number of bumblebee species exploit the opportunities
provided by the selfless efforts of the workers of the social species. These are the
cuckoo bumblebees, and they are, indeed, cuckoos in the nest. They are very
closely related to the social bumblebees, now included in the same genus, and
it seems likely that their ancestors were once also social species. The female
cuckoo invades an already established nest, often killing the incumbent queen,
and lays her own eggs. The resulting larvae are fed and tended by the host
workers.

This chapter is concerned with the life cycle of the social species, leaving the
story of the cuckoo bees and other enemies and friends of the social bumblebees
to Chapters 4 and 5. The pattern of life sketched above is shared by the social
species, but with some fascinating variations of detail from species to species.
Bumblebees are mostly to be found in the temperate regions of the world, and
their social life is accordingly adapted to the seasons. Most obviously, there is the
challenge of surviving the winter. Usually, it is only the daughter queens that

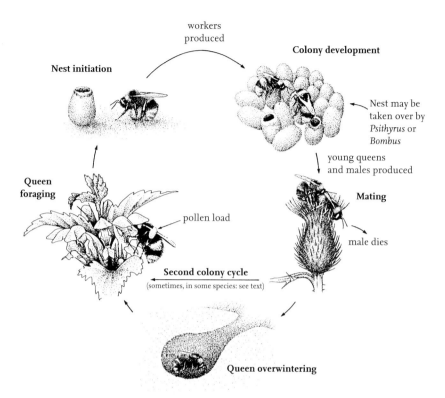

workers
produced

Colony development

Nest initiation

Nest may be
taken over by
Psithyrus or
Bombus

young queens
and males produced

**Queen
foraging**

Mating

pollen load

male dies

Second colony cycle
(sometimes, in some species: see text)

Queen overwintering

FIG 27. The colony cycle of a social bumblebee. (Drawing © Tony Hopkins, reprinted from Prŷs-Jones & Corbet, 1991, with permission)

survive the winter, so that the life cycle is commenced in the spring and has to be completed before the following winter sets in. This contrasts with the perennial colonies of their cousins, the honey bees. There are some bumblebee species in the tropics, where, of course, there is no winter hibernation of the queens. In the tropics, colonies may last several years, producing 2,000 or more workers (Michener, 1974). In recent years, possibly under the influence of global climate change, there is evidence even in southern Britain that a few colonies of some species remain active through the winter. Also, some species are known to be capable of completing two full colony cycles in a single year – possibly more in favourable seasons. As insects well adapted to cold climates, some bumblebees are also to be found at high altitudes in mountains, and far north in the Arctic. Here, the short spring and summer seasons impose a very tight timetable on the bumblebee colonies, and their exceptional efficiency as food gatherers is stretched to its limit.

Much of the fascination of studying bumblebees comes from the discovery of unexpected complexities in the ways they organise their lives – and also from our growing recognition of the variations from species to species in the ways they deal with the challenges of social existence. One key argument of this book is that we need to keep in mind the features shared by all the bumblebee species, whilst never forgetting that each one is the unique outcome of its own evolutionary history. Some species are easier to study than others, and there is a risk of over-generalisation. The detail of the lives of some of our species – including some of our most seriously threatened – has been almost completely unknown until very recently. So a recurrent pattern in this book is one of 'theme and variations'. The present chapter is no exception. There is a common sequence of events and processes making up the life cycle of our social bumblebees, but as the different species come to be studied we become increasingly aware of the variations. Often, but not always, it is possible to link these variations to differences of habitat, developmental rhythms, foraging behaviour, or differences in anatomy or physiology.

Some parts of the life cycle can readily be studied by attentive observers – the queens' search for suitable nest sites in the spring, the movements of worker-foragers into and out of the nest, the strategies used by the males to find mates later in the year, and so on. However, much of the most fascinating detail goes on inside – almost literally – a 'black box'. This is the nest itself. What we know about life inside the nest has come mainly from the pioneering efforts of earlier students of bumblebees, notably F. W. L. Sladen, who devised ways of inducing queens to establish nests in captivity. Nest boxes have been designed which enable captive colonies to be continuously observed through from initiation by the queen to the emergence of the new generation of males and daughter queens. Subsequent observers have developed these methods and refined what is known about the secret life of the colony. A coauthor of an earlier New Naturalist volume on bumblebees, John B. Free, made particularly valuable discoveries, but dedicated amateur naturalists have also pioneered techniques for persuading wild bumblebees to nest in specially designed nest boxes. One exceptionally successful observer is Manfred Intenthron, who regularly has 20 or more nests of all six common species in his suburban garden (Intenthron & Gerrard, 2003). Still, much remains to be discovered. Studies so far have concentrated on a few of the more common species only, and, of course, we cannot be entirely certain that the artificial circumstances under which the captive bees are observed do not affect their behaviour: how do they behave when we are not 'snooping' on them?

Despite these limitations, we do now have a great deal of knowledge of the life cycles of many of our bumblebee species. For convenience we can divide the history of a colony into five overlapping phases. First is the period between the queen's emergence from hibernation and her initiation of a nest. Second comes the period of growth of the colony, through increasing numbers of workers, to the point of transition to production of males and daughter queens. Third is the period of this crucial transition itself. Fourth is the emergence of males and females, their mating, and the entry of the fertilised queens into hibernation. Fifth is a period of overt conflict among the workers and between them and the queen, associated with attempts at egg laying on the part of the workers. This competition phase eventually leads to the decline and extinction of the colony.

SPRING QUEENS

Queens of some species, especially *Bombus terrestris* (the buff-tailed bumblebee), can be seen visiting the catkins of sallow or garden flowers on warm days as early as February. Depending on weather and locality, they are soon joined by the other familiar species. In southern Britain, the rest of the six common species will have emerged from hibernation by the end of March. Their first priority is to maintain their energy levels, and restore the greatly depleted fat store that has sustained them through their long hibernation. When weather permits they feed actively and opportunistically on such early spring flowers as are available. The catkins of sallows are especially popular. As they come into flower, white and red deadnettle are particularly favoured by the early queens of some species, but they will also visit dandelions, blackthorn, lesser celandine, and a wide range of early garden herbs and shrubs, such as flowering currant, *Ceanothus*, *Erica* species, crocus, japonica and even daffodil (Figs 28–32). Bouts of foraging are often interspersed with periods of sunbathing, on exposed leaves, or pale reflecting surfaces such as paving stones or walls (Fig. 33).

At night and during spells of inclement weather the queens take shelter, often in deep leaf litter or among mosses in rough grassland. Some authors suggest that they return to their hibernation sites, and sometimes large aggregations of queens are found close to each other in a suitable sheltered bank. An observer in south Essex has observed queens emerging from the bells of crocus flowers as they opened in the early morning (Fig. 34) (D. Down, pers. comm.).

The queens of some species, however, emerge from hibernation later than our common six. A localised and declining species, *B. ruderarius* (the red-shanked carder bumblebee), is usually first seen in early April, but others, including some

FIG 28. Blackthorn blossom, a valuable early forage source for several common bumblebee species.

FIG 29. An overwintered queen *Bombus terrestris* foraging from blackthorn blossom in March.

FIG 30. An overwintered queen *Bombus pascuorum* foraging from sallow catkins.

FIG 31. An overwintered queen *Bombus hortorum* visiting white deadnettle.

FIG 32. An overwintered queen *Bombus lucorum* foraging from red deadnettle.

FIG 33. An overwintered queen *Bombus pascuorum* sunbathing on a garden wall.

FIG 34. An overwintered *Bombus lapidarius* queen in the bell of a crocus flower.

of our increasingly scarce carder bumblebees (see below) do not venture out of hibernation until late May or even June (Figs 35–37). The reasons for this are not clear, and they may not be the same for all the late-emerging species. In the case of *B. muscorum* (the moss carder bumblebee), there are few suitable nectar or pollen sources in its marshland habitats in early spring. In other cases, such as *B. humilis* (the brown-banded carder bumblebee) and *B. sylvarum* (the shrill carder bumblebee), it has been suggested that they are physiologically suited to higher temperatures. As we shall see, the late-nesting species may be particularly adversely affected by current grassland management regimes.

Soon another pattern of behaviour emerges, and alternates with foraging and sunbathing. This typically involves low-level exploratory flights over rough grassland, along hedgerows or overgrown banks. The bees 'contour' irregular features they encounter, and can often be seen entering small holes and crevices, disappearing into the base of tufts of grass, or under shrubs. Usually they reappear in a few minutes and continue with their exploratory flights, eventually flying off, sometimes high and fast. All the common species exhibit this behaviour, and it seems the queens are now prospecting for suitable nest sites. At this time of year one also frequently encounters queens flying fast and direct, and there is evidence that this is a key period during which the queens disperse to colonise habitats at some distance from their own place of origin.

FIG 35. Late-flowering grassland habitat of the scarce carder bumblebees, *Bombus sylvarum* and *B. humilis.* Note the red clover in flower, late May.

FIG 36. A queen *Bombus humilis*, recently emerged from hibernation in late May, foraging from red clover.

FIG 37. Late-flowering coastal grassland, Essex, habitat of *Bombus muscorum*. Late May.

When a suitable location is found the queen begins to establish her nest (Figs 38–40). All the familiar species show some adaptability in their choice of nest sites, and there is also considerable variation between species in their preferences. *Bombus lucorum* (the white-tailed bumblebee), *B. terrestris* and *B. lapidarius* (the red-tailed bumblebee) generally establish their nests underground. Commonly the disused nest of a small mammal is used, and the nest chamber is linked to the surface of the ground by a narrow tunnel. The new incumbent uses available nest materials present in the chamber, such as dead grasses, leaves, fine roots or mosses. Sometimes a false nest of plant debris is also constructed on the surface, around the entrance hole, but this is by no means general. In some cases, the entrance hole may be narrowed by impacted sand or soil, presumably to exclude larger, potentially predatory animals (Fig. 41).

The group of bumblebees sometimes referred to as the carder bumblebees, including one of our most common species, *B. pascuorum* (the common carder bumblebee), as well as some of our most endangered (for example, *B. humilis*, *B. sylvarum*), also generally take over and adapt disused small mammal nests. However, they usually establish their nests on or slightly above ground level (Fig. 42). *Bombus pascuorum* seems more adaptable than the others, and it frequently nests in abandoned corners of gardens, in compost heaps or under sheds. The other carder bumblebees seem to require tall grassland, with a relatively open sward, and a plentiful supply of leaf litter or moss at ground level. Presumably,

FIG 38. Tussocky grassland nesting habitat for common woodland edge bumblebees.

FIG 39. A wide woodland ride in early spring, nesting habitat for woodland edge bumblebees.

FIG 40. An overwintered queen *Bombus terrestris* prospecting for a nest site.

FIG 41. A worker *Bombus lucorum* emerging from the entrance to its underground nest.

FIG 42. A surface nest of *Bombus pascuorum*, composed of fragments of dry grass-blades.

also, the local small mammal population is a very significant factor, although there is little systematic evidence on this. The carder bumblebees are so-called because of their nest-building activity. The queens gather adjacent nest material and bind it together. Later in the season the workers may combine together to extend the nest in this way, or to repair it after damage (Fig. 43). As we will see later, the individual species of carder bumblebee also differ from one another in their exact requirements – some, such as *B. humilis*, seem to require a more open sward exposed to the sun, whereas others, such as *B. muscorum*, are associated with more dense, damp, and often cooler grasslands, such as coastal grazing marshes. Other species, such as *B. pratorum* and *B. hortorum*, appear to be more adaptable, and their nests may be found below or above ground, in ivy-covered walls, old birds' nests or nest boxes, and even, apparently, the pocket of a fur coat! (Free & Butler, 1959).

It is often held that the availability of abundant sources of pollen and nectar is a key factor limiting bumblebee populations. Given the immense losses of flower-rich grasslands to intensive agriculture and building development in lowland southern and central England this could hardly be denied. However, these massive environmental changes may have affected bumblebee populations in other ways. As well as losing sources of food, they will also have lost many suitable nest sites. If suitable nesting sites for voles, shrews and mice are lost, then this must have

FIG 43. House-bee worker *Bombus pascuorum* carrying out repairs to the nest.

FIG 44. Overwintered queen *Bombus sylvarum*, still foraging in July. The partial pollen load suggests she has at last established her nest.

a knock-on effect on the bumblebees that make use of their old nests. Where permanent grassland is lost, or management regimes are altered, potential nest sites, especially for the carder bumblebees, will be lost as well as the flowers they formerly visited for food. There is some evidence that shortage of suitable nesting sites is a limiting factor. The dead bodies of queens are sometimes found at the entrance and inside occupied nests, indicating competition, and even direct conflict for them. A further indication is the length of time often taken for the early-emerging queens to establish their nests (Fig. 44). Prospecting for nest sites is often observed well into May, even for early-emerging queens such as *B. lucorum* and *B. terrestris*. Following a very wet spring in 2001 many queens of *B. humilis* in south Essex had still not established nests by 28 July, possibly because waterlogging of their habitat had reduced the availability of suitable nesting places.

The mortality rate of overwintered queens is very high indeed – some estimates put it at more than 80 per cent. Some fall victim to predation by birds, including blue and great tits, others may simply fail to find sufficient nutrition, particularly if there are long periods of inclement weather after their emergence from hibernation. Another cause of mortality at this time of year is infestation by a species of nematode worm, *Sphaerularia bombi* (see Chapter 4 for more details). Infested females feed actively after emergence, as do healthy queens, but unlike the latter, they do not turn to nest-site prospecting and do not establish nests. On some measures, as many as 70 per cent of overwintered queens in some populations may be infected (Alford, 1975). To these casualties, we should add those that fail to find a suitable nest site, or are defeated in a contest for one.

ESTABLISHING THE COLONY

Before long, the surviving queens can be observed carrying clumps of pollen in their corbiculae. Instead of directly consuming the pollen that they comb from their furry bodies, the queens now pass the pollen forward to be mixed with regurgitated nectar, and then brush it back onto their hind legs. This is an indication that the second phase of the life cycle has already begun (Fig. 45).

Spring queens with pollen loads are not just foraging for themselves, but are either preparing a food store for their future offspring, or already feeding their first brood of larvae. To discover how they have arrived at this point, we need to gain access to the 'black box'. Thanks to Sladen, Free and others who have followed on and developed their techniques for persuading queens to initiate nests in captivity, we now have a great deal of information about the interior life of bumblebee colonies. From the time of her emergence from hibernation, the queen's ovaries have been undergoing development. Once a suitable nest site has

FIG 45. Queen *Bombus pratorum* with partial pollen load, early spring.

been occupied, she lines in with fine materials, and builds a cup-shaped cell with
thin layers of wax exuded from between the plates of her abdominal segments.
The pollen loads she brings back to the nest are scraped off into the cell and
bedded down. In some species the queens form a clump of moistened pollen first,
and build the wax cell on it. Either way, the first batch of eggs is then laid, with a
primer of pollen to feed the future larvae. Close by the brood cell the queen
constructs a honey pot with wax, in which she stores nectar from her subsequent
foraging trips (Fig. 46).

The eggs are white, sausage-shaped and 3–4 millimetres long (Fig. 47).
The first batch may number from 8 to 14. When the clutch of eggs has been laid,
the queen extends the wax cell to enclose them, and proceeds to incubate them
by stretching her body over the cell. Bumblebees have a remarkable ability to
maintain their body temperature well above that of their surroundings – above
30°C through a wide range of ambient temperatures. This seems to be important
for the development of the eggs and the resulting larvae, though it must fall
periodically while the queen is out on a foraging trip. An ingenious series of
experiments carried out by Heinrich (1979, 1993) showed that while queen
bumblebees are able to maintain both thoracic and abdominal temperatures well
above their surroundings while incubating, the main transfer of heat energy to
the brood is through the abdomen, which is stretched out and flattened against
the brood cell. The increase in metabolic rate required when surrounding
temperatures are low exceeds that achieved by many warm-blooded vertebrates.

In four to six days the eggs hatch, and the resulting tiny larvae are white,

FIG 46. A queen bumblebee soon after founding her colony, with pupal cocoons, larval
cells and honey pot.

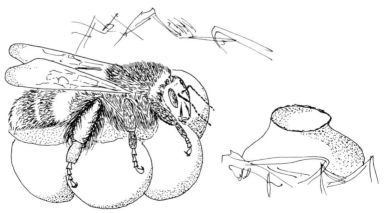

FIG 47. Nest of *Bombus lucorum*, showing eggs in an open cell attached to a cocoon.

grub-like and have little in the way of external features or sense organs. Initially the larvae feed on the pollen mass provided for them by the queen, and they grow rapidly. As Sladen discovered, the species of bumblebee differ in the ways they feed the developing larvae. The pocket makers deposit pollen to a pocket, or pouch on the side of the brood cell, and the larvae inside feed themselves from it. Because this may involve some competition, and some may be better placed in the cell to reach the pocket, it is supposed that the resulting workers of the pocket makers are likely to vary considerably in size. The other group of species, the pollen storers, make a separate store of pollen, and the larvae are fed individually by the queen (and, later, workers) squirting regurgitated mixtures of pollen and nectar into the brood chamber through a hole in the wax walls. As they grow, the larvae of the pollen storers spin separate compartments for themselves within the brood chamber. As the larvae of the pollen storers can be fed individually, the expectation is that the resulting workers will differ in size less than those of the pocket makers. This appears to be the case, but even in pollen-storer colonies there are still considerable differences in size among the workers. It has recently been suggested that these differences in size do not reflect 'poor parenting', but may be adaptive, in predisposing different workers to the various roles in the colony's division of labour (Goulson, 2003). Since at least some of the pocket makers switch to feeding larvae individually by regurgitated food in the later stages of those destined to develop as queens, it could be that these differences in feeding methods are also related to the way the female castes develop – either as future workers or as daughter queens.

Throughout the period of development of her first batch of larvae, the queen continues to incubate the brood cell, and enlarges it as the larvae grow by adding more wax to its walls. As with the larvae of other insects, the bumblebee larvae grow by shedding their 'skin' several times (Fig. 48). Their growth thus takes the form of a series of stages or instars, the timing of which is determined by a combination of hormones. Interestingly, the rear end of their gut is not open, so waste materials remain within the body cavity, and fouling of the larval chamber is avoided. When fully grown, each larva spins a more substantial cocoon of silk, and its final skin-moult reveals the shape of the pupa – a new stage in its life history (Fig. 49). The pupa is also whitish in colour, and shows many of the external features of the future adult insect, with the shape of the head, thorax and abdomen, wing-buds, legs, eyes, antennae and proboscis clearly visible. With the formation of the pupa, the accumulated waste products of the larva are expelled into the cocoon. The resulting meconium contains husks of pollen consumed during the development of the larva, and so is an interesting source of evidence about which flower species are used.

At this stage the queen removes the wax covering from the brood chamber and constructs one or more cells on the outside of the cocoons. After priming these with pollen, she lays more eggs. After roughly two weeks, the adult workers begin

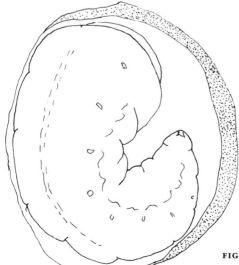

FIG 48. A full-grown larva, cell opened.

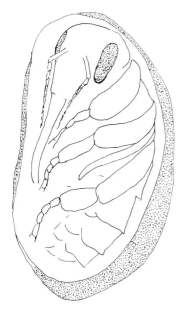

FIG 49. A pupa, cell opened.

to emerge from their pupae, and to bite their way out of their cocoons – often aided by the queen. At first they are tinted silvery-grey, lacking the full adult coloration, and the wings are soft, but after a day or so their colour pattern is acquired, and the wings have hardened. These new adults – all infertile females, generally much smaller than the queen – are the first cohort of the worker-caste, whose destiny is to aid the queen in foraging for their siblings, feeding and tending them, and carrying out various other tasks of colony maintenance.

GROWTH OF THE COLONY

The colony is now a fully social unit. Initially the queen continues to forage along with the workers, but after a few days she remains in the nest, confining her activities to egg laying and household tasks. All subsequent provisioning of the nest is carried out by the foraging activity of an increasing 'army' of worker bees.

Bumblebees feed their larvae on a mixture of pollen and nectar, sometimes combined with regurgitated droplets of proteins (Fig. 50) (Pereboom, 2000). Pollen is the main source of protein for the larvae, while nectar is a primarily a mixture of sugars which provide energy for both the larvae and the adult workers and their queen. Nectar is also important in maintaining an appropriate water balance in the

FIG 50. A worker *Bombus pratorum* feeding a larva.

diet. With foraging behaviour we are back out of the 'black box', and into a topic
that has been exhaustively studied. Chapter 6 is devoted to the fascinating
complexity and rival interpretations of bumblebee foraging behaviour. Here we
need note only the key points. Both main components of the bumblebee diet are
produced by flowering plants, as part of their own reproductive strategy. Over tens
of millions of years bumblebees have become adapted to collecting their food
from flowers, while the latter have evolved to attract bees and other visitors and
to regulate their behaviour in such a way as to enhance their own chances of
pollination (Proctor, Yeo & Lack, 1996). Bumblebees are famously effective
pollinators of many wild and cultivated plants, and some types of flower are held
to be adapted specifically to attract the pollinating services of bumblebees.

As social foragers, which have to bring food back to the nest at the end of each
foraging trip, bumblebee workers have to cover the energy costs of their flight to
and from the flowers they visit, with a surplus to feed the other nest inmates.
Energy is also required to maintain the nest temperature: the cooler the outside
temperature, the more energy will be required. Worker bumblebees are adapted
in several ways to be effective nectar collectors, being able to forage even in cold
weather, early and late in the day, and having honey-stomachs capable of carrying
back to the nest a nectar load up to 90 per cent of their body weight. They are also
good at learning how to access the complex structures some flowers have evolved,

and at identifying flower species and rewarding localities for foraging. The important thing to note here, however, is that the workers can only supply the energy requirements of the nest if there is a continuous seasonal succession of suitable flowering plants, in sufficient quantities, to meet the ever-expanding energy demands of the growing colony through its whole cycle. Furthermore, these food sources must be within the effective flying and navigating range of the nest.

At the same time, the colony must be provisioned not just with nectar, but also with pollen, particularly crucial for larval development (Fig 51). Although the problems of pollen collection have been studied far less than nectar collection, it is already clear that most bumblebee species are much more selective about pollen sources than they are about sources of nectar. The local abundance of a small number of flower species may be more important to colony survival than floristic diversity. Red clover and other Fabaceae, several members of the deadnettle family (Lamiaceae), some of the figwort family (Scrophulariaceae) and bramble, as well as some common garden herbs and shrubs, are among the most important pollen sources for the majority of the British bumblebees.

More than merely foraging efficiently, the workers have to bring back to the nest food of the right sorts and in the right proportions to meet the shifting needs of the larvae and the other inmates of the nest (Fig 52). This must involve a division of labour among the foragers that changes as the colony itself develops, and as the

FIG 51. A worker *Bombus muscorum* with full pollen loads.

FIG 52. A worker *Bombus monticola* returning to its nest with nectar.

availability of food sources in the local environment changes through the season. There is also a division of labour between the workers that go out on foraging trips and those that stay in the nest and perform various household tasks, including feeding, incubating and tending the larvae, cleaning out empty cocoons for use as food stores, extending the wax covering of larval groups, repairing and extending the nest and maintaining its temperature (Fig. 53). These house-bees also play a role in defence if the nest is under threat from predators, such as badgers (Fig. 54). In those bumblebee colonies that have been studied, it seems that workers do often change from one sort of task to another over the longer term, but may remain constant to a particular task for several days. In J. B. Free's studies of *B. pascuorum* (then called *B. agrorum*), freshly emerged workers generally began as house-bees. Some of these never left the nest throughout their lives, whilst others later took to making intermittent foraging trips outside the nest. These bees then tended to become committed foragers. However, some 30 per cent of the workers showed no clear specialisation of function. Free also noted a tendency for the larger workers to begin foraging at an earlier age, so that at any one time, the foragers were on average larger than the house-bees.

Whilst a division of labour among the workers could be expected to enhance the efficiency of the colony, too great a rigidity in the division of labour would put it at risk in the face of changing conditions. In social insects other than

FIG 53. A worker *Bombus pratorum* pressing its body against the comb to maintain brood temperature.

FIG 54. Part of the comb of a *Bombus lapidarius* nest (a pollen storer), showing honey and pollen stored in old cocoons. One worker (bottom left) has adopted a threat posture, on its back, with tip of the abdomen pointing at the source of disturbance to the nest.

bumblebees there is quite a variety of ways to adjust colony activity to changing conditions. In some ant species, specialist castes increase their work rate, while other workers diversify their activity. In other groups, notably honey bees, there is a reserve of inactive workers who take up new tasks as required. In some insects, including *B. pascuorum*, as discovered by Free, there is a broad age-related division of labour. In these species colony effort can be adjusted by workers slowing down or speeding up the shift from early to late life-time specialisms. However, in some bumblebee species there seems to be no particular link between age of workers and their role in the division of labour, and most respond to short-term emergencies or changes in environmental conditions by significant numbers of workers simply shifting from one task to another to meet the prevailing pattern of demand.

In a series of ingenious experiments, Free showed that the commitment of workers to different tasks was relatively flexible, and influenced by the changing needs of the nest. Removing foragers from a captive nest resulted in house-bees, many of which had not previously left the nest, switching over to foraging. Removal of house-bees also tended to result in a return of foragers to housework, but this was less marked. Similar results were obtained in relation to the division of labour among foragers, as between pollen and nectar collection. Proportions of nectar to pollen collected by workers in pairs of colonies were measured, and then the larvae were removed from one of each pair. The workers in the colonies from which larvae had been removed did continue to collect pollen, but proportionally less.

Free showed that the state of food stores in the nest also influences foraging behaviour. He artificially filled some of the honey pots with syrup and observed the subsequent behaviour of foragers. Those that had previously been foraging for nectar abandoned foraging and remained in the nest for some hours. However, pollen collectors continued to forage as usual. Adding pollen artificially had corresponding results. Pollen was added to the pollen stores in the case of pollen storers, and balls of pollen were attached to the comb in the case of pocket makers. In both cases, relatively less pollen was subsequently collected by the workers. Interestingly, in neither experiment did workers switch between pollen and nectar collecting, indicating the bees' constancy to their specialisation, though switching might have occurred if the experiments had been continued over a longer period (Free & Butler, 1959).

Cartar (1992) followed up Free's experiments with three North American bumblebee species, and his results were broadly similar, showing considerable short-term flexibility in the overall colony division of labour. In Cartar's study an attempt was made to identify which bees shifted to new tasks in the face of changes in colony food supply. In general, those that switched tasks were the less experienced and so less efficient ones at the original task. The one exception to this was the shift from nectar to pollen collecting, where no differences in efficiency were discovered between those who did, and those who did not switch tasks. Cartar interprets this as evidence that nectar collection may be harder to learn than pollen collection, but this seems unlikely. Another possibility could be that energy shortfall in the colony has immediate and serious consequences, so calling for an efficient response, whereas pollen shortage, no less crucial in the long run, does not provoke an immediate crisis. This interpretation is supported by Cartar & Dill's (1991) experimental study of colony responses to a simulated attack by a vertebrate predator and the introduction of a cuckoo bee. Energy-rich colonies responded aggressively to both, whereas workers in the energy-depleted colonies either remained stationary on the comb, or merely adopted threat postures. A further study by O'Donnell *et al.* (2000) investigated flexibility in the division of labour in another North American species, *B. bifarius*. Their research showed that some individual bees continued as specialists in the various foraging and housekeeping tasks, whilst others more readily shifted between tasks in response to short-term changes in environmental conditions or patterns of demand in the nest. The specialists contributed proportionately more labour to the colony than the non-specialists.

On the assumption that these patterns are adaptive, it may be that they con-stitute a compromise between the benefits of specialism in enhancing efficiency by learning, and the need for the colony to be able to respond to short-term fluctuations in external resources or internal demand. It remains unclear what cues provoke individual workers to switch tasks, and why some individuals do so whilst others do not. In some species genetic predispositions may be involved, or experienced and efficient specialists may possibly be more motivated to continue in their specialism. However, the use of chemical signals (pheromones) as a means of communication among bumblebees is gaining increased attention from researchers, and it may be that they play a more complex role in the division of labour in the nest than has so far been shown. Honey bees have the well-known waggle dance by which workers communicate to each other the best places to for-age (von Frisch, 1967). Bumblebees have no direct equivalent of this, and it seems that workers find their own way to suitable foraging sites by individual searching. However, here again, it seems that communication by scent plays an important role. We will return to a more detailed discussion of this in the next chapter.

Given favourable conditions, the number of workers continues to grow until it reaches a critical size. In some species colony growth is relatively slow, and at full maturity the nest may number several hundred workers. In others, maturity is reached relatively quickly, and the maximum number of workers may be well under 100 – perhaps as few as 20 in some of the rarer carder bumblebees. Whatever these differences in timing, however, successful colonies of all species reach a critical point at some time in the late spring or summer.

INVESTING IN THE FUTURE: MALES AND DAUGHTER QUEENS

This is the moment at which the adult bees that hatch from their pupae are not infertile workers, but males and gynes, or daughter queens (Fig. 55). Only if a generation of sexuals that go on to find mates is produced can the colony be counted a success. From growth and development, the colony has now shifted to its reproductive phase – but, of course, the key 'decisions' involved must have taken place some time earlier, either (in the case of males) as the eggs were laid, or (in the case of females) at some time during their larval development. Recent studies have focused on the moments at which male eggs are laid, and the future caste of female larvae is determined, rather than on the moment of actual emergence of the males and daughter queens. The timing of these decisions varies from species to species, and may also vary between different colonies of the same species. In some species the switching point occurs surprisingly early, and the queen may continue to lay eggs destined to develop as workers, so that there is considerable overlap in time between the growth and reproductive phases of colony development (Müller *et al.*, 1992). In those species studied so far, the developmental stage at which female larvae are determined as future workers or queens has been shown to be surprisingly early: in *B. terrestris* larvae, for example, not later than the seventh day after hatching from the egg. In the case of males, their sex is determined from the moment the egg is formed. Given what is known about the length of time it takes for full development of each sex and caste it is possible to read back from emergence times to estimate the point at which the decisions to produce future reproductive individuals were made.

In a study conducted on three bumblebee species by Müller *et al.* (1992) it was shown that these decisions were made very early in the life cycle of the colony. In the majority of *B. lucorum* colonies studied, the first decisions determining the production of future queens were made before any adult workers had emerged. In the two other species (*B. terrestris* and an American species, *B. terricola*), the determination of future sexual cohorts began when only a few workers were present. One interpretation of these findings is that early sex and caste determination allows the queen to control the key reproduction decisions in the colony.

FIG 55. Part of the comb of a *Bombus pascuorum* nest (a pocket maker), showing cocoons, honey stores and a recently emerged male (top right).

These decisions are taken during the phase in the life cycle of the colony when reproductive conflicts with workers are least likely. The study also revealed that the majority of the workers in each species emerged from eggs laid after the initiation of male and daughter queen-production. The growth and reproductive phases of the colony thus overlap very considerably, by as much as a third of the growth phase in the case of *B. lucorum*. One possible adaptive consequence of this is that foraging workers are still present after the emergence of the males and daughter queens. For the daughter queens, particularly, food sources in the nest will reduce the need for them to forage prior to hibernation, and so reduce the risk of predation.

Despite an increasing focus of recent research on this crucial development in the life of the colony, there remain many unanswered questions. What factor or combination of factors is responsible for the transition? Why does its timing differ so much among the different species? What triggers the change? How early in the life of the developing female larva is its future caste determined? What are the respective roles of queen, workers and, perhaps, the larvae themselves in the transition?

In bumblebees, as in other bees and their relatives, fertilised (diploid) eggs develop into females. So the females have two sets of chromosomes, inherited equally from male and female parents. There is no difference in genetic constitution between the two female castes – workers and queens – so a fertilised egg can develop into either a worker or a queen, depending on environmental influences. Males (usually) result from unfertilised (haploid) eggs, and so inherit their genetic constitution from their mother only. Since the workers do not have an opportunity to mate, only the queens can lay eggs that produce workers or daughter queens. In the small number of species studied so far, it seems that queens predominate in producing male offspring, too. The queen has sperm from her mating the previous year stored in a special organ, the spermatheca. She is able to switch the laying of haploid and diploid eggs on or off by regulating the release of sperm during the process of egg laying. Under some circumstance, the ovaries of workers are activated and they also lay eggs. These go on to develop as males, if they are allowed to survive. If the colony loses its queen, one or more workers may become dominant and lay eggs. Generally, however, the workers do not attempt to lay eggs until the final competition phase in the life of the colony, to which we will return later.

Colonies vary a great deal in their success at rearing males and daughter queens. Many never reach the stage of producing either. In those that do, some produce all or mainly males, others mainly daughter queens, while others may produce considerable numbers of both sexes. Where both sexes are successfully reared, the queen has usually switched to male-production earlier. It is generally thought that males which emerge early in the season are more likely to find a mate than later ones.

Several connected problems have engaged the ingenuity of bumblebee researchers. One is why the workers do not lay eggs sooner, but rather altruistically tend their sisters and the sons or daughters of their queen. We will return to that question a little later in this chapter and again in Chapter 3. Other issues are what prompts the shift to the reproductive phase in the colony's development, and what are the mechanisms that bring about the shift? In the case of the queen's switch to male-production, the main question is what prompts the queen to begin laying haploid eggs? In the case of the shift from the production of workers to production of daughter queens, the question is a complex one concerning alternative developmental pathways: what environmental influences shape or determine which will be followed, and at what stages in the life history of the insect?

An important step forward in unravelling some of these puzzles was the impressive synthesis of a wide range of scattered studies by M. V. Brian, a researcher at the Furzebrook research station in Dorset (Brian, 1980). His synthesis covered the control over caste and sex-determination in social bees, wasps and ants (his own research subjects). So far as the bumblebees were concerned, he made an important distinction between 'simple' and 'complex' species. *Bombus pratorum* is an example of the former. J. B. Free had shown that colonies of this species kept in the laboratory, if provided with ample food and a sufficiently high ratio of workers to larvae, could produce daughter queens even in the first broods. This happened even in the absence of a queen. These observations suggest that the transition from worker- to young queen-production is a process not directly controlled by the queen. It seems that food supply and the ratio of workers to developing larvae are both important factors. In some species (including the 'new arrival' to Britain, *B. hynorum*) the caste of female larvae is not determined until late on in their development. Those destined to develop into young queens are fed more and for longer, and pupation is delayed. Yet another factor could be day length. Early transition to daughter queen-production in captive colonies of *B. hortorum* and *B. pascuorum* was triggered by artificially shortening day length in spring, apparently simulating the onset of autumn (Grinfeld & Zakharova, cited in Brian, 1980).

Complex species include *B. terrestris* and its close relative, *B. lucorum*. These are distinctive in that the queen has a more dominant role in the nest, and is able to control the timing of transition to daughter queen-production, as well as the production of males. In the simple species it is believed that the queen maintains her dominance in the nest mainly or wholly through her greater size and behavioural cues. However, in the complex species chemical signals – pheromones – play an important role. There is strong evidence that pheromonal communication is important in suppressing the activation of the workers' ovaries so that the queen monopolises reproduction of male offspring until the onset of the competition phase. The queen is also able to control the switch from worker- to queen-production. Even when there is a high ratio of workers to larvae and food is abundant the queen is able to delay the transition to daughter queen-production. Instead, large workers are produced. Since it is the workers who feed the larvae, the queen exerts her control indirectly, and it seems that she can exert this influence over the workers only through close contact with them. Larvae destined to become young queens are set on this course of development by the action of a pheromone produced by the queen, and are subsequently fed for longer, taking some three days more to reach the pupal stage, and remain as pupae for several days longer than those that emerge as workers.

Further important insights into the reproductive strategies adopted by complex species were provided by Duchateau & Velthuis (1988) in their study of 26 nests of *B. terrestris* (see also Duchateau *et al.*, 2004). Their colonies showed two quite different patterns. In some, the queen switched early to laying haploid eggs, between 6 and 13 days after the emergence of the first workers. These early-switching colonies produced mostly males. A second group switched to producing their reproductive generation significantly later (18–32 days after the emergence of the first workers). These colonies produced fewer males on average, but more daughter queens. Overall, the colonies produced four males to each daughter queen. The study showed that there was no direct causal link between the queen's beginning to lay haploid eggs and the switch to queen-production. It also failed to confirm any of the available explanations of the timing of the switch to production of males, leaving open the possibility that this is innate in the queen. For queen-production, however, there was a clear relationship to worker:larva ratios. Queen larvae require three times as much food for their full development as do workers, and the presence of a sufficiently large worker cohort during the last stage of larval development is crucial. In the early-switching colonies, the few that did manage to rear daughter queens did so when this ratio was high. In late-switching colonies with high worker to larva ratios, nine out of ten colonies managed to rear daughter queens (Fig. 56).

FIG 56. A diagram of the average pattern of production of workers, queens and males assuming a constant rate of egg production, and the resulting number of individuals in early- and late-switching colonies respectively. Also shown is the average biomass of reproductives. I = colony initiation; S = switch point; C = competition point (reproduced from Duchateau & Velthuis, 1988, with permission).

Early-switching colonies:

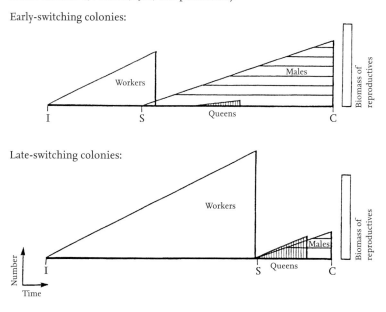

Late-switching colonies:

There is evidence that a pheromone, secreted by the queen and transmitted by way of close contact with the workers, destines the female larvae to develop as workers. The switch to producing daughter queens is apparently triggered by the queen's ceasing to secrete the pheromone. As we shall see, there is still some dispute about the processes involved, but the development and final emergence of the fully developed males and daughter queens marks the culmination of the colony's development.

COMPETITION AND CONFLICT

In late-switching colonies, the shift to queen-production is closely followed by the onset of a phase of aggressive interactions among the workers, and between them and the queen. It seems that the onset of this competition phase is not correlated with the switching point, though it generally occurs some seven to ten days after the first eggs that will develop into queens have been laid. However, Duchateau & Velthuis could find no clear social or environmental explanation for its timing: the queen remains active, can continue to lay eggs, and timing is also unaffected by worker numbers, or whether the colony is an early or late switcher. During this phase, some workers attempt to lay eggs, but these attempts are resisted by the queen and other workers. Those that are successful have to defend their own egg cells from attempts by others to eat their eggs, or expel the resulting larvae, and eggs laid by the queen are also eaten by some of the workers. Sometimes groups of workers harass and bite the queen, even killing her or expelling her from the nest (van Honk et al., 1981a; Bourke, 1994). Some observers report that few of the eggs laid during the competition phase ever reach adulthood, whereas others note that a significant proportion of the males produced by some colonies are offspring of workers. Lopez-Vaamonde et al. (2004a) used genetic sampling to study worker-produced males in 32 B. terrestris colonies, and showed that they were, indeed, a very small proportion of the total number of males produced (3.6 per cent). However, one remarkable result was that almost half of these were the offspring of non-resident 'drifter' workers. These workers showed more aggressive interactions and were more likely to lay eggs prior to the competition point than were resident workers.

The outbreak of conflict within the bumblebee nest raises fascinating questions about the balance between co-operation and conflict, and its evolutionary explanation. Co-operation, such as we find in bumblebee colonies, seems to involve the caste of workers sacrificing their own reproductive interests in favour of their queen. This seems to fly in the face of common understanding of the way natural selection works in the evolution of both bodily and behavioural traits of living organisms. In so far as patterns of behaviour are inherited, we would expect them to be geared to enhancing the survival and reproductive chances of the individual. However, if we take the 'gene's-eye view' it can be argued that there may be circumstances in which an individual's genes may be more likely to be passed on to the next generation if it acts to boost the reproductive success of another individual. This is most likely to be the case if that other individual is a close relative: that is, one with which it shares a large part of its genetic constitution. So-called altruistic behaviour is thus most likely to be shown towards close kin: the closer the kinship, the more altruistic the behaviour. The evolutionary process leading to this outcome is known as kin selection, and its theoretical working-out is attributed to W. D. Hamilton. Since worker bumblebees share up to 75 per cent of their genes with one another and with their sisters who will develop into daughter queens, they are very closely related – more so than each of them is to their mother, the queen, with whom they share 50 per cent of their genes.

So the bumblebee colony is essentially a family grouping, but, as in all families, there is plenty of room for conflict (Müller *et al.*, 1992). Kin selection theory offers an explanation of the puzzling phenomenon of altruism, but it also predicts the situations in which conflict and the reassertion of self-interest is likely to arise. Since workers share only one half of their genes with the queen, their reproductive interests are not identical. However, since they have no opportunity to mate, workers cannot produce female offspring, so their inability to prevent the development of the queen's female larvae into daughter queens makes evolutionary sense. However, if they can avoid the queen's power to inhibit the activation of their ovaries they are able to produce males. The workers will be more closely related to their own male offspring than they are to the males produced by their queen. So kin selection theory predicts that they will sometimes seek to lay their own eggs, and to be in conflict with the queen over whose male progeny survive.

Initial applications of kin selection theory (Hamilton, 1964; Trivers & Hare, 1976) led to the expectation that the competition phase should coincide with the queen's shift to laying haploid (future male) eggs, because this is the point at which the reproductive interests of queen and workers diverge. However, Duchateau & Velthuis showed that the competition point was not correlated with the shift to male-production on the part of the queen. Rather, there was an association between the onset of competition and the shift to daughter queen-production in both early- and late-switching colonies. This finding has been partially confirmed in later studies, but experimental manipulation of colonies of *B. terrestris* has exposed more complexity: the timing of the onset of competition is influenced by worker numbers and numbers of male larvae as well as by the transition to production of daughter queens (for example, Bloch, 1999).

The application of kin selection theory has implications for the way we think about the queen's dominance in the nest. Most accounts have tended to see the queen's ability to prevent workers laying their own eggs, and to control the points in the development of the colony at which male eggs are laid, and the production of daughter queens commences as a result of her power over them. This suggests a conflict of interests between queen and workers. On the other hand, kin selection theory predicts that up to the competition point the queen and workers have common reproductive interests. On this interpretation, we should see the queen's role not as coercing or determining events in the nest, but, rather, as emitting 'signals' that are acted on by their recipients because it is in their reproductive interests to do so. The onset of the competition phase is thus seen not as the result of declining queen dominance, but, rather, as a direct expression of the divergence of the reproductive interests of the different castes.

Duchateau & Velthuis argued that ratios between males and daughter queens in the colonies they studied showed a bias in favour of the queen's reproductive interests, suggesting that queen control enhances her reproductive interest, in this respect at least, at the expense of that of the workers. Later work by Cnaani and others seems consistent with this interpretation, suggesting that the queen's perception of actual or impending conflicts with workers may be what triggers her 'decision' to shift to production of daughter queens (for example, Cnaani *et al.*, 2000). The alternative view, that 'queen control' should be seen as 'honest signalling' between social partners with shared interests has recently been developed in ingenious ways to account for some of the puzzling results of experimental work. We will consider in more detail some of the issues involved in Chapter 3.

The assumptions about degrees of kinship in the nest made in the above discussions suppose that the queen has mated with only one male. This holds good for most species, but the queens of at least one, *B. hypnorum*, are known to mate more than once. This produces a situation in which the workers are more genetically heterogeneous, and may be more closely related to the queen than to each other. One consequence is that the workers aid the queen in 'policing' the attempts of other workers to lay eggs. Newly developed techniques of DNA analysis now allow more definitive measures of the degrees of genetic related-ness between individuals. It seems likely that future research will yield more information about these complex patterns of conflict and co-operation, and at the same time illuminate the strengths and possible limitations of the kin selection approach.

Much still remains to be discovered about the social processes that take place in the nest. This is true even for species such as *B. terrestris*, which have been most thoroughly studied. Studies such as that by Müller *et al.*, discussed above, illustrate the diversity in colony life histories even for three closely related species. It seems likely that future studies of other species, including those designated simple, will reveal still more diversity.

Not all colonies reach maturity: inclement weather, limited resources in foraging range, the effects of parasitism and predation and other factors may lead to premature collapse. Even those that do reach maturity may produce only males or only daughter queens, while other colonies are successful in producing both. One study, conducted by Cumber, concerned 80 nests of *B. pascuorum*. More than half of them (48) produced no males or young queens. Nine produced males only, and only 13 produced more than eight queens each (Cumber, 1953). It seems very likely that ratios between males and females produced, and the probability of a colony reaching full maturity, will differ greatly between captive and wild colonies. From the point of view of conservation, the success rates of colonies of the various species under different environmental conditions and land-management regimes are of great importance, but little is so far known.

FINDING A MATE AND PREPARING FOR WINTER

On emergence from their pupal case, males take from two to four days to dry their wings, acquire their full adult coloration, and feed from the nest's store of pollen and nectar. They then leave the nest and are generally believed not to return to it. In contrast, daughter queens spend more time in the nest after emergence. They consume some of the nest's food stores, but in some species also play a part in tending the larvae and in foraging. After foraging trips they return to the nest, and shelter there at night and in inclement weather, sometimes remaining associated with the maternal nest until they find a place to hibernate.

Young queens have two main priorities. One is to mate, so they will have a store of sperm with which to fertilise their eggs after the foundation of their own nests. The other is to build up their food reserves for the coming winter hibernation. Although at least some bumblebee species can be induced to mate in captivity, mating of wild bumblebees is rarely observed. But before it can take place, males and females must first find each other. It is the mate-locating strategies of the males that have been most studied. There are three basic patterns. One is for the males to gather round a nest entrance and pounce on fresh females as they emerge. Another is to establish a fixed 'perch' from which to intercept and mate with a passing female. The third, and most curious, is repeated patrolling of scent-marked routes.

The first strategy is described by Sladen as used by *B. subterraneus* (now believed extinct in Britain) and *B. ruderarius* (the red-shanked carder bumblebee). He also reports having seen 'a male of *B. ruderatus* ride away upon a queen as she was flying from the nest' (Sladen, 1912). The second strategy is reported for several bumblebee species, but is not used by any of the British species. According to Free & Butler (1959), males select a prominent perch and remain close to it for 'hours on end'. They may stand motionless, with erect antennae and half-spread wings, or hover close to the perch. From this vantage point they dart after anything flying by of about the size of a queen bumblebee – including a stone thrown into the air close by. Accurate recognition of a potential mate apparently requires a close encounter!

The third strategy, patrolling, can easily be observed, and is the one most studied. There are variations from species to species, and each species is also capable of altering its pattern of patrolling according to habitat features. Perhaps the earliest account of patrolling male bumblebees is that given by Darwin. He observed males of *B. hortorum* following one another at intervals of a few minutes along a fixed route, stopping every few yards at what he called 'buzzing places' (Fig. 57). These included a patch of bare earth, a hole at the base of an ash tree and an ivy leaf. He was able to mark out the circuit followed by the bees by recruiting exceptionally agile research assistants:

> 'The flight paths remain the same for a considerable time and the buzzing places are fixed within an inch. I was able to prove this by stationing five or six of my children on a number of separate occasions each close to a buzzing place, and telling the one farthest away to shout out "here is a bee" as soon as one was buzzing around. The others followed this up, so that the same cry of "here is a bee" was passed on from child to child without interruption until the bees reached the buzzing place where I myself was standing.'
> (C. Darwin, tr. R. B. Freeman, 1965)

Darwin noted that the middle of a warm day was the best time to observe this behaviour, and was deeply puzzled by it. He experimentally altered the appearance of the buzzing places, and observed that this made no difference to the behaviour of the bees. He also observed bees following exactly the same route on successive years, and was astonished by this. He presumably had some inkling that the behaviour was linked to mate-location, since he noted that he had never witnessed

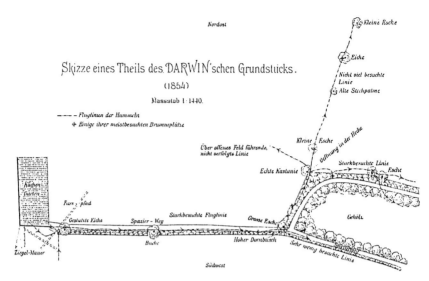

FIG 57. Darwin's sketch map of the patrolling route of *Bombus hortorum* males in his garden (from Darwin, 1965).

a queen on the flight path, despite looking out for them. He also noted variations of this patrolling behaviour in *B. pratorum* and *B. lucorum*.

Since Darwin's observations, patrolling behaviour in males has been described for several species, and it is now somewhat better understood. Darwin's 'buzzing places' are now referred to as 'approach places', and at least one of Darwin's mysteries has been solved: the bees scent-mark points along their patrolling routes with pheromones, and these are repeatedly visited as they continue their circuits. It is supposed that these scent patches are attractive to young queens, which are then discovered by the males. However, there are few observations of this actually occurring! Males appear to be sexually attracted to virgin females only at marked approach places, though such reports as exist suggest that males merely attach themselves to females at these points, with actual mating taking place at some distance – on the ground, on flowers or in the tree canopy.

Systematic observations of this patrolling behaviour have provided rather few clear patterns. Patrolling behaviour is reported for males of most British bumblebee species, most commonly in *B. hortorum*, *B. lapidarius*, *B. pratorum* and *B. terrestris*, as well as the cuckoo bumblebee, *B. vestalis*. However, it has been observed, though less frequently, in most other British species – *B. lucorum*, *B. pascuorum*, *B. jonellus*, *B. monticola* and others. Close studies of several species in alpine and subalpine zones in northern Sweden during the 1970s provided some significant insights into male patrolling behaviour (Svensson 1979b). It was established that patrolling began early in the day, and the bees marked their approach places with pheromones within the first hour of activity. If the weather was variable, they would repeat their marks at intervals through the day. In all species where patrolling was regularly observed, the bees followed a constant route through the day and on successive days. In some species, the same routes and approach places were adopted in successive seasons – as Darwin had observed for *B. hortorum*. The bees would fly swiftly and directly between approach places (usually located within a few metres of one another), but adopt a different flight pattern when close to one, before moving on again. There is evidence that the change in behaviour of the bees as they approach the points they have scent-marked is a response partly to visual cues and partly to the scents emanating from them.

Several male bees of the same species (and possibly from the same nest) often arrive at approach places simultaneously, and either together or in sequence will follow the same route. However, when the full circuit of each bee is traced, it turns out that they are all different. The flight paths of the patrolling bees thus intersect and run together for a part of the route and then separate out again. Some approach places are thus much more intensively visited than others (Fig. 58).

In favourable weather, patrolling is most intensive up to the middle of the day, with bees occasionally diverting to feed from a wide range of flowers close to the patrol route. Later in the day more time is spent foraging. When the weather is more variable, foraging and patrolling are alternated through the day.

FIG 58. Individual flight paths of *Bombus lapponicus* males. Four, and part of a fifth patrol routes are shown. The upper part of the map indicates fairly dense and tall birch forest, and the lower part an open area with low scattered willows and dwarf birch (reproduced from Svensson, 1979*b*, with permission).

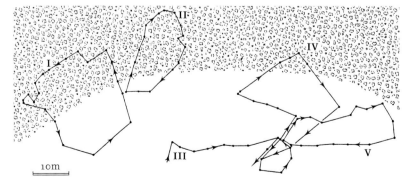

Of particular interest are the comparisons between the patrolling behaviours of the various species. In the Swedish study, there was considerable differentiation in the habitats used for patrolling by different species in the alpine zone. However, in the subalpine zone there was much less evidence of this, with as many as four species sharing the same patrolling areas. In some cases, the patrolling routes followed by different species intersected, and the same object, such as a birch tree, would be marked by more than one species. However, where this happened, the routes and approach places would be differentiated vertically, with flight paths and approach places at different levels above the ground (Fig. 59). So, for example, of three species which also occur in Britain, *B. pratorum* tended to follow flight paths from low bush to ground level, *B. lucorum* flew around the middle level, whilst *B. jonellus* flew at tree-top height. Even so, there was considerable overlap between the flight paths of some species.

Svensson (1979b) considered the likelihood that differences in flight paths played a part in reducing the chances of mating between different species. This was confirmed by the fact that where flight paths were similar, and habitats shared, the species concerned tended to have either incompatible genital structures, or pheromones with very different chemical composition. A study of patrolling behaviour carried out in very different habitats in the UK and New Zealand yielded similar findings, in that species sharing the same habitat tended to mark points and patrol at different levels in relation to habitat features. However, both studies indicate that most species are very flexible both in their habitat preferences and in the kinds of feature used for marking (Fig. 60).

FIG 59. Simplified pattern of flight paths and approached places (circles) of six male bumblebee species patrolling in subalpine birch forest in northern Sweden (reproduced from Svensson, 1979b, with permission).

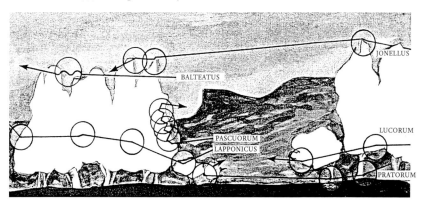

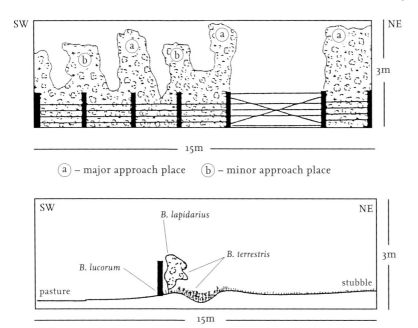

FIG 60. Approach places of patrolling bumblebees in farmland: (above) approach places of *Bombus terrestris* along a 15-metre stretch of a south-east facing gappy hedgerow at Cambridge University Farm on 4 August 1989; (below) approach places of *Bombus terrestris* (bush and nettles in the ditch), *B. lucorum* (base of fenceposts) and *B. lapidarius* (tops of bushes) on a field boundary at the same locality, 2 August (both drawings reproduced from Fussell & Corbet, 1992d, with permission).

There are rather few reports of patrolling by males of some species, even some common ones such as *B. pascuorum*. Such reports as exist suggest that this species' method is intermediate between patrolling and waiting at the nest. This method involves patrolling, but with marked approach places at or near the entrances to nests of the same species. It seems that other carder bumblebees as well as *B. hortorum* might also adopt this method of mate location. If so, it would explain Darwin's observation that the *B. hortorum* males he watched showed particular interest in a hole at the base of a tree.

Most observers comment on the rarity of sightings of mating bumblebees, and these appear to be always away from patrolling routes. There are reports of several males – up to five – attached to the same female, and all attempting to mate with her. In my own field work, I have observed mating on very few occasions. Two involved *B. lapidarius*, with the much smaller male perched rather absurdly on the

FIG 61. A pair of *Bombus lapidarius* mating.

dorsal surface of the lower abdominal segments of the female (Fig. 61). In one case the pair were stationary on the ground, but in the other, the female was actively foraging on knapweed flowers, with the male beating his wings rapidly to stay on board. Two other cases involved entanglements between two species: one involved a male *B. lapidarius* mounted on the back of a female *B. lucorum*, while the other was a mating pair of *B. lucorum*, with a male *B. lapidarius* firmly attached to the back of the female (Fig. 62). In view of Svensson's comments on reproductive isolation, it would be interesting to know if this particular confusion is more widespread.

Fertilised queens continue to feed and to return to the parental nest, building up their fat store – large, whitish clumps of cells, which eventually fill much of the abdominal cavity. They also fill their honey-stomachs prior to settling into their chosen place for hibernation. Little is known about where or when the different species hibernate. Favoured places are said to be north-facing banks, where they dig into deep leaf litter, or into loose soil, forming a small chamber. In some species, at least, the fertilised young queens enter their winter quarters as early as July or August, but individuals of other species (such as *B. pascuorum* and *B. terrestris*) may be seen on the wing well into October.

Sometimes daughter queens can be seen returning to their nest of origin with full pollen loads (Fig. 63) (for example, *B. hortorum*, own obs.). One possibility is that

FIG 62. A pair of *Bombus lucorum* mating, with a male *B. lapidarius* attached to the body of the *B. lucorum* queen.

FIG 63. A daughter queen *Bombus hortorum* returning to her nest of origin with pollen loads.

they are foraging for the maternal colony, but it is also believed that if the original queen is very weak or dead, daughter queens may lay their eggs in the nest, and begin the cycle over again without first going into hibernation (M. Intenthron, pers. comm.). Alternatively, in some species with short, early colony cycles, such as *B. pratorum* and *B. hortorum*, young queens may start new nests and succeed in completing two cycles in a single year.

DECLINE AND FALL

With the death or eviction of the queen, workers may continue for some time to raise their own male offspring, or forage for themselves, but soon the colony disintegrates and dies out. Meanwhile, the males continue to patrol and forage for themselves. They roost outside, often clinging to the underside of a flowerhead, such as a thistle or knapweed. Their foraging is under much less pressure than that of the workers, and they tend to be more sluggish in their movements while foraging, often seeming almost motionless on a flowerhead. Those that escape predation are increasingly worn, with tattered wings, and often faded colours. All die off before the onset of winter. In southern England a small number of colonies of *B. terrestris* and *B. lucorum* continue into the winter in favourable years.

CHAPTER 3

Bumblebee Psychology

O F   C O U R S E, no one can have direct access to the 'inner life' of bumblebees: what philosophers call the phenomenology of bumblebee experience of the world is of necessity inaccessible to us. So it might seem that my chapter title is inappropriate – perhaps imputing to bees something like our own conscious experience of the world.

However, as with other groups of animals, we can make reasoned inferences about their mental life from two important sources of evidence: the anatomy and physiology of their sensory organs, brain and central nervous system, together with observations and experiments on their behaviour in different contexts. A useful way of putting this evidence together is to consider the overall mode of life of bumblebees, and the range of sensory, mental and motor challenges it poses.

First, we consider the challenge of successful foraging. As central place foragers (see Chapter 6), worker bees (and queens prior to the emergence of the first cohort of workers) are faced with the challenge of finding rewarding sources of nectar and pollen. These resources are patchily distributed spatially, and subject to time constraints on various timescales, from minutes to weeks, depending on prior visits by each bee itself, or other foragers, on the timing of pollen release and nectar secretion, or on the seasonality of the flowers it visits. Discriminations have to be made between patches, and, within the patches, between more-or-less rewarding flowers or flower types, 'decisions' have to be made about how long to stay and when or where to move on. The bee must learn how to handle each flower to gain the reward it is seeking. If it is to do this efficiently, it must have some ability both to recognise flower types similar to ones it has handled before, and to remember how to access their rewards.

Furthermore, if it is to return to the nest to deliver its load of pollen or nectar, and repeat its journey on a subsequent occasion, it must have some way of recalling its route between nest and foraging patch, and an ability to navigate between the two.

However, each foraging worker is not just acting to meet its own needs, but is playing a part in an overall division of labour among the cohort of foragers from its colony. If the needs of the non-foraging workers, queen and brood are to be met, then the foragers need some way of assessing the resource requirements of the nest, and adjusting their foraging activities accordingly: how much nectar? How dilute or concentrated? How much pollen? This involves not only perceptual and cognitive abilities, but also a degree of flexible adaptability: while some of the challenges of foraging can be solved by learning fairly fixed routines (see Chapter 6), these cannot be so fixed that the individual workers fail to respond to changing availability of resources in the environment and the shifting needs of the colony.

How are these shifting needs communicated? How do individual workers 'know' what part they are to play in meeting them? Within the nest, successful reproduction depends on the sustained dominance of the queen over her workforce. Both behavioural cues and chemical secretions appear to be involved in this: so a complex system of communication, involving both motor powers and sensory discrimination between scents and behaviours, on the part of both queen and workers, must exist among the members of the colony. Among the bees that stay in the nest, there are many tasks that have to be accomplished: brood care, nest cleaning and maintenance, thermoregulation and defence. These tasks must be allocated, and the requisite skills learned. As the colony grows, and the queen switches from production of workers to production of males and daughter queens, further adjustments are required to the division of labour in the nest, to ensure appropriate treatment of the brood destined to become sexually reproductive adults. Again, how far is it crucial that workers tending the brood are able to distinguish between these, and how is their treatment regulated? Finally, a basic division of labour has to be established between house-bees and foragers, and among the latter between pollen and nectar gatherers. How is this achieved? How is it revised to meet contingencies, such as the loss of foragers to predation or parasitism?

When fully adult males and daughter queens emerge from the nest, the next challenge is locating a mate. This involves discrimination between the castes and sexes, as well as recognition of a potential mate as of the same species. Since most bumblebee queens mate only once, males have the added challenge of finding virgin queens. Finally, for the fertilised daughter queen, there is the challenge of finding an appropriate place to hibernate, and, the following spring, a suitable nesting site.

To summarise, the complexity of these challenges is such that any simple notion of 'instinct' to characterise bumblebee behaviour must be inadequate. The bees require not only perceptual, cognitive and motor-learning abilities, but also a high degree of flexible adaptability on the part of both individuals and the colony as a whole. This latter also implies a sophisticated system of communication. For a long time bumblebees were seen as the poor relations of honey bees, lacking the complex division of labour and waggle dance mode of communication used by the latter. The more recent acceleration of research effort devoted to bumblebees leaves many so-far unsolved mysteries, but at least begins to undermine the older view of the 'primitive' character of bumblebee social life.

BUMBLEBEE PERCEPTION

Perhaps because of the dominance of vision in our own experience of the world, this is the sense which has been most studied by bee researchers. However, bees are also sensitive to touch, temperature and humidity. But only in recent decades has systematic research begun to reveal the importance and complexity of the ways bumblebees use the chemical senses – tastes and scents – in all aspects of their lives.

Vision

The role of vision in navigation, recognition of flower types, perception of behavioural signals of dominance, threats and so on has been well researched. The large compound eyes of bumblebees can detect colour, shape and movement, whilst the three simple ocelli are thought to be sensitive mainly to light intensity (Fig. 64). Research on the importance of visual cues in bumblebee foraging has tended to concentrate on the abilities of bees to discriminate between different colours and shapes, and the role of colour and shape in identification of rewarding flowers.

The initial detection of suitable flowers and flower patches seems to depend primarily on colour contrast. Interestingly, however, bee colour vision is rather different from that of humans: colour contrasts perceptible to us may not be so for bees, and vice versa. This is because bee colour vision is, like ours, trichromatic (with receptors stimulated by light of three wavelength bands), but responds to a different spectrum of wavelengths. Bees, including bumblebees, do not have receptors sensitive to the red end of the spectrum, but are sensitive to ultraviolet light. So their three basic colours are UV, blue and green (compared with the red,

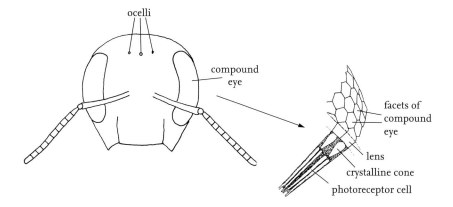

FIG 64. Head of a bumblebee showing the compound eyes and ocelli.

green and blue colour perception of humans). Interesting research by Chittka and others has related the patterns of light reflection from flowers, leaves and other background objects to the 'visual colour space' of bees (see Chittka *et al.*, 1994). What these researchers discovered was that of a sample of more than 500 flower species, more than 85 per cent fell within one or other of only five basic colour groups as perceived by bees: in terms of the wavelengths perceptible to the bees, these mainly reflected green, blue, blue-and-green, blue-and-UV, or green-and-UV (none reflected light in the UV range only). Because some of these flowers reflect light in the red end of the spectrum, and because human observers cannot detect UV, some of these colour clusters look quite different to us: for example, common bird's-foot trefoil, a popular bee forage source, is seen by us as yellow, but is 'bee-green' to its pollinating visitors.

The research showed that not only were the basic five clusters of flower colours clearly distinguishable from one another in the bees' visual colour space, but that also all were clearly demarcated from likely backgrounds. Leaves that appear green to us, for example, appear grey or colourless to bees, contrasting sharply with the highly chromatic reflectances the bees can detect from the flowers. The same is true of other likely backgrounds – soil, or rocks, for example. So bee colour vision seems to be well adapted to detecting flowers, or flower patches, against likely backgrounds, and for at least a provisional sorting of flower types into colour categories. However, from the point of view of the plants, efficient pollination services might be best served by a species-specific colour signal, encouraging constancy on the part of the pollinator (although see Chapter 7 on the risks of extreme specialisation). Chittka *et al.* argue that there are constraints in the form of available pigments and plant physiology that limit the adaptability of plants in this respect.

Colour is, of course, not the only flower character that can be varied. Specialisation on the part of plants to insect pollination often takes the form of distinctive floral shapes: bilateral symmetry, and greater or lesser depth of the corolla. Research by Gegear & Laverty (2001) on *Bombus impatiens* suggests that the combination of variability in colour with other variable traits, such as shape, encourages specialisation on the part of bee pollinators because of the more demanding visual processing involved. The size of flowers, too, affects the discriminations that can be made by foraging bees, so that the cues used in searching for small flowers use different visual processing abilities (Spaethe *et al.*, 2001).

At close range bees are capable of perceiving and learning different flower shapes. Some have an innate preference for bilaterally symmetrical ones, or are even restricted to a single flower species, whilst others, including the great majority of bumblebees, seem not to have strong innate preferences, but learn to recognise flower shapes and make choices between them based on past experience of handling difficulty and reward (Chittka & Thompson, 1997). In mixed arrays of flowers of similar (bee-) colours, bumblebees constant to one species will often mistakenly approach a flower of the 'wrong' species whilst searching for the preferred one by recognising its shape or scent. For example, a queen *B. humilis* foraging exclusively from flowers of yellow-rattle dispersed among buttercups (presumably similar in colour both to bees and to humans) repeatedly approached and quickly rejected buttercups as it searched (own obs.). Goulson (2000a) found that workers of *B. pascuorum* took on average twice as long to locate (yellow) flowers of common bird's-foot trefoil when these had a background of yellow flowers than when they did not. Also, experiments suggest that bumblebees will switch more readily between flowers of similar colours than they do between those of similar shape but different colour (see Chapter 6). (See also Chittka & Waser, 1997; Chittka *et al.*, 1999 and Chittka *et al.* in Chittka & Thomson, 2001.)

Hearing

Most research on the sense of hearing in insects has been focused on groups such as the Orthoptera (grasshoppers, crickets and their allies) in which sound production (stridulation) plays a central role in mating behaviour, or others (such as night-flying moths) that are able to detect the ultrasound of predatory bats. The sense of hearing in bumblebees has attracted much less attention. The buzz of bumblebees as they fly from one flower to another or between patches (often of different pitches in the two modes) is presumably an incidental effect of their activity in flying. However, bumblebees do sometimes buzz as a sign of aggression when they are disturbed during foraging, or when the nest is under attack. Since this aggressive response is probably mainly directed against vertebrate predators, it does not follow that the bumblebees themselves can hear it.

Buzzing is also used in the interactions between colony members. It was once thought that a 'trumpeter' bee would rouse the colony to activity by buzzing its wings early in the morning, though there are several other possible explanations for this buzzing activity, such as ventilation (see Alford, 1975). Workers also buzz at moments of conflict with the queen. Sometimes the workers touch the queen with their antennae or mandibles before buzzing rhythmically by means of short wing vibrations (Van der Blom, 1986), and this is generally interpreted as an aggressive signal (Röseler & Röseler, 1977; van Honk *et al.* 1981*b*). Sladen also noted buzzing as a sound made by bumblebees when they were irritated. He thought the sound was made by air passing over the edge of a membrane in the spiracles of the thorax, and cited an experiment by Burmeister to the effect that covering the thoracic spiracles stops or greatly weakens the sound of the buzz (Sladen, 1912). Whatever the truth of this, it seems that the buzzing sound made by bumblebees is at least greatly amplified by the vibration of the wing membranes.

Recent research has revealed that in honey bees, perception of the various components of the dance performed to recruit workers to a forage source involves the sense of hearing (Goodman, 2003). The organ involved does not, as in other insects, and many other species including humans, operate by perceiving sound waves as pressure gradients. Instead, the sensory apparatus of the honey bee detects particle movements in the air, and it does so by means of receptor cells in the antennae, collectively termed Johnston's organ (after the scientist who discovered it) (Fig. 65). These are located in the pedicel, and are attached at one end to the inner wall of the pedicel, and, at the other, to the membrane connecting the pedicel to the flagellum. They are thus able to detect the tiny vibrations of the flagellum caused by moving air particles as sound is transmitted to the antennae.

Honey bees can also detect high frequency vibrations in the comb caused by a bee vibrating its wings and pressing its thorax against it. These vibrations are picked up by sensory organs in the legs. It is possible that bumblebees have similar sound-sensitive organs, but this has not yet been established. The buzzing used in aggressive encounters is accompanied by bodily posturing, and wing vibrations can also be perceived visually in some circumstances. However, since these interactions most often take place in the dark of the nest cavity, other senses are presumably involved. Foraging bumblebees show no reaction to sudden electronic sounds within the human hearing range (own obs.). So it

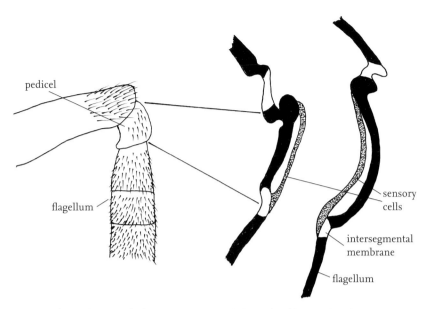

FIG 65. Johnston's organ, the hearing apparatus of a honey bee (drawing based on Goodman, 2003, with permission).

remains unclear whether bumblebees can hear, and, if they can, what they hear and how.

Touch

The sense of touch in insects is mainly a function of receptor cells at the bases of differently shaped tiny hairs and spines distributed widely over the surface of the body, but particularly numerous in the antennae. Movement of a hair as a result of mechanical contact is detected by the receptor cell, and communicated via a nerve pathway to the insect's central nervous system – usually the ganglion governing the relevant part of the insect's body. The hairs are often placed asymmetrically in membranous sockets in the cuticle, so that the direction of their movement on contact is restricted, giving the bee information about the direction of mechanical impacts or physical pressure. In some insects, these sense organs may be so sensitive that they can detect sound waves, as well as direct contact. There is a significant concentration of sensory cells (sensilla) at the junction of the antennal pedicel with the scape, and it is believed this plays a crucial role in the interpretation of tactile inputs from the rest of the antenna.

Other receptors for the sense of touch include variously shaped campaniform and chordotonal sensilla, which are important in informing the insect about its own posture and limb movements. The campaniform sensilla are dome- or bell-shaped mounds set in thin areas in the cuticle in bees (Fig. 66), and they detect bending or twisting of the cuticle. They are present at the base of the antennae, and many of them are also concentrated near the wing bases. Sensory inputs from these organs, as well as chordotonal sensilla, or stretch receptors, that are also present in the wing bases of bees, are believed to be important for regulating wing movements in flight. Sensory hairs in the antennae are also involved in regulating flight movements by detecting the flow of air across the antennal surface. Other sensilla, made up of variously shaped pegs in sunken pits or hollows in the cuticle of the antennae, are believed to be sensitive to temperature and humidity (Goodman, 2003).

In bumblebees a combination of visual and tactile cues is involved in a wide variety of social interactions, most notably in the pushing and mauling behaviours through which queens or cuckoo females attempt to assert dominance over workers – particularly in the later phases of colony development. As we saw in Chapter 2, this sort of contact is thought to play a bigger role in the maintenance of social order in the colony in the simple species than in the complex ones, where chemical communication is believed to play a more significant role. In foraging, too, once a flower is selected, tactile cues must play the primary role in the bee's handling of it to obtain nectar or pollen. As a heavy insect, it must be able to assure

FIG 66. Greatly enlarged views of the surface of the antenna of a honey bee, showing several different types of sensilla (drawing based on Goodman, 2003, with permission).

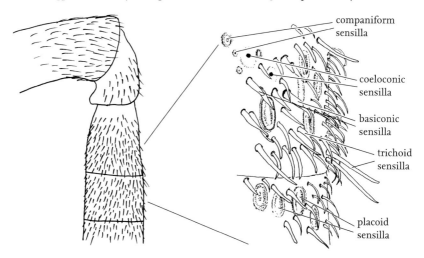

companiform
sensilla

coeloconic
sensilla

basiconic
sensilla

trichoid
sensilla

placoid
sensilla

stability by gripping the flower parts or other plant structures as a platform, and be able to adopt an appropriate posture to manage the physical task of probing the nectar stores in the flower, or to brush against its anthers. It is thought that minute sculpturing of the surface of petals can be detected by sensilla in the antennae of honey bees. These help the bees to distinguish flower species and may also guide them to the nectar source. It may be that bumblebees have similar abilities. However, depending on the complexity of floral structures, all these tasks will require more-or-less acquired skill, and so both learning and memory are, as we shall see, involved.

Chemical senses

Finally, we consider the least fully understood, but possibly most important of the bee senses: smell and taste. These are often treated together as the chemical senses, because they involve discrimination between, and responses to, a vast range of chemical compounds. The only differences are that taste receptors rely on contact whereas the sense of smell detects scents at a distance. Honey bees can distinguish hundreds of different scents, and learn to recognise them with remarkable speed and accuracy: 90 per cent after just one visit to a rewarding source (Menzel & Erber, 1978). The organs of chemical sense are minute sensilla concentrated on the surface of the antennal segments, but also present on the mouthparts and the tarsi. Like the main touch receptors, many of the organs of chemical sense are minute hair-like structures with attached sensory cells that communicate nerve impulses to the bee's central nervous system – usually, in the case of olfactory information, directly to the brain. The hair-like, or trichoid, sensilla that detect scents have a porous cuticle. The scent molecules either pass through the pores directly from the surrounding air, or are trapped on the surface of the sensillum, and then pass through the pores. Here they make contact with receptor sites on fine extensions (dendrites) of the sensory cells. Interspersed with the trichoid sensilla are many other olfactory sense organs. These are variously shaped – stout pegs, fluted pegs in pits in the cuticle, or oval, dome-shaped plates of cuticle (placoid sensilla). These, too, have minute pores through which scent molecules can pass to activate sensory cells below (see Fig. 66). The olfactory sensilla vary in their degree of specialisation, some responding to only a very narrow range of chemical stimuli. The importance of scent perception in honey bees is indicated by the number of olfactory sensilla on the antennae (some 3,000 trichoids, and 2,700 placoids), and there is no reason to suppose this is less true of bumblebees.

The sensilla responsible for the sense of taste are peg-like projections. Each has an aperture at the tip, filled with fluid. The substances tasted have to be in contact with the sensillum, whereupon molecules are taken up into the fluid, and stimulate the nerve endings of connected sensory cells.

Possibly because scent plays a relatively minor role in human sensory awareness, but also because of the technical difficulties of identifying and analysing the roles of chemical scents, understanding of this aspect of bee experience and communication is relatively undeveloped. That scent plays a significant role has long been recognised, especially in honey bees (Free, 1987). But a detailed analysis of the role of chemical communication in bumblebees, and identification of the compounds involved, has only been carried out in recent decades. Even now, many results are contradictory or ambiguous, and there is little firm knowledge. However, what is known suggests that scent plays a central and very complex role in both the social organisation and foraging behaviour of bumblebees.

We can distinguish two sorts of role played by the chemical senses. The first, and most readily understood, is that tastes and scents, as aspects of the bee's environment, can be used as cues to orient its behaviour, just as the other sensory inputs can. Most obviously, the scents emitted by flowers provide cues for close orientation and guides to the nectaries, as well as signalling the species of the plant, indicating the age of the flower and state of its available reward. The scent of a flower may be formed by a blend of 40–50 volatile compounds, but the foraging bees use only a proportion of these as the scent 'signature' of that species (Goodman, 2003). However, it is the second sort of role played by the chemical senses that is now attracting much research attention. This is their function in communication between bees. Central to this is the secretion of more-or-less volatile compounds that can be detected and interpreted either by contact ('taste') or at a distance ('scent') by other bees of the same species. These compounds are known collectively as pheromones and are highly complex and variable in their chemical nature.

Just as the hormones secreted by endocrine glands evoke or regulate internal physiological processes, so the pheromones, secreted by a number of exocrine glands, affect physiological and behavioural activity in other bees through external communication. The best known exocrine glands are the mandibular, labial and hypopharyngeal glands, situated in the head, and Dufour's gland, situated in the abdomen. The tarsi, too, are equipped with exocrine glands that secrete complex chemical compounds on contact (see Billen & Morgan, 1998).

Some experimental work has investigated the distinct functions of secretions from these glands by either removing them or exposing other bees to extracts taken from them. Other work has concentrated on chemical analysis of the secretions themselves, independently of their functions in social communication.

In the latter category, a recent analysis of the chemical compounds extracted from the main exocrine glands of a queen *B. terrestris* yielded well over 400 distinct compounds, including 188 hydrocarbons, 18 alcohols, and many acids and esters (Hefetz *et al.*, 1996). Some of these compounds were present in the secretions of all the glands, whilst others appeared to be more specialised products of one or more. It seems likely that many of these compounds may not function individually as pheromones, but the sheer diversity and complexity of the secretions does suggest the possibility of an elaborate system of chemical communication that has still to be explored.

In some cases, it is not clear whether a particular use of scent cues should be understood as social communication or more simply as an environmental indicator. It is now established that scent is used extensively in recognition of fellow colony members and of intruders in many social insect species. Cuckoo bumblebees have also been shown to recognise the scent of their host species. In such cases as these it is not clear that the scents are secreted specifically to communicate identity – and in the case of the use of host nest odour by cuckoo females, this is presumably not at all likely! It seems probable that in such cases as recognition of nest mates and intruders, scents are acquired incidentally in the course of participation in the life of the colony, and their uses in recognition are subsequently learned.

The organisation of the bee's behaviour depends on its ability to integrate the inputs from its various sensory systems, and to interpret them in the light of its past perceptual and sensory-motor learning. The bee's brain is the main organ for receiving and integrating sensory inputs, as well as co-ordinating behavioural responses. The sense organs for vision and the chemical senses are concentrated on the head and antennae, and nervous pathways connect them directly to the brain. Many of the touch-sensitive sensilla are also situated on the head and antennae, but these sensilla are also distributed over the whole body surface. Much of the sensory information from these is relayed to ganglions (concentrations of cells in the bee's central nervous system) situated along the length of the bee's body (see Fig. 26). The motor responses to these signals are often decentralised to the ganglion closest to the relevant part of the body, so that many touch responses may be continued even after decapitation of the insect. In the living insect, however, the overall co-ordinating role of the brain involves selective inhibition of these decentralised responses.

LEARNING AND MEMORY

The capacity for learning and memory in insects has generally been much underestimated, but research on bees, and honey bees in particular, has done much to correct this. Both bumblebees and honey bees have complex problems of navigation and orientation to solve in order to locate and relocate their nests and rewarding foraging patches, and to travel efficiently between them (see Chapters 6 & 7). Since repeated trips to the same patch are frequently required, routes have to be learned and remembered between one trip and the next so that they can be repeated. Also, individual bumblebees will often (temporarily) specialise in foraging from one flower species. Again, learning and memory are involved in recognising flower species by a combination of traits including colour, shape and scent. Since most bumblebees lack strong innate preferences for particular floral structures, learning and memory must play the major role in identifying, choosing and handling appropriate flower types (Laverty, 1994; Laverty & Plowright, 1988; Chittka & Thompson, 1997; West & Laverty, 1998). Depending on the structure of the blossom concerned, the bee may also have a complex set of handling skills to learn and memorise. Finally, with declining reward, bees may be prompted to switch from one flower species or patch to another. Tracking the fluctuating resource in this way requires further exploratory and learning abilities.

Menzel's work on honey bees (Menzel, 2001) shows them to be able to navigate by integrating information from the direction of light from the sun, visual estimation of distances and visual landmarks to form a 'specialised route memory'. This SRM is put into operation when the bee follows its regular course between nest and foraging patch. However, disturbances to the environment or to the bee itself may make this method of navigation ineffective. So when bees, including bumblebees, are released away from their regular routes, they begin by attempting to follow their SRM. When this fails, they are still able to reorient themselves and find their way back to the nest or, sometimes, to the forage patch.

Menzel's work shows this to be made possible by bringing into play what he calls a 'general landscape memory' (GLM). When they first leave the nest, both bumblebees and honey bees perform an elaborate orientation flight, involving ever-wider circles round it. Discovery of a new and rewarding foraging patch, physical relocation of the nest, radical alteration of the immediate surroundings of the nest, or release of the bee in unfamiliar surroundings all may elicit the same behaviour. These orientation flights lead to the formation of an integrated memory of the overall landscape including nest, forage patches and landmarks. This GLM is what enables the bees to navigate between any two points in the landscape, independently of any previously learned route. Osborne *et al.* (1999) used harmonic radar to follow the movements of foraging bumblebees and were able to detect one forager flying directly from its regular foraging patch to a new one without making a prior journey back to the nest (see Chapter 6). A study designed to test the homing ability of *B. terrestris* found that when released 1.1 kilometres from the nest, at least nine out of ten workers were able to return quickly to it (Goulson & Stout, 2001). Bees released well beyond what we may suppose was their 'home' foraging range – up to 9.8 kilometres away – did sometimes manage to return, but only after a considerable delay. Here, the likely method of orientation was a systematic search for landmarks.

The memory processes required by a foraging bee need to work over a series of different timescales – a few seconds as the bee moves from one flower to another, perhaps minutes as it moves from patch to patch, and from four or five minutes to hours, days or even months (in hibernating individuals) between one foraging trip and the next. In the honey bee, Menzel found evidence for five memory phases, with transfers between them, both consolidating and revising information in the light of new experience (Menzel, 1999). Early short-term memory involves general arousal for up to one minute, during which time the bee is likely to encounter similar stimuli (for example, as it moves from one flower to the next). Reinforcement by rewards leads to the transfer of short-term memory to longer-term storage. Subsequent memory processes store more specific memories for both medium- and long-term retention. The longest term storage includes lifelong memories, such as nest location, and the general landscape memory.

However, the successive choices to be made by a forager as it moves between flowers and foraging patches entail acquisition of new short-term memory, as well as continuous and simultaneous retrieval of medium- and long-term memory from storage, and flexible application of these diverse sources of expectation. The concept of 'working memory' is used to account for the way this is achieved. It suggests that during foraging, the bee is simultaneously retrieving memories from longer-term storage and also learning and acquiring new memory from its current activity. But short-term memory is dominant so long as stimuli recur within a timescale up to approximately one minute. However, with greater intervals, as when the bee leaves a foraging patch, longer-term memory is activated, and the pattern of reward and floral signals continuously updates the longer-term memory stores.

One important and well-researched aspect of learning for foraging bumblebees is their development of the necessary skills to access more complex floral structures. Heinrich pioneered this study, both by field observation, and experimentally. He screened off a section of a flowery meadow, introduced a bumblebee nest, and released fresh workers into the meadow one by one. He then observed them through the day, noting which flowers they visited, how they handled them and how long it took them to collect a full load of nectar. He followed the foraging patterns of the individual bees through several successive days, noting their acquisition of foraging skills. These results were compared with observations of freely foraging bees. The inexperienced bees were inefficient foragers in three respects. First, they foraged indiscriminately on their first trips, visiting flowers irrespective of whether they had nectar or pollen or neither. Second, they did not follow fixed routes to minimise travelling time on the foraging trip, and third, they were unable to successfully handle morphologically complex flowers. It took from two to six foraging trips for the bumblebees to become 'expert shoppers', by which time they could collect a full nectar load from jewelweed in 6 or 7 minutes. Inexperienced bees, foraging from simpler but less rewarding flowers, took about an hour to collect a full load (Heinrich, 1979).

This provides one hypothesis to explain the supposed flower constancy of bumblebee foragers (see Chapter 6): once having learned the flower structure of a particular species, greater efficiency in foraging can be maintained by remaining constant to it, rather than switching to alternatives. A common interpretation of this hypothesis is that bees are very limited in the number of handling skills that they can remember at the same time. If this is right, bees trained to access one flower type, then trained to another, should forage less efficiently when returned to the original type. This might be because of 'interference' with the first set of learned skills by the process of acquiring the second, or simply because of the intervening lapse of time.

In fact, most studies do show an increase in handling time when bees are switched back after learning to handle a second flower type. However, the loss of efficiency is variable, depending on the complexity of the flowers, and is relatively small. Bees subjected to these tests still foraged from 10–50 times more efficiently then inexperienced bees encountering the same floral structures for the first time. Moreover, studies that allowed the bees the opportunity to become experienced at switching between flower types reduced the switching 'penalty' to zero. However, requiring the bees to switch between three or more flower types did substantially reduce their efficiency (Dukas, 1995; Chittka et al., 1999; Gegear & Laverty, 2001).

These results suggest that bumblebees are capable of retaining in their long-term memory both sensory signals and handling abilities for several types of flower. Flower constancy is not the result of constraints imposed by the bees' memory capacity. However, switching from one flower type to another does take longer than continuing to forage from the same type. One likely explanation of this is that retrieval of the memory of an alternative flower type from long-term memory, even though it is familiar from past experience, is more demanding that continuous use of active short-term, or working memory. In other words, constraints imposed by the bees' limited powers of memory *processing*, as distinct from *capacity*, might be what disposes them to flower constancy (Chittka *et al.*, 1999).

Most research on bee learning and memory has – not surprisingly – been conducted on the more easily observed activities such as foraging and navigation. However, many complex tasks are performed within the nest – tasks such as tending the brood, maintaining humidity and temperature balance and cleaning and maintaining the nest structures. It seems highly probable that learning and memory are involved here, too, as indicated by research on specialisation to various domestic tasks in the American species *Bombus bifarius* (O'Donnell *et al.*, 2000), and by Cartar's study of task-switching in three Canadian species (see Chapter 2). This is a promising field for future research.

COMMUNICATION

As we have seen, communication within a bumblebee colony makes use of a wide variety of cues, involving several of the bee's senses. It is generally thought that in the so-called simple species the social order of the colony is maintained mainly by behavioural means. Queens can assert their dominance by mauling or pushing workers, or by issuing postural threats. This is thought to be effective where colony sizes are relatively small. However, it is now known that chemical com-munication – by taste and scent – plays an indispensable role in the colony cycle of at least one of the complex species. This is *B. terrestris*, the most widely domesticated and researched bumblebee species. Increasingly, it seems likely that scent plays a much larger role in the social lives of all bumblebee species than previously thought.

As we saw above, scents incidentally acquired in the course of participation in the life of the colony may be utilised for recognition or other purposes, but communication in a fuller sense involves the secretion of specific chemical cues in the form of pheromones. It is conventional to distinguish two biological roles that pheromones can play. Some are designated releaser pheromones, and these directly elicit a specific behavioural response. Those involved in mating, alarm signals and so on are included in this group, and they are relatively well researched. Others, termed primer pheromones, bring about or regulate longer-term physiological processes in their recipients, eventually eliciting a behavioural response. These pheromones are at work in some of the more extended and complex processes in the development of the colony, most notably the suppression by the queen of ovary activation and egg laying in her workers, and the determination of caste in the case of female brood.

Releaser pheromones

Among the earliest uses of pheromone communication among bumblebees to be noticed and researched were the marking of patrolling routes by males. As we saw in Chapter 2, Darwin noted but was also puzzled by the behaviour of patrolling males of *B. hortorum* in his garden. Sladen appears to have been the first to recognise that patrolling males were following trails marked with scents they had secreted. As so often, Sladen's account can hardly be bettered:

> 'This strange behaviour of the male humble-bee has puzzled many observers, but I have noticed certain facts about it that point to an explanation. A sweet fragrance, like the perfume of flowers, is perceptible about the pausing places. This same fragrance may be detected in the scent produced by a male if he be caught in the fingers, although it is now blended with an odour like that of sting-poison emitted in fear. Evidently, therefore, the males emit the perfume in their pausing places; and I think it extremely likely that in doing so they attract not only one another, but the queens. The males of the one species do not pause at spots frequented by those of the other species, and we may infer from this that each species emits a different scent.' (Sladen, 1912)

Haas, Frank and others conducted more systematic research from the 1940s onwards, with attempts to localise the source of the pheromones. At first it was supposed that the mandibular glands were responsible, but it was later established that the male marking compounds were produced by the cephalic portion of the labial glands (Kullenberg *et al.*, 1973). With the availability of sophisticated methods of analysis, the chemical constituents of these glandular secretions were identified for most species during the 1980s and '90s, the lead being taken by Scandinavian researchers. In the case of the Scandinavian species it was shown that the pheromone blends extracted from the labial glands did correspond closely with those deposited on marked sites by the males, and also that always complex blends of several compounds were used – averaging 5.5 compounds in each blend (Fig. 67).

This important body of work succeeded in showing that the blends of marking pheromones are, indeed, as Sladen guessed, unique to each species. However, patterns of similarity and difference between species can be correlated with other characteristics to inform discussions of the evolutionary relationships between

FIG 67. The chemical composition of the male-marking compounds of some British bumblebees (reproduced from Prŷs-Jones & Corbet, 1991, with permission).

	BOMBUS	B. pratorum	B. jonellus	B. soroeensis	B. lapidarius	B. pascuorum	B. monticola	B. terrestris	B. lucorum	PSITHYRUS	P. rupestris	P. bohemicus	P. campestris	P. barbutellus	P. sylvestris
Geraniol	○														
Citronellol	○											◉			
Geranyl acetate	○														
Citronellyl acetate	○														
Farnesene isomers	○														
All-*trans*-farnesol	●													●	
2,3-dihydro-6-*trans*-farnesol		●					●								
2,3-dihydro-6-*trans*-farnesal			◉												
All-*trans*-farnesyl acetate	◉													◉	
2,3-dihydrofarnesyl acetate							○								
Geranylgeraniol	◉								○						
Geranylcitronellol								◉			○				
Geranylgeranyl acetate	◉	●							○		◉				
Tetradecanal											○				◉
Tetradecanol					○						○				
Hexadecenol				●	●						●	●			●
Hexadecanal															○
Hexadecenal						●						○			◉
Hexadecanol	◉			◉		◉	○	○		○					
Octadecenol	◉												◉		○
Eicosenol											●				
Hexadecenyl acetate							●								
Hexadecyl acetate							◉	○							
Octadecyl acetate													○		
Eicosyl acetate								○							
Docosyl acetate								○							
Ethyl decanoate								○	○						
Ethyl dodecanoate								◉	●						
Ethyl tetradecenoate								○	●						
Ethyl tetradecanoate									○						
Ethyl hexadecatrienoate									○						
Ethyl hexadecadienoate									○						
Ethyl hexadecenoate									○						
Ethyl octadecatrienoate									○						
Ethyl octadecadienoate									○						
Ethyl octadecenoate									○						
Ethyl octadecanoate									○						
Tetradecenoic acid															◉

Symbols indicate relative amount present: minor component (○), major component (◉) and main component (●).
Adapted from Bergström *et al.* (1981), Cederberg *et al.* (1984) and Descoins *et al.* (1984).

species. For example, the cuckoos *B. vestalis* and *B. bohemicus* have 22 and 16 compounds, respectively, in their labial gland secretions. Each species has a distinctive chemical profile, but 12 compounds are shared, confirming the closeness of the evolutionary relationship between the two species (Bergman *et al.*, 1996). In another example, chemical analysis of male-marking pheromones played an important part in Bergström & Svensson's (1973; Svensson, 1979a) demonstration that the taxon *Bombus lapponicus* in fact included two species – now recognised as *B. lapponicus* and *B. monticola*.

This research has also highlighted the biological functions of the marking pheromones. As we saw in Chapter 2, Svensson (1979b) showed that they play an important part, along with other factors, in reducing the chances of cross-species mating. Species differ in the seasonal timing of their emergence, in their habitat preferences and so on, but often males of several species are patrolling in an area simultaneously. Where this happens, the height of the routes and the sort of object scent-marked differ from species to species, with greater differentiation in these behavioural elements when the pheromonal mixes are similar. The co-presence in the environment of many scents may also explain why the marking pheromones of male bumblebees always consist of complex blends of compounds. Only in this way could specific information be communicated against the chemical background 'noise' (Hefetz, 1990).

Sladen's expectation that unmated queens are attracted by the scents is widely accepted, but there is relatively little direct observation of this happening. However, the scents may also have a function of sexual excitation in males, as they do not respond to daughter queens unless they encounter them at or close to a marked place (Awram, 1970; Free, 1971; Kullenberg, 1973; Awram & Free, 1987a). The males mark their trails early each morning, and then follow a consistent route through the day, although during inclement weather they replace the scent marks at more frequent intervals. It has been suggested that the scents may help the males themselves to remember their routes. However, experienced males whose antennae have been removed are able to continue patrolling on their established routes by relying on visual signals and route memory. Unable to perceive their own scent marks, these males repeatedly re-mark their approach places (Awram, 1970; Awram & Free, 1987b).

In some species, several males patrol a common route in procession. This suggests that males are attracted to the scent marks established by other males of the same species, or, possibly, that groups of males may share in the scent-marking of a route. It is difficult to understand this in terms of assumed competition between males for access to females. It may be that by joining forces in this way each male increases his chances of finding a suitable mate. A possible mechanism here might be that the presence of numbers of males on a route is required if a daughter queen is to be attracted to it. There is some evidence that queens prefer spots that have been marked by more than one male (Maccagnani *et al.*, 1994). Alternatively, it might be that if the males are closely related – for example, if co-patrolling males are all derived from a single nest – co-operation might be favoured on the basis of shared genetic inheritance. Resolving this puzzle would be an interesting research topic.

Initial recognition of queens by patrolling males depends on visual cues – colour and pattern – but actual mating seems to require the presence of the male's own marking pheromone, as well as a sexual excitant emitted by the queen herself. As in other bees, it seems that daughter queen bumblebees secrete a sex pheromone that is necessary to induce mounting and copulation on the part of the male. The source of this pheromone has been shown to be the queen's mandibular glands (van Honk *et al.*, 1978).

Many social bee species make use of scent-marking in their food gathering. This has been most fully researched in the honey bees, which use pheromones as well as the famous waggle dance to indicate to one another the whereabouts of newly discovered food sources (von Frisch, 1967). As well as communication of information at the hive, honey bee foragers also lay scent trails that can be followed by nest mates, and they scent-mark particularly rewarding food sources with an attractant pheromone. The trail pheromones are secreted by glands in the tarsi, but seem to be present over the body surface, too. The attractant pheromones are secreted by another gland, the Nasanov gland, situated towards the rear of the dorsal surface of the abdomen of worker honey bees. The secretions from this gland play a part in swarming and in orientation to the nest, as well as in foraging.

It is now generally thought that, unlike honey bees, bumblebees do not use attractant scent marks for rewarding flowers. However, they do make other uses of pheromonal communication in their foraging. Foraging workers leave behind volatile compounds as they visit each flower during a foraging trip. If the same or a subsequent bee visitor encounters a recently visited flower it may approach or briefly alight on it, but then move on without attempting to forage from it. These scents thus have a repellent, rather than attractant effect on behaviour, and save the bee time and effort in foraging from flowers that have recently been emptied. Corbet *et al.* (1984) showed that the time interval between visits to previously depleted flowers, as cued by repellent scent marks, coincided with the time taken for the flowers to resupply their nectaries. In this way it is supposed that the scent marks indicate to the bee the length of time that has elapsed since a flower was previously visited by itself or another forager. However, since different flower species replenish their nectar supplies at very different rates, and weather conditions also affect nectar secretion, bees must learn ways of 'interpreting' these scent signals in a very flexible way. In fact, the situation must be still more complex, since other factors affect the reward threshold at which the bees are willing to forage. These include competition from workers of other colonies, or flower visitors of other species, as well as the nutritional state of the colony.

More recent research on the chemical composition of the scent marks deposited on flowers has shown close correlation between the scents deposited and the contents of the tarsal glands. But the compounds involved are also found generally on the outer surface of the bee's body, and are also widespread across other insect groups. The particular blends deposited are now known to be species-specific, at least in the common species so far studied – *B. lapidarius*, *B. terrestris*, and *B. pascuorum* (Goulson *et al.*, 2000). However, the scents deposited by foragers of one species induce flower-rejection by subsequent visitors of other species, and it also seems that bumblebees can 'read' the scents left by honey bees, and vice versa. It may even be that scents left by flower visitors from other insect orders can also be detected, but so far the evidence is inconclusive (Stout, Goulson & Allen, 1998; Goulson *et al.*, 1998; Stout & Goulson, 2001).

This raises interesting questions about how this particular use of scent communication could have evolved and what its function is. Recent work using genetic markers has shown that for at least some species workers from each colony are widely dispersed across sites and foraging patches. Foragers of two species, *B. terrestris* and *B. pascuorum*, were sampled from urban sites by Chapman *et al.* On the assumption that non-siblings must be from different colonies, the samples showed that, averaging over the sites studied, 96 colonies of *B. terrestris*, and 66 colonies of *B. pascuorum* were represented, per site, by foraging workers (Chapman *et al.*, 2003). Similar results were obtained by Darvill *et al.* (2004) using a somewhat different method. Many colonies were represented at each of a series of foraging patches along a transect, whilst full sisters were found distributed at considerable distances from each other – up to 312 metres in the case of *B. pascuorum*, and 625 in the case of *B. terrestris*. Research on the foraging patterns of other common species is currently being carried out.

This suggests that information left by a scent mark is unlikely to benefit nest mates. On the contrary, it might increase the foraging efficiency of subsequent flower visitors of other colonies or even species, and so might entail costs in a competitive situation. On the other hand, being able to tell whether a flower had been recently depleted of nectar by another visitor, of whatever species, would be advantageous. It could be that the current pattern represents some sort of provisional compromise between these two pressures. However, it also seems likely that repellent scent marks play an important role in providing information to individual foragers about their own past movements. Some foragers pursue a repeated track through a foraging patch (traplining) and it may be that such foragers make use of their own scent trails as well as visual landmarks and directional cues in following them. But not all foragers behave in this way. In a complex and heterogeneous foraging patch, where the target flower species is dispersed and often hidden, foraging often appears much more like fairly random searching behaviour. Here, encounters with previously visited flowers may aid orientation or trigger departure for another patch (see Chapter 6). Finally, it is quite possible that the scents left behind are simply incidental, and have no adaptive significance for the individual leaving the signal, although the response of subsequent visitors may be adaptive.

Very recent research has shown that, as well as scent-marking flowers, some bumblebees also communicate foraging information to siblings at the nest. Unlike the waggle dance of the honey bees, this does not convey positional information about food sources. In studies by Dornhaus & Chittka (2001), foragers of *B. terrestris* that had discovered a new and rewarding forage source ran about on the nest surface, buzzing their wings and bumping into other workers. This activity was shown to stimulate other workers into foraging activity, and these newly recruited foragers showed a strong tendency to forage from sources with the same scent as that carried by the initial forager. It seems that chemical communication is involved, and that this activity conveys information about which flower species are currently rewarding.

Whilst some authors have seen the lack of an equivalent to the honey bees' waggle dance as indicating a more primitive level of sociality in the bumblebees, it may be that conveying positional information is simply less relevant to the foraging patterns of bumblebees. Their food sources are often scattered in small patches that can be exploited without the need to recruit large numbers of workers to the same locality. It may also be that spatial dispersal of the foragers reduces the risk of loss of large numbers of foragers to predation. With their larger workforce, honey bees may be less susceptible to this risk. For bumblebees, being able to discover and access a continuous series of suitable forage sources throughout the whole colony cycle is a crucial condition of reproductive success. If, as Dornhaus & Chittka suggest, the communication of information about rewarding flower species enables the colony to monitor and adjust its foraging activity to the seasonal changes in availability of food sources, then this is potentially more useful than positional information. Presumably this newly discovered means of communication within the colony complements the already well-known practice of 'minoring' by individual foragers. Whilst constant to a main flower species, foragers will periodically sample other species, as a way of monitoring the changing pattern of rewards in their environment (Chapter 6). It now seems likely that bumblebees not only adapt their own individual foraging specialisms in this way, but can also communicate their discoveries to other members of the colony. This may be one means whereby overall co-ordination of the foraging effort of the collectivity of foragers belonging to a colony can be orchestrated.

It seems likely that pheromone communication may play a much larger role in other aspects of the social lives of bumblebees besides mating and foraging. Their close relatives the honey bees have been much more intensively researched, probably because of their commercial use and relative ease of domestication. As a result, much more is known about both the chemical composition and biological functions of their systems of chemical communication. Given the honey bees' much larger colony size and complexity of social organisation, it is perhaps not surprising that their systems of communication appear to be much more complex than those of the bumblebees. However, this may be to some degree an artefact of the latter having been less fully studied, and the growing body of recent research on bumblebee communication does suggest previously unsuspected complexities. As with honey bees, bumblebee colonies that are disturbed by predators, or by human interventions in the case of captive colonies, show an immediate 'alarm' reaction. In *B. terrestris*, guard bees, situated close to the nest entrance, are the first to react, but soon numbers of other workers leave the nest and fly towards the intruder, and others react with behavioural threat postures (possibly also associated with pheromonal signals). Other common species all show an alarm reaction, though it is a relatively mild one compared with *B. terrestris*.

Where there is a long passageway linking the nest with the outside world – especially in the case of underground nesting species – workers entering and leaving the nest have been shown to follow a scent trail. Cederberg demonstrated this for *B. terrestris*. He initially restricted the path to be followed by workers of a captive colony, but then gave them access to a wider area. The bees continued to use the initial trail, even when its physical alignment was altered (Cederberg, 1977). It seems likely that the pheromone used is secreted by the tarsal glands. From the point of view of the colony, however, the marked trail entails some risk. There is evidence that female cuckoo bees use these scent trails in conjunction with visual cues to locate and enter host nests. In cuckoo species that parasitise nests of only one or a few related species, scent may be important in identification of the appropriate host. Cederberg has shown that this is true of the cuckoo *B. rupestris*, females of which follow natural or artificial trails of its host *B. lapidarius* (see Chapter 4).

Chemical communication is also used by guard bees, which palpate returning workers with their antennae. Presumably the scent or 'taste' of the individual bee enables it to be recognised as a colony member or an outsider. It is probable that the aggressive response sometimes provoked by the entry of a cuckoo female into the nest is mediated by its alien odour. It is commonly observed that the cuckoo will often attempt to lay hidden in the host's nest until it acquires the colony odour. This is presumably a tactic to avoid recognition (see Chapter 4).

The use of pheromones in mutual recognition may also be important in co-ordination of activities within the nest and in maintaining or altering the division of labour among workers. In the honey bees, pheromones emitted by the queen stimulate foraging behaviour, brood nursing and comb construction among the workers. These processes have been less fully researched in bumblebees, but a broad division between house-bees and foragers is maintained with considerable flexibility. As we saw in Chapter 2, available evidence suggests that commonly workers start out their adult life as house-bees, leaving the nest on foraging trips later on. Also, the foragers tend to be larger than the house-bees. However, when foragers are removed from a colony, or food stores are removed, house-bees convert to foraging. Conversely, a shortage of house-bees is compensated by conversion of foragers back to domestic work. Foragers also respond flexibly to the nutritional demands of the brood, queen and house-bees, shifting between pollen and nectar collection, as well as selecting nectar concentrations (or even foraging for water) in response to the water balance in the nest. It is unclear whether these adaptations are mediated by pheromonal communication between the workers, or between them and the queen, or whether they are the result of direct monitoring of the internal state of the nest by individual workers. In the honey bees, pheromones emitted by the brood play an important part in stimulating foraging on the part of workers, and this may also be the case for bumblebees. This is particularly likely in the case of the pollen storers, whose larvae are fed individually (O'Donnell et al., 2000; Van Doorn, 1987; Cartar, 1992; Cartar & Dill, 1991; Ribiero et al., 1999).

The workers treat larvae destined to be queens, workers and males differently from each other, at least at certain developmental stages. This suggests they are able to distinguish the different castes and sexes among the brood, and it seems likely that chemical compounds on the larval cuticle may be involved in this. Furthermore, during the final phase of the colony's life, when conflicts break out and some workers both lay their own eggs and eat those of the queen or other workers, it seems that workers can recognise and protect their own offspring. Again, whether they do this by remembering their position in the nest, or whether chemical cues are involved, is unknown.

Primer pheromones

The primer pheromones are involved in complex and long-term processes in the life cycle of the colony, and their action and identity is more difficult to establish than is the case with the more immediately effective releaser pheromones. Research has had two main foci. One is the role of pheromones in determining the switch to producing the new generation of males and daughter queens. The other is the hypothesised role of pheromones in maintaining the queen's dominance and preventing colony workers from reproducing.

As we saw in Chapter 2, when a colony reaches a certain stage in its growth, there is a shift from production of new workers to production of males and daughter queens. In simple species it seems that this transition is mainly the result of food availability and ratio of workers to larvae in the nest. However, for complex species, of which *B. terrestris* is the most-studied example, the queen seems able to exert more control over the timing of these events. There is no firm evidence that any special food is delivered to larvae destined to develop as queens in this or any other bumblebee species (Pereboom, 2000). However, in *B. terrestris* there is good evidence that future queen larvae are treated differently in other respects. Larvae kept segregated from their queen by a screen develop as queens, unless workers are frequently removed from the queen's side of the screen and placed with the larvae. This suggests that the queen secretes a non-volatile pheromone that is transferred to the larvae by workers that have been in contact with the queen, or by the queen herself. At two to four or five days after hatching from the egg, female larvae are sensitive to this pheromone, and exposure to it sets them on an irreversible course to develop as workers.

The shift to production of daughter queens apparently results from the mother queen ceasing to secrete the pheromone. Larvae not exposed to it will go on to develop as queens, provided that in their last larval stage they are fed more frequently and for longer by the workers. They are much larger when they enter the pupal stage and they remain in it longer. In *B. terrestris* (and possibly other complex species) it seems that queens exert more control over the timing of the transition to the reproductive phase of the colony cycle, and that pheromone communication plays an important part in this. There is evidence that the pheromone works by inhibiting the production of juvenile hormone in the larvae. This, in combination with one or more other hormones, induces earlier moulting, and pupation at a smaller size (Cnaani *et al.*, 2000; Hartfelder *et al.*, 2000). However, the chemical identity of the queen's pheromone has yet to be established.

Pheromonal communication seems to be intimately involved in another, related, long-term process in the life of the colony. This is the continued subordination of the workers to the queen, apparently sacrificing their own chances of reproduction in favour of contributing to the nurture of her offspring. For most of the colony's development, this holds good, but it is now known that towards the end of the life of the colony some workers start to lay eggs, and, as we have seen, conflicts break out among them and between them and the queen. There is great research interest in how queen dominance is maintained, and why it appears to break down when it does. Much of the controversy about these issues turns on two different levels of explanation, and the bearing they have on each other. Much research has concentrated on identifying the mechanisms at work in maintaining or triggering changes in these relationships in the nest. This is sometimes referred to as a search for 'proximate' explanations. However, it should also be possible to explain how these mechanisms could have come into being through the operation of well-known evolutionary processes of selection. Since kin selection theory (see Chapter 2) has a central role in understanding the evolution of social modes of life in social insects such as the bumblebees, this idea should be able to provide an 'ultimate' (that is, evolutionary) explanation of their peculiarities.

Research conducted especially since the end of the 1970s produced strong evidence that the suppression of reproductive activity by the workers was under the control of the queen. The queen, it is argued, secretes a pheromone that acts on the workers to suppress the action of the glands (corpora allata) whose secretion of juvenile hormone (JH) would otherwise stimulate the activation of their ovaries. For most of the colony cycle this is effective, and tests on workers usually show low levels of juvenile hormone and little ovarian activation. Röseler et al. (1981) provided evidence that the queen pheromone is secreted by the mandibular glands, but spread over the rest of the queen's body by grooming. A queen without mandibular glands can still inhibit worker reproduction to some extent, and it is supposed that under normal circumstances her dominance is maintained by a combination of behavioural and pheromonal cues. However, as we have seen, some time after the queen has switched to laying haploid eggs (future males) the colony enters a phase – the competition phase – of increased aggression and rivalry among the workers, and loss of full queen dominance.

It had been thought that the transition to the competition phase occurred as a result of the declining ability of the queen to secrete the queen pheromone, allowing the workers to assert their own reproductive interests. However, recent experiments have shown that queens taken from colonies that have entered the competition phase are no less able than ones removed from colonies prior to that point to inhibit egg laying in small groups of fresh workers. This suggests that a declining power to achieve dominance by pheromonal secretion may not be the complete explanation of the outbreak of worker reproduction and conflict in the colony (Bloch *et al.*, 1996). Other factors may influence the onset of the competition phase, such as the sheer number of workers in the colony and consequent reduction in pheromonal communication between workers and the queen. Further experiments (Bloch & Hefetz, 1999*a*) suggest that the queen continues to exercise some inhibitory influence over worker reproduction into the competition phase, but that a brief period of reproductive activity by workers is soon suppressed by dominant workers. These workers develop the ability to prevent ovarian activation and egg laying in other workers (but cannot prevent female larvae developing into queens). In *B. terrestris*, at least, the queen continues to be responsible for most of the output of male offspring even in the competition phase (Lopez-Vaamonde *et al.*, 2004*a*).

However, it has been argued that the use of pheromones to suppress the reproductive activity of workers against their own reproductive interests is unlikely to have evolved. This is because workers could be expected to have evolved immunities to the pheromone, requiring ever higher doses, and also because the pheromone might impede the queen's own reproduction. For these and other reasons it has been argued that the queen pheromone is better understood as an 'honest signal': in other words, the pattern of secretion and the reaction to it by recipient workers is likely to have evolved in such a way as to enhance the reproductive chances of the workers themselves, as well as the queen. Only where subordination of workers is achieved by physical coercion should we expect one partner to the relationship to be enhancing its reproductive chances at the cost of the other (Keller & Nonacs, 1993).

Returning to *B. terrestris*, it is difficult to see how the reproductive interests of the workers are enhanced by their refraining from laying their own eggs and tending the resulting larvae, especially in those colonies that switch to mainly male-production early on. Since workers would be more closely related to their own sons (sharing 50 per cent of their genes) than to their brothers (the male offspring of the queen – 25 per cent of genes shared), their reproductive interests would presumably be best served by destroying the queen's eggs, and replacing them with their own. As queens of *B. terrestris* and most other bumblebee species mate only once, workers would also be more closely related to their nephews (37.5 per cent of genes shared) than to the queen's sons. This contrasts with the multiply mated social species such as the honey bees, where workers are more closely related to the queen than to their half-sisters, and so 'police' one another's attempts at reproduction (Ratnieks, 1988; Bourke, 2001).

Despite these anomalies, a novel and persuasive attempt has recently been made to explain the known patterns of co-operation and conflict over reproduction in *B. terrestris* colonies in terms of kin selection theory (Bourke & Ratnieks (2001), building on proposals made by Crespi (1992) and Kukuk (1992)). This supposes that the pheromones involved act as 'honest signals', and that individual bees act so as to enhance their reproductive interests. As we saw in Chapter 2, *B. terrestris* colonies adopt either of two reproductive strategies, at least in some populations. In some, the queens switch to laying haploid eggs (destined to develop as males) early on, whilst others switch to rearing reproductives later on, and produce mainly daughter queens. In early-switching colonies, it is argued that it is not in the interests of workers to lay their own eggs prior to the queen's switching to laying haploid eggs. To do so would impose a cost on the growth of the colony's workforce that could undermine both their and the queen's chances of successful reproduction in the long run. However, in fact, the change to worker egg laying and conflict (the competition point) occurs much later – some 21 days later – than the point at which the queen switches to laying haploid eggs. What accounts for the delay? Bourke & Ratnieks (2001) argue that the workers are unable to detect the sex of larvae until they are a few days from pupation (some 15 days after the eggs are laid). At this stage, the workers have little or no interest in destroying the queen's offspring in favour of their own, since the resulting sons of the workers would arrive much later on the scene, and probably suffer a much lower chance of mating success. The reproductive interests of the workers thus might favour allowing the queen's sons (with whom they share 25 per cent of their genes) to continue their development. Destroying the queen's offspring at this stage would also confer no benefit, as they would not in any case compete for nutrition with possible (male) offspring of the workers, as the former would already have pupated by the time the latter's eggs hatched. However, any haploid eggs laid by the queen after the point at which the workers retrospectively discover they have been tending the queen's male offspring are in direct competition with any eggs the workers might lay, and do not have the advantage of early mating success. At this point, it is in the reproductive interests of the workers to begin laying their own eggs, and to destroy those of the queen or other workers. Hence the shift to the competition phase. Unfortunately for this part of the explanation of the onset of the competition phase, further experimental work carried out by Lopez-Vaamonde *et al.* found that the timing of the competition point was unaffected by the age of male larvae introduced into *B. terrestris* nests (Lopez-Vaamonde *et al.*, 2004b).

In late-switching colonies, the competition point is reached about seven to nine days after the queen switches to laying eggs that are destined to develop as queens. The cue that prompts this shift of developmental pathways is, as we have seen, the cessation of the queen's pheromonal signal. Bourke & Ratnieks (2001) argue that the workers can detect the cessation of this pheromonal signal. It is now in their interests to start laying their own eggs, and the competition phase begins.

Despite the success of this construction in resolving some puzzling features of the *B. terrestris* colony cycle, there are some remaining anomalies. One is the unexplained gap between the switching point and the onset of the competition phase in the early-switching colonies. A potentially more serious anomaly concerns the explanation of the timing of the competition point in the late-switching colonies. The anomaly is this: it is clearly in the reproductive interest of the workers that daughter queens are successfully raised by the colony. However, if they begin laying their own (male) eggs during the period of development of the daughter queens, and disruption of the social harmony of the colony ensues, this is put at risk. Resources will be diverted from nurture of the immature daughter queens in favour of the workers' own offspring and of generalised conflict among workers and between them and the queen. Meanwhile, the offspring of the workers are at risk from destruction by the queen and competing workers before reaching maturity (evidence suggests that few, in fact, do survive), and even if they do reach maturity, they are at a disadvantage, compared to earlier-emerging males, in the competition for mates.

However, these male offspring of workers may still have some, however small, chance of successful mating. It might still be in the reproductive interests of workers to attempt to raise their own sons, so long as this imposes little or no cost to the colony's success in rearing daughter queens. This seems intuitively very unlikely, as considerable diversion of foraging and nursing effort, as well as time and energy spent in aggressive interaction, is associated with the competition phase. But a recent study of the production of daughter queens in *B. terrestris* colonies found no evidence that worker aggression reduces either numbers or biomass of daughter queens. Lopez-Vaamonde *et al.* (2003) removed aggressive or egg-laying workers from half of eight paired late-switching colonies, and replaced them with non-aggressive ones. Non-aggressive workers were also removed and replaced in the control colonies. The colonies with artificially reduced aggression did not differ significantly in their production of daughter queens from those in which aggressive and egg-laying workers were allowed to remain: in fact there was a weak tendency for the latter to be slightly more productive.

This result supports the kin selection explanation for the onset of the competition phase in the late-switching colonies. However, it also poses new questions. If it turns out that aggression and egg laying by workers do not impose detectable costs to the colony's production of daughter queens, then it is difficult to see why the workers should not attempt to reproduce much earlier in the colony cycle, and, in particular, to compete with the queen's production of males in the early-switching colonies. The male offspring of workers produced early in the colony cycle would presumably have more chance of successful mating, and no cost to the future success of the colony in producing daughter queens might be incurred. However, against this, it could be argued that the cost to colony fitness of worker reproduction early in the colony cycle would be greater than at the later stage when the colony is more populous (Bourke, pers. comm.).

A second question posed by this new finding is how damage to daughter queen rearing is avoided during the competition phase. One possibility is that the outcome of this experiment may have been affected by the way the captive colonies were fed. With immediate availability of food provided by the experimenters, the bees had few, if any, foraging costs. In freely foraging colonies, competition within the colony for food gathered by foragers, and reduced colony investment in brood-nursing relative to foraging might have made a difference. However, the study by Müller & Schmid-Hempel (1992b) to mimic the effect of conopid infestation of foragers suggested that reduced food availability did not depress the numbers of daughter queens produced, though they were generally smaller. A further, intriguing possibility is that the queen larvae are themselves active in regulating the feeding behaviour of the workers, so offsetting the potential costs to their development of the competition phase. A study by Ribiero et al. (1999) of the feeding of B. terrestris larvae showed different patterns of inspection of larval cells and frequency of feeding as between male, worker and queen larvae. Workers would often inspect larvae briefly and move on without feeding them, even when those workers had food in their crop and would go on to feed other larvae. Ribiero et al. hypothesise that the larvae can emit a 'hunger signal', and that frequency of feeding is a function of communication between nurse-workers and larvae. Bumblebee larvae are known to move their heads and mandibles as a response to touch. It is well known that honey bee larvae emit pheromones that prompt workers into increased foraging, and also either signal or determine the inhibition of ovarian activation in them (Free, 1987). There is a brood pheromone in bumblebees, too, but it is unknown whether this is involved in the communication of hunger.

Cnaani et al. (2000) provide evidence on the correlation between the timing of the competition phase and the onset of queen-production. One interpretation of this is that the queen shifts to daughter queen-production first, and that workers detect this as a signal that now is the last opportunity for them to reproduce. The alternative is that overt worker/queen conflict occurs first, and the existing diploid larvae provide the last opportunity to rear daughter queens. If this latter interpretation were upheld then it would rather reverse the relationships between these events as portrayed by Bourke & Ratnieks (2001) giving support to the earlier view that the competition phase is a result of declining dominance on the part of the queen.

We are clearly some way from a full understanding of the forms of communication that prompt the shifting patterns of relationship in the bumblebee colony. Discovery of the chemical identity of the key pheromone or pheromones involved would be a big step forward, enabling experimental evidence to be obtained on the precise biological functions of chemical communication in these complex processes. Finally, it should be noted that none of the earlier researchers claimed that queen dominance prior to the competition phase was maintained entirely by chemical communication. Since physical domination also plays a part, and can result in some inhibition of worker ovarian development by queens without mandibular glands, it may still be that queens in some respects override the reproductive interests of their workers. Further research on the timing of the competition phase in relation to the other phases in the colony cycle in species other than *B. terrestris* would also be illuminating.

CHAPTER 4

The Usurper Bumblebees

I T HAS COMMONLY been observed that bumblebee queens sometimes come into conflict over possession of nest sites. Dead queens may be found in or near established nests, and it is reasonably assumed that these are the remains of losers in such struggles. Sometimes, intruder queens succeed in taking over already established nests – sometimes of their own species, sometimes of another. In one Canadian study, 93 such usurpations were recorded, the majority within species, but 17 per cent involving takeovers of nests by different species (Richards, cited in Pamilo *et al.*, 1987). Queens of *Bombus affinis*, a North American species, often take over the nests of *B. terricola* where their distributions overlap (Fisher, 1983*a*; Plath, 1934). In some extreme environments, particularly at high altitudes in southern mountains, and in the far north, a few bumblebee species occasionally take over the established nests of other species, persuading the 'host' workers to rear their own brood (see Yarrow, 1970; Richards, 1973).

This habit of social or nest parasitism, sometimes called inquilinism, has become an obligatory mode of life for one distinctive group of bumblebees. These are the cuckoo bumblebees. There are ten species in Europe, of which six occur in Britain. There is no worker caste in these species, and although they very closely resemble the social bumblebees, there are some distinguishing structural features. The most obvious of these are probably related to their parasitic habit. The females lack the corbiculae and other structures associated with pollen collection (Fig. 68). They are also generally more sparsely covered with hair, and have a thick cuticle (Fig. 69). They lack the ability to secrete wax from their abdominal segments, and have variously shaped outgrowths, or callosities, on the ventral surface of the last abdominal segment (Fig. 70). These differ in shape between species and are a useful character for identification. Cuckoo females also

FIG 68. A female cuckoo bumblebee (*Bombus sylvestris*). Note the lack of a corbicula on the hind tibia.

FIG 69. Cuckoo bumblebee *Bombus sylvestris* (female) showing the thin covering of hair on the abdomen.

FIG 70. A female cuckoo bumblebee (*Bombus vestalis*). Note the callosities just visible at the tip of her abdomen.

have larger and differently shaped mandibles than those of the social species, as well as longer and more curved stings (Fig. 71). These, too, are considered by some to be adaptations to their nest parasitism (see Fisher & Sampson, 1992). Finally, cuckoo females have differently structured ovaries, with more ovarioles than the social species, and their eggs are generally smaller and narrower.

The males are less obviously different from the males of the social species, but they, too, have differently shaped hind tibiae, usually with a covering of hair on the outer surface, and generally have a less dense covering of hair on the body (Fig. 72). This is often most noticeable on the dorsal surface of the first two or three abdominal segments. Of course, the males do not need the structural and physiological adaptations for conquering and dominating the host nest that are present in the females. Both sexes typically have short, rounded faces (Fig. 73).

According to Sladen, the distinction between the cuckoos and the 'true' bumblebees was first noted in 1803 by Kirby, but it was not until 1832 that Lepeletier assigned them to a distinct genus, *Psithyrus*. The separation of the bumblebees into two genera, *Bombus* and *Psithyrus*, persisted until more systematic taxonomic work in the 1980s began to call it into question. Even as early as 1912 Sladen noted how very similar the two groups were, suggesting a common origin of the cuckoos from a social bumblebee ancestor, with subsequent differentiation

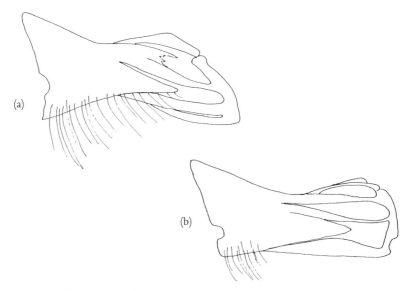

FIG 71. Mandible of: (a) female cuckoo bumblebee (*Bombus vestalis*) and (b) female social bumblebee (*Bombus terrestris*).

FIG 72. A male cuckoo bumblebee (*Bombus bohemicus*). Note the thin covering of hair on the abdomen.

FIG 73. A view of the face of a female cuckoo bumblebee (*Bombus sylvestris*). Note the short, rounded face, typical of cuckoo bumblebees. She is cleaning her antenna with her right front leg.

occurring as a result of their adaptation to their parasitic mode of life. In a series of studies, Paul Williams (1985, 1991, 1994) identified a large number of structural details that varied between bumblebee species. These included 22 features of the male genitalia, and a further 22 characteristics from head, thorax and abdomen of males and females. These provided data for a statistical grouping of the bumblebee species, from which a provisional estimate could be made of their degree of relatedness, and the evolutionary history of the group. Earlier groupings of the social bumblebees into subgenera were only partially confirmed, but there were two clear implications for the cuckoo bumblebees. One, which had been widely indicated by previous work, was that the cuckoos were all derived from a single common ancestor. The second was that the position of this group in the overall family tree of the bumblebees did not justify their status as a separate genus. To maintain this consistently would have required the division of the bumblebees into at least nine genera. His proposal, now widely accepted, and supported by subsequent biochemical and molecular analysis (Koulianos & Schmid-Hempel, 2000; Pamilo *et al.*, 1987; Pedersen, 1996, 2002), was to include the cuckoo bumblebees as a subgenus within a wider genus, *Bombus*. However, for the purposes of the field naturalist and ecologist, the division between the cuckoos and the social bumblebees remains an important one (and for clarification in this chapter the distinction is indicated by inclusion of the initial 'P.' in parentheses in the scientific names of cuckoo species).

In Europe, most cuckoo bumblebees specialise in usurping the nests of a single host species. However, some may also parasitise the nests of a small number of other species, often ones closely related to the preferred host. Løken's study of Scandinavian cuckoos and their hosts, for example, includes *Bombus jonellus* as an alternative host for *B. (P.) sylvestris*, whose usual host is *B. pratorum*, and *B. pascuorum* and *B. sylvarum* as alternatives for *B. (P.) rupestris*, which usually parasitises nests of *B. lapidarius* (Table 2). However, it cannot be ruled out that some of these reports concern cuckoos merely taking brief refuge in nests of non-host species. By contrast, the associations between *B. terrestris* and its cuckoo, *B. (P.) vestalis*, and that between *B. lucorum* and its cuckoo, *B. (P.) bohemicus*, seem to be unvarying. Among North American cuckoo bumblebees, some are, like the British species, specialised to one or a small number of closely related species, but others are generalists, capable of usurping the nests of a wide variety of *Bombus* species.

TABLE 2. Records of host nests usurped by the European cuckoo bumblebee species. + = 5–10 colonies recorded; + + = > 10 colonies (adapted from Løken, 1984, with permission).

SOCIAL PARASITE	HOST	N
P. bohemicus	B. (s. str.) lucorum	++
P. vestalis	B. (s. str.) terrestris	++
P. barbutellus	B. (Megabombus) hortorum	+
	B. (Pyrobombus) hypnorum	1
P. rupestris	B. (Melanobombus) lapidarius	+ +
	B. (Melanobombus) sicheli ssp. alticola	2
	B. (Thoracobombus) pascuorum	2
	B. (Thoracobombus) sylvarum	2
P. campestris	B. (Thoracobombus) pascuorum	++
	B. (Thoracobombus) humilis	+
	B. (Rhodobombus) pomorum	1
	B. (Pyrobombus) pratorum	1
P. quadricolor	B. (Soroeensibombus) soroeensis	3
P. sylvestris	B. (Pyrobombus) pratorum	++
	B. (Pyrobombus) jonellus	1
P. flavidus	B. (Pyrobombus) jonellus	?1
P. norvegicus	B. (Pyrobombus) hypnorum	+

In some cases, most notably *B. lapidarius* and its cuckoo, *B. (P.) rupestris*, there is a close resemblance in colour pattern between host and parasite. Whilst it is a possibility that this aids the parasite in avoiding recognition by host bees when it invades their nest, it seems more likely that such visual resemblances are examples of Müllerian mimicry. Among the bumblebees there are several clusters of similarly coloured species as, for example, *B. lapidarius* and *B. ruderarius* (black with red tails) and the larger group of black-and-yellow banded species. If predators that are stung by one of the group learn these patterns, then the others might be expected to get some protection as a result of future avoidance behaviour on the part of the predator. This is a widely accepted explanation of the strong convergence in colour patterns among the bumblebees, and the consequent difficulty in identifying them reliably by colour pattern alone.

The parasitic mode of life brings with it a life history quite different from that of the social bumblebees. In its broadest outlines, this life history is common to the various cuckoo species, but there appears to be a great deal of variation in the details, both within and between species, and much remains to be discovered.

This is Sladen's colourful summary:

'The way in which the Psithyrus queen proceeds in order to ensure the success of her atrocious work has all the appearance of a cunning plan, cleverly conceived and carried out by one who not only is a mistress of the crime of murder, but also knows how to commit it at the most advantageous time for herself and her future children, compelling the poor orphans she creates to become her willing slaves.' (Sladen, 1912)

Shed of its moralising tone, Sladen's account pinpoints some of the key problems the cuckoo bumblebees have to solve if they are to complete their reproductive cycle. On emergence from hibernation, the cuckoo females, like the queens of the social species, have to replenish their depleted food stores by foraging on spring flowers. Next, they must locate an already established nest of their host species, and subsequently gain entry into it. As Sladen notes, the timing of this is quite crucial. If the potential host colony is too far advanced, the cuckoo female may be successfully repulsed by the defenders. If, on the other hand, a colony is invaded too early in its development, the cuckoo may have too few host workers available to nurture its offspring. Once inside the nest, the cuckoo must somehow establish its own dominance over the host workers, at the expense of the incumbent queen. For the species studied most closely by Sladen, this invariably meant 'murder' of the host queen, but more-or-less lengthy periods of cohabitation have also been noted by other observers, as well as by Sladen himself.

Even where the host queen is deposed, the cuckoo faces the same problem as the social queens in unparasitised nests. As we have seen, the workers have reproductive interests of their own, and may individually or collectively rebel when it is in their interests to do so, or when a queen is weakened and incapable of maintaining full dominance. How does the successful invader secure the submission of the host workers? This is a particularly interesting question, given the differences amongst the host species themselves in this respect, notably between simple and complex species (see Chapters 2 & 3). Do the cuckoos mimic the control methods of the queens of their particular host species? Once the cuckoo is established in the host nest, and has begun to lay its own eggs, these have to be defended against any continuing hostility from host workers, and the latter somehow have to be 'tricked' into providing nourishment for the resulting larvae until they reach maturity as cuckoo sexuals, and, of course, for the cuckoo female herself. Here, too, there is added complexity since the modes of larval feeding differ among host species (between the pollen storers and pocket makers), as do the mechanisms involved in caste and sex determination.

NEST SEARCHING AND IDENTIFICATION

It is generally assumed that the cuckoo females emerge from hibernation rather later than their hosts, though some species are certainly to be seen very early in spring, foraging from *Salix* catkins and other early flowers. Sladen observed cuckoo females in the nests of a wide variety of non-host species, and it seems likely that post-hibernation cuckoos take temporary shelter in such nests, without attempting to usurp them. Soon, however, the predominance of foraging behaviour is replaced by active searching behaviour, which closely resembles the prospecting for nest sites exhibited by the queens of the social species (Fig. 74).

In the cuckoos, the search is for already established nests of the host species. Nest searching is particularly commonly observed in *Bombus (P.) vestalis*, which quarters areas of rough ground, 'contouring' tufts of grass, and investigating hollows and holes in the same manner as its host. However, this behaviour is less often observed in other cuckoos, and it may be that they have different methods of locating potential host nests. There is decisive evidence that scent plays an important role in nest location. Sladen (1912), for example, observed a strong response of a captive *B. (P.) vestalis* female to the scent of queen *B. terrestris*, its host species. In some species, underground tunnels of up to 5 metres connect the nests

FIG 74. A female cuckoo bumblebee (*Bombus rupestris*) searching for a host nest in which to lay her eggs.

with their entrances, and in some of these species (including *B. terrestris, B. lucorum* and *B. hypnorum*), scent trails are used by workers in their movements between foraging patches and the nest. In an ingenious series of experiments, Cederberg (1983) was able to show both that these scents are species-specific, and that in one cuckoo species, scent trails of the host species are distinguished and preferred. Scent trails of *B. lapidarius* workers were collected from a captive colony, and the response of females of its cuckoo, *B. (P.) rupestris*, were observed. The latter, on making contact with the *lapidarius* scent, became 'strongly activated and excited'. They pointed their antennae down onto the scent marks, with tips bent almost at right angles, they 'eagerly palpated' the surface, and periodically vibrated their wings (Fig. 75). Queens exhibited the same host recognition behaviour on being confronted with scent marks artificially provided from extracts taken from the bodies of previously killed queen *lapidarius*. However, they did not initially respond to similarly prepared extracts from the bodies of five non-host species.

When presented with single scent marks of the host, *B. (P.) rupestris* females eventually lost interest and moved on. However, their response to trails was more persistent, taking up to 230 seconds, and covering 360 centimetres. In each case, the cuckoo became increasingly less focused as time went on, and where the scents of other species were present, they eventually began to show some interest in these. So far as this host/parasite association is concerned, it seems that the cuckoo

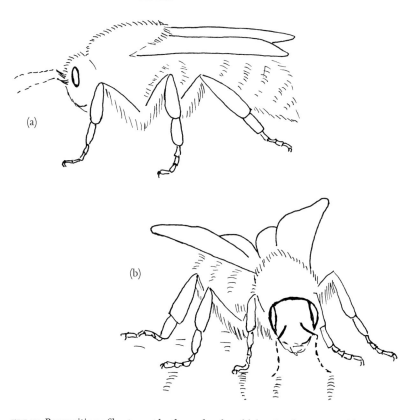

FIG 75. Recognition of host scent by the cuckoo bumblebee *Bombus rupestris*: (a) female in normal relaxed posture; (b) the same female showing host recognition behaviour in response to an extract from *B. lapidarius* queen tarsi. The odour spots are outlined. Note the position of the antennae and the slightly spread wings (drawn from photographs in Cederberg, 1983, with permission).

female is able to recognise the scent trail of its host workers, and to follow it for a sufficient distance to reach even quite secluded nests. There is also some evidence that sampling of the nests of other potential host species might be an alternative behaviour if preferred host nests are not available, as indicated in Table 2 above.

Further evidence of the use of scent both to locate nests, and to identify those of the host species comes from the work of R. M. Fisher. He studied the behaviour of *B. (P.) ashtoni*, a nest parasite of both *B. terricola* and *B. affinis* (a North American species). In this case, the cuckoo female cannot use the scent trails left by workers, as nest searching begins before the emergence of the first worker brood. Fisher's experiment involved placing cuckoo females in cages adjacent to nests of host and non-host species, as well as a control containing only nest material, with wire mesh separating them. The cuckoo females showed strong attraction for nests of both host species, compared with the non-host and the control, and chewed at the wire mesh in apparent attempts to enter the host nests (Fisher, 1983a).

It seems likely that nest-searching cuckoo females use a combination of visual cues in their generalised searching for potential nest sites, together with scent for close-range location and discrimination of host nests.

ENTRY AND CONQUEST

Once a suitable nest has been located, the female cuckoo enters it. According to some accounts, she may remain for some days concealed in nest materials without attracting hostility from the hosts. It is assumed that during this period she acquires the host scent, and is subsequently not recognised as an intruder. Other accounts suggest that the intruder is met with immediate resistance from host queens or workers, and a fight to the death ensues. It seems likely that timing and circumstances produce quite different scenarios, and also that characteristic patterns of host/parasite interaction may differ considerably from species to species.

It is, of course, extremely difficult to obtain clear evidence on these questions, as introduction of cuckoo females into captive colonies is necessarily an artificial process which may well distort the behaviour of both partners, and unmanipulated wild colonies are by that fact not open to continuous observation. However, we do have some valuable accounts from Sladen, and from subsequent researchers, most notably R. M. Fisher. According to Sladen (1912), intruding cuckoo females may be met initially with some aggressive responses from either workers or the host queen. However, they tend to avoid conflict, slipping away to hide in nest material. Other observers even report a submissive behavioural response on the part of the cuckoo, in which it draws its legs up tightly against its body. In any case, the cuckoos are well protected by their thick cuticle and the reduced, thicker 'hinges' between their abdominal segments. However, if a cuckoo attempts to enter a nest that is in an advanced stage – after the emergence of the second batch of host brood – she is likely to attract a much more aggressive response from the defending workers.

Sladen gives two examples of advanced *B. terrestris* nests in which there were dead cuckoo females. In one, the bodies of two cuckoo females were accompanied by those of 15 *B. terrestris* workers, presumably killed in the course of defeating the intruders. Sladen excavated many parasitised nests of *B. terrestris* and *B. lapidarius* and found none in which the host queen and cuckoo cohabited. On the evidence of one parasitised nest of *B. hortorum* he supposed that its parasite, *B. (P.) barbutellus*, also killed its host queen.

However, there was already contrary evidence of prolonged cohabitation between *Bombus* queens and their parasites. Sladen was aware of studies by Hoffer (1889), in Styria, on other cuckoo species. Hoffer's observations focused on two host/parasite relationships: *B. pascuorum* (then called *agrorum*) and its nest parasite, *B. (P.) campestris*, and *B. pratorum* with *B. (P.) sylvestris* (then called *Psithyrus quadricolor*). These studies indicated prolonged cohabitation and successful rearing of both host and parasite sexuals from the same nest. In Sladen's opinion, the striking differences between Hoffer's observations and his own might be explained by the less aggressive nature of these two host species than *B. terrestris* and *B. lapidarius*. A case in point is the *B. pratorum/sylvestris* association observed by Küpper & Schwammberger (1995). In three parasitised nests they studied, the level of aggression exhibited by hosts varied, but cohabitation persisted for several weeks, and both host and parasite succeeded in rearing sexual progeny.

In a remarkable series of studies by Fisher (1987, 1988), cuckoo females of three species were introduced into freely foraging but captive colonies of their respective hosts. Females of *B. (P.) vestalis* were introduced into two nests of *B. terrestris*. Both were at an early stage of colony development. In the first, the host queen and her three workers attacked the cuckoo female. However, this struggle appeared to be inconclusive and the cuckoo eventually left the nest. In the second case, the queen and workers attacked the cuckoo, which in turn mauled them. The host queen left the nest temporarily, but later returned, and by the end of an hour's observation both queen and cuckoo jointly occupied the comb, and there was no hostility from the workers. However, other studies of the same host/parasite association (van Honk *et al.*, 1981; Frehn & Schwammberger, 2001) give support to Sladen's view that successful invasion of *B. terrestris* nests by *B. (P.) vestalis* is generally fatal for the host queen. In three parasitised nests observed by Frehn & Schwammberger, the host queen was found dead in the nest after six hours, two days and six days, respectively.

An instructive comparison is provided by another of Fisher's introductions. In this case females of *B. (P.) campestris* were introduced into a captive but freely foraging colony of *B. pascuorum*. However, with 32 workers, this colony was clearly more advanced than either of the *B. terrestris* nests used in the previous study. The *B. pascuorum* workers attacked the cuckoo, forming a ball around her as they attempted to sting her (a pattern of behaviour noted from several other studies). Seven workers were stung and killed by the cuckoo female before she was herself

killed. Interestingly the host queen took no part in the conflict and left the comb
for seven minutes during it. The introduction was repeated with a second cuckoo
female, but it elicited the same aggressive response. Fisher succeeded in getting
the cuckoo queen adopted only by removing all workers for 16 hours, and then
reintroducing only five. In the absence of the workers, neither queen nor cuckoo
attacked one another, and the return of the smaller group of workers elicited no
further aggression. The cuckoo female remained beside the comb, largely inactive,
but occasionally grooming itself, for the first eight days.

Such accounts as are available indicate marked differences between host bee
species in their patterns of response to the cuckoo female's entry into the nest.
A host colony of *B. lucorum* studied by Fisher showed no initial hostility to their
intruder, and neither did a colony of *B. lapidarius* invaded by *B. (P.) rupestris*.
In marked contrast, both *B. pascuorum* and *B. terrestris* hosts responded violently.
Even here, though, there were differences, *B. terrestris* queens and workers jointly
attacked their cuckoo, whereas *B. pascuorum* workers took on this hazardous task
unaided by their queen. Given the central role of the queen in the life of the
colony, this latter pattern would seem to make good evolutionary sense.

To some extent these observed differences may be species-specific, but there
is evidence that host responses to intruders also vary, for the same parasite/host
pair, according to circumstances. These include both the stage of development of
the host colony (that is, the number and age of the host workers) and the state of
its energy stores at the point when the parasite makes its entry into the nest. Both
the *B. lapidarius* and the *B. lucorum* colonies discussed above were at an early stage,
with few workers, and neither responded aggressively. However, the *B. terrestris*
colonies were also at an early stage, but still actively resisted the introductions
of their cuckoos, in one case successfully. The aggression shown by Fisher's
B. pascuorum workers contrasts with Hoffer's account of the generally non-
conflictive relationship between *B. pascuorum* and its social parasite. However,
this might be explained by the more advanced stage of colony development in the
former case.

Cartar & Dill (1991) showed that the level of energy reserves in the nest affects
the response of hosts to the entry of a female cuckoo. Existing nectar stores in
five captive colonies of a Canadian species, *B. occidentalis*, were removed, but food
supplies maintained for 24 hours. After this, the colonies were starved for a day,
and feeding subsequently resumed. Colony responses to the introduction of
a female cuckoo (*B. (P.) insularis*) at different times during this procedure were
recorded. Depletion of energy resources in the colonies led to a progressive 'shut
down', with workers becoming torpid, ceasing to incubate the brood and allowing
nest temperature to fall. When cuckoo females were introduced into these

energy-depleted colonies the host workers responded with passive threat postures. These included a range of characteristic bumblebee threat postures from raising one leg, through raising two legs and pointing the abdomen tip towards the intruder, to lying on their backs, legs spread, and with sting pointing at the enemy. These were generally not effective in seeing off the cuckoo. By contrast, colonies that were well supplied with nectar tended to respond with active aggression, chasing off the cuckoo, or attacking it, often with fatal consequences for the workers. It seems likely that periods of inclement weather that prevent foraging in wild colonies will reduce the ability of colonies to resist intruding cuckoo females, giving them time to take on the odour of the colony and escape further aggressive responses if energy resources are subsequently restored.

Another of Fisher's studies (1985) sheds some light on the evolutionary significance of species-specific differences in host responses to invasion by social parasites. The interactions between a North American cuckoo bumblebee, *B. (P.) citrinus*, its preferred host, *B. vagans*, and a secondary host, *B. impatiens*, were Fisher's subjects in this study. *Bombus vagans* colonies do not respond aggressively towards intruding females of *B. (P.) citrinus*, and so the latter have a very high rate of success in usurping nests of this species. By contrast, *B. (P.) citrinus* females introduced into nests of *B. impatiens* were attacked by both queens and workers of the hosts, and experienced much lower levels of success in taking over the nests. A minority of queens of both host species continued to cohabit with the intruder for some time. Fisher notes that *B. vagans* queens are smaller than female *B. (P.) citrinus*, and would be unlikely to succeed in ousting them by an aggressive response. Non-aggression may possibly give them a chance of staying in the nest and reproducing, or leaving to found another nest. From the point of view of the nest parasite, its greater success in usurping the nests of *B. vagans* suggests that specialising to this host gives it a selective advantage. But the cuckoo's attraction also to nest-scents of *B. impatiens* suggests there may be an advantage in the ability to usurp the nests of this species if those of *B. vagans* are unavailable. In Fisher's studies, the cuckoo was able to reproduce successfully in nests of both its hosts.

CUCKOO DOMINANCE, AND BROOD CARE IN THE NEST

In Fisher's observation of a *B. terrestris* nest with an introduced female of the cuckoo, *B. (P.) vestalis*, the host queen and parasite cohabited for more than two weeks. During this time the cuckoo attempted to dominate the host workers and queen by pushing and mauling them, and it also began to eat host eggs and eject their larvae. It began laying its own eggs some six days after being introduced into the nest, and continued to defend its own brood from host workers, as well as spending some time incubating both its own brood and that of its host. After some 17 days, the host queen was found dead on the comb. It was not clear how she had died, but, interestingly, the host workers were very active, and attacked the cuckoo. In addition, some of the cuckoo's brood clump had been destroyed, and despite restoration of the dominance behaviour of the cuckoo, the host workers eventually destroyed all its remaining brood. Meanwhile, the cuckoo female had eaten the eggs of a host worker. The host workers also engaged in conflict with each other in defence of their broods. In this case, egg laying by workers and the disintegration of the colony resembled the response of workers to the onset of the competition phase, or loss of the queen in an unparasitised colony. A possible interpretation of this, in the light of the prolonged cohabitation prior to these events, might be that at least in this association, the cuckoo experiences difficulty in maintaining its dominance over the host workers in the absence of the host queen.

In two of the three parasitised *B. terrestris* nests observed by Frehn & Schwammberger (2001) the cuckoo female experienced similar difficulties. Despite showing dominance behaviour, these cuckoos were unable to prevent host workers from laying eggs, and successfully rearing male offspring. In these nests, the cuckoo was not successful in rearing offspring. However, in the third nest, whose workers were both younger and fewer at the time of introduction of the parasite, the cuckoo was successful in dominating the workers and ensuring the survival of its own brood. In the case of Fisher's introduction of a female *B. (P.) campestris* into a nest of *B. pascuorum*, mentioned above, the cuckoo began to eat host eggs and eject their larvae some eight days after its introduction. At the same time it began to lay its own eggs in wax cells built from materials derived from destroyed host cells. *Bombus pascuorum* is a pocket maker, and it appears that the cuckoo brood were fed in the same way as the host larvae by the workers. These deposited pollen in the pockets constructed on the larval cells, and subsequently collected the pollen to feed it to the larvae. The cuckoo fed its own larvae in this way by biting holes in the larval cell and regurgitating the food. In 30 per cent of observed feeding episodes, the cuckoo simply bit small holes in the cells of its own larvae, while the host workers fed its larvae and resealed the cells. The cuckoo was not observed to feed host larvae. Eventually, 33 days after its introduction, the cuckoo female was attacked by host workers and expelled from the nest. The host queen remained in the nest and continued to lay eggs.

Some general conclusions can be derived from the above accounts. Queens of the host species and cuckoo females may cohabit for long periods in the same nest, although conflict does eventually occur. In all cases the cuckoo depends on the resources brought into the nest by host workers, for its own nutrition and for that of its brood. However, contrary to widespread assumptions, some cuckoo females participate in the care of their own brood. These include both *campestris* and *vestalis*, as well as *bohemicus*, a close relative of the latter. According to Fisher's account, females of *B. (P.) vestalis* even incubate brood of the host. The species studied so far lay their eggs in cells constructed from wax derived from destroyed host cells. The few available detailed accounts of brood-rearing cover both pocket-making and pollen-storer host species, though there is little clarity on the exact feeding regimes used by the cuckoo females and host workers. However, Fisher's observation of brood care by *B. (P.) campestris* is one of particular interest. Though both host workers and cuckoo females attempt to destroy one another's brood, the cuckoo leaves some of the host brood to develop. This presumably ensures that there are sufficient workers to provision itself and its own brood. Finally, the cuckoo female generally faces eventual worker rebellion against its dominance, as do queens of the host species in unparasitised nests.

The evidence we have so far suggests there are also some interesting differences between the various host/nest parasite associations. *Bombus (P.) vestalis* exhibits dominance behaviour, described as 'mauling' and 'pushing' host queens and workers, as well as 'head-rubbing', and chasing away of workers. Fisher also describes this behaviour on the part of *B. (P.) bohemicus* females, inquilines in the nests of *B. lucorum*, a very close relative of *B. terrestris*, and in *B. (P.) citrinus* in the nests of both its hosts (Fig. 76). By contrast, no such behaviour was noted in the case of *B. (P.) campestris*, which appeared to be quite passive by comparison with the other cuckoos that have been studied. The dominance behaviour described as 'mauling' consists of the cuckoo grabbing its victim as if to sting it, but then releasing it, a behaviour also shown by social bumblebee queens in asserting dominance over workers.

As we saw in Chapter 2, some social bumblebees (complex species) use chemical cues as well as behavioural ones in dominating workers and suppressing the activation of their ovaries. In the case of *B. (P.) citrinus*, Fisher established that physical contact between parasite and host workers is needed for ovarian activation in the latter to be suppressed (Fisher, 1983b). This suggests that this cuckoo species has to rely on dominance behaviour alone, though it remains possible that chemical cues are communicated through contacts such as head-rubbing. There is evidence that cuckoos are able to detect the development of ovaries in host workers and that they respond with renewed dominance behaviour (Frehn & Schwammberger, 2001). Overall, the extent to which the cuckoo's attempt to gain reproductive control of the colony involves behavioural dominance,

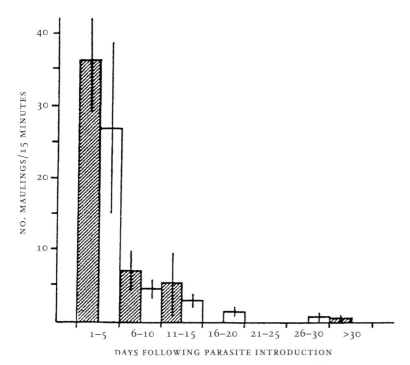

FIG 76. Mauling frequencies displayed by females of the cuckoo bumblebee *Bombus (P.) citrinus* in parasitised nests of *Bombus impatiens* (hatched lines) and *Bombus vagans*. Bar heights represent the average number of maulings observed per 15-minute observation period (reproduced from Fisher, 1983*b*, with permission).

chemical cues (as in the complex social species), or direct but selective destruction of host brood may well differ from species to species. It could be, for example, that *B (P.) vestalis* cannot mimic the pheromonal signals by which *B. terrestris* queens suppress the ovarian activation of workers in unparasitised nests. This is a possible explanation of the more aggressive behaviour of *B. (P.) vestalis* compared with some other cuckoo species. This aspect of nest parasitism deserves further research, and could shed light on some of the issues discussed in Chapter 3.

In at least some accounts, relatively peaceful cohabitation between hosts and cuckoo females continued for some time after the entry of the latter into the nest, even through the whole nest cycle in some cases. Still, conflict usually erupts in the end, but there are considerable differences from case to case in the points at which it does. Sladen's study of a spontaneously parasitised nest of *B. lapidarius* led him to suppose that it was the development of the intruder's ovaries and her readiness to begin laying eggs that sparked a conflict in which the host queen and three workers were killed. This seems plausible, and parallels the queen's aggressive response to egg-laying workers in unparasitised nests. However, in the other cases, cohabitation was much more prolonged than this, and the eventual conflict did not invariably result in the death of the host queen.

Finally, it should be emphasised that no easy generalisation can be drawn from these accounts. Detailed observations of the interactions between hosts and cuckoos inside the nest are unavoidably subject to distorting effects of captivity and observation, and, in most of the studies, also to the artificiality of the introductions themselves. Sladen's accounts of the contents of excavated nests are very instructive, but also limited in that they give us only a 'time-slice' of the colony's development, together with what can be reconstructed about its past from the structure of the nest. Clearly much more research is needed on the intricate relations between the various cuckoo species and their hosts within the nest.

REPRODUCTIVE SUCCESS

Parasitised nests generally produce fewer workers than they would otherwise do, owing to the limitations on the host queen's reproduction imposed by the female cuckoo. Successful control by the cuckoo over the reproduction of the colony would imply the eventual emergence of males and fertile females that were exclusively her own offspring. Again, Sladen, with his more adversarial view of cuckoo/host relations, says that he never observed a *Bombus* queen or male produced from a parasitised nest of either *B. terrestris* or *B. lapidarius*. However, Fisher's studies give a rather different picture. In the *B. lucorum* colony, some males of the host species, derived from eggs laid prior to the entry of the cuckoo, emerged as adults. None of the cuckoo progeny survived. In the *B. terrestris* nest, 18 host males and 14 cuckoo males reached adulthood. The *B. pascuorum* colony yielded 16 host males in addition to three cuckoo females and ten males (Table 3). In Frehn and Schwammberger's study, host workers successfully reproduced in two out of three nests. Though some significant depression on the reproduction of the host must result, they may still succeed in rearing some sexuals from parasitised nests. Fisher (1987) acknowledges that successful reproduction on the part of hosts in parasitised nests may be an artefact of laboratory conditions. However, if it also occurs in the field, it suggests that adaptive behaviour on the part of hosts might evolve, and social parasitism may not be an 'all or nothing' matter.

TABLE 3. Records of host reproduction in bumblebee colonies parasitised by various species of cuckoo bumblebees. Letters in parenthesis: L = laboratory reared and confined host colonies; F = field or freely foraging host colonies; B, D and A, host reproduction from eggs laid before, during or after the occupation of the comb by the parasite, respectively (reproduced from Fisher, 1987, with permission).

PARASITE	HOST	HOST REPRODUCTIVE SUCCESS	REFERENCE
P. ashtoni	B. terricola (L, F)	Yes (B, D)/No	Fisher (1985); Plath (1934)
	B. affinis (L, F)	Yes (D, A)/No	Fisher (1986); Plath (1934)
P. bohemicus	B. lucorum (F)	Yes (A)	Fisher (unpublished data)
P. vestalis	B. terrestris (L, F)	Yes (A)/Yes (B)	van Honk et. al (1981); Fisher (unpublished data)
P. variabilis	B. pennsylvanicus (F)	Yes (B)	Webb (1961)
P. citrinus	B. vagans (L)	Yes (B)	Fisher (1985)
	B. impatiens (L, F)	No/Yes (A)	Fisher (1985)
P. campestris	B. pascuorum (F)	Yes (A)	Fisher (unpublished data)

AFTER LEAVING THE HOST NEST

The new generation of cuckoo bees are most often seen foraging on flowerheads. Males are more often seen than females, frequently in clusters on the same patch of flowers such as thistles and knapweeds. They tend to be more lethargic than workers of the social species. However, as well as foraging, both males and females engage in reproductive behaviour. Little is known of the mating activity of the females, but the males engage in patrolling scent-marked routes, as do many of the social species.

Patrolling behaviour of males has been observed in all the species that occur in Britain, but there are rather few accounts in the literature. To some extent the relatively low numbers of the cuckoos may explain this. *Bombus vestalis* is currently the most abundant cuckoo species in southern Britain, and its patrolling behaviour is correspondingly more often observed. In most respects it resembles the common pattern of the other *Bombus* species, involving a repeated pattern of flight with occasional approach places that are regularly scent-marked with pheromones from the labial glands. The bees sometimes patrol singly, and sometimes collectively, with ten or more flying along a shared route in succession. The approach places are usually relatively tall features, but much depends on the topography of their local habitat, and possibly also on the co-presence of other *Bombus* species. Cederberg, Svensson and colleagues (for example, Svensson, 1979*b*; Cederberg *et al.*, 1984) carried out studies of male cuckoo bee patrolling behaviour in northern Europe, and also analysed their marking pheromones. The main chemical constituents are various blends of isoprenoids and fatty acid derivatives. The precise blends are different for each species, and, with one exception, the cuckoos have no constituents in common with their host species. That these marking compounds have a significant role in species isolation is suggested by the fact that species with chemically similar pheromones tend to have quite different patrolling habits. Cederberg *et al.* (1984) never saw a male cuckoo using the same approach place as males of a social species.

As with the social species, males do not return to the nest of origin, but roost at night on or under flowerheads, and die off before winter sets in. Fresh females are relatively rarely seen, but they, too, like their social sisters, forage to build up their fat stores before entering hibernation. There are a few scattered reports of chance discovery of hibernating cuckoo bees, such as that given by Sladen:

> '*I have dug up the hibernating queens of* Ps. rupestris, vestalis, barbutellus, *and* campestris *from banks facing north-west, occupying little cavities in the ground, about two inches below the surface, exactly like the queens of* B. lapidarius *and other Bombi.*' (Sladen, 1912)

In general, as with other host/parasite relationships, the host species are considerably more abundant than their cuckoos. However, this difference may be exaggerated by the absence of a worker caste in the case of the cuckoos. There is very little information about levels of infestation of the various social species by cuckoos. In Britain, the six cuckoo species take as their main host species the six most common and widespread of the social species. However, there is probably a good deal of variation from place to place and time to time in the proportions of host nests which are parasitised. For example, Sladen reports that in east Kent some 20–40 per cent of *lapidarius* nests were parasitised by *B. (P.) rupestris*. By contrast, *B. (P.) rupestris* has been the rarest of the cuckoos since Sladen's time, though showing a strong recovery in the late 1990s. In this case, it seems unlikely that the changes in abundance of the parasite are connected with changes in the status of its host. Alford (1975) cites a study by Awram according to which more than 50 per cent of *B. pratorum* nests obtained in Hertfordshire were parasitised by its cuckoo, *B. (P.) sylvestris*. The 36 *B. lucorum* nests studied by Müller & Schmid-Hempel (1992*a*) in Switzerland suffered a 30 per cent invasion rate by *B. (P.) bohemicus* females, and several were reinvaded after removal of the first usurper by the experimenters. In recent years, males of *B. (P.) vestalis* have appeared abundantly in coastal districts of Essex, but without noticeable effects on the abundance of its host, *B. terrestris*. In general, Alford's judgement that the cuckoo bees are 'not usually a major problem' for the populations of the social species seems justified. However, along with other parasites and predators, they may still significantly affect the species composition of local bumblebee assemblages, one of the issues addressed in the next chapter.

CHAPTER 5

Predators, Parasites and Lodgers

BUMBLEBEES, like other social insects, are a very attractive target for predators and parasites. Their colonies have evolved ways of collecting large stores of food, and the insects themselves, together with their brood, are concentrated together. Enemies may attack colonies to rob their food store, or to consume the colony members themselves. We saw in the previous chapter the complex ways in which one group of nest parasites succeed in harnessing the labour and food resources of the host colony to the benefit of their own offspring. True parasites, which attach themselves to or enter the bodies of their hosts, may also benefit from the social density, close kinship and physical interactions between the members of the host colony, since this provides many opportunities for transmission from one host body to another.

These elementary features of the mode of life of the social bumblebees go some way to explaining the immense diversity of other species that live in close association with them, either invading the bodies of individual bees, or cohabiting with them in their nests as nest parasites, inquilines or scavengers. However, there is another side to this. A bumblebee nest may be a cornucopia for any predator or parasite that gains entry to it, but this feat first has to be achieved. Bumblebee colonies and individual bees are well defended against their various enemies. Bumblebees have strong outer cuticles and the queens and workers are armed with poisonous stings. Their warning colour patterns, too, are generally supposed to deter birds and mammals that might otherwise prey on them. The nests are generally well concealed, and in the case of underground-nesting species, in particular, often very inaccessible. It may also be that the use of foraging patches well away from the nest is an adaptive behaviour that reduces the chances that nest parasites or predators will find it (see Chapter 6).

There are other, more direct, behavioural defences, too. We have seen the aggressive reactions of some colony workers and queens to the entry of cuckoo females. These behavioural responses include various levels of threat display, encircling and repeatedly stinging the intruder and, in the event of its penetrating this first line of defence, consuming its eggs. Recognition of the intruder is a precondition for such methods of defence, and it is now widely accepted that scent is the key to this. But, of course, such defences are not infallible, and there is often supposed to be an evolutionary 'arms race' between parasite and host. However, this is an arms race that the parasite cannot afford to win outright, on pain of losing its host! It is even possible, in the case of some associations between cuckoo bumblebees and their hosts, that there is a degree of evolved adaptation to coexistence (see Chapter 4).

It may also be that other features of colony organisation, the division of labour and the evolution of the social mode of life itself are related to defence against parasites and other nest invaders. Then, at the level of the individual bee, there is an effective immune system carried in the haemolymph, which circulates in the body cavity, comprising chemical antibodies and cellular defenders. These latter engulf and consume smaller foreign bodies, or encapsulate larger ones. The encapsulation response involves the aggregation of blood cells around a pathogen, sometime several layers deep, with an associated darkening (melanisation). Encapsulation works by immobilising, killing or simply cutting off the foreign body from the tissues of the bee. The melanisation that occurs with encapsulation is used by researchers to measure the extent of the immune response. Though less complex than the immune system of vertebrates, that of insects, including bumblebees, is effective, though largely lacking the 'immunological memory' of the former. That is, successfully beating off one infection confers no extra protection the next time the same pathogen is encountered (Schmid-Hempel, 1998).

So would-be invaders have some quite tough obstacles to surmount if they are to access the bounty of the bumblebee nest, and successfully reproduce their own kind in association with it. Relatively little is known about how this is achieved, and the natural history of only a tiny fraction of the great variety of bumblebee cohabiters has been thoroughly studied. Because of their economic importance, these relationships are much better known in the honey bees. However, in recent decades there has been a growth of interest among biologists in the wider issues of host/parasite interactions and their implications for the behaviour, mating strategies, genetic variability, population dynamics and community ecology of host species. Because of their (normally) annual colony cycles, the relative ease with which they can be reared artificially and experimentally treated, and, of course, their parasite-richness, bumblebees have become a much-favoured group of organisms for testing the theorists' models. The sustained work of Paul Schmid-Hempel and co-workers such as Regula Schmid-Hempel, Christine Müller, Stephan Durrer and others has played a central role in yielding many new insights into the fascinating and unimaginably complex world that is the bumblebee nest. Much of what follows is drawn from their work and that of Alford, who was a pioneering student of bumblebee parasites in Britain.

PREDATORS

Though it seems very likely that bumblebees or their nests regularly fall victim to predation by mammals and birds, there is little beyond anecdotal evidence about its frequency and possible implications for bumblebee populations. It is known that disused mammal nests are commonly used by bumblebees as nest sites, and for some species the availability of these may set a limit to the bumblebee population that can be supported in a given area. It may also be that competition for nest sites is a selective pressure affecting both the population structure of the species concerned, and also the wider bumblebee community. But some mammalian species are also predators on bumblebee nests. These include some of the same species – mice, shrews and voles – whose discarded nests are used by the bumblebees. Alford cites a mid-nineteenth-century claim that two-thirds of bumblebee nests were destroyed by field mice (Alford, 1975) while Sladen adds moles and weasels to the list of nest predators. Christine Müller describes a nest predated by a dormouse, which killed all the workers by biting through the thorax, and consumed all the larvae (pers. comm.). There are frequent contemporary reports of nests destroyed by badgers, and foxes also attack bumblebee nests. However, it is relatively common to find partially excavated nests in which many workers are carrying out repairs, or which have evidently survived to successfully rear sexuals (males and daughter queens) (Fig. 77).

Presumably at least some mammalian predators are effectively driven off by the aggressive response of numbers of defending workers. *Bombus terrestris* and *B. lucorum* respond aggressively when their nests are disturbed, but Sladen's account of the response of two *B. muscorum* colonies is worth quoting at length:

> '*In July 1911, having been informed by some labourers in these marshes who were mowing the hay there, that they frequently came across the nests of a savage yellow bee which they feared to disturb more than a wasp's nest, I asked them when they next found a nest to let me know, and on July 21 was summoned to take two nests, both of this*

FIG 77. Nest entrance of *Bombus monticola*, damaged by a mammalian predator. Despite the damage, the colony went on to complete its cycle, producing both males and daughter queens in August.

species, situated only about ten yards apart in a hay field. So great was the men's fear of getting stung that they did not dare to approach near enough to show me the exact spots, and I found that, as soon as I disturbed the nests, the workers flew round my head in a most menacing manner; they also had the disagreeable trick of persisting in doing this, following me wherever I went for a minute or two.' (Sladen, 1912)

Birds, too, will take individual bumblebees as prey. A meeting of the Essex Field Club in 1884 discussed a member's observation of many dead bumblebees lying beneath lime trees. The consensus was that the bees had become intoxicated from imbibing the nectar of the lime trees, and so rendered themselves vulnerable to attack from red-backed shrikes. However, it is still common to find the bodies of bumblebees with the tip of the abdomen neatly snipped off, and the abdominal contents (presumably including the nectar-filled crop) removed. Sometimes the thorax, too, is entered via the dorsal surface and the contents removed. Indeed, several dozens of bodies (of worker *B. lapidarius* and *B. terrestris/lucorum*) in this condition were seen under an avenue of limes, just as described above, on 3 July 2003 (own obs.). Since red-backed shrikes can now be confidently taken off the list of suspects, it seems likely that some other bird species – probably blue or great tits – have mastered the art of capturing bumblebees without getting stung (see Saunders, 1896; Alford, 1975). I have one report of a great tit first pecking out the sting, and then consuming the body contents of a bumblebee (P. Talbot, pers. comm.).

Bumblebees also have their invertebrate predators. These include robber flies (Asilinae), though it seems likely that in Britain only one species, the rare *Asilus crabroniformis*, is large and powerful enough to take bumblebees. Robber flies lie in wait for their victims, finally attacking them with short, fast, darting flights. The victim is pierced with the rigid mouthparts and immobilised (Colyer & Hammond, 1968). Alford reports the solitary wasp *Philanthus bicinctus* as a bumblebee predator in America, whilst its relative, the bee wolf (*P. triangulum*) has become well established in Britain in recent years (Fig. 78). Though known to include honey bees among its prey, it is unclear whether it also takes bumblebees. Recently hornets have been added to the list of the invertebrate predators on bumblebees. In one reported case, the hornet stung the bee and then bit off its wings (Cham, 2004). Spiders perhaps represent a more widespread and formidable threat to foraging bumblebees. The crab spider *Misumena vatia* lies in wait on flowerheads, with which it is often perfectly camouflaged. It remains motionless until foraging insects, including worker bumblebees, come between its outstretched front legs, whereupon it grabs and poisons them (Figs 79–81). The venom is highly toxic and death results in a few seconds. The spider feeds by sucking out the body contents of its prey, leaving a complete husk (Jones, 1983).

FIG 78. The bee-wolf (*Philanthus triangulum*).

FIG 79. A crab spider lying in wait on a flowerhead.

FIG 80. A crab spider with its prey: a male *Bombus pratorum*.

FIG 81. A crab spider with a captive worker *Bombus lucorum*.

However, a study by Morse (1986) of *M. vatia* lying in wait on milkweed inflorescences indicated a very low level of risk to bumblebees from this predator, and no behavioural response to its presence. So far as web-spinning British spiders are concerned, Alford knew of none that regularly included bumblebees in their diet. In fact, however, males are frequently found in webs spun in the flowerheads of thistles, knapweed and bristly ox-tongue in late summer. Victims are almost all male *B. lapidarius*, but even queens of some species may be taken (Figs 82 & 83) (own obs.).

PARASITES AND PARASITOIDS

Parasites are organisms that live in or on their hosts' bodies, feeding from their nutrients. Parasitoids also do this, but kill their host in the process. Parasites and parasitoids of bumblebees include viruses, bacteria, fungi, protozoa (or protoctists, in current classifications), nematodes, mites and insects, including some members of the Hymenoptera, many Diptera species, and some species of Lepidoptera (Table 4).

There is space here to give brief accounts of the natural history of only a few of the best known of these.

FIG 82. A male *Bombus lapidarius* caught in a spider's web.

FIG 83. A queen *Bombus sylvarum* caught in a spider's web.

TABLE 4. Reported bumblebee parasites, with brief comments on their effects (reproduced from Schmid-Hempel, 2001, with permission).

GROUP	PARASITE	REMARKS
Virus	Acute Bee Paralysis virus	Uncertain status in nature
	Entomopox virus	
Bacteria	Spiroplasma	In haemolymph
	Aerobacter cloaca and other unidentified bacteria	
Fungi	Acrostalagmus	Possibly shortens hibernation
	Beauveria bassiana, Candida	
	Hirsutella, Metarhizium, Paecilomyces	
Protozoa	Apicystis bombi	Can completely destroy the fat body
	Crithidia bombi	A study object
	Nosema bombi	Can kill entire colonies but highly variable in expression. A creeping disease
	Neogregarina sp.	
Nematodes	Sphaerularia bombi	Infects hibernating queens and castrates them. Known from almost all species
Hymenopoteran parasitoids	Syntretus splendidus	Probably attacks spring queens exclusively
	Melittobia acasta; M. chalybii Monodontomerus montivagus Pediobius williamsoni	

TABLE 4. – *cont.*

GROUP	PARASITE	REMARKS
Dipteran parasitoids	*Apocephalus borealis*	Feeds on thoracic muscles
	Boettcharia litorosa	
	Helicobia morionella	
	Brachioma devia: B. sarcophagira; B.setosa	Can be extremely destructive
	Conops algirus; C. argentifacies; C. elegans;	Investigated, particularly in *B. terrestris*
	C. flavipes; C. quadrifasciatus; C. vesicularis	
	Melaloncha sp.	
	Physocephala brugessi; P. dimidiatipennis;	Pupa can be hyper-parasitized by
	P. dorsalis; P.nigra; P. obscura; P. rufipes;	pteromalid wasps
	P. sagittaria; P. tibialis; P. vittata	
	Senotainia tricuspis	
	Sicus ferrugineus	Investigated, particularly in *B. terrestris*
	Zodion sp.	
Lepidoptera	*Ephestia kühniella*	Feeds on provisions
Acari (mites)	A large number of species	Unclear status as parasites

Single-celled organisms (Protozoa)

Crithidia bombi

This is a single-celled flagellate, which infects the intestines of a wide range of bumblebee species. The parasite reproduces rapidly in the gut of infected bees, passing through many generations in the lifetime of a single worker. After infection, the cells of *Crithidia* line the walls of the mid-gut and rectum, from where infective cells are released. Within colonies, *Crithidia* is spread by spores that are deposited in faeces. Spores may be released from two days after initial infection, and then in increasing numbers for 10–12 days afterwards. Transmission between workers within the colony occurs through ingestion of infected material and faeces. Transmission between colonies takes place mainly by way of spores left on flowers by foraging workers. The frequency of infection by this route is dependent on the density of the host population. Once deposited on a flower, the *Crithidia* spores must be picked up by another forager quickly, as they deteriorate rapidly when exposed to UV light. There is evidence that infection can be transmitted by this route both to other colonies of the same species, and also between bumblebee species. Simple inflorescences have also been shown to offer less chance of infection than complex ones (Durrer & Schmid-Hempel, 1994; Schmid-Hempel & Schmid-Hempel, 1999). Because of transmission between colonies, levels of infection increase through the season, so that most colonies in a locality may be infected as they reach maturity. There is also evidence of adaptation on the part of the parasite to its host, so that it becomes more virulent later in the season (Schmid-Hempel, 2001).

Transmission from one season to the next (vertical transmission) depends on the parasite infecting daughter queens and their survival to establish new nests the following spring. In otherwise healthy bees *Crithidia* is only mildly pathogenic, causing a reduction in ovary size, and slower colony development, but also delaying the development of egg laying in workers. However, under unfavourable environmental conditions *Crithidia* infection can be very damaging.

Nosema bombi

This is another single-celled organism, which belongs to the phylum Apicomplexa (formerly Sporozoa), along with many other parasites, including the malarial pathogen. Its close relative, *N. apis*, is a serious pest of honey bees. Unlike its relative, *N. bombi* is particularly infective of larvae. The parasite lives in the intestines, and reproduces very rapidly, reaching a peak in two to three weeks. Spores are deposited in the faeces, from five days to as much as three weeks after infection. Given average lifespans of bumblebee workers of 20–30 days, and high mortality rates among foraging workers, this parasite stands to gain from infecting its hosts early in their development. This may explain its ability to infect larvae as well as adult bees (Schmid-Hempel & Loosli, 1998). Within the colony, transmission between individual hosts is through ingestion of infected material such as faeces. Transmission between colonies and between species presumably takes place mainly by way of infected material on flowers, although 'wandering' from one colony to another by infected workers is another possibility. Infected queens go into hibernation later than uninfected ones, and emerge earlier, possibly because of depletion of their fat bodies. The parasite is believed to be an important cause of mortality in overwintering queens. Infection rates among spring queens are relatively low – from just 'a few' to some 10 per cent. However, by the end of the season as many as 60 per cent of colonies may be infected.

Nematodes
Sphaerularia bombi
The nematode S. bombi (Fig. 84) was one of the first insect parasites to be described (by Reamur, in 1742). These nematodes live and mate in the soil, and fertilised females invade queen bumblebees during their winter hibernation. They are supposed to enter through the mouth. Sphaerularia infestation is rare in queens that emerge early from hibernation, but as many as 12 per cent are infected altogether, and as many as 50 per cent of late-emerging queens (Schmid-Hempel et al., 1990). Initially there are between one and eight nematodes in a single queen, but many more are occasionally recorded. At this stage the female nematode appears as a tiny appendage to its huge everted ovary.

The eggs of the nematode are released over a period of one to two weeks, and hatch from four to seven days later. As many as 50,000–100,000 offspring may result, occupying the body cavity and intestines of the queen. These subsequently move to the rectum, and, in lesser numbers, to the oviducts. Infestation causes a degeneration of the queen bee's ovaries and sterilisation. Also, her behaviour is radically altered. Some accounts suggest that, instead of proceeding to search for a suitable nest site and founding a new colony, she turns to inspecting suitable hibernation sites. Here, the juvenile nematodes are released into the soil in the queen's faeces. However, a detailed study carried out in Sweden by Lundberg & Svensson (1975) revealed a more complex pattern of disorientation in the behaviour of infected queens (mainly Bombus lapponicus). These foraged widely and inefficiently, often landed clumsily, and exhibited searching behaviour for both nest and hibernation sites. They frequently dug shallow holes, but often in places unsuitable for hibernation (Fig. 85). Lundberg & Svensson suggest that these behavioural characteristics are likely to result in widespread transmission of the parasite, and that healthy queens searching for hibernation sites may be attracted

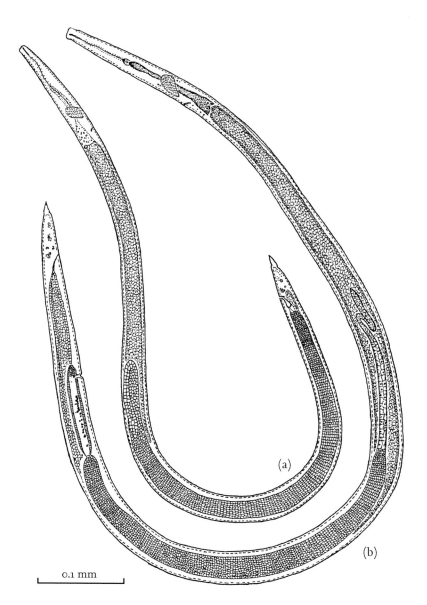

0.1 mm

FIG 84. Adult *Sphaerularia bombi*: (a) male; (b) female (reproduced from Poinar & van der Laan, 1972, with permission).

FIG 85. An overwintered queen *Bombus lapidarius*, infected with *Sphaerularia bombi*, attempting to dig into a bank as if to hibernate.

to holes dug by infested ones. After being deposited in the soil, *Sphaerularia* juveniles take some ten weeks to develop, after which they may mate, and are ready to invade a new host (Fig. 86).

Diptera

Flies belonging to four genera of the Family Conopidae are recorded as parasitoids of bumblebees in Britain. These are *Conops* (Fig. 87), *Physocephala* (Fig. 88), *Sicus* (Fig. 89) and *Myopa*, and members of the first three look remarkably like solitary wasps, or *Nomada* bees. The prevalence of conopid infestation is high, with averages of 20 per cent to 30 per cent of workers affected, and seasonal peaks of over 70 per cent. Although the parasite is fatal to the individual bee, it is generally workers that are affected. The colony may suffer significant depletion of its worker cohort if infestation is high, but this may still not be fatal to the colony (see below).

The females have prominent genitalia, and are equipped with modifications of the final abdominal segment. These are a specialisation to aid in attaching themselves to their victim and penetrating its outer cuticle. The female conopids spend much of their time basking on flowers, attacking passing bumblebees from the air, while the latter are in flight, or foraging on a flowerhead. The conopid then prises apart the strong cuticle of two adjacent abdominal segments of its victim, and inserts an egg through the softer membrane between them. The conopid eggs

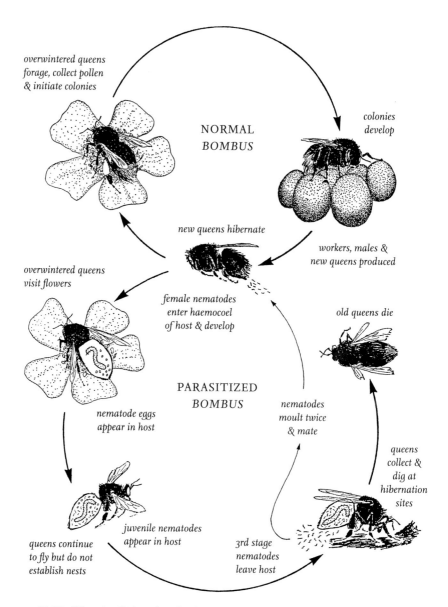

overwintered queens forage, collect pollen & initiate colonies

NORMAL
BOMBUS

colonies develop

new queens hibernate

workers, males & new queens produced

overwintered queens visit flowers

female nematodes enter haemocoel of host & develop

old queens die

PARASITIZED
BOMBUS

nematodes moult twice & mate

nematode eggs appear in host

queens collect & dig at hibernation sites

queens continue to fly but do not establish nests

juvenile nematodes appear in host

3rd stage nematodes leave host

FIG 86. The life cycle of *Sphaerularia bombi* and a *Bombus* host (reproduced from Poinar & van der Laan, 1972, with permission).

FIG 87. *Conops quadrifasciata*, a common conopid parasitoid of bumblebee species.

FIG 88. *Physocephala rufipes*, another common conopid bumblebee parasitoid.

FIG 89. *Sicus ferrugineus*, a conopid parasitoid of *Bombus* species.

are usually armed with hooks, spines or ribbons at one end, and these serve to anchor them to internal tissues of the host – usually to the bee's respiratory system, ensuring the resulting larva has an air supply (Clements, 1997). Depending on the general levels of conopid population relative to the abundance of bumblebees, a bee may suffer one or more subsequent attacks, by the same or other conopid species. The eggs are generally found in the fat body of the bee, which may explain the limited immune response they provoke. The larvae pass through three stages or instars in their development. In the first instar, they possess a sabre-shaped egg tooth, which may be used in conflicts with rival larvae sharing the same host. During the first two stages, the larva lives on the haemolymph of its victim, but then consumes its internal organs. Full development of the larva takes from 10–12 days (and varies between conopid species), by which time only one parasitoid larva remains, and fills the abdominal cavity of the host. Pupation takes place inside the host, and the pupa overwinters in the remains of its body.

Single conopid larvae have very low mortality rates, but are much less likely to survive in a multiply parasitised host bee. In this case, at most one of the competitors survives, but sometimes none does. Where more than one conopid species is capable of infesting the same host species, there may be direct competition between larvae of the different species in a single host. Also, where the various conopid species may affect several host species in a given area, competition between them may be played out through species-specific patterns of infestation of the host community.

A series of studies carried out in north-west Switzerland by Schmid-Hempel & Schmid-Hempel has disentangled some of the intriguing complexities in these relationships. Three conopid species parasitised seven bumblebee species: *Bombus terrestris, B. lucorum, B. pascuorum, B. lapidarius, B. hortorum, B. pratorum* and *B. humilis.* However, each conopid species has its own distinctive pattern of host preferences, which is sustained despite season-by-season shifts in relative abundance of the hosts. Two conopid species, *Sicus ferrugineus* and *Physocephala rufipes,* commonly parasitise *B. pascuorum. Sicus ferrugineus* larvae develop more rapidly in the earliest stages of development, which gives them a competitive advantage over larvae of *P. rufipes* where eggs of both species have been laid in a single *B. pascuorum* worker. However, this may be offset by differences in the preferences shown by ovipositing females of the two conopids for various host species. Both species parasitised *B. terrestris/lucorum* (pooled), and *B. pascuorum.* However, *S. ferrugineus* was a far more prevalent than its competitor in *B. terrestris/ lucorum,* whilst in *B. pascuorum* they were present in roughly equal proportions, and *B. lapidarius* was parasitised virtually exclusively by *P. rufipes* (Schmid-Hempel & Schmid-Hempel, 1989, 1996a, 1996b).

Where parasitoid numbers were high, relative to their hosts, the incidence of parasitoids laying eggs in already parasitised bees increased. Despite the higher mortality rates of larvae sharing a single host, parasitoids might still gain a reproductive benefit from laying eggs in already parasitised hosts so long as there remains a finite chance of them surviving. It is unclear whether the parasitoids can distinguish between parasitised and unparasitised potential hosts, or whether the rise in multiply infected bees with increased parasitoid pressure is a result of random encounters. Either way, since this increases the likelihood of premature death for either or both of the larvae sharing a common host, the result is a stabilisation of the population dynamics of host and parasitoid.

As with *Sphaerularia,* the conopid larvae are able to modify the behaviour of infected bees. Although some observers find no detectable difference in the foraging behaviour of infected bumblebee workers, others note that they are more prone to nectar from shallow flowers, in which the nectar is accessed more easily. Schmid-Hempel & Müller (1991) compared levels of infestation of workers entering and leaving known colonies with those of workers caught while foraging nearby. Far higher proportions of workers in the latter category were infested than in the former, suggesting that conopid-infested workers tended to stay out of the nest (Table 5). This was confirmed by direct inspection of nests during the night.

A later study showed that parasitised workers preferred cold sites to spend the

TABLE 5. Observed numbers and percentages of conopid infestation in foragers from known colonies (Colony foragers) and foragers caught in surrounding meadows (Field foragers) (reproduced from Schmid-Hempel & Müller, 1991, with permission).

	NON-PARASITIZED	PARASITIZED	TOTAL
Colony foragers	80 87·9%	11 12·1%	91
	(53·7)	(37·3)	
Field foragers	18 24·0%	57 76·0%	75
	(44·3)	(30·7)	

Numbers in parentheses represent expected values. $\chi^2 = 69 \cdot 445$, $df = 1$; $P < 0 \cdot 0001$.

night, thus slowing down the development of the conopid larva, and prolonging the life of the bee (Müller & Schmid-Hempel, 1993). In another study (Müller, 1994) it was shown that the behaviour of the parasitised bees was altered in another respect. Before dying, they dug themselves some 5–10 centimetres into the soil.

There is some disagreement about the significance of these behavioural changes. Poulin (1992) interpreted the parasitised workers' departure from the nest as adaptive for the bee colony, in that it might reduce the chances of predation or further conopid infection of the infected bee's kin. In fact, patterns of bumblebee foraging, and what is known about predation make this interpretation improbable (Müller & Schmid-Hempel, 1992a). However, the behaviour of the parasitised bees in slowing down the development of the conopid larva could benefit the host colony, particularly if the parasitised bee was able to continue foraging, even if less efficiently. However, the digging behaviour of parasitised workers that occurs when the conopid larva (in at least some species) is fully developed has advantages for the parasitoid. Müller's study provided evidence that spending the winter underground brought several benefits to the conopids. Compared with pupae that overwintered on the ground, they suffered less from scavengers, and from attack by parasites, were larger and suffered fewer deformities in wing development. These findings suggest that if the parasite-induced behavioural alterations are adaptive, they benefit the host initially, but finally benefit the parasitoid. On this interpretation, the digging behaviour is manipulated by the conopid larva. However, Cumber (1949) found conopid pupae in the nests of four bumblebee species, as many as 19 in one (*B. ruderarius*), so their leaving the nest may not be universal. It is possible that there are significant differences in the behavioural effects of parasitism by different conopid species, and also that at least some behavioural changes that occur are non-adaptive consequences of the parasite attack.

A tachinid fly *Brachicoma devia* (Family Sarcophagidae) is a common parasite of bumblebee nests. Adult flies, which are viviparous, emerge early in May, and deposit their tiny larvae in the cells or brood clumps in bumblebee nests. The larvae do not feed until the bumblebee larvae spin their cocoons, prior to pupation. They feed on the body contents of the bee larvae, and develop rapidly. When full grown, they leave the comb, and pupate nearby. Several generations may be completed in a season. The fly overwinters in the pupal stage. Cumber (1949) found over 200 puparia and larvae in one nest, and over 100 bumblebee cocoons had been destroyed in another (of *Bombus terrestris*). In Cumber's view this parasite took a heavy toll of bumblebee populations, and had been found in the nests of the following species: *Bombus agrorum* (now *B. pascuorum*), *B. hortorum*, *B. humilis*, *B. ruderarius*, *B. lapidarius*, *B. sylvarum*, *B. lucorum*, *B. pratorum* and *B. terrestris*. Nests constructed near the surface and with exposed entrances were thought to be more heavily parasitised than those below ground.

Lepidoptera

Several moth species breed in bumblebee nests, and most are believed to be harmless. However, the pyralid 'bee' or 'wax' moth, *Aphomia sociella*, is a serious threat. The moth attacks a range of bumblebee species as well as wasps, and is widespread in Britain and the rest of Europe. The adults are on the wing from June to August, and lay their eggs in bumblebee nests. They are believed to locate host nests by scent, and to invade the nests of surface-nesting species more frequently than those which nest underground (Beirne, 1952; Alford, 1975). Goulson *et al.* (2002) found that *B. terrestris* colonies sited in artificial nests in gardens were very heavily infested by wax moths, and much more so than those sited in farmland, but this may have been because they were more easily discovered by the moth than naturally established nests. The eggs are laid in masses on the comb, and the larvae, usually over 100 in a single infested nest, hatch in about one week. They begin to feed gregariously on old cells, droppings and detritus in the nest, but then turn to feeding on the bumblebee larvae, burrowing silk-lined tunnels through the clusters of brood cells (Fig. 90).

When full grown, in September, they leave the nest and spin tough silken cocoons, which are often massed together under cover. The larvae remain in their cocoons over the winter and pupate in the spring. They subsequently emerge as adult moths and the cycle is repeated.

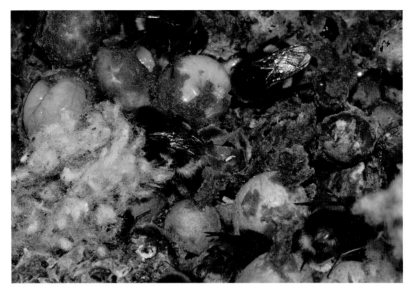

FIG 90. Damaged caused by a wax moth infestation of a *Bombus terrestris* nest.

OTHER NEST ASSOCIATES

Mites

Mites are among the most obvious and pervasive of the associates of bumblebees. Most are believed to be harmless commensals, and there is even some evidence that they may be beneficial, as they consume moulds and detritus in the nest. However, there is also the possibility that they may act as vectors for virulent microorganisms, as does the *Varroa* mite in honey bees. Mites that live as nest commensals spread from colony to colony, and are passed on from one season to the next by means of juvenile stages that attach themselves to the bodies of adult bees – particularly daughter queens. Other mite species develop as internal parasites, penetrating the spiracles to attach themselves to the respiratory organs of the bees. Bumblebee colonies support a high diversity of mite species, as well as large populations. Schousboe (1987) found four species of the genus *Parasitellus* (Fig. 91) on the Danish bumblebees he studied, as well as two species of tracheal mite. Schwarz *et al.* (1996) found as many as ten species of mesostigmatic mites on 141 queens collected in an area near Zurich (also see Schmid-Hempel, 2001). Corbet & Morris (1999) found nine species of mites on queens and workers of three bumblebee species in West Cornwall, and a further species in a nest of *B. terrestris*. Studies show a wide range of infestation rates, but some suggest up to 83 per cent, with more than one hundred individuals having been counted on individual queens of some species.

Mites live freely in the bumblebee nest, and pass through several generations in a season. The females lay eggs that hatch into an initial larval stage, followed by protonymphal and then deutonymphal stages. In several species, it is this pre-adult, non-feeding stage that attaches itself to the cuticle of forager-workers, males and daughter queens, but with a definite preference for the queens (Richards & Richards, 1976; Schousboe, 1987; Schwarz & Huck, 1997). Young queens in summer, or overwintered queens in spring, are commonly festooned with these mite nymphs, which attach themselves among the hairs, particularly around the junction of the thorax and abdomen, or head and thorax.

Other mite genera show variations on this pattern, though there are some

FIG 91. Deutonymph of *Parasitellus* (reproduced from Alford, 1975, with permission).

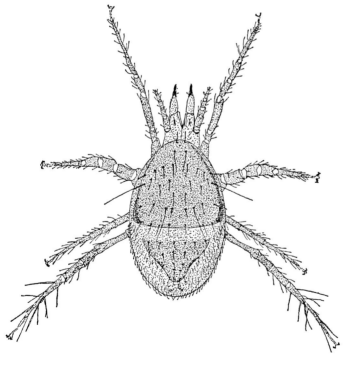

1 mm

that occur as parasites on the bodies of other mites! Queens of *B. lapidarius* and *B. lucorum* seem particularly heavily infested, though cuckoo bees, also frequently carry large numbers of mites (Fig. 92). The mite nymphs overwinter still attached to the queen, but once she founds a new nest in the spring they detach themselves and move off into the nest. They subsequently live and reproduce in the nest. Horizontal spread between bumblebee colonies is achieved by attaching themselves to workers (Fig. 93) and then dismounting onto flowerheads, where they may be able to hitch a lift on another visiting bee (phoresis).

Schwarz & Huck (1997) showed that mites placed on inflorescences quickly entered flowers, where they were most likely to be in contact with subsequent visiting bumblebees. They were able to remain in the flowers for up to 24 hours, and could mount an introduced bumblebee within three seconds, climbing up by way of its legs or proboscis. In another study, it was demonstrated that mites are able to distinguish between host bee species by scent, and show definite preferences to particular host species (Schwarz *et al.*, 1996). Host preferences were also indicated by the distributions of mite species across the species of bumblebee in the study carried out by Corbet & Morris (1999), who were also able to show associations between the foraging preferences of host species and the mite species found on their forage plants (bluebells).

FIG 92. Phoretic mites often attach themselves to cuckoo females as well as host queens. This female *Bombus rupestris* has a particularly heavy load of mite nymphs.

FIG 93. Mites will also accept a lift from worker bumblebees: in this case a worker *Bombus terrestris*.

The natural history of the tracheal mites is somewhat different. Alford (following Cumber, 1949) describes the life history of one species, *Locustacarus buchneri*. Females overwinter in the tracheal system of the queen bumblebee. In spring they pierce the wall of the trachea and feed from the haemolymph. They grow rapidly, and subsequently lay up to 50 eggs within the air-sacs of the host. These develop into males and females, and after mating some of the females leave the queen's body by way of the spiracles, and subsequently enter the bodies of worker bees. Others remain in the body of the original host, and complete further generations in a season. However, survival of the mites over the winter depends on their infesting daughter queens. Alford regarded this mite as a relatively benign parasite, though it could have some harmful effects, especially on weakened bees late on in the season. However, Schmid-Hempel considers it potentially very damaging, and capable of imperilling whole colonies (Schmid-Hempel, 2001).

Diptera
Among the assortment of other invertebrates that live among the detritus in bumblebee nest are several hover flies (Syrphidae), most notably the common and distinctive bumblebee mimic, *Volucella bombylans*.

The female fly is reputed to 'flip' its eggs into the bumblebee nest from the entrance. The eggs are covered with a sticky coating that subsequently hardens,

FIG 94. A larva of *Fannia canicularis*, a scavenger in a nest of *Bombus pratorum.*

attaching them to nest material. Egg laying is a reflex action, and even after being killed by guard-workers, the fly may continue to deposit eggs. The resulting larvae mainly scavenge on detritus below the comb, though there are some reports of their feeding on bumblebee brood. They overwinter as pupae, and emerge from the nest as adults the following spring. Another fly whose larvae are nest scavengers in bumblebee nests is *Fannia canicularis* (Fig. 94).

PARASITES AND THE NATURAL HISTORY OF BUMBLEBEES

It seems likely that the mode of life of bumblebees may have been shaped in many ways as a result of the selective pressures exerted by such a wide variety of predatory and parasitic enemies. Theoretical models have been devised which predict such effects, and there is a growing body of experimental and observational studies that sets out to test them. From the point of view of the invader, a key problem to be solved is how to locate and gain access to the nest, which, as we have seen, is often both well hidden and well guarded. This leads to the question of how far the selection of nest sites, the behaviour of males, queens and foraging workers outside the nest, and so on, can be understood as evolved responses to the various ways that invaders have developed to gain access.

In the case of parasites, there are the further problems of transmission from one individual host to another within the colony, and transmission from colony to colony, together with the difficulty of surviving the winter to infest new colonies the following spring. Again, this raises the possibility that key features of bumblebee natural history may have evolved at least partly in response to selective pressures exerted by their many parasites. For example, colony organisation and division of labour in social insects is thought to be shaped by such pressures. Where colonies are dependent on a single queen for their reproductive success, a division of labour that reduces her chances of becoming infected by parasites is likely to be an important condition of colony success. In many bumblebee species, younger workers are more likely to be involved in nest maintenance and brood care, turning to foraging as they get older (see Chapter 2). The house-bees, which are thus more likely to be in contact with the queen, are also less likely to be infected by such parasites as *Crithidia* and *Nosema* than are foragers (Schmid-Hempel & Schmid-Hempel, 1993; Schmid-Hempel, 1998). Again, since foraging involves considerable risk of attack by predators and parasitoids, as well as infection by protozoan parasites, it seems probable that it, too, will have been shaped to some degree by this, as well as by the more commonly recognised factors to do with economic efficiency. This is one explanation for the tendency of at least some species to forage at long distances from the nest, and for foragers to be dispersed over many foraging sites (see Chapter 6).

Aspects of bumblebee biology that are of direct relevance to their conservation may also be illuminated by considering host/parasite interactions. If different species are variably susceptible to prevalent and virulent parasites this may significantly affect the local composition of bumblebee communities in ways that are not immediately obvious from more readily measurable indicators of the quality of the habitat, such as the availability of sufficient quantities of suitable forage sources through the season, nesting and hibernation sites. It may also be that notable declines in range and abundance of some bumblebee species could be connected directly or indirectly with changes in parasite load or virulence. For example, if, as has been shown, the infectiveness and virulence of some parasites varies with the condition of the host, then adverse climatic conditions, or a deterioration in the availability of local food resources may lead indirectly to local decline or even extinction through increased vulnerability to infection on the part of the host population. Again, if gene flows between local populations of parasites or hosts affect the intensity of infections or their virulence, the fragmentation of habitats and erection of barriers to movement between them will have implications for the parasite-induced dynamics of isolated subpopulations. The increasing use of imported bumblebee colonies in horticulture also raises serious questions about the potential impact on indigenous populations of the incidental introduction of non-native parasite species and strains (S. A. Corbet, pers. comm.).

Detailed studies of the interactions between bumblebees and their parasites, combined with experimental work conducted with some of the above questions in mind, are now available for at least some parasites of one or two bumblebee species. Because these systems are immensely complex, and consequently very difficult to investigate experimentally, many of the intriguing questions that have been asked still do not have definitive answers. However, the accumulating body of evidence has its own intrinsic interest, is thought provoking, and has brought to light a number of unexpected aspects of bumblebee natural history. Here we will explore current research findings on a small selection of these interactions between bumblebee natural history and the challenges mounted by their many parasites and predators.

THE IMPACT OF PARASITES ON REPRODUCTION AND POPULATION DYNAMICS OF THEIR HOSTS

Field studies suggest that many bumblebee nests never produce a fertile sexual generation, whilst some produce only males, and others both males and daughter queens. The levels of reproductive success probably vary considerably both within and between species, between different localities and from season to season. Since the late 1980s a few studies have explored the conditions that most affect reproductive success in colonies, showing, in particular, the effects of parasitism. One such study was conducted by Müller & Schmid-Hempel (1992*a*) in Switzerland. From wild-caught queens of *Bombus lucorum*, they reared colonies in the laboratory and relocated them in the field when five to ten first-brood workers had emerged. Thirty-six colonies were regularly monitored, with removal of samples of workers to test for presence of conopid fly infestation. Any cuckoo nest parasites (*Psithyrus* – now *Bombus* – *bohemicus*) present were removed. Of the 36 nests, almost half (16) did not produce sexuals. The remaining 20 produced variable numbers of males (from one to 65) only, whilst only 5 produced both daughter queens and males.

This study showed that reproductive success was correlated with early date of nest establishment, the size of the first worker brood, longevity of the colony, size of the colony at its maximum, size of the colony at the time of first appearance of conopids (late June), and, for those colonies that produced sexuals, with the size of the colony at maturity. These variables were also generally correlated with one another. More specifically, maximum colony size explained the numbers of sexuals produced, whilst size of the colony at the time of first appearance of conopids was a good predictor of the overall biomass of sexuals. Cuckoo females entered ten of the nests, but were removed within three days, so the longer-term impact of the cuckoos on reproductive success was not measured. Some nests were subsequently invaded by other cuckoo females – up to four in the case of one nest. Cuckoo invasions were recorded between 10 May and 29 June, whilst the conopid infestations began on 24 June and continued until early September (Fig. 95). Samples of workers from the nests revealed relatively low frequencies of conopid

FIG 95. *Top*: Average colony size of *B. lucorum* nests in the course of a season. QM colonies produced both males and daughter queens, M colonies produced males only; NR colonies did not produce either queens or males.
Bottom: The timing of cuckoo bumblebee nest invasions (first horizontal bar) and conopid infestations (second horizontal bar). Note that colony size decreased markedly at the time when conopids appeared (reproduced from Müller & Schmid-Hempel, 1992*a*, with permission).

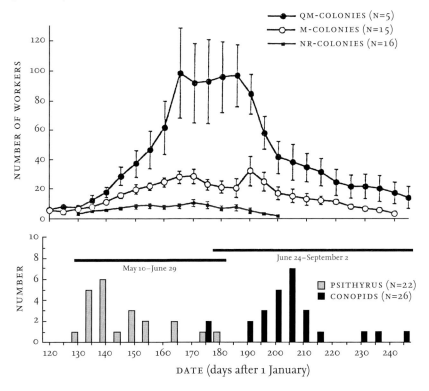

infestation, a finding consistent with the discovery that infested workers tend to stay outside the nest (Schmid-Hempel & Müller, 1991). One indication of the level of infestation was the steep decline in worker numbers in all colonies during the flight period of the conopids.

These correlates for reproductive success provide a useful framework for considering the likely impact of various parasitic organisms on the reproduction and population dynamics of their bumblebee hosts. At 30 per cent, the level of attack by the cuckoo suggests a high risk to the host species early in the season. Interestingly, in this study, the cuckoos disproportionately invaded nests with larger numbers of first brood workers – ones which, if they remained unparasitised, could be expected to go on to be among the more reproductively successful. Although, because of the experimental procedure, we do not know how many of these invasions would have been successful, the implication is that early invasion by cuckoos must exert a high toll. This is particularly so given the high proportion of nests that fail to reach maturity for other reasons. In the case of the conopid infestations, since they occur later in the season, a high premium is set upon rapid colony growth earlier on. Since sexual brood are already developing at the time of onset of conopid attack, infestation does not reduce the numbers of sexuals produced. However, it does limit the resources available to nourish them, so that the overall biomass of the sexuals is reduced, shifting the ratios of males to daughter queens, and resulting in smaller queens. Again, the longer-term population effects could be significant, as it is known that smaller queens are less likely to survive the winter hibernation.

The single-celled parasite *Crithidia bombi* is considered to be a rather mild pathogen, though widespread. Under normal circumstances, overwintered queens infected with *Crithidia* develop their ovaries more slowly, and start their nests later. This is likely to reduce, but not eliminate, their chances of successfully completing the colony cycle. The prevalence of infection among workers increases through the development of the colony, and the ovaries of infected workers develop more slowly than those of uninfected ones. In a laboratory study of infected and uninfected colonies of *Bombus terrestris* reported by Shykoff & Schmid-Hempel (1991b) there was no impact of infection on the overall production of sexuals. However, it seems likely that under the more resource-limited conditions encountered by wild colonies, the delayed reproductive development of infected workers would tend to prolong the dominance of the queen, so increasing the chances of the colony reaching the size threshold for production of daughter queens, and also reducing the production of male offspring by workers. This parasite-induced increase in the colony's investment in producing daughter queens would favour the transmission of the parasite to the next season's host population, since this can be achieved only by infecting daughter queens which successfully hibernate and establish new colonies the following spring. If this is so, then it might to some extent offset the costs to the fitness of the host imposed by the parasite earlier in the season.

However, the virulence of *Crithidia* infection is variable. There is evidence of coevolution between strains of the parasite and host lineages, affecting both infectiveness and severity of symptoms in the host. One study, for example, suggests that infections from distant strains of the parasite produced higher levels of mortality than did locally sourced strains (Imhoof & Schmid-Hempel, 1998). But it is well known that the vulnerability of organisms to disease also varies considerably with environmental stress. That this applies to *Bombus terrestris* in relation to *Crithidia* has been shown by Brown *et al.* (2000). In laboratory colonies with abundant food supplies, both infected and uninfected workers showed very low mortality rates, with no significant difference between the two conditions. However, some reallocation of resources from ovaries to the fat body was confirmed, as expected. In a separate experiment, workers were starved and in this case the infected workers suffered higher rates of mortality. Again, there was reallocation of resources away from reproduction to the fat body. This may be an indication of an immune response on the part of the host, or, as suggested above, it may be a physiological change induced by the parasite to reduce the likelihood of egg laying by the workers, thus enhancing queen-production (though see p. 100).

The underlying hypothesis is that with limited resources, and a range of different vital functions to be carried out, there will be trade-offs between different activities. If deploying the immune system imposes costs, then we might expect immune defence to result in reduced levels of investment in activities that meet other needs – such as reproduction or foraging for food (and vice versa). This idea was tested by Konig & Schmid-Hempel (1995), for the bumblebee *Bombus terrestris*. In order to investigate the effect of foraging activity on one immune response – encapsulation of foreign bodies – they used implants of tiny nylon threads to mimic conopid eggs. Comparing workers that were allowed to forage with non-foragers, they showed that this immune response was depressed in the former group. Similar results were later recorded for colonies situated in natural surroundings (Doums & Schmid-Hempel, 2000). This is interpreted in terms of the physiological costs of deploying immune responses. With unlimited resources, both active foraging and immune responses can be sustained, but under conditions of environmental stress, deploying resources away from immune defence in favour of (for example) foraging might increase the overall fitness of the colony. A further study involving captive colonies and controlled feeding regimes (Schmid-Hempel & Schmid-Hempel, 1998), found no direct relationship between food availability and the encapsulation immune response, suggesting that it is increased foraging activity to compensate for food shortage, rather than shortage itself, that may be the cause of the depressed immune response.

However, the situation is even more complex, as illustrated by subsequent work on immune responses on the part of *Bombus terrestris* workers to doses of molecules derived from a bacterial pathogen, and injection of latex beads to mimic a bacterial infection. There were differences in the bees' immune responses to each of these, and the effect of starvation on these immune responses was very marked. 'Infected' bees that were able to compensate for the costs of their immune responses by extra feeding showed no increased mortality compared to non-infected ones. Bees subjected to starvation, as expected, died within a few hours, but infected ones died significantly more quickly. Bees facing both types of immune challenge died more quickly than did bees facing only one (Moret & Schmid-Hempel, 2000). The mutual independence of immune reactions to different types of pathogen was also suggested in an experiment by Allander & Schmid-Hempel (2000). Using the nylon implants to mimic conopid eggs, and then infecting workers with *Crithidia*, they found that the latter did not cause a reduction in the encapsulation immune response to the implants under laboratory conditions. However, naturally acquired cross-infection by *Crithidia* of worker bees already 'infected' with nylon implants did depress the encapsulation immune response under natural conditions in the study conducted by Doums & Schmid-Hempel – presumably because of the greater environmental stress they encountered.

Thus, there is a growing body of evidence that the various parasites of bumblebees have highly significant effects on the reproduction and consequently on the population dynamics of their hosts. However, these effects are very complex and variable in their timing and intensity. Conopids mainly affect workers late in the colony cycle, and despite their extreme effects on individuals, may be compatible with successful reproduction of the colony. *Sphaerularia* causes sterility in overwintering queens, and so impacts directly on populations of the species affected in proportion to its prevalence. *Crithidia* exacts a toll through the colony cycle, but has a particularly damaging effect by limiting and delaying nest-founding by infected overwintered queens. There is some evidence that cuckoo bumblebees may disproportionately invade early nests, which would otherwise have been more likely than average to successfully reproduce. Interestingly, however, there is some evidence that *Nosema* infection may actually increase the production of sexuals in its hosts, especially daughter queens (Imhoof & Schmid-Hempel, 1998). This makes sense for a parasite wholly dependent on successful daughter queen-production for its transmission from one season to the next. If this is confirmed, it suggests that the association of *Nosema* with *Bombus terrestris* may under some circumstances be symbiotic rather than parasitic.

Perhaps the most significant outcome of experimental research has been the evidence that vulnerability to a range of parasites varies with environmental stress. This may impact particularly on colonies during the early part of the colony cycle, when nectar and pollen supplies may be limited, and periods of inclement weather are likely to inhibit foraging. Heavily parasitised colonies at this time of year would be more severely affected than others, either because their immune defences are depressed, or because they cannot sustain the extra costs of mobilising them. Similar considerations apply to deteriorations in bumblebee habitats brought about by human activities. To the extent that these increase the environmental stress on bumblebees (because of more dispersed or seasonally discontinuous forage, for example) then they will be more vulnerable to parasitic attack than they would otherwise be. Increased vulnerability to parasites could thus play a significant part in local declines and extinctions of some species, by rendering them less able to cope with adverse conditions. Conversely, the effort of coping with environmental stress may impose costs in terms of their reduced ability to resist parasitic attack.

BREEDING STRATEGIES, GENETIC DIVERSITY AND PARASITE VIRULENCE

As we saw in Chapters 2 and 3, kin selection theory is used to explain the altruistic behaviour needed for workers to sacrifice their own reproductive activity, and to sustain the cohesion of social insect colonies. Kin selection theory predicts that colonies of social insects will be made up of close relatives. We would therefore expect social insects to have evolved reproductive strategies which maximise the relatedness of colony members: in other words, to favour genetic homogeneity in the colony. These strategies might include foundress queens mating with only one male, colonies being dominated by only one queen, and possibly even high levels of inbreeding. In fact, it seems that the colonies of many social insects are much more genetically heterogeneous than the concept of kin selection might suggest. Queen honey bees mate with many males, and queens of a minority of bumblebee species commonly mate more than once. In some social insects, particularly among the ants, colonies are dominated by two or more queens. In bumblebees, inbreeding is avoided by dispersal of daughter queens, rapid abandonment of the nest by freshly emerged males, and possibly by other mechanisms.

For such systems to have evolved suggests that there are selective costs involved in genetically homogeneous colonies which to some extent counterbalance the advantages derived from the social integration of the colony. Crozier & Page (1985) considered a range of possible explanations for the evolution of mating strategies favouring genetic diversity in the offspring of social species. There are probably several reasons why inbreeding should be avoided. The clearest one is that inbreeding runs a heightened risk of producing males from fertilised (diploid) eggs. These males are infertile, so from the point of view of the reproductive success of their colony, investment in raising them would be wasted. But there are other reasons why reproductive strategies that increase genetic diversity might be favoured, even at some cost to social cohesion. One is that genetic variability might contribute to a more effective division of labour between castes. This might be applicable even to bumblebees, despite their relatively flexible division of labour (see Goulson, 2003, and Chapter 3). Another selective advantage that more genetic diversity could confer is that it might make the colony less vulnerable to environmental fluctuations. Sherman *et al.* (1988) added a further possibility, really a special case of this: that genetic variability in the host population might make colonies less vulnerable to disease and parasitism. This would be particularly likely in the case of pathogenic organisms capable of rapid evolution of new strains. Resistance to these on the part of the host species would have to cope with unpredictability, and one way of doing this might be by genetic diversity within the colony. Sherman *et al.* went on to suggest experimental work that could test this idea. Subsequent experimental studies by Schmid-Hempel and colleagues have shown that there are, indeed, strong links between patterns of parasitic infestation and genetic diversity in the colony in several bumblebee species. Some of these patterns are linked in sometimes unexpected ways with the mating strategies of the bees.

The hypothesis that mating strategies and thus the genetic structure of colonies is strongly influenced by the selective pressure exerted by parasites involves three related claims. The first is that there is genetic variation among the bees, affecting their susceptibility to parasites, and also variation in virulence (usually defined in terms of the effects of parasite infestation on colony success) among strains of parasites. Second, it needs to be shown that greater genetic diversity in a colony confers enhanced resistance to parasitism. Third, the hypothesis implies that the overall reproductive success of colonies is affected by the levels of parasitism they suffer.

Schmid-Hempel and colleagues have provided evidence that there is within-species variability in susceptibility to different strains of parasite for *Bombus terrestris* and two of its prevalent parasites. In one experiment, Shykoff & Schmid-Hempel reared colonies from locally caught queens, some of which were infected with *Crithidia bombi*. They observed the two groups of resulting colonies in the laboratory. They isolated groups of workers of varying degrees of relatedness from uninfected colonies and introduced workers taken from the infected colonies. They then tested for levels of transmission of the parasite to the various groups of workers. They were able to show marked differences between source colonies in the levels of infection they induced, and also in transmission rates as between more and less closely related individual workers. Freshly emerged workers taken from infected colonies (and shown to be uninfected from their source colonies) were significantly more likely to become infected, and transmission rates between full sisters were higher than those between less closely related individuals. Close behavioural observation provided evidence that these differences could not be explained in terms of more frequent physical contacts between close relatives (Shykoff & Schmid-Hempel, 1991*a*).

Subsequent experimental work by Schmid-Hempel & Loosli (1998) on the parasite *Nosema bombi* tested the relative effects of artificial infection from two sources of the parasite on previously uninfected workers from three colonies of *Bombus terrestris*, and also on colonies of two other species: *B. lapidarius* and *B. hypnorum*. Three measures of the effect of the parasite on its hosts were adopted: prevalence (proportion of individuals infected), intensity of infection (concentration of spores in bodies of individual hosts), and mortality rates. In this host/parasite relationship it was possible to show that there was variation in susceptibility of workers from different colonies, variation in the infectiveness of *Nosema* from the two sources, and interaction between them. These results strongly suggest association and coevolution between strains of the parasite and bumblebee family lines. A further finding was that *Nosema* spores derived from infected *Bombus terrestris* hosts were on average rather less successful in infecting workers of the other two species tested. However, this difference was less significant than the differences between individual colonies in their vulnerability to infection. These findings suggest that *Nosema bombi* is capable of cross-infecting different species in a given habitat, but the extent of this may vary according to the parasite strain involved and the mix of *Bombus* species. The wide variation in infection rates between colonies within species is further evidence for a strong genetic component in patterns of infection.

The next step in testing the hypothesised role of parasite-resistance in favouring genetic diversity in colonies is to compare more and less diverse colonies with respect to parasite attack in the field. In a field experiment, Liersch & Schmid-Hempel (1998) transferred previously established colonies of *B. terrestris* to underground nest sites in a field in the Jura mountains. In addition to frequent monitoring of the colonies, they manipulated them so that some colonies consisted of closely related (full sister) workers, whilst others were much more genetically diverse. This was achieved by replacing a proportion of the brood of those colonies destined to be heterogeneous with an equal number of brood taken from several donor colonies that were known to be parasite-free. This was repeated through the colony cycle. Apparently the introduction of the 'foreign' brood caused no behavioural disruption in the heterogeneous colonies. Samples of workers taken at regular intervals from the two groups of colonies showed marked differences in levels of parasitism. Three measures were used: prevalence (proportion of workers infected in the colony), parasite load (defined here as the number of infections per worker), and parasite richness (the range of parasite species present per colony). Significantly lower parasite levels by all three measures were shown in the heterogeneous colonies. The same general pattern was consistently shown when the results were broken down for particular parasite groups: for *Nosema bombi*, *Crithidia bombi*, nematodes, mites, conopid fly larvae, and others. Owing to poor weather the actual reproductive success of the colonies was low, and the authors used a substitute measure of fitness: colony size. On this measure, the lower levels of parasitism experienced in the heterogeneous colonies were weakly correlated with greater fitness.

In the above experiment, partial replacement of brood was used to mimic the effects of multiple mating (or multiple queens governing a colony) for genetic diversity in the offspring. An even closer model has been devised by Baer & Schmid-Hempel (1999, 2000, 2001), using artificial insemination of daughter queens. In their experiments, a combination of multiple inseminations with sperm from variously related males, and single inseminations of sperm-mixtures from numbers of males were used to measure the impact of different levels of genetic diversity on both parasitism and reproductive success of freely foraging colonies. Since this methodology eliminated the possible effects of enhanced risks of predation and variations in the genetic quality of males in actual multiple mating by the queens, it allowed for direct relationships between genetic diversity, parasitism and fitness to be studied. Strong and quantifiable associations between increasing degrees of genetic diversity and lowered parasitic infestation were confirmed. However, the outcomes for reproductive success were more complex and equivocal. Apparently the initial move from single mating is correlated with reduced fitness, and only with increasing numbers of effective matings does a fitness benefit emerge.

This offers one possible solution to the paradox that despite an apparent fitness benefit from multiple mating due to increased parasite resistance, most bumblebee queens, including *B. terrestris*, are believed to (usually) mate only once. Baer & Schmid-Hempel suggest that if the ancestral strategy is single mating, then the shift from it to reap the benefit of multiple mating would be inhibited by the 'fitness valley' illustrated in their findings. Though it is yet to be established experimentally, it seems likely that this fitness valley is a result of the costs to the social cohesion of the colony induced by greater genetic diversity. However, a further complication is introduced by the discovery that males directly interfere with the mating behaviour of the young queens. They transfer a sticky 'mating plug' to the queen during mating (Baer *et al.*, 2001). This alters the future behaviour of the queen and prevents her mating for some hours or days afterwards. Since daughter queens, like workers, run high risks of parasite attack (especially from conopids) at this stage in the season, there are strong time-pressures for entering speedily into hibernation. It could be that a male's reproductive interest in having sole paternity of his mate's offspring overrides any benefits that both of them might otherwise have gained by the genetic diversity of the queen's future colony.

Though much remains to be disentangled in this extraordinarily complex field, enough is known to suggest that the mating strategies and genetic structures of bumblebee colonies, local populations and, indeed, communities of bumblebee species cannot be understood without bringing into the picture the dynamics of their interactions with their numerous parasites. A particularly interesting avenue for further research would be studies using bumblebee species other than *B. terrestris*. Recent research suggests that single mating is the most common pattern in *Bombus* species, though a study using molecular techniques to determine the paternity of workers showed multiple mating in queens of *B. hypnorum*. Colonies of *B. terrestris*, *B. lucorum*, *B. lapidarius* and *B. pratorum* were all the products of singly mated queens, but colonies of *B. hypnorum* investigated were the offspring of queens that had mated with from one to four different males (Estoup *et al.*, 1995).

PARASITES, BUMBLEBEE COMMUNITIES AND DISTRIBUTION

We have already seen that parasitism may have a role in mediating and intensifying the effects on bumblebee populations of adverse seasonal conditions or deterioration in habitat. Given that there is considerable variation both within and among species of bumblebees in their vulnerability to different parasitic species and strains, it seems likely that the composition of local bumblebee communities, and their wider distributions, might also be affected. There is some evidence that this is indeed the case.

A study of bumblebee parasites close to London (Cumber, 1949) illustrated not only the extent to which different bumblebee species shared the same parasite species, but also how infestation rates differed across the different host species making up a local bumblebee community. The nematode *Sphaerularia bombi*, for example, was found in six out of eight species of overwintered queens dissected by Cumber (including the cuckoo *B. barbutellus*). However, prevalence of the parasite differed widely among the species affected, varying from 60 per cent in *B. lucorum* queens down to a mere 11 per cent for *B. lapidarius*. Subsequent work, including a study by Lundberg & Svensson (1975) added further social species known to be hosts of *Sphaerularia*, to a total of 17 species. Cumber listed seven bumblebee species as parasitised by conopid flies, and a further nine species parasitised by the fly *Brachicoma devia*. Further research on conopid fly infestation reveals a very complex situation, with several species of fly parasitic on a varying array of host species, and with varying prevalence in each (see, for example, Schwarz *et al.*, 1996; Schmid-Hempel *et al.*, 1990; Schmid-Hempel & Durrer, 1991; Schmid-Hempel & Schmid-Hempel, 1996a). For the protozoan *Nosema bombi*, again, there is evidence of its ability to infect several species of bumblebee, but it appears to vary in its infectiveness and virulence both among colonies of the same species, and also among the species it affects (Liersch & Schmid-Hempel, 1998).

Most discussions of variation among localities and regions in the number of bumblebee species they support place their emphasis on physiological climatic tolerances, physical barriers and climate on the largest geographical scale, combined, at the more local levels, with availability of suitable nest sites, appropriate forage through the colony cycle, and interspecific competition (see Chapters 10 & 11). However, there is good evidence that many parasite species are shared by a range of bumblebee species that often fly together in a locality, and that there are variations among parasites in their incidence and virulence, and among host species in their vulnerabilities. This strongly suggests that parasites may play a significant role in shaping bumblebee communities. This could arise either from the direct effects of differential parasitism on mortality in the different host species, or from the more indirect effects of vulnerability to other parasites and predators, lowered foraging efficiency or altered timing of colony development on the reproductive success of colonies. Given the complexity and likely interaction of all these factors, not to mention the frequency of multiple parasitic infestations in many colonies, it would be difficult to demonstrate these effects empirically.

However, some patterns can be predicted on theoretical grounds. One such hypothesis is that on a regional scale, widespread and common species of bumblebee host should be more intensively parasitised than rare and more localised species. The reasoning behind this is that the commoner and more widespread species are likely to encounter a greater diversity of parasites than more local and rarer ones. In part, at least, the more widespread species can be seen as 'winners' compared with more localised ones in their ability to cope with parasites.

Durrer & Schmid-Hempel (1995) set out to test this expectation. They selected 12 sites at lower elevations in a region of the Jura mountains in Switzerland. Of the 13 species recorded, three were sampled in such small numbers that they were discounted from some of the calculations, and the sibling species *Bombus lucorum* and *B. terrestris* were pooled. This study showed correlations between regional distribution and local abundance: on average, the more widespread the species, the more common they were at the particular sites where they occurred. Both local abundance and distribution were correlated with parasite diversity and with parasite load (corrected for sample size): the more common and widespread species on average carried a greater number of parasite species per host species, and per host individual. This finding is consistent with the argument that parasites may play a significant role in shaping the structure of local bumblebee communities, as well as affecting their distribution on wider geographical scales. The study also showed an inverse relationship between parasite load and the diversity of local bumblebee communities: that is, the localities with more bumblebee species tended to have lower parasite loads (parasite species per average host worker). As Schmid-Hempel notes, there are two possible ways of explaining this. One is that higher levels of parasitism in a locality drive populations of some host species to local extinction. Alternatively, it may be that the parasites themselves encounter more difficulty in infecting more diverse assemblages of bumblebees (Schmid-Hempel, 2001). Either way, the correlation strongly indicates that parasite load is implicated in the structuring of local bumblebee communities – in exactly what ways awaits further research! The association that Durrer & Schmid-Hempel found between the breadth of distribution of a species and its local abundance is also predicted by Williams (1988; forthcoming; and see Chapter 10).

Parasites may also affect the structure of local bumblebee communities by influencing the timing of the stages in the colony cycle (see Wcislo, 1987). We saw above that the protozoan *Crithidia bombi,* when present in overwintered queens, slows down the development of their ovaries and delays nest-founding. At least for the species studied, late establishment of nests reduces the chances of their successfully rearing sexuals. Another seasonal effect is the intensity of attacks by conopid flies. As the study by Müller & Schmid-Hempel (1992*a*) showed, the conopids they studied are most abundant from late June onwards, when the numbers of host workers of most species are also at their peak. However, some early-nesting species have already completed a full colony cycle by this time, and so are unlikely to be so significantly affected by these conopids. Schmid-Hempel *et al.* (1990) showed that in their study sites around Basel, Switzerland, *Bombus pratorum* and *B. hortorum*, both of which complete their colony cycle early in the season were, indeed, less parasitised by the conopids (Fig. 96).

It is possible that early completion of the cycle in these species is an adaptation that reduces their vulnerability to a virulent parasitoid, as well as enabling them to avoid the more intensive resource competition later in the season.

Because they are associated with so many predators, parasites and nest commensals, bumblebees are an outstandingly rich source of general insights into these relationships. Many issues remain to be investigated, but already there is

FIG 96. Levels of conopid infestation in two *Bombus* species with different flight periods. Parasite frequency refers to the proportion of bees (worker, males) that were sampled in the field and were discovered to contain a conopid puparium when dissected in the laboratory. The horizontal bars represent the flight periods of the two species, the whole length representing the flight period of the workers, the shaded part that of the males. N = number of conopids found. Note the much lower impact of conopids on *Bombus pratorum*, the earlier of the two species (reproduced from Schmid-Hempel *et al.*, 1990, with permission).

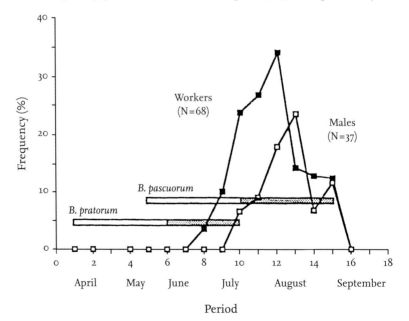

sufficient evidence to suggest that many aspects of bumblebee natural history and ecology are strongly influenced by parasitism. Infestation by several groups of parasites and parasitoids has been shown to have significant effects on the relative reproductive success of bumblebee colonies. There is evidence to suggest that many aspects of bumblebee social life, foraging behaviour and mating strategies may have evolved at least in part as responses to the risk of parasitic infestation. Finally, from the point of view of conservation, it seems highly probable that levels of predation and parasitism affect the species composition of local bumblebee assemblages. It also seems likely that the interactions between incidence and virulence of parasite infestation, on the one hand, and the challenge posed by agricultural change, on the other, have played a significant role in causing the steep declines and local extinctions of so many of the British bumblebees. A vicious spiral of reduced availability of forage leading to depressed immune responses and consequently greater intensity and virulence of parasitic infestation might well have accelerated the decline of the more vulnerable species (see Chapter 10).

CHAPTER 6

Bumblebees and Flowers I: Foraging Behaviour

E VERY KEEN GARDENER will be well aware of the intense foraging activity of bumblebees, their preferences for certain groups of garden flowers, and their ability to forage early in the morning, late into the evening and during inclement weather. Other insects, including their relatives the honey bees, are much more readily 'grounded', starting work later, finishing earlier, and taking shelter much sooner in the face of overcast or rainy weather. The more observant may also have noticed the different colour patterns of the bees' coats – some black, yellow and white, others mainly ginger-brown, still others black with red tails – and that these differences correlate with different preferences for various shapes and colours of garden flowers. Different preferences also follow each other in sequence as plant varieties come into flower, die off and are replaced by others through the season. Commercial growers will be still more aware of the significance of bumblebee activity, as they increasingly take advantage of the value of bumblebees as pollinators of economically important horticultural and agricultural crops.

These general observations pose many questions about how the lives of bumblebees are intertwined with those of the flowers they visit so industriously. Flowers are quite fundamental to bumblebees, sometimes giving them shelter in inclement weather as well as supplying their nutritional requirements (Figs 97 & 98). As we saw in Chapter 2, overwintered females depend on nectar and pollen in the spring to replenish their depleted stores of food, to fuel the development of their ovaries, and to provide the initial nourishment for the first cohort of larvae. Subsequent cohorts of workers visit flowers for nectar and pollen both for the brood in the nest, and for their own nutrition. The males that emerge later from the nest seek out nectar from flowers to meet their own nutritional needs only,

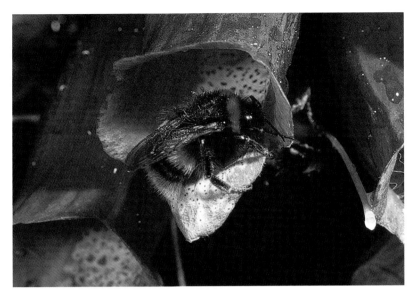

FIG 97. A male *Bombus terrestris* sheltering on the platform of a foxglove flower.

FIG 98. A male *Bombus hortorum,* drenched after a night's rain, despite its shelter of a thistle flowerhead.

while daughter queens feed actively to build up their fat store for the coming winter hibernation. This short sketch already begins to explain some puzzles: the sheer intensity of worker-bee activity is linked to the fact that they are providing for the developing larvae back in the nest, as well as to maintain their own energy. Males (and cuckoo bumblebees) are often noticeably less energetic or persistent foragers.

But it is essential to recognise that the relationship between flowers and bees works both ways: it is an association presumed to have developed over many millions of years between the foragers and the plants whose flowers they visit. With some exceptions, it is a mutualistic association: one from which both partners derive a net (though not necessarily equal) benefit. The bumblebees are entirely dependent on flowers to meet their nutritional needs throughout their life history (though I have one fascinating report of a queen *B. hortorum* feeding from bird droppings (M. Heywood, pers. comm.)). For their part, many plant species have evolved to be dependent upon insects, and in a few cases almost exclusively on bumblebees in particular, for their sexual reproduction. The crucial role the bees play is to carry pollen from the anthers of one flower and deposit it on the receptive stigma of a flower of the same species.

As we will see in the next chapter, plants often have remarkable adaptations to increase the chances that an insect visitor will play its part in their sexual reproduction. The arrangement of flowers into inflorescences of various sorts, and the colour patterns, shapes and scents of the flowers all contribute, along with the reward of pollen or nectar, both to attracting foraging insects and to guiding their behaviour so as to increase the likelihood of pollination. Commonly this is achieved by placing the nectar stores deep in the flower so that the visiting insect has to brush against the anthers in its efforts to reach the nectar. However, the nectar stores are sometimes beyond the reach of shorter-tongued bumblebees, some of which use their powerful mandibles to bite a hole into the side of the corolla tube. They can then probe their tongues through the hole and access the nectar. Since this bypasses the anthers, and enables the foragers to cheat the plant of their pollination services, it is sometimes called nectar robbery or larceny (Figs 99–101). Other species of bumblebees and other insects often make use of the holes once they have been opened up, and this is known as secondary larceny (Fig. 102). By contrast, the 'proper' way of getting at the nectar is known as legitimate foraging (Fig. 103). But bumblebees (and other insects) also forage for pollen, so they have an interest in legitimate foraging, too. Sometimes the same forager will rob a flower for nectar and collect pollen legitimately from flowers of the same species in a single foraging trip (Fig. 104) (own obs.).

In some cases, special behaviour is needed to get the flower to release its pollen. One of the most remarkable of these is sometimes called buzz-foraging, or

FIG 99. A worker *Bombus terrestris* robbing nectar from red campion flowers.

FIG 100. A worker *Bombus pratorum* robbing nectar from a flower of comfrey, after a bout of pollen collecting.

FIG 101. A worker *Bombus monticola* robbing nectar from a flower of bell heather.

FIG 102. Secondary nectar robbery: a large heath butterfly sips nectar from a flower of cross-leaved heath through a hole presumably made by a bumblebee.

FIG 103. A *Bombus hortorum* worker foraging 'legitimately' from a comfrey flower.

FIG 104. A *Bombus terrestris* worker robs nectar from a comfrey flower, after also collecting pollen from comfrey in the same trip.

sonication (Fig. 105). The bees emit a high-pitched whine by rapidly contracting their wing muscles (quite unlike the lower-pitched buzz emitted during flight) whilst running rapidly over the anthers. The vibrations cause the partial release of pollen from the anthers (King, 1993; Larson & Barrett, 1999; Harder *et al.*, 2001). In other cases, the weight of the bee as it lands on a flower causes the anthers to brush against either the dorsal or ventral surface of the bee.

However, pollination is only one step in the whole process of sexual reproduction of flowering plants. Seed-set and effective dispersal are also important processes, and they are affected by factors other than pollination (Corbet, 1998). Not all plants are dependent on insect pollination: some are pollinated by other groups of organisms, such as bats or birds. Some plant species can be either cross-pollinated or self-pollinated, and so may be less dependent on pollinating visitors than others. However, in these cases it is generally accepted that heavy dependence on self-pollination, with resultant inbreeding, is deleterious to the plant population. In other plant species (such as many grasses) pollination is achieved by wind or other non-living vectors, and, finally, many plant species can reproduce vegetatively by sending out runners or underground tubers (Richards, 1997).

So the reproductive strategies of flowering plants are immensely diverse, and many that are pollinated by insects such as bumblebees, or other visitors,

FIG 105. A *Bombus lucorum* worker buzz-foraging for pollen on a garden variety of *Hypericum*.

have fall-back options. Studies of the role of bumblebees in the pollination and overall reproductive success of flowers have to take these complexities into account. Similarly, pollinators themselves vary greatly in their sizes, shapes, bodily processes, sensory and learning abilities and behavioural patterns. Some may be specialised to get their food from just one or a small number of flower species, whilst others are very effective generalists. Different bumblebee species themselves have quite different foraging strategies, which can often be related to structural traits, such as tongue length, to size, or to physiological differences, such as their ways of regulating body temperature.

Through all this diversity, there are many examples of remarkable 'fit' between species (or groups of species) of pollinators, and the structure, flowering time and pollination mechanisms of the flowers they commonly visit. Some of the most elaborate and sophisticated mutual adaptations between flowers and pollinators are to be found among the bees and the flowers they specialise in visiting. However, in bumblebees, this specialisation is hardly ever complete: most bumblebees (and all the British species) are capable of accessing the food sources provided by a wide variety of flowers, and very few flowering plants are entirely dependent on the pollination services of a single species of bumblebee.

The study of such highly evolved mutualisms between many flowering plants and their pollinators is ideal territory for the integration of diverse biological approaches: animal behaviour and its evolution, pollination biology and ecology, the genetics of animal and plant populations, and wider fields of ecology and conservation. In recent years such integrated approaches have been developed, but earlier studies of flowers and their visitors have tended to be strongly rooted in zoology, with the emphasis on animal behaviour, or in botany, with the emphasis on plant reproductive strategies and population genetics (often closely related to agricultural and horticultural plant breeding). The most influential approach from the zoological side has been optimal foraging theory, whilst the concept of pollination syndromes, linking the reproductive strategies of flowering plants with broad classes of animal pollinators, has come mainly from the botanists. More integrated approaches have come from studies that set pollinator-plant interactions in their wider ecological context. Here I aim to show how the different approaches have each illuminated different aspects of the bee–flower relationship.

But theory-based expectations have sometimes not been met, illustrating limitations in the starting assumptions of both approaches. Bumblebee behaviour is complex, flexible and very adaptable in ways not easily captured by any single theoretical approach. This chapter is devoted to discussion of the most influential zoological approach – optimal foraging theory. Chapter 7 focuses on the idea of

pollination syndromes, concluding with a brief discussion of the idea of
pollination webs as a way of integrating the studies of bumblebee behaviour and
plant pollination.

ECONOMICAL FORAGERS

The most influential approach to the foraging behaviour of bumblebees is usually
referred to as optimal foraging theory (henceforth OFT), though it is rather a set
of general principles that are variously appealed to in the construction of
mathematical models of different foraging 'decisions'. OFT drew its inspiration
from the new version of Darwinian evolutionary theory that became established
from the late 1930s onwards. Neo-Darwinism placed great emphasis on the
evolutionary role of environmental pressures acting on the relative reproductive
success of individual organisms as carriers of heritable variation. The most
general influence of the new approach to behaviour was that, in general, talk
about the interests and survival of species dropped away, in favour of analyses
which focused on the way individual animals tended to optimise their chances
of survival (and so reproduction) through their inherited behavioural patterns or
dispositions. Different aspects of animal behaviour could be tested against
theoretically derived models of 'optimal' strategies, given assumptions about the
goal of the behaviour in question, and the various means, opportunities and
constraints available to the animal (Parker & Maynard-Smith, 1990). Among the
fields of behaviour subjected to this approach was the crucial one of foraging for
food. The key assumption was that there would be a direct association between
the most efficient behavioural strategy for gaining food, and the overall 'fitness'
of the animal. Given that, it could be expected that evolutionary pressures would
tend to shape behaviour towards an optimal foraging strategy. OFT soon became
the dominant way of thinking about feeding behaviour, and a huge research
effort has gone into devising appropriate theoretical models and testing them by
experimentation and systematic observation (Charnov, 1976; Pyke, 1980; Stephens
& Krebs, 1986).

Bees, and bumblebees in particular, have proved to be very popular choices
of subject matter for this research effort, and because of it a great deal of light has
been shed on bumblebee behaviour. The main assumptions and models used in
the theory closely resemble those of the most influential approach in modern
economics. Perhaps because of this, researchers in this tradition generally
describe bumblebee behaviour in terms of an economic analogy. Like owners
of capital seeking profitable investment, or consumers seeking the best purchases

in the market, bumblebees (or any other forager) are treated as actors who attempt to maximise their gains whilst minimising the costs of achieving them. As with economic markets, there is a 'currency' in terms of which costs and benefits can be measured and compared, and profits calculated. The currency that bumblebee foragers are expected to be maximising is generally considered to be energy, usually measured in terms of the calorific value of nectar. 'Profit' may be defined as the surplus energy content a forager gains over and above its energy cost in foraging. But, as we will see, difficulties in applying these simple assumptions have led to more complicated definitions and measures of both currency and profit – perhaps the point at which we might ask whether the basic assumptions of the approach are the right ones.

Although OFT is meant to apply quite generally to foragers, and was originally mainly applied to predator–prey interactions, the models derived from it need to be adapted to the peculiarities of the animals under study. To build plausible and testable models, some distinctive traits of bumblebees have to be taken into account. The most obvious is that they are social species, in which the foragers are (mainly) infertile females. If OFT is to be applied to individual workers it has to be assumed that there is a direct relationship between their optimal foraging and the reproductive success of the colony as a whole. Intuitively this seems reasonable, as the workers are foraging not just for their own nutritional benefit, but also to maintain the overall nutritional and other energy requirements of the larvae and any non-foraging nest members. However, this is a testable assumption, and may not be confirmed by the evidence. Also, the fact of sociality itself has to be taken into account: each individual forager is making its contribution to the overall food and energy requirements of the whole colony as just one member of a larger team of sisters. It might not be possible to tell what is the optimal contribution for any individual to make without knowing what part it plays in the team. This is a key problem for the OFT approach, and its implications will be discussed later.

Second, bumblebee workers have to return to the nest at the end of each foraging trip to deliver their accumulated pollen and/or nectar load. The constraints affecting them are therefore quite different from those which affect the behaviour of animals which forage just to meet their own nutritional needs, or which carry their offspring around with them. Workers need to set out from the nest with enough food energy stored in their bodies to fuel the flight to their foraging site, and their foraging efforts once there have to cover the energy costs of their foraging and return flight, with a surplus to be transferred to non-foraging nest members. The time- and energy-budgeting of flights between nest and foraging sites, the ability of workers to carry large loads, and foraging efficiency while at the foraging sites will all affect and be affected by the need to leave and to take food back to a fixed point – the nest. It is by virtue of this that they are referred to as central place foragers, and optimal foraging models are designed to take it into account (Schoener, 1979; Plowright & Laverty, 1984; Ydenberg et al., 1994; Cresswell et al., 2000).

Third, the food sources of bumblebees are distributed in a patchy way in both space and time: different flower species offer different levels and types of reward, and are distributed in patches of varying size and density, at various separation distances from one another. Moreover, the rewards from different flower species vary at different times of day, according to secretion rates of nectar, availability of pollen from the anthers, weather conditions, and prior visits by other foragers, and at different seasons in the year according to the succession of flowering periods (phenology) of the various plant species. Bumblebees have to be able to move between patches, or from one flower species to another, according to the changing relative costs and rewards available in their environment.

So OFT as applied to bumblebees makes several generalised assumptions about the problems faced by bumblebee workers in foraging efficiently, and it predicts the most profitable solutions available to them. The expectation is that their behaviour will approximate to these solutions, as a result of successive generations of selective pressures. One such implication is that, other things being equal, central place foragers should adopt nest sites close to rewarding foraging areas, thus minimising the energy costs of travelling between the two. Other predictions have to do with the diversity and patchiness of forage sources. Bees have to learn how to access rewards offered by flowers, and some flower types are more demanding than others. Optimal foraging expectations are that foragers will tend to be constant to one or a few flower species once they have learned to handle them efficiently. Similarly, once bees have found a rewarding patch of flowers, they are likely to remain in it and to revisit it.

However, these tendencies will be offset by declines in the rewards offered in relation to the time and energy expended. So, for example, as a favoured flower species comes towards the end of its flowering period, the benefits of specialising on it decline. The same happens with a patch of flowers within a single foraging visit. As the bee removes nectar from the flowers its own foraging activity reduces the resources available in this patch, and it forages less and less efficiently. At some point, the bee must 'decide' to leave the patch and search for resources elsewhere. Charnov (1976) provided a complex mathematical model, based on optimal foraging assumptions (for example, the 'predator [forager] is assumed to make decisions so as to maximise the net rate of energy intake during a foraging bout'). This predicted the point at which a forager would respond to declining energy gains by leaving a patch: a forager whose resources are distributed in a patchy way will continue to forage in a rewarding patch until the rate of reward declines to that which can be expected on average for the environment as a whole. This is known as the marginal value theorem, and it has been applied to the decisions of foragers to depart from inflorescences of single plants, from patches of flowers, and from favoured flower species. To the extent that it accurately models the behaviour of actual foragers, it raises interesting questions, as we shall see, about how foragers are able to assess the availability of alternative sources, the costs of searching for and accessing them, and so on.

Another use for OFT is to take a regularly observed pattern of behaviour and devise testable explanations of it in terms of the theory. One such pattern is the observation that bumblebees foraging on vertical inflorescences generally begin foraging on the lower flowers and often move vertically upwards, departing before reaching the topmost flowers (though, in fact, they often move in an upward spiral, and sometimes move downwards!). Where the plants concerned are protandrous (that is, the anthers mature before the stigmas become receptive) and the lower flowers mature first, this pattern of behaviour would benefit the plant. An upward-foraging bee would be likely to deposit pollen from the previous inflorescence visited on the stigmas of the older, lower (effectively female) flowers in the inflorescence, and take pollen from the younger, higher flowers on to the next plant, so enhancing cross-pollination (Best & Byerzychudek, 1982; Heinrich, 1979). But how would such a 'movement rule' in each inflorescence benefit the bees? The conventional explanation of this in terms of OFT is that the nectar rewards are greater in the lower flowers, and decline as the bee moves up until they reach the lower threshold of profitable foraging (sometimes called the 'giving up density' or GUD), whereupon they leave for the next inflorescence – as predicted by the marginal value theorem. However, as we shall see, the key assumption that nectar rewards decline as the bee moves up the inflorescence is open to question and to empirical testing. So, also, is the assumption that the bees are foraging for nectar, and not pollen, or a combination of the two.

There is much to be said in favour of OFT. It has provided a widely shared set of assumptions for a huge research effort, ranging from abstract theoretical model-building through to systematic field observation and experiments and laboratory tests. Its high level of generality has stimulated comparison between the behavioural strategies of widely different groups of animals and it is firmly grounded in a deeper-level theory (a version of Darwinism that is itself, however, open to criticism). OFT also conforms to a strongly held view of what sort of explanations science should aim at: it lends itself to quantitative predictions and research designed to test them. However, the assumptions underlying the most frequent applications of the approach to bumblebees are questionable, and expectations derived from it have often not been fulfilled by experimental studies of the ways foraging bumblebees actually behave. Next, we will explore in more detail some of the fascinating complexities and challenges that have emerged from attempts to study bumblebee foraging in the light of OFT.

HOW FAR TO FLY?

The key expectation that central place foragers will site their nests close to abundant food resources is a good illustration of the difficulties. Perhaps the most original and fruitful studies consistent with the principles of OFT have been those of Bernd Heinrich and his colleagues. Heinrich's *Bumblebee Economics* (1979) remains a classic. In it he presented a view of the overall energy and materials that flow into, through and out of the bumblebee nest, highlighting the crucial role of forager efficiency in ensuring that the nutritional needs of the larvae, queen and workers themselves were met, as well as carrying out nest maintenance and temperature regulation of the nest (Fig. 106).

By measuring the rates of energy use by bumblebees in flight, the energy demands of regulating their thoracic temperature (essential for the working of the flight muscles), and their uptake of energy from given rates of flower visitation, he calculated the consequences of long-distance flights for foraging profitability. His model revealed that the energy cost of flight was relatively small compared to the overall energy cost of foraging, even with long-distance flights. However, there was a high indirect cost. Time taken flying to and from forage sites was time that might otherwise have been spent foraging, so long-distance foraging considerably reduced the *rate* at which energy gains could be made compared with foraging close to the nest (economists refer to this as opportunity cost).

However, Heinrich, unlike some of the more theoretically inclined advocates of OFT, observed the foraging of wild bumblebees in a systematic way, and, in some of his studies, used electronic tagging of bees to track their foraging movements. He clearly recognised that, like honey bees, they travel long distances, possibly several kilometres, to forage sites. On the face of it, this is inconsistent with OFT expectations, though the high speed of bumblebee flight (11–20 kilometres per hour in his calculations), and their extraordinary capacity to carry large loads of both pollen and nectar (up to 20 per cent of body weight of the former and 90 per cent of body weight of the latter – Heinrich, 1979) can both be seen as adaptations that either shorten flight times, or increase the economic return of each foraging trip. Either of these would compensate for greater costs of long-distance travel.

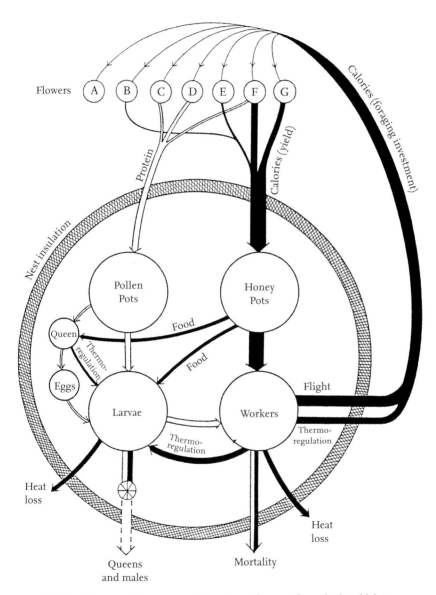

FIG 106. A flow diagram of the movement of matter and energy through a bumblebee colony (reproduced from Heinrich, 1979, with permission).

Implicit in Heinrich's discussion is the assumption that bumblebees have to make long-distance flights because their food sources are so widely scattered. However, more recent studies of bumblebee foraging at the landscape scale provide some evidence that challenges this assumption. Schulke & Waser (2001) carried out a field experiment on transfer of pollen between source populations of *Delphinium nuttallianum* and artificially isolated plantings at varying distances up to 400 metres away. They reported that there was substantial pollinator (bumblebee and hummingbird) activity in the isolated arrays, and the quantities of pollen deposited and seed set in the isolated arrays were only slightly less than the levels recorded in the (closer) source patches. In mark and recapture experiments, they recorded flights by bumblebee queens of up to 300 metres.

In another study, harmonic radar was used to track bumblebee movements over a landscape, including agricultural crops, hedgerows, woodland, and, at the margin, domestic gardens (Figs 107 & 108) (Osborne *et al.*, 1999). Nests of *Bombus terrestris* in plastic boxes were placed in the study area and the foraging behaviour of workers tracked over two ten-day periods, in June and August. Some individuals were tracked over the course of two to three days. Most bees flew more than 200 metres to their foraging sites, the mean outward journey was 275 metres, and the range of distances tracked over the two trials was from 70–631 metres. These distances represent tracking results, and it seems likely that many bees were flying further, since tracking was limited by obstacles to the range of the radar responders. Numerous flights were, for example, in the direction of gardens beyond the limits of radar tracking and subsequent research has tracked *B. terrestris* workers foraging up to 1.5 kilometres from the nest (Osborne, pers. comm.).

This study shows that bumblebees can and do frequently fly long distances from the nest, but its implications for OFT are unclear. The nests were placed in the study area by the researchers, and might have been located quite differently by wild bees occupying the same site. The study site was a mixed arable farm, with associated dispersal of suitable forage patches. It could be argued that the bees were flying further than might be expected on the assumptions of OFT because of the artificial constraints imposed by these features. Nevertheless, it could still be argued that the bees may have been foraging optimally given those constraints.

However, evidence against the 'meagre resources' interpretation is that long-distance flyers in this study had apparently suitable forage, visited by other bees (presumably from other nests), at closer range. Other studies, carried out by Dramstad, Saville and others also suggest that bumblebees fly long distances between nests and forage sites, even when apparently suitable forage is available close by. Dramstad (1996) reported three mark and recapture studies carried out in Norway, and located literature references, all indicating that bumblebees do

FIG 107. (a) *Bombus terrestris* with radar transponder attached (with permission, Rothamsted Research, photograph by A. Martin). (b) Harmonic radar equipment set up in the field. The Landrover contains a computer with radar screen output and log.

FIG 108. Modified figure of outward forager tracks over farmland in June 1996. Key: green lines = hedges, blue = mass-flowering crops, black lines = radar tracks with symbols representing individual bees, small green square = position of the colony, red circle = radar position. The range rings are at 200 metres and 400 metres from the radar. (Rothamsted research, with permission J. Osborne.)

forage at considerable distances from their nests. They do this even when there are suitable foraging patches close by, and these are used by bees of the same species. Saville *et al.* (1997) report another study of bumblebee foraging in an agricultural landscape – also in Norway. The research included a dawn-to-dusk study of foragers entering and leaving a naturally established nest of *B. lucorum*. Foragers were marked leaving and re-entering the nest, while scattered forage sites up to 250 kilometres from the nest were monitored. Very few individuals marked at the nest were recaptured at these forage sites, yet other bumblebees, including those of the same species, were observed and marked there. Bees marked while foraging were frequently recaptured, often at the same forage patches, but none were seen entering the nest. It seems very likely that the nest-marked foragers were generally foraging outside the 250 metre limits of the study area, whilst foragers from other nests were feeding at patches much closer to the nest under study. The bees marked while foraging exhibited the well-established pattern of 'patch fidelity' (of which more later), but it could not be assumed they were foraging close to their nests. The nest-marked bees appeared to be avoiding patches close to the nest, and many were observed to fly up and off rapidly as they left the nest.

This study was based on a naturally established nest of wild bees, and the implication is that, at least for the bee species under study, in agricultural landscapes, workers fly long distances from the nest to forage, even when there is available forage much closer to the nest. In the absence of quantitative assessment of the actual distribution of resources at the appropriate landscape scale, it cannot entirely be ruled out that long-distance flights are constrained by inadequate local resources. It seems that the ability to forage at long distances from the nest may explain the success of some species in coping with increasingly intensive agricultural landscapes, and that some version of OFT, focusing on energy and time optimisation, might still be capable of explaining long-distance foraging in such environments. A model developed by Cresswell *et al.* (2000) compares the costs and benefits of foraging close to and at greater distances from the nest, yielding a prediction for the maximum distance at which foraging can be profitable. This may be as great as several kilometres if greater rewards can be gained from the more distant sources. However, this model still assumes that distant foraging is a response to relative lack of local resources. It does not address the question why foragers seem to avoid rewarding patches close at hand.

Rather different models have been designed to predict the optimal spatial distribution of central-place foragers (Dukas & Edelstein-Keshet, 1998). These assume evenly distributed foraging patches at various distances from the nest. Like those of Cresswell *et al.*, these models predict that long-distance flights between nest and forage patch, of up to several kilometres, may still provide a net energy gain. Their models distinguish between solitary and social foragers, and take into account the effects of competition between nest members in the case of social foragers. Bumblebees are non-territorial foragers, so there is no overt behavioural interaction when they compete for resources (that is, there is generally no 'interference competition'). However, when numbers of foragers converge on a single patch, the foraging efficiency of each can be expected to be reduced by the depletion of the resource as a result of the foraging of the others. This is termed 'exploitation competition'. In social insects such as bumblebees, a forager strategy of avoiding exploitation competition between itself and members of the same colony by flying further away might increase its net contribution to the provisioning of the colony, despite some cost to its individual foraging efficiency. Dukas & Edelstein-Keshet's models predict that this would be the case. So while the numbers of foragers in solitary species should fall with greater distances from the nest, social foragers should be more evenly distributed between close and distant foraging sources. Proportionally more foragers of the social species, such as bumblebees, would be expected to forage at greater distances. On their models, the predicted difference between solitary and social foragers varies according to the 'currency' assumed. They also concede that their models do not take account of the effects of competition between different colonies of the same or of other species occupying the same or overlapping foraging ranges.

However, evidence from the empirical studies suggests that the bumblebees under study, rather than being evenly distributed at different distances from the nest, actually avoided local foraging patches that were apparently rewarding. Also, in the field studies, the foraging ranges of foragers from nests under observation overlapped with those of other nests, of both the same and other species. This is the normal situation of bumblebee foragers, so even if they avoid exploitation competition with foragers from their own nest, they certainly do not avoid competing with those from other nests. Finally, while these newer and more biologically realistic models show how long-distance flights might still be profitable, this is not quite the same as showing how they could be optimal. Optimality involves the stronger claim that the foraging strategy adopted is more profitable than available alternatives. One key difficulty in getting a clear empirical test of optimality in relation to such large-scale studies is the problem of quantifying the available food supply present and its spatial distribution in relation to the shifting nutritional requirements of the colony. Comparative studies of bee-foraging in landscapes less affected by agricultural change would probably shed more light on the issues, as would studies of other bumblebee species, which are likely to have different foraging ranges.

There are other possible explanations for the observed patterns of long-distance and apparently more costly foraging, and some of these seem to expose serious limitations in OFT – or at least to suggest that some of its most commonly made assumptions need to be abandoned. One of the alternative explanations is that both opportunities and preferences for nest sites are shaped by factors other than closeness to forage sites. Many species occupy disused mammal nests, and so are dependent on the availability of these. Others make use of nest material above ground in grassland habitats, and have particular requirements of vegetation structure around the nest, particularly with respect to incidence of solar energy (see Westrich, 1996; Edwards, M., 1998; Carvell, 2000). Finding a suitable nest site is a fundamental necessity for successful reproduction, and it imposes constraints that may be independent of the requirement for foraging efficiency.

Another possibility is that positive avoidance of forage sites close to the nest may be a strategy for limiting predation or parasitism (Dramstad, 1996; Dukas & Edelstein-Keshet, 1998; Dukas in Chittka & Thomson, 2001). One possible explanation might be found in the nest-location strategies of mammalian predators, such as badgers, or the nest parasites, such as the various species of cuckoo bumblebees (subgenus *Psithyrus*). If these strategies include following foragers back to the nest, then long-distance flights might well reduce levels of infestation or predation. A concentration of foragers close to a nest might increase the risk of predation on the foragers themselves, and also increase the likelihood of predators discovering the nest. More distant foraging, in dispersing the foragers from their nest, would reduce both risks (Dramstad, 1996). As we saw in Chapter 5, most social bumblebee species suffer very high levels of infestation by cuckoos and other nest parasites and it seems quite likely that they will have evolved behavioural adaptations in response to them. Dramstad considers the possibility that the scent-marking of flowers by foraging workers might provide a 'scent-guide' to the nest for cuckoo bumblebees if they foraged close to the nest. This is certainly plausible, as it has been shown that cuckoos do recognise and respond to the odour of their host species (Fisher, 1983a). However, cuckoo bumblebee females can often be seen directly searching for host nests, rather than following workers. Given that they invade nests at an early stage, there would be rather few workers to follow, in any case. Mammalian predators such as badgers probably also search for nests directly, and are in any case nocturnal.

Finally, dispersal of foragers might reduce the risk of a colony being harmed by loss of individual foragers to predation or parasitism. Foragers are at direct risk of predation from birds, hornets and crab spiders, but they also suffer very high levels of fatal infestation from conopid flies. This has been shown to negatively affect the reproductive success of colonies of *B. terrestris* and *B. lucorum*, reducing the investment in males and daughter queens (Müller, 1993, and see discussion in

Chapter 5). Remarkable new evidence derived from the use of genetic markers shows that foragers of at least some species disperse very widely from their nests, so that few nest mates forage together at any one patch (Chapman *et al.*, 2003; Darvill *et al.*, 2004). If we assume that the risk of predation, or of infestation by conopid parasitoids, is greater at some sites than others, then dispersal of foragers would reduce the risk of a high proportion of foragers being attacked at any one time. Ability to forage at long distance, making possible widespread dispersal of the forager-cohort of a nest, could thus be adaptive in reducing the risk to the colony of a sudden loss of a high proportion of its food gatherers.

Dukas & Edelstein-Keshet take up this line of argument and offer further models based on the supposition of a trade-off between foraging efficiency and risk of mortality through predation. This is of interest in that it involves inventing a currency that departs from the standard ones used by OFT, which are generally concerned solely with net energy gains, or rates of energy gain. In this model, two quite distinct determinants of overall fitness are run together as 'lifetime food delivery under predation risk'. This might well be understood as an implicit shift away from the basic assumptions of the original theory. The situation is still more complex, however, because there is evidence that some viral and protozoan infections are spread from one colony to another by way of flower visits. The strategy of dispersal is likely to increase the risk of contracting infections from flowers previously visited by foragers from another colony. So avoiding risk from parasitoids might increase risks of other sorts. Unfortunately, the implications of these models for predicting how far bees will fly to foraging patches are unclear in the absence of evidence about the distribution, and relative seriousness of these risks to foragers, through both time and space. It seems that some species may have adapted to the risk of conopid infestation by timing key reproductive events in the colony cycle away from the period of population peaks of adult conopids. For other species (including *B. terrestris* and *B. lucorum*) large worker numbers at the peak of colony development may also be understood in terms of these risks (Müller, 1993). We might speculate that the much larger colony size and greater food-storage ability of honey bees makes them less vulnerable to predators and parasitoids attacking foragers, so making possible greater concentrations of nest mates at rewarding foraging sites.

Finally, the few landscape-scale studies so far reported have all used fragmented agricultural areas as study sites, and are confined to a small number of bumblebee species which can forage profitably in such mosaic habitats. However, given the very rapid pace and profound transformations that have occurred in agricultural landscapes in recent decades, the ecological context in which inherited behavioural dispositions were acquired may no longer apply. It seems reasonable to guess that at least some of these dispositions will have become maladaptive, or at least suboptimal, under the new conditions. It may also be that species vary in their ability to adapt to habitat fragmentation, and those that are capable of profitable long-distance foraging are, other things being equal, more able to cope. Available cross-species comparisons suggest that foraging ranges do differ from species to species, with good evidence that *B. terrestris*, *B. lucorum* and *B. pascuorum* are all capable of long-distance foraging, though *B. pascuorum* may have a rather shorter range than the other two (see Darvill *et al.*, 2004). Evidence that *B. muscorum* forages relatively close to the nest is provided by Walther-Hellwig & Frankl (2000). Although their study is open to serious criticism (Edwards, 2000), it may be that some of our scarce and declining bumblebees could have shorter foraging ranges, and, if this is so, it may be important for conservation (see Chapters 10 & 11).

WHEN TO STAY AND WHEN TO LEAVE

As we saw above, OFT yields other expectations of bumblebee behaviour. The marginal value theorem predicts when bees will abandon a food source, whether this is an individual inflorescence, a flower species, or a foraging patch.

Inflorescences

At the level of inflorescences, OFT has been used to explain the 'bottom upwards' pattern of foraging on vertical inflorescences (such as foxgloves, purple loosestrife, and many Lamiaceae, such as the deadnettles and woundworts). As we saw, the theory explains this pattern of foraging behaviour in terms of an assumed decline in nectar rewards as the bee moves up the inflorescence. Best & Bierzychudek (1982) confirmed the energy-gain model for foragers on foxglove, and support has been forthcoming from subsequent studies (for example, Rasheed & Harder, 1997*b*). However, a study by Pyke (1979) yielded conflicting results. He measured the rate of nectar secretion for flowers at different levels in the inflorescences of five plant species – two *Delphinium* species, monk's-hood, rosebay willowherb and *Pentsemon strictus*. Expectations from OFT were confirmed for four out of the five plant species. They were protandrous, lower flowers opened first, the expected nectar gradient was confirmed, and the bees tended to move upwards through the inflorescences. However, *Pentsemon strictus* was anomalous, in that neither the timing of flower opening, nor the nectar gradient, were as expected, yet the bees still tended to forage upwards.

Further complexities were revealed in a study by Corbet *et al.* (1981), showing that the flower-handling methods of different species of forager need to be taken into account. The study compared foraging by wasps and two species of bumblebee on water figwort and common toadflax. In this study, actual quantities of nectar were measured at hourly intervals in flowers at the various levels on the inflorescences. This direct measure of 'standing crop' was considered more appropriate than the measure of secretion rate used by Pyke. In the figwort, there was no nectar gradient in the inflorescence, but the wasps still moved upwards. In toadflax, there was an upward gradient, with greater nectar content in the higher flowers. However, this did not translate directly into available reward. The toadflax was visited by both *Bombus hortorum* and *B. terrestris*, but the latter robbed the flowers by accessing the nectar through holes in the spur, as well as taking nectar from unopened buds. For this species, the lower buds of the toadflax offered the greatest accessible rewards, with declining benefit both upwards and downwards. For the longer-tongued legitimate forager, *B. hortorum*, accessible rewards increased upwards on the inflorescence, but against the expectations of OFT, these bees generally moved upwards through the inflorescence. Foragers of *B. terrestris* were observed to move both upwards and downwards on inflorescences, in a pattern related to their postures when accessing nectar, rather than nectar gradient. This study, then, did not confirm the energy budget explanation for these plant and forager species.

Corbet *et al.* went on to offer an alternative explanation in terms the relative ease of movement between flowers for bees adopting different postures. The 'head-up' posture of the wasps, given the structure of the inflorescences, would have favoured upward movement, as would also be the case for *B. hortorum*. However, in *B. terrestris*, it was observed that some robbed 'head down' and others 'head up'. These postures were associated with downward and upward movement through the inflorescence respectively. La Ferla, too, in a study of *B. pascuorum* foraging from specially planted beds of marsh woundwort at Cambridge Botanic Gardens, confirmed the upward pattern of flower visitation, but did not find the expected gradient of nectar rewards (La Ferla, 2000). She searched the literature and found several suggested alternative explanations (including that of Corbet *et al.*) to the standard OFT one in terms of nectar gradients (Table 6; Figs 109–112).

It might be that the flowers are so oriented that bees get a better view upwards than downwards. Alternatively, it might be that having a constant pattern of foraging minimises the risk of the bees revisiting flowers just emptied of nectar (though this would explain only the benefits of having *some* rule of movement, not that this should generally be upwards). Another possibility, not encountered in La Ferla's review, is that moving up the inflorescence puts the bee in a better position to view other adjacent inflorescences at the point of departure. Indirect

TABLE 6. Explanations why bees exhibit directional movements when visiting flowers (reproduced from La Ferla, 2000, with permission).

FACTOR	EXPLANATION	SUGGESTED BY
Nectar	Bees visit flowers in a pattern dictated by the distribution of nectar	Pyke (178, 1979) Best & Bierzychudek (1982)
Avoid revisitation of flowers	Bees visit flowers in a sequence to ensure they do not visit flowers they have already drained.	Heinrich (1979) Pyke (1979)
Avoid visiting buds	Bees start at the bottom and move upwards on spikes so they avoid visiting closed buds first, from which they cannot drink nectar.	Waddington & Heinrich (1979)
Gravity	Bees move upwards because they are negatively geotactic.	Waddington & Heinrich (1979)
Vision	The constant orientation of flowers is such that when a bee leaves them, it has a better view of flowers in one direction than in the other.	Waddington & Heinrich (1979)
Posture	The bee's position during a visit is such that movement in one direction is easier than movement in the other.	Corbet *et al.* (1981)

effects of interactions between different pollinators attracted to an inflorescence may also be relevant (Harder *et al.*, 2001).

OFT also predicts that in patches of lower floral density, foragers will visit more flowers per inflorescence before moving on (Beattie, 1976; Heinrich, 1979; Cresswell, 1997), a finding confirmed in a study by Mustajärvie *et al.* (2001) on experimental plots of sticky catchfly in Finland. Less easily interpreted are studies of the effects of variable nectar rewards in flowers on the same inflorescence. Large, many-flowered inflorescences are advantageous to plants in enhancing their attractiveness to pollinating visitors. However, there is a dilemma, in that the more flowers the visitor probes before leaving, the greater the likelihood that pollen will be transferred from one flower to another on the same plant, as against

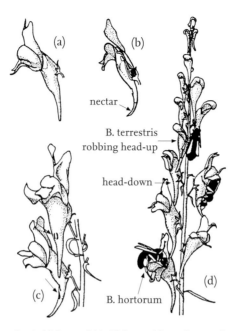

FIG 109. *Linaria vulgaris*: (a) flower; (b) half-flower; (c) two flowers showing holes made by nectar-robbing bumblebees (arrows); (d) a raceme, showing postures adopted by *Bombus hortorum* and *B. terrestris* when taking nectar (reproduced from Corbet *et al.*, 1981, with permission).

FIG 110. A *Bombus muscorum* worker collecting pollen from a vertical inflorescence of tufted vetch.

FIG 111. A black male *Bombus ruderatus* foraging upwards on a vertical inflorescence of marsh woundwort.

FIG 112. *Bombus hortorum* foraging from white deadnettle. This species often works up the inflorescence in a spiral pattern.

the (presumed optimal) transfer of pollen from one plant to another. The reproductive success of the plant might be optimised by encouraging pollinators to leave early, whilst not sacrificing initial attractiveness. A Canadian study by Biernaski *et al.* examined the effects of varying nectar rewards in artificial inflorescences on visiting behaviour of hummingbirds (*Selasphorus rufus*) and bumblebees (*Bombus albifrons*) (Biernaski *et al.*, 2002). Both species departed from inflorescences with variable rewards earlier than they did from ones with constant ones, even though the mean reward was equivalent (and in some instances despite individuals having greater uptake of nectar from the inflorescences offering variable rewards). As well as indicating a possible adaptive strategy on the part of plants with many-flowered inflorescences, the study suggests that foragers may not always optimise on energy economy, or rate of profit, but may also show risk aversion. Foraging to reduce the risk of falling below an energy threshold in the longer term may take precedence over short-term gain.

Flowers

Another expectation from OFT assumptions is that individual bees will tend to specialise in foraging from blossoms of one type. However, this 'flower constancy' will be qualified by occasional sampling of other species as a way of checking that other, equally rewarding and accessible blossom types are not being overlooked. As predicted by the marginal value theorem, bees will switch to such alternatives if they experience relatively declining rewards from their current specialism. Heinrich explains that flower constancy enhances the profitability of foraging by eliminating or reducing the time and energy costs of learning how to handle different blossom types. These are likely to be higher with more complex and specialised floral morphologies, so increasing the benefits of constancy for bees adapted to forage from them. Heinrich uses the terms majoring and minoring to describe the expected pattern of constancy to one flower species, combined with less frequent sampling of others (1979). Heinrich observed tagged bees of the same species, each constant to a different flower type, showing constancy to the same species and patch for up to a month. He experimentally removed one of the flower species, and observed its former specialists experiment with other species until they established a new major. The marginal value theorem was supported by simple experiments involving artificially enriching minors, and observing bees switching to them (Heinrich, 1976).

However, again, the evidence from studies of flower constancy is rather mixed in its implications for OFT, and provides a more complex picture than might be expected. Heinrich is quite clear that constancy is a feature of individual foraging behaviour only: at the level of species, local populations and colonies, bumblebees may be more-or-less generalised in their foraging preferences (subject, of course, to the actual availability of suitable forage plant species in the range of the colony). Thus the preferences for particular flower species shown by bumblebee foragers are what Heinrich terms labile preferences: they may be constrained by tongue length (and, we might add, a whole suite of other variable morphological, physiological and behavioural traits), and are acquired by learning by individual workers. His claim is that each bee learns by experience which flowers are rewarding and continues to major on that species until minoring indicates that at least equivalent gains can be made by switching (it is now known that in some species, at least, there is communication between workers about rewarding forage plants – see Chapter 3). Optimal foraging on the part of individual workers is then supposed to aggregate to optimal provisioning of the nest. Profit maximising by individuals is assumed to translate automatically into the common benefit of all, and Heinrich refers to the analogous assumption made by the classical economist, Adam Smith, in his famous assertion that the market operates as a providential 'invisible hand' (Heinrich, 1979). As we shall see, there are serious problems with this analogy, and with the energy budget approach that is based on it.

Other studies have shown a complex relationship between flower density, flower diversity in a patch, patch size, and the degree of isolation of foraging patches. For example, Stout, Allen & Goulson studied the foraging behaviour of visiting bumblebees of three species (*B. pascuorum*, *B. terrestris* and *B. hortorum*) to experimental plots containing various mixtures of four flowering plant species (Stout *et al.*, 1998). The arrays were arranged so as to test the effects on foraging behaviour of the relative rarity of each plant species, and also of various mixtures of species in the same array. Individual bees were marked and their subsequent visits noted. It was observed that bees were more likely to be constant to a flower species if it was in a mixture with dissimilar species, less likely if it was planted together with similar species. This held good for flowers with complex floral morphologies as well as simple ones, with *B. hortorum* workers switching easily between snapdragon and toadflax, apparently contrary to expectations from OFT.

Patches

What about fidelity to a particular foraging patch, and when to leave it? The patch-fidelity of foraging bumblebees is well established. Heinrich electronically tagged individual bees and tracked their foraging routes to, through, and back from their foraging areas. These routes were very similar over successive trips and on successive days, saving time and energy in searching for new sites. Mark-and-recapture studies, such as those reported by Dramstad (1996), generally report high levels of reobservation of the same marked bees close to the location of their initial capture (for example, 80–100 per cent within 50 metres of patch-marked bees in one of Dramstad's studies). The landscape-scale study carried out by Saville *et al.* (1997) also found high levels of patch-fidelity, as indicated by recapture of marked individuals. Osborne *et al.* (1999) were also able to track the movements of individual bees on successive trips and days. Tracked bees showed constancy in both flight direction and distance, with remarkably direct routes to their foraging areas, indicating that they were not foraging en route and in some sense 'knew where they were going'. However, patch-fidelity, like constancy to a particular flower species, cannot be inflexible. OFT predicts that patches, like species and inflorescences, will be abandoned if there is expectation of equal or better foraging elsewhere. Osborne *et al.* were able to track one bee apparently doing just this. Their 'R33' was tracked for three days, during which she switched from having been constant to hedges to the north-west of the study area to forage sites on the north-east. They were able to track a flight directly from north-west to north-east, which presumably established the new pattern (Fig. 113).

FIG 113. A series of eight tracks performed by bee R33. Tracks 1–4 go north-west, then the fifth goes from west to east without first returning to the nest. Subsequent tracks are to the north-east. Range rings are 200 metres and 400 metres from the radar. (Rothamsted research, with permission J. Osborne.)

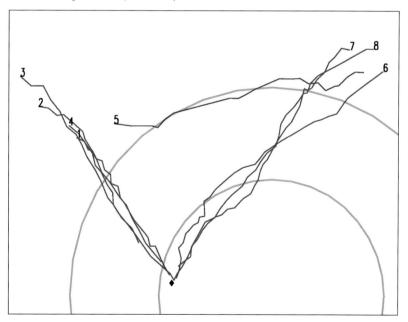

When and why do bumblebees switch from one patch to another? Foraging patches vary in several ways. We have already considered some of the evidence about isolation, and distances between patches and nests, but patches also differ in size, floral density and diversity and also in the extent to which they are visited by other foragers of the same or different species. Distinguishing the relative influence of these different variables on bumblebee foraging presents major experimental challenges, but some interesting patterns have emerged from such studies. Pyke (1980) developed mathematical models of the rate of net energy gain for foraging bumblebees in terms of the energy reward per flower visited and the number of flowers visited in a unit time, set against the energetic cost of foraging in terms of the physical activity involved and energy expended on maintaining an appropriate thoracic temperature. He designed an experimental test of OFT using these models and applying them to the foraging behaviour of workers of *B. flavifrons* on two adjacent patches, one of larkspur and the other of monk's-hood, observed during August in 1977 and 1978. The expectation derived from OFT's marginal value theorem is that the densities of workers on the two patches would be such as to equalise the average rate of net energy gain. Pyke acknowledges that some energy costs, especially those associated with thermo-regulation, are difficult to estimate, but the results of his experiment do show very similar values of rate of energy gain for the bees foraging on the two patches, as predicted by the marginal value theorem: if substantially higher rates of reward could be obtained by switching patches, the theorem predicts that this would have happened. In this case, the flowers of larkspur were less rewarding, but handled more speedily than the monk's-hood.

It is well established that foragers spend longer and visit more flowers in large patches, as one might expect on OFT assumptions. However, less obviously, it appears that foragers visit a smaller *proportion* of flowers in large patches compared with smaller ones. Models developed by Goulson (1999) and Ohashi & Yahara (1999) assume that foragers are able to work more systematically in small patches, and so avoid revisiting flowers they have already depleted. The likelihood of such 'mistakes' increases with larger patches, so that the bees will experience declining reward (relatively) more quickly. Goulson tested this model experimentally, using specially prepared patches of white clover and visiting *B. lapidarius* (Goulson, 2000b). Observed departures corresponded closely with those predicted by the model, and indicated that the bees respond to declining rates of reward at the patch. He also showed that a simple departure rule: 'depart when two consecutive visits are to previously visited flowers', yielded predictions very close to the behaviour observed. Though consistent with marginal value theorem expecta-tions, these results do not, of course, demonstrate that this or any other

FIG 114. *Anthidium manicatum.*

departure rule was in fact being followed by the bees. In other respects there were
inconsistencies between expectations of the model and observed behaviour.

Sowig, comparing bumblebee foraging on patches of varying sizes, also
concluded that the bees are able to forage more systematically on smaller patches,
and assess likely rewards from them more readily. They are thus more likely to
'make mistakes' when foraging from larger patches, where nectar availability is
much less evenly distributed between blossoms (Sowig, 1989). Premature departure can also be triggered by disturbances to the patch, including the behaviour
of other species. A solitary bee, *Anthidium manicatum*, for example (Fig. 114),
takes up territories over flower patches and induces immediate departure in
bumblebees on contact (see Comba *et al.*, 1999*b*) – including queens of *Bombus
pratorum* and *B. terrestris* (own obs.).

GOOD TIMES TO FORAGE

Finally, it is well established that floral rewards vary according to plant species,
time of day, weather conditions, and seasonal change, as also do the patterns of
visitation by different groups of foragers (Corbet, 1978; Corbet *et al.*, 1979;
Zimmerman, 1988; Herrera, 1990; Corbet *et al.*, 1993; Corbet *et al.*, 1995; Comba *et al.*,

1999*a* & *b*). Optimal foraging behaviour should show a temporal fit with these patterns of variation. This expectation was tested by a study of insect visitors to a summer-flowering Mediterranean shrub, *Lavandula latifolia*, carried out by C. M. Herrera (1990). Some 80 species of visitors were observed, but a subset of 34 species accounted for the overwhelming majority of visits. These included species from the insect orders Hymenoptera, Diptera, and Lepidoptera, and the patterns of their foraging activities through the day were observed, and related to both the availability of floral rewards and pollinating effectiveness. A complex pattern of matches and mismatches was recorded, and Herrera concluded that this could be explained as adaptive to either the plants or their visitors only by introducing complicated extra assumptions. A simpler and more plausible explanation could be given in terms of the needs of the flower visitors to achieve a thermal balance through the day, and, for the plants, the effects of water stress on nectar secretion.

In the bumblebees (*B. terrestris* and *B. lucorum*) activity peaked early (5–7 a.m.) and again later (5–7 p.m.), with a notable decline around the middle of the day. Measurements of floral rewards showed two peaks for pollen-bearing flowers, shortly after midday and around sunset. Nectar-producing flowers offered approximately constant rewards through the day, declining sharply after 4 p.m., whilst flowers offering both peaked around midday. There was, therefore, no clear match between the timing of the foraging activity of the two bumblebee species and the availability of nectar and pollen from *Lavandula latifolia*. Instead, Herrera explains the pattern of bumblebee activity in terms of their large size and ability readily to raise their temperature above that of the environment, enabling them to forage early, or in dull conditions. However, bumblebees conversely run a higher risk than most other insects of overheating in the middle of the day. Another relevant factor may be the need to maintain water balance. Bumblebees are often assumed to gain all their water intake from nectar. In fact they are sometimes observed to take water directly (see Ferry & Corbet, 1996), but it is likely that the water content of nectar provides most of their needs. It may be that in Herrera's study the greater viscosity of nectar in the middle of the day, due to evaporation, did not suit their water balance requirements.

OPTIMAL FORAGING THEORY: A PROFITABLE INVESTMENT?

Overall, the empirical study of implications of OFT has produced mixed results. Some observed patterns, such as patch and flower species constancy, majoring and minoring, seem to match the predictions of OFT models fairly well. Others, such

as nest siting in relation to forage sources, daily patterns of foraging in relation
to floral rewards, and risk-averse behaviour, seem to be inconsistent with the
expectations of OFT. Attempts to deal with this have led to increasingly complex
models, which turn out to be very difficult to test by experiments. In view of this,
some critics have objected to the approach as circular and untestable. At its most
fundamental, this criticism is addressed to the version of evolutionary theory
on which optimality models such as OFT are based, and raises complex and
fascinating philosophical and theoretical issues beyond the scope of this chapter
(see Gould & Lewontin, 1979; Parker & Maynard-Smith, 1990; Pierce & Ollason,
1987; Goodwin, 1994; Rose, 1997).

Convertible currencies?

The accumulated evidence, however, reveals some quite serious difficulties for
the approach. First, there are problems in defining the currency whose rate of
acquisition is predicted to be maximised. Models can be devised on various
assumptions about what, in any specific case, is to be maximised, and why.
However, as with cost/benefit approaches in economics and political science, there
are difficulties in dealing with activities which have multiple, incommensurable
aims: where, in other words, costs and benefits cannot be measured in the same
units, so that there is no single currency. In bumblebees, almost all tests of OFT
involve studies of nectar collection. This is to be expected as the theory assumes
that foraging decisions are made in terms of energetic costs and benefits. This
may be more appropriate in the study of honey-bee foraging (given their
development of large honey stores). In bumblebee colonies, demands are for a
balance of nutritional goods supplied by both pollen and nectar in quantities and
proportions that are liable to change through the life cycle of the colony. Also, as
we saw in Herrera's discussion, maintaining water balance for both individual
workers and within the colony as a whole is a further constraint on foraging
behaviour.

Water stress is particularly likely to be of significance in arid habitats, where
achieving an adequate water balance, to maintain both the physiological
functioning of the individual forager and the requirements of the nest, will be a
high priority. Willmer (1986) carried out a study of *Chalicodoma sicula*, a central
place foraging but non-social bee, in Israel. She showed that these bees were able
to forage from different flowers according to the water content of their nectar at
different times of day. They restored their own water balance by absorbing water
from nectar at the end of foraging trips, but also 'topped up' the water content
of the food store left for their larvae just prior to sealing the cells in which they
deposited their eggs. There was some evidence that patch choice as well as

choice of flower species was strongly influenced by the demand for water.

At least in hot or arid habitats, obtaining appropriate amounts of water may be a critical priority governing foraging behaviour. Although water stress is less likely to be a problem for individual bumblebees foraging in temperate conditions, aspects of microclimate at the nest, humidity and density of honey stores may affect foraging behaviour for them, too. That this may at least sometimes be the case is indicated by observations reported by Ferry & Corbet (1996). Workers of *Bombus lucorum* were observed over a four-day period of unusually warm and dry weather to drink from a concrete water tank. One hundred and three visits were noted, and two marked bees visited up to 12 times a day. It seems likely that the water was being taken back to the nest either to dilute larval food supplies, or for evaporation-cooling of the nest. It could be that bumblebees use non-floral sources of water more frequently than is currently believed, but in so far as they are constrained by lack of accessible direct sources of water, appropriate choice of forage plants is likely to be influenced by the need for water balance. As with the *Chalicodoma* studied by Willmer, bumblebees may well forage suboptimally in relation to energy gains by choosing more dilute nectar for its water content (see Prŷs-Jones & Corbet, 1991).

As well as maintaining an appropriate water balance, foragers need to supply to the nest an appropriate, and probably changing, mix of pollen and nectar. The implications of this are considerable. There is much evidence from field observation and from pollen load analysis that the mix of flower species used as pollen and nectar sources are often very different. Some species have a much narrower menu of pollen sources than nectar sources, and most species seem to be 'choosey' about the plants they visit for pollen. Recent research suggests that the protein contents of the pollen of different flower species varies, possibly explaining the strong preferences shown by some bumblebee species for a restricted range of pollen sources (Fig. 115) (Edwards, 1998, 1999, 2000*a*, 2001*b*; Benton, 2000; Goulson & Darvill, 2004; Goulson *et al.*, 2004). At least some of the observed bumblebee movement (at the level of individual, colony, local population and species) at all spatial scales must be due to availability of the right type of nutritional reward, rather than simply energetic gain. The behavioural implications of the requirement to achieve a balance of nutrients have been studied for ant species in southern Arizona, USA, by Kay (2002), and also for the solitary bee *Osmia lignaria* (cited in Harder *et al.*, 2001).

For solitary bee species, requirements for balanced nutritional intakes involve compromises between economical pollen and nectar collecting, especially as these often require visits to different plant species. In social species such as the social bumblebees, balance at colony level can be achieved by varying the proportions of

FIG 115. A queen *Bombus pascuorum* combing pollen from its fur.

workers committed to pollen or nectar collecting (Brian, 1952; Free & Butler, 1959; Cartar, 1992; Plowright *et al.*, 1993). This raises difficult questions about the relationship between individual forager efficiency and colony requirements, to which we will return later. For now, the realisation that there are qualitative as well as quantitative considerations in foraging poses problems for defining the currency which foragers are supposed to be maximising according to OFT. Since water, pollen and nectar provide resources that cannot be substituted for each other, none of them can by itself serve as an overall measure of foraging success.

Without a single currency governing all foraging behaviour, mathematical cost/benefit analysis just cannot be applied. One way of addressing this problem has been to invent a more complicated currency that includes in its definition the various different costs and benefits encountered by foragers. For example, Rasheed & Harder (1997a, b) and Ydenberg *et al.* (1994) have produced models, based on OFT, of the economics of pollen collection, taking into account the mixed nutritional demands and travel requirements of central place foragers. To do this, they suggest different currencies for measuring optimality such as 'gross efficiency' in the case of pollen collection, and 'maximum overall daily delivery of resources' for central place foragers collecting more than one resource. But this is just defining the problem away: any attempt to apply such a formula would still have to deal with which of a range of different balances of nectar, water, or pollen (of which species) was going to count as 'maximal'.

Theoretical generalisations versus peculiar species

The general models derived from OFT have usually been intended to apply to a wide range of different animal groups. They have consequently paid relatively little attention to the particular characteristics of the animals used to test the models. Whatever the particular morphology and physiology, or the perceptual, cognitive and learning abilities of the groups under study, the general expectations of the theory should be met. However, these particular characteristics clearly do shape the framework of opportunities and constraints within which hypothesised optimising strategies may evolve. This is acknowledged by reflective defenders of the theory, such as Stearns & Schmid-Hempel (1987), who distinguish between slowly evolving traits that can be treated as invariant within lineages, and other traits that vary within species and evolve more rapidly. The more slowly evolving traits are best treated as a more-or-less fixed framework that sets limits on the range of foraging behaviours that any given species can evolve. So what counts as optimal foraging has to be understood in terms of the limitations imposed by the inherited character of the group of animals under study. OFT can only be made appropriate by building into its models of foraging behaviour detailed knowledge of the inherited biological traits and ecological relationships of the organisms concerned. As Harder *et al.* remark: '…the details of pollinator behaviour (and the associated pollination) are often context dependent' (2001). 'Optimal' thus means 'optimal under boundary conditions', which can be stated and, in principle, independently tested.

This approach to optimality modelling allows it to claim explanatory relevance, whilst strictly limiting its scope. However, it could then be argued that the need to develop a new model for each group of foragers implicitly acknowledges that the specific patterns of relatively fixed inherited traits and ecological conditions of life have a greater role in explaining foraging behaviour at the level of particular species or local populations than the abstract generalisations of the theory. Unfortunately for OFT, it is the hoped-for explanatory power of these generalisations that is the main attraction of the approach for many of its advocates.

Foraging strategies: nature or nurture?

A further issue for the application of OFT to bumblebee foraging has to do with the evidence we now have about the complex learning and information processing abilities of bees and the adaptability shown by many species in the face of environmental stress (Laverty, 1994; Menzel, 2001 and Chapter 3). Since the rationale for the approach depends on assumptions about the outcome of natural selection for inherited behaviour patterns, its predictions apply to behaviour that is under strong genetic control. Applying the theory to bumblebees requires the case to be made that the range of learned adaptive strategies adopted by them is in some way governed by inherited learning dispositions or behavioural biases. It seems likely that some such inherited dispositions do shape bumblebee foraging, but there is little hard evidence, and even where there are inherited elements, specific foraging behaviours still have to be learned (see Thomson & Chittka, 2001). The considerable plasticity of bumblebee foraging behaviour, both at individual and colony level, suggests that learning and cognition play a large part in shaping it.

Fitness and foraging

Perhaps still more challenging for OFT is the problem of modelling the interaction between foraging and other activities that are important to the bees' chances of surviving and reproducing. The theoretical justification of the approach depends on assuming that there is a direct functional relationship between optimal foraging by the workers and 'fitness', defined in terms of reproductive success. But there are other conditions for reproductive success, and these may well set limits on the foraging strategies that can be adopted. As we have seen, at least one plausible interpretation of apparently suboptimal long-distance foraging in bumblebees is that foraging strategies are constrained by availability of suitable nest sites, and/or by avoidance of parasitism and predation. Predation-avoidance strategies may also be relevant to other aspects of bumblebee foraging. For example, workers of *Bombus sylvarum* are observed to forage predominantly on flowers overtopped by long grasses and other vegetation (Benton, 2000), often on scrub margins, rather than on open, short-grass patches even when these are available (Fig. 116). This may make them less susceptible to predation by birds, or reduce competition with other foragers. In principle, such survival- and reproduction-related constraints as these might be built into more complicated models of foraging behaviour, but the problems of quantifying the potential trade-offs between these different ecological and behavioural contributions to fitness seem formidable. Mangel & Clark (1986) proposed such a model of what they termed 'unified foraging theory', calculating trade-offs between various activities in terms of a common currency of fitness defined as reproductive success. However, the complexity of the calculations involved (admittedly beyond then-available computer power!) would seem hard to reconcile with the mental abilities of bumblebee foragers (notwithstanding the remarkable perceptual and learning abilities that the bees do have, as we saw in Chapter 3).

FIG 116. A *Bombus sylvarum* forager weaving its way through rank vegetation. A possible way of avoiding predation?

Individuals and the collective worker

The problem of the relationship between optimal foraging and overall fitness is particularly acute in the case of social foragers like bumblebees. Since the flights of workers are devoted to foraging, without the distraction of ovipositing or mate location, it is thought by some researchers that the optimality approach would be more appropriate (Goulson, 2000b): that is, the lack of distraction to meet other exigencies should make for a direct relationship between foraging success and fitness. However, in the social bumblebees, it is the reproductive success of the *queen* (and her mate from the previous season) and *not* that of the individual, usually infertile, worker that is at stake. So, for these species, fitness has to be understood in terms of the reproductive success of the colony as a whole. Since individual workers may make different sorts of contribution to this, any adequate model would have to take into account the overall division of labour within the colony.

As we have seen, Heinrich short-circuited this difficulty by drawing on the economic analogy and appealing to Adam Smith's 'invisible hand': optimising the foraging of individual workers automatically translates into success for the colony as a whole (1979). But this assumption is unwarranted. The 'invisible hand' of the market is supposed to work by sensitively communicating the demands of consumers to producers, thus ensuring efficient modification of producer activity to what consumers require. As an account of the way actual markets work, this is very questionable, but it is doubly implausible as an account of the relationship between the foraging of individual bumblebee workers and the reproductive success of the colony. Unlike participants in market exchanges, they are not connected to each other as producer and consumer, but each gathers from an independent source, and delivers most of its gains to a collective 'pot'. If suitable balances of nutrients and water are to be maintained through the lifetime of the nest, through variations in the environmental availability of different resources, and shifting patterns of demand, there must be some form of regulation of the division of labour at the colony level. The unit of analysis for foraging success in social bumblebees is therefore the whole cohort of foragers working for a colony.

Any notion of 'optimality' would have to be understood in terms of quantitative balances between qualitatively appropriate resources (pollens, nectar and water), gathered by the *collectivity* of foragers in relation to the complex of nutritional and thermoregulatory needs of the various categories of nest members, and the various costs of the foraging activity. At colony level, this necessarily involves both a division of labour and transfers among the nest members, including the immature stages (elsewhere Heinrich implicitly accepts this, likening bee colonies to 'communistic polities' (1979)). As we have seen, bumblebee foragers are often specialised to pollen or nectar collection, or to both for significant periods, but show high levels of flexibility in response to short-term fluctuations in demand or in environmental conditions.

The energy budget must balance

Even if a method could be devised for measuring optimal foraging at colony level, the other difficulties would remain. Foraging efficiency is only one prerequisite of colony success. The timing of nest establishment (Müller & Schmid-Hempel, 1992a), the siting of the nest, defence against predators and parasites, and maintenance of social order in the nest are other variables that affect the chances of a colony producing males and daughter queens. The interactions between these various conditions of colony success, and their relative importance, probably vary greatly from one species to another, and even among colonies of the same species. Under some ecological and climatic conditions abundant energy supplies might be critical, but in others availability of suitable nest sites might be a more severe limitation.

Many of these problems have been addressed in the research inspired by OFT, and the approach is now usually adopted in a more cautious and provisional way, often with the admission that its general principles need to be modified to take account of the biological and ecological peculiarities of the species under study.

Whatever its analytical weaknesses, the theory has provided researchers with a coherent basis for generating quantified hypotheses, the testing of which has revealed a great deal of previously unsuspected complexity in the behaviour of foragers, and bumblebees in particular. Independently of whether the main assumptions of OFT are accepted, the relevance of a quantitative analysis of the energy-flows into and through colonies could hardly be denied. Whether or not foraging is deemed 'optimal', the overall foraging success of the collectivity of workers in any nest must at least enable its energy budget to balance through the lifespan of the colony. Unless this minimum condition is met, the reproductive cycle of the colony will not be completed.

CHAPTER 7

Bumblebees and Flowers II: Flower Arrangements

O NE OF THE key conclusions of our discussion in the previous chapter was the need to see the foraging behaviour of bumblebees in the context of their biological (morphological, physiological, perceptual, cognitive, etc.) traits and ecological relationships, with appropriate sensitivity to variation between species. As Prŷs-Jones & Corbet (1991) argue:

'... *mathematical treatment of biological systems requires simplifying assumptions, and the selection of assumptions that are at once realistic and productive requires, perhaps, a deeper understanding of bumblebee biology than is yet available. We should not underestimate the extent to which major theoretical advances will depend on patient observational studies of natural history*'.

Central to the natural history of bumblebee foraging is, of course, their relationship to the flowers on whose rewards they depend. So we now turn to some of the contributions that have come primarily from botanical researchers. There are two main themes here. One has to do with the way floral traits have evolved to attract animal visitors, and then to regulate their behaviour to increase the chances of pollination. The second theme is the way pollinator-assisted flows of genes through plant populations affect their genetic structure and reproductive success. This has obvious implications for commercial growers as well as conservationists.

As we saw earlier, flowering plants have many different reproductive strategies, so it would be wrong to think that most species are entirely dependent on pollinating visits from just one forager species, or even on flower visitors more generally. However, some plants are thus dependent, and it is widely held that animal-mediated cross-pollination is important to the reproductive success, and viability of populations of very many plant species. According to Steffan-Dewenter & Tscharntke (2002), 80 per cent of European flowering plant species are insect pollinated. The benefits to plants of insect pollinators vary from species to species. Some rely on insect visitors to move pollen from anthers to stigma in the same flower (for example, oil-seed rape) whilst others, if self-incompatible, rely on insects to transfer pollen from the flowers of one plant to another. In still other cases, cross-pollination may increase seed-set or the size of fruit, or improve the genetic constitution of the progeny (Corbet *et al.*, 1991; Corbet, 1996). Though forager species often show preferences in their foraging behaviour, most visit a wide range of flowers. According to Jordano (1987) plant species tend to be pollinated by a rather smaller spectrum of visitors. So, while there is strong evidence of mutual adaptation, with net benefits to both parties in the pollinator/plant relationship, it is generally believed that competition among plants for the attention of pollinators has been a more powerful source of selective pressures than competition among pollinators for floral rewards. However, this may not be universally true. For example, in their study of two English meadows, Dicks *et al.* (2002) found that the plant species were more generalist than their insect visitors, although this study did not measure the effectiveness of the different insect visitors as pollinators. The issue of specialism versus generalism as pollinator strategies remains controversial, and we will return to the topic later in this chapter.

Among the most obvious adaptations shown by the plants are the flowers themselves, visually striking, often brightly coloured and/or scented, sometimes with distinctive, complex shapes, and offering varying rewards to foraging visitors. The visitors cover a wide spectrum including members of several insect orders, most notably Hymenoptera, Lepidoptera, Diptera and Coleoptera, through to vertebrates such as some mammals (bats) and birds (most famously hummingbirds, but other species, such as sunbirds, honeyeaters and several European warblers, commonly take nectar from floral sources).

POLLINATION SYNDROMES

The concept of pollination syndromes is an attempt to link together typical spectra of flower visitors with the different types of floral adaptation exhibited by plants. Implicit in it is the assumption that mutualistic ties will have evolved, through which plants with a particular array of floral traits will have developed special relationships with a subgroup of pollinators that have complementary behavioural and structural features.

Animal-pollinated flowers tend to share a range of traits that have definite functions in relation to attracting and regulating the behaviour of pollinators. These functions can be assigned to a variety of different structures, depending on the evolutionary history of the flower types. Typically, however, the key function of 'advertising' is played by large, brightly coloured petals, contrasting with their backgrounds. Sometimes dense clusters of smaller flowers on the same plant (inflorescences) have the same function, and in pollination ecology the floral unit is generally taken to be the blossom, including inflorescences as well as single flowers. Scents also play an important role in advertising.

But the advertising would not attract pollinators consistently unless it was associated with (at least the promise of) some biologically important reward. In some bee/flower associations, notably the relationships between some orchid and bee species, the flower deceives the visitor by posing as a potential mate. In most pollination systems, however, the reward is food: usually nectar and/or pollen. These food sources have different nutritional contents, and also play different roles in the sexual reproduction of the plant. Nectar is produced as a reward, or 'primary attractant', for foragers, as a means of securing their pollination services. Nectar is secreted and stored, usually within the flower, in various locations such that forager behaviour in reaching it is likely to contribute to pollination. It is the main calorific reward offered by flowers (hence the focus on it in energetics-based optimum foraging studies), and it is high in sugars, mainly glucose, fructose and sucrose. It also contains nitrogen and other essential chemicals in smaller quantities. For bumblebees it is their main external source of water. Pollen, on the other hand, contains the male gametes, and thus is essential to the sexual reproduction of the plants that produce it. Its role as reward for pollinating flower visitors is presumably a secondary adaptation. In part the nutritional content of the pollen, which includes carbohydrates, proteins, lipids, enzymes and minerals, is determined by its role in penetrating the stigma to reach the ovules in the female part of the flower.

Pollen is formed in the anthers, which, together with the filaments that carry them, form the male part of the flower, and it is released by a variety of mechanisms. Fertilisation takes place when pollen is transferred to a receptive stigma, and the male gamete travels within the style to reach the ovules, usually located at the base of the carpels. Successful pollination leads to the formation of fruit and seed-set. In some plant species separate male and female flowers are carried on the same or different plants. In others (more commonly), flowers carry both male and female parts (hermaphrodite flowers). However, the sequence of events during the flowering period varies. In some species the anthers mature first (protandry), and the flower is functionally male. Later, the stigma becomes receptive, and the flower is effectively female. In other species the sequence may be reversed. These ways of sequencing events through time, especially when co-ordinated with visual or scent cues, and the provision of rewards to pollinators, are held to be adaptations likely to increase the chances of cross-pollination. The fine-tuning of pollinator behaviour once foragers have been attracted is achieved by such devices as these, along with guide-marks on the corolla, scent signals, and floral structures themselves. It is these which have been the prime focus in distinguishing the various pollination syndromes, and the concept is based on an assumed coevolutionary past through which traits of both blossoms and pollinators have become adapted to one another (Fig. 117).

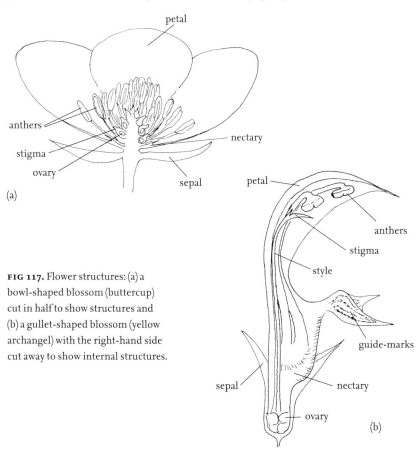

FIG 117. Flower structures: (a) a bowl-shaped blossom (buttercup) cut in half to show structures and (b) a gullet-shaped blossom (yellow archangel) with the right-hand side cut away to show internal structures.

BLOSSOM TYPES

There are several classifications of blossoms in relation to pollination strategies, but perhaps the most influential is that presented in Faegri & van der Pijl (1979). Their classification is not based on how closely related the plant species are, but rather on the functional organisation of the blossom in relation to expected pollinator behaviour. Of the main types they distinguish, six are of interest to us.

A. Dish- to bowl-shaped blossoms (Figs 118–123). These are usually radially symmetrical, with the sexual parts of the flower towards the centre, and with the outer parts, serving as 'advertisements', either flat or shallowly upcurved. As single flowers, this group includes buttercups, roses and brambles. Compound inflorescences include 'daisy'-type members of the Asteraceae. Blossoms in this group are held to be relatively unspecialised, their floral rewards being relatively easy to access for a wide spectrum of foragers. Pollination is effected by foragers scrambling around the blossom and brushing against the sexual parts. This is referred to as 'mess-and-soil' pollination. Higher temperatures in the blossom may also be attractive to insect pollinators.

FIG 118. Mallow, a dish-shaped blossom.

FIG 119. Cherry blossom, a dish-shaped blossom.

FIG 120. A hover fly feeding from buttercup, a bowl-shaped blossom.

FIG 121. *Bombus sylvestris* foraging from a buttercup.

FIG 122. A compound dish-shaped blossom provides food and a place for 'courtship' for two hover flies.

FIG 123. *Bombus lucorum* foraging from a compound dish-shaped blossom (Asteraceae).

B. Bell- and funnel-shaped blossoms (Figs 124–126). Like type A blossoms, these are radially symmetrical, the two subtypes being distinguished by their outline when viewed from the side – convex in bells, straight or concave in funnels. They have a greater surface exposed to view from the side than do the members of type A, and their sexual parts and nectaries are concealed. The stigma and anthers are usually carried on elongated styles and filaments, often grouped together as a column within the blossom. Some have outer rims, which may serve an advertising function, or form a landing platform for visitors. This group of blossoms requires the forager to enter if it is to access the rewards, though, in some cases that are intermediate between this and type F, larger visitors may use the platform to probe the blossom with head and proboscis. In some cases the forager clambers down the central column formed by the sexual parts, collecting or depositing pollen from its ventral surface as it does so. In other cases it may crawl down the inner surface of the bell or funnel itself, collecting or depositing pollen from its back. Examples of bells include bellflowers, and of funnels, bindweeds. These blossoms also provide shelter for pollinating insects during inclement weather.

FIG 124. *Convolvulus*, a funnel-shaped blossom.

FIG 125. Clustered bellflower, bell-shaped blossoms.

FIG 126. *Bombus hortorum* collecting pollen from bluebell.

C. Brush-type blossoms (Figs 127 & 128). In this group the external surface of the blossom is mainly made up of the sexual parts. The perianth (corolla plus calyx) is much reduced, or split into fine segments. The most familiar examples used by bumblebees are the sallows, but the group also includes myrtles, rampions and, within the Lamiaceae, mints and thymes.

FIG 127. A queen *Bombus jonellus* foraging from a sallow catkin, a brush-type blossom.

FIG 128. A hover fly feeding from ivy, a brush-type blossom.

D. Gullet-type blossoms (Figs 129–132). These are generally bilaterally symmetrical (zygomorphic). The sexual parts are not central, but placed in the upper side of the blossom. The forager enters the blossom from the front, commonly using the lower part of the perianth as a platform, and probes for nectar towards the base of the blossom. As it does so, it brushes against the anthers and/or stigma with its back. Iris flowers are composed of three connected gullets, and there are compound inflorescences of the gullet type, but most are single flowers. Common examples used by bumblebees in Britain include many members of the plant families Lamiaceae and Scrophulariaceae, such as sages, deadnettles, woundworts, black horehound, foxglove and snapdragon.

FIG 129. Yellow archangel, a gullet-type blossom. Note the sexual parts of the flower in the 'hood'.

FIG 130. A worker *Bombus pascuorum* foraging from sage, a gullet-type blossom. Note the position of the sexual parts in the flower below the one being visited by the bee.

FIG 131. A *Bombus hortorum* male reverses out of a foxglove flower, a gullet-type blossom.

FIG 132. A male *Bombus ruderatus* foraging from marsh woundwort. Note the spent anthers in the flower to its left.

E. Flag-type blossoms (Figs 133–137). Like the gullets, these are also bilaterally symmetrical, but the carpels and stamens are in the lower part of the blossom, the upper part of the perianth functioning as advertisement. The pollinator approaches from the front, using the lower part of the blossom (often called the keel) as a platform and probing into the flower for nectar. In many examples it is the weight of the forager that mechanically releases the sexual parts and they brush against its ventral surface (or, in a few cases, curve over to deposit pollen on its back). In some cases, such as broom, no nectar is produced, and foragers visit for pollen only, though they often probe the base of the blossom with their probosces as if seeking nectar (own obs.). There are some examples among the species of *Pelargonium* and *Corydalis*, but the most widespread flag-type blossoms are members of the Fabaceae (pea family). The blossoms are generally single flowers, but may be carried in dense inflorescences (for example, tufted vetch).

FIG 133. Bird's-foot trefoil, a flag-type blossom popular with bumblebees.

FIG 134. A worker *Bombus lapidarius* collecting pollen from spiny restharrow, a flag-type blossom.

FIG 135. A flower bee triggering the pollination mechanism of a vetchling flower. Note the pollen grains on the exposed stigma (Mt. Parnassos, Greece).

FIG 136. A queen *Bombus terrestris* collecting pollen from broom. Note the positions of the sexual parts of the flower.

FIG 137. A queen *Bombus sylvarum* foraging from red clover, a compound of flag-type blossoms.

F. Tube-type blossoms (Figs 138–141). In this group, nectar is stored in structures (usually the corolla tube) that are too narrow for many foragers to enter. The whole flower may be a tube (as in comfreys and many garden shrubs such as *Hebe*, *Buddleia* and heathers) but more usually tubes form part of a blossom of one of the other kinds. Bell-type blossoms with tubes include alkanet and bugloss and more complex combinations are found in monk's-hood, *Delphinium* and *Aquilegia*. Many of the compound inflorescences of the Asteraceae (thistles and knapweeds), Apiaceae (eryngos and sea holly) and Dipsacaceae (teasels and scabious) are composed of aggregations of tubes on a single head, or capitulum. Tubes are believed to enable the plant to offer greater rewards to foragers, allowing a greater volume of nectar to be stored, and limiting competition from shorter-tongued foragers. The greater specialisation and learning-time involved in accessing the nectar may in this way be compensated by greater reward to the forager, whilst encouraging constancy, and hence greater likelihood of cross-pollination from previously visited flowers of the same species.

Although the above list of blossom types is not a linear spectrum, there is a broad contrast between the earlier and later groups in the list, in terms of morphological complexity, irregularity of shape, the 'depth' of the blossom, and

FIG 138. A male *Bombus pascuorum* foraging from verbena, a compound inflorescence made up of tube-type blossoms.

FIG 139. A hummingbird hawk moth using its very long proboscis to take nectar from tube-type florets.

FIG 140. A worker *Bombus ruderarius* foraging from viper's bugloss, a combination of bell and tube.

FIG 141. A male *Bombus pratorum* foraging from alkanet, a combination of dish and tube.

associated degrees of difficulty in accessing the rewards on offer to foragers. Generally, dish- to bowl-shaped blossoms are accessible by a wide spectrum of visitors, implying relatively generalised patterns of interaction. By contrast, some complex flowers, such as monk's-hood, a combination of gullet and tubes, require considerable learning ability and manoeuvrability on the part of the forager. Heinrich (1976) observed the difficulties experienced by bumblebees that had not encountered this flower before, compared with the ease developed by specialists. The more specialised forager types, such as birds and bees, are thus associated with the more complex and specialised floral morphologies, clustered towards the end of the list (especially, in the case of bumblebees, with gullets, flags and tubes). It is here that we find the strongest suggestion of evolved mutualisms between flowers and their pollinators.

SOME REASONS FOR CAUTION

Users of the idea of pollination syndromes have generally signalled the need for caution in its application, and some recent studies suggest more deep-rooted difficulties with the concept. First, not all blossoms fit clearly or unambiguously into the classification. Some dish-types (such as *Hibiscus* and *Lavatera*) have the sexual parts on projecting central columns, and require different approaches from foragers. Others, such as *Hypericum vouytcheuse*, are visited for pollen only by *Bombus lucorum* and *B. pascuorum* workers using buzz-foraging. In Britain, only a relatively small number of bee species, including bumblebees, are known to use this method of foraging. However, a significant portion of the native Australian flora depend on buzz-pollination (sonication), and it is reported that introduced honey bees represent a threat to such plants, as they effectively displace native pollinators, but do not trigger the pollination mechanism as they do not buzz (Buchmann & Nabhan, 1996). Anthers that depend on buzz-pollination to release their pollen can therefore be seen as a specialised adaptation that limits the spectrum of pollen collecting visitors. Such specialised traits can thus be found in blossoms whose overall morphology is associated with the more generalised type-A syndrome. But the situation is still more complicated! In the buzz-pollinated *Hypericum* just described, pollination is also effected by pollen beetles, *Meligethes aeneus*, which access the pollen by chewing the anthers with their mandibles (Fig. 142). As Mayfield *et al.* (2001) point out, flowers may possess some features adapting them to attract one group of pollinators, while other features are adapted to attract other types (Fig. 143).

A further complication has to do with the taxonomic level at which the concept

FIG 142. A worker *Bombus lucorum* buzz-forages pollen from *Hypericum*, while pollen beetles bite their way into the anthers of the same flower.

FIG 143. Honeysuckle, a blossom that attracts moths by night and long-tongued bumblebees by day.

of pollination syndromes is supposed to apply. The concept involves linking general types of floral morphologies, and other associated traits, such as colour and scent, with typical spectra of pollinating visitors. At a very general level, the blossoms of insect-pollinated plants (entomophilous blossoms) are distinguished from those that are pollinated by bats, or birds, as so many distinct syndromes. Within the class of entomophilous blossoms, subgroups are distinguished in terms of the typical insect group that visits and pollinates them. So there are syndromes for fly-pollinated blossoms (myophily), beetle-pollinated (cantharophily), butterfly- and moth-pollinated (psychophily and phalaenophily), and bee-pollinated (melittophily). However, while syndromes are described in terms of these broad taxonomic groupings of visitors, it is clear that within each group of flower visitors there may be a great range of different foraging adaptations. So, for example, some flies are capable of accessing complex, melittophilous blossoms (and apparently become their main pollinators when bees are absent – Hagerup, 1951, cited in Faegri & van der Pijl, 1979), while many solitary bees are unspecialised and fly-like in their foraging patterns. The labelling of syndromes thus refers to what are held to be 'typical' examples of the insect visitor group, and should not be applied unreflectively to all members (see Figs 144–148).

FIG 144. The hairy-footed flower bee has a long tongue and is able to access many of the blossom types also visited by bumblebees.

FIG 145. A hover fly can collect pollen from the exposed anthers of deep flowers such as willowherb.

FIG 146. The beetle *Strangalia maculata* is able to access complex flowers such as orchids.

FIG 147. The bee fly *Bombylius major* can access a deep gullet-type blossom.

FIG 148. The broad-bordered bee hawk moth has a very long tongue but can feed from shallow, dish-shaped blossoms.

Yet another reason for caution in the use of the idea of syndromes is that many blossom types are visited by a wide spectrum of visitors from different insect orders, calling into question the assumption of specialised co-evolved associations. However, the observation of a large spectrum of visitors to a particular plant species does not necessarily imply that the reproductive strategy of the plant is a generalist one. To test this it is necessary to discover the relative *effectiveness* of the various visitors as pollinators. For example, nectar robbing (Fig. 149) is supposed to cheat the plant of the pollination services of the forager (though this assumption is open to question – see Morris, 1996, and Stout *et al.*, 2000).

As we saw, Herrera observed 80 species of visitors to *Lavandula latifolia*, but a mere 34 accounted for 88–96 per cent of visits. Visits that achieve cross-pollination are likely to be a still smaller subset, suggesting that flower visitors may vary considerably in terms of their pollination effectiveness. If this is right, then it is reasonable to suppose that selective pressures would lead plants to adapt to attracting and securing the services of their most effective pollinator, and it is here that we should expect the strongest mutualisms. From the point of view of plant reproduction, the rest of the spectrum of visitors are incidental 'free-riders'.

FIG 149. Another way to rob: a queen *Bombus sylvarum* sidesteps the pollination mechanism of a flag-type blossom.

EFFECTIVE POLLINATORS?

The expectation that flowers will be adapted to attract pollinating visits from the most effective pollinator of the plant concerned, but exclude or discourage others, was formulated by Stebbins (1970) as the 'most effective pollinator principle', but, as with optimal foraging theory, the results of empirical testing are mixed. Mayfield *et al.* (2001) conducted an experiment with *Ipomopsis*, a plant whose complex flowers are 'quintessentially' of the hummingbird syndrome. The effectiveness of a pollinator has two aspects: a qualitative and a quantitative one. The qualitative aspect is the reproductively effective transfer of pollen per visit. The quantitative one is frequency of visits. It is assumed that natural selection will tend to bring about a strong association between the two: that the plant would become adapted to increase the frequency of visits from a pollinator which gave the best pollination service per visit. However, the results of the experiment did not confirm this. Although hummingbirds accounted for most visits, supposedly out-of-syndrome bumblebees also visited the flowers, but much less frequently. However, the bumblebees were much more successful pollinators per visit. On average, each bumblebee visit yielded four times the seed production of single hummingbird visits.

This might be explained in several ways. One is that while selective pressures may operate to restrict the range of flower visitors to the most effective pollinators, there could be constraints in floral design that still allow opportunist foragers to gain access (the case of honeysuckle, a moth-syndrome flower often visited by *Bombus hortorum* and other bumblebees, may be similar). Another possible explanation is that there are selective pressures operating against too great a narrowing of the pollinator spectrum, especially if the most effective pollinator fluctuates in availability. Earlier discussions have tended to assume that a plant's adaptation to attracting one group of pollinators will reduce its ability to attract others. But this may not be true. If attracting a less effective pollinator does not reduce its ability to continue attracting a more effective one, a plant may adapt to both (Aigner, 2001).

To gain further insights into the complex interactions between plants and pollinating insects, the pressures making for either mutual specialisation or more generalist foraging and pollination strategies, it is necessary to study the interactions in the wider context of the ecological communities to which the animals and plants concerned belong. Such studies are being carried out, and they have important implications not only for bumblebee conservation, but also for understanding the genetic structure and patterns of flow of genetic information through the communities of plants that they pollinate. We will return to discussion of some of these studies towards the end of this chapter.

A BUMBLEBEE SYNDROME?
HOW DO BUMBLEBEES FIT IN?

First, however, we need to consider, in relation to bumblebees, one of the key implications of the idea of syndromes: that there is a fit between the morpho-logical and other features of the flowers commonly visited by bumblebees and the evolved traits of the insects themselves. A distinct 'bumblebee syndrome' is sometimes alleged: robust flowers, often with a landing platform, deep corolla, complex morphology and typically pink, purple or yellow in colour. The advantage of specialisation for the plant is that if it can attract repeated visits of the right sort from the same species of bee, then its chances of cross-pollination are enhanced: that is, there is a greater chance that the plant whose flowers were visited previously and the one to be visited next will be of the same species. So specialisations that encourage strong preferences at the level of bee species, as well as for flower constancy on the part of individual workers, by, for example, providing high nectar rewards for learning specialised handling skills, are likely to enhance the reproductive success of the plant. If these specialisations simultaneously discourage or exclude visits from non-pollinating visitors, then so much the better for the reproductive strategy of the plant.

Tongue length

Implicit in the idea of a syndrome, therefore, is a range of assumptions about the capacities, constraints and dispositions of the foragers. Morphological fit has received most attention, especially the key variable of tongue length in relation to corolla-depth. Compared with many other flower visitors (though not, for example, butterflies and moths), bumblebees are long-tongued. This provides opportunities to access rewards from blossoms not available to other foragers. However, they differ significantly among themselves in their tongue length, partly in relation to size, and partly by species, which also plays a part in explaining observed differences in floral preferences among the various bumblebee species. Tongue length provides the basis for a putative subdivision between long-tongued/deep corolla and short-tongued/shallow blossom associations within the bumblebee syndrome. As we will see in Chapter 10, this distinction is often considered important in explaining the dramatic decline in several of the long-tongued species in recent decades.

But some caution is needed. Tongue length varies at the level of species, but also, within each species, among individuals, depending on their overall body size (Fig. 150). Even in the pollen storers (see Chapter 2) the size differences among workers are very great. For example, for *B. terrestris*, eightfold weight differences have been reported among the workers in a single nest, with almost a threefold difference in thorax width (Goulson, 2003). If we keep in mind the contribution to food gathering of the whole cohort of foragers, the range of actual, as distinct from relative, tongue lengths represented, is considerable. On this view, the constraint imposed by species-specific differences in relative tongue length may not be as limiting as is sometimes claimed. If we add to this the remarkable ingenuity shown by bumblebee foragers in accessing 'difficult' floral structures, by nectar robbing, by thrusting head and thorax as well as tongue into the corolla, and other inventions, then the constraint seems still less decisive (Figs 151 & 152). The ability of some species to access exotic garden flowers, such as *Fuchsia* and *Tricyrtis* (Figs 153 & 154), which have evolved among radically different pollinator communities, is also significant.

There is experimental evidence to show that bumblebees may forage less efficiently on flowers whose depth does not match their tongue length, but even here it seems that it is the short-tongued species that are most affected when they

FIG 150. The large queen of *Bombus terrestris*, a short-tongued bumblebee, can access the deep flowers of red clover.

FIG 151. A worker *Bombus pascuorum* forages from comfrey by pushing her head and thorax into the narrow bell.

FIG 152. A queen *Bombus pascuorum* forages from a shallow, bowl-shaped blossom, despite the length of its tongue.

FIG 153. This *Bombus pascuorum* worker has learned how to access the nectar of an exotic *Tricyrtis* flower from the outside.

FIG 154. A *Bombus pascuorum* worker foraging from *Fuchsia*.

attempt to access deep flowers (Harder, 1983). The efficiency costs of long-tongued bees foraging from shallower flowers rise less steeply, suggesting that there may be more complex relationships between the longer-tongued species and the menu of flowers they visit than simply matching tongue and corolla lengths. It seems likely that the nutritional value of the pollen collected from these species is an important factor (Goulson, unpublished).

Weight, size and temperature

Other features of bumblebee morphology may be either directly or indirectly relevant to the fit between foraging patterns and blossom types. The dense coat of bumblebees, for example, while playing a part in temperature regulation, also is crucial in collecting pollen, probably enhancing the bumblebee's pollination effectiveness as well as being a means of gathering a key source of nutrients. It is arguable that worker bumblebees' combing of pollen from their body hairs onto the corbiculae counteracts pollination effectiveness, but in fact bees tend to visit a series of flowers between combing episodes. The relatively large size of bumblebees may also affect the range of accessible blossoms in either direction, because of the need for robust structural support to carry the bee's weight, the relative dimensions of the corolla-tube, or the strength required to open some blossoms (most notably snapdragon, which tends to be visited only by queens or large workers) (Fig. 155). Indirectly, size affects physiological opportunities and constraints, because, other things being equal, larger size involves higher energetic demands for flight and other activities, and also affects temperature regulation.

Bumblebees cannot fly if their thoracic muscles are too cold, and they have a remarkable capacity to maintain body temperatures above environmental values. When in flight, heat energy is released from the flight muscles, so maintaining the temperature of the thorax at a sufficiently high level (30–40°C). They are also able to generate heat mechanically by contracting their flight muscles when at rest. This is important for maintaining a high nest temperature, and for commencing activity when ambient temperature is low. Heat loss is also significantly reduced by the dense pile of hair on the bumblebee body and legs. In addition bumblebees have been held to possess a remarkable capacity to generate heat by using an energy-releasing biochemical process known as substrate cycling (Newsholm *et al.*, 1972; Prŷs-Jones, 1986; Prŷs-Jones & Corbet, 1991). However, this is strongly contested by Heinrich (1993) who argues that heat generation in bumblebees is always associated with muscular contraction. Whatever the mechanisms, there is no dispute as to the remarkable capacity bumblebees possess to maintain body temperatures well above ambient levels, and to use heat energy from their bodies to maintain similarly high nest temperatures, irrespective of the physiological

FIG 155. A heavy queen bumblebee gets extra support by using a conveniently placed leaf as a platform.

mechanisms underlying it. In view of these features, bumblebees are regarded as adapted to cool climates (though there are a few tropical species). Whilst (as Herrera (1990) noted) there is a risk of overheating in hot weather, bumblebees have a great advantage over other insect pollinators in being able to forage at low ambient temperatures, and so forage effectively early and late in the day, and during inclement weather, when other foragers may not. However, this has to be set against the increased energetic costs incurred in temperature maintenance.

Corbet *et al.* (1995) distinguish three main morphological and physiological determinants of bumblebee foraging patterns: the energy costs of foraging, minimum temperature threshold for activity, and tongue length. Though bumblebees as a group may be distinctive with respect to these features, it is also clear that there is considerable variation between species. The three variables can thus be used as a template to define a 'competition box', which can be used to compare the variations among bumblebees in foraging behaviour, detect the influence of other determinants of foraging activity or assess the likely effects on competitor species of planned introductions of new species to a specific habitat. The idea could also be adapted as a contribution to explaining the radical declines of some species both in Britain and across lowland Europe (see Chapter 10).

Bumblebee psychology

These physiological and structural adaptations could not have evolved independently of the psychological abilities and dispositions of the bumblebees: their sensory-motor, cognitive and learning abilities. Both OFT and the idea of pollination syndromes assume that pollinators have complex navigational, decision-making, sensory-motor, learning and memorising abilities. OFT tends to generalise about these across the range of foragers, whereas the idea of pollination syndromes tends to point in the opposite direction: to varying degrees of specialisation and mutualism between pollinators and plants. As we saw in Chapter 3, current research suggests that both honey bees and bumblebees have complex memory-processing abilities, involving both short- and long-term elements, and ability to retrieve memories over long timescales when required. There is evidence that flower constancy in bees may be favoured not by limited memory capacity, but rather by problems of memory processing. Bees have been shown to have extraordinary navigational abilities, comprising integrated learning and memorising of particular routes using landmarks and both visual and scent cues, as well as developing internal general 'maps' of landscapes around the nest. Increasing evidence is emerging of the importance of the use of scent marks both to identify previously visited flowers, and to communicate information among the foragers (see Chapter 3).

SPECIALISTS AND GENERALISTS

Most field studies of foraging behaviour and pollination ecology indicate that very close mutual associations between individual plant and pollinator species are quite rare. Animal-pollinated plants and their pollinators both tend to interact with a more-or-less wide spectrum of partners. In my local Essex study, for example, I recorded visits to over 40 plant taxa by workers of each of three common bumblebee species (*Bombus lucorum*, *B. pratorum* and *B. pascuorum*), and in each case different foraging patterns exhibited by queens and males added to the list. Even though the spectrum of flower visitors in this study was limited to the locally occurring bumblebees, generalisation on the part of the plants was also evident, with six plant species each recorded as receiving visits from seven or more bumblebee species (red clover ten species, bird's-foot trefoil nine, knapweed nine, black horehound eight, white deadnettle seven and bramble seven (Benton, 2000)). These recorded visits include all castes, but still almost certainly understate the full spectrum of bumblebee visits to these plants at the local level, let alone wider geographical scales.

A national survey of forage plants used by bumblebees was co-ordinated by Fussell & Corbet, using amateur volunteers (Fussell & Corbet, 1992c, 1993). Though the bees were grouped according to colour pattern rather than species, sex and caste, the results showed that each bee type visited a very wide spectrum of flowers (and all visits totalled more than 150 plant taxa). At the same time, the numbers of recorded visits showed quite strong associations, with some flowers attracting very large numbers of visits from all bumblebee types (rhododendron, bramble, white deadnettle, white and red clovers, thistles, knapweed, *Cotoneaster* and lavender). Visitors to other flowers were strongly skewed to some bumblebee types, as against others. Dandelion, hogweed and rosebay willowherb, among others, were frequently visited by some species but rarely, or never, by 'three-banded white-tails' (presumably mostly *B. hortorum*). In general *B. hortorum* was recorded less often than the others (though, as the authors point out, this may have been an artefact of the recording criteria), but it showed a relatively strong preference for deep flowers such as red clover, foxglove, monk's-hood and *Delphinium*. These observations and those by Williams (1989), Benton (2000), Bäckman & Tiainen (2002) and others suggest a complex pattern of broad-spectrum foraging, but with distinguishable, if overlapping, preferences linking groups of foragers with sets of plant taxa. The idea of pollination syndromes, as proposed by Faegri & Pijl and others, implies that each blossom type should attract a restricted spectrum of insect visitors. However, many attempts to use data from studies of plant-visitor systems to identify pollination syndromes have tended to find only limited evidence for this (Herrera, 1988; McCall & Primack, 1992; Dicks *et al.*, 2002).

The problem for the concept of pollination syndromes is the apparent conflict between the expectation of strong mutualistic interdependencies between coevolved plant and pollinator pairs on the one hand (Janzen, 1980) and, on the other, evidence that actual pollination systems involve mainly quite generalised interactions. In their wide-ranging contribution to the debate, Waser *et al.* (1996) reviewed several ecological studies of pollination systems, reported on an experimental test of pollinator colour preferences, and provided models of their own which imply that across a wide range of common ecological conditions, selective pressures will tend to favour generalised as against specialised strategies on the part of both plants and pollinators. They and Jordano (1987) analysed sources of bias on this issue in existing studies, limiting their usefulness for settling it. Most studies are small in scale, concentrating on a limited range of plant or pollinator taxa, and so they are likely to exaggerate the degree of mutual specialisation. Also, the background assumption of specialisation may often lead to unconscious bias, as, for example, when researchers simply discount 'out-of-syndrome' visits as incidental to the study. However, as Waser *et al.* concede, there are also sources of bias in the opposite direction. Listing the number of visitor-taxa may be misleading, as many of these may involve very few visits per taxon, with the great majority of visits being made by members of a small subset of total visiting taxa (as shown in Herrera's study). Also, of course, visitor frequency does not translate directly into pollination, or to pollination effectiveness. It could also be noted that mere lists of visiting taxa do not represent the nutritional importance to the pollinators of the flowers they visit. As we have seen, many bumblebees appear to be much more specialised for pollen sources than for nectar, and this also varies greatly between species. However, Waser *et al.* conclude that biases in both directions may balance each other out, suggesting that the studies (most of which indicate high degrees of generalisation, as against specialised mutualisms) probably provide an accurate picture of reality.

They go on to provide models of the conditions under which natural selection would have favoured either specialisation or generalisation, for both plants and pollinators, and in both the short and long term. These models predict that, for plants that are dependent on cross-pollination for their reproductive success, specialisation to a single pollinator may be favoured in the short term if there is one pollinator that is both abundant and markedly more effective than any other. Under these conditions, the model agrees with the 'most effective pollinator principle'. However, in the longer term, generalisation may be favoured if the gains from specialisation in the short term are relatively low, flowering episodes are infrequent, there is variation (in time or space) in the abundance and identity of the most effective pollinator, and/or relatively slight differences among pollinators in their pollination effectiveness. In the most extreme case, complete dependence on a single 'obligate' pollinator would lead to the extinction of the plant in the event of the loss of its pollinator.

Similar considerations apply to pollinator strategy. In the short term, where handling costs are high (involving investment by the bees in learning) and travel costs low, specialisation to a high-reward flower species may be favoured over generalised foraging nearby. However, where travel is costly, and nectar rewards of different flowers are similar, generalisation is favoured. The latter condition is likely to be satisfied commonly, because of competition between pollinators, and generalisation is likely to be favoured even in the short term. In the longer term, generalisation is favoured by two main conditions: where there is non-coincidence between the flight-period of the pollinator and the flowering period of the plant, and where there is variation in space and/or time in the abundance of the plant. The broad qualitative expectation from these models, then, is that generalisation is likely to have been selected for more widely than specialisation. The latter is likely to be the exception rather than the rule. In fact, both the conditions

Waser *et al.* specify for pollinators to become generalists in the longer term apply to bumblebees, but the implications for them are more complex than for solitary species that have short adult flight periods. With their relatively long colony cycles of from two to seven months or more, survival of the colony depends on foragers being able to forage from a succession of suitable flowers through the cycle. But the selective pressure in favour of generalisation at the level of the colony is consistent with high (but variable and flexible) levels of learned specialisation (flower constancy) at the level of the individual foragers.

The arguments presented by Waser *et al.* lead us to expect generalised patterns of association between flowers and insect visitors, but what sense can now be made of the observed patterns of fit between pollinator and blossom morphology which the idea of pollination syndromes tries to capture? Waser *et al.* do concede that the longevity of the concept suggests that it has some purchase on reality, but argue that this is quite limited. Mutualistic fits are neither so constraining nor so inflexible as they are commonly taken to be. Waser *et al.* review the evidence on the behaviour, morphology and physiology of the main groups of pollinators to illustrate the case. All groups of pollinators have broad-spectrum colour vision and can discriminate between the main colour clusters into which blossoms can be grouped. They report a study of their own that did not find statistically significant differences in the colour preferences of the main groups of pollinators, concluding that colour differences among blossoms probably related more to the chemistry of plant pigments than to co-evolution with specific groups of pollinators. Many groups of pollinators have been shown to learn associations between rewards and flower colours, make foraging choices on this basis and remember the associations. Again, this indicates generalisation. Waser *et al.* do agree that morphological differences among pollinators, such as size, structure of mouthparts and so on, will affect both foraging and pollination efficiency, but only rarely to such an extent that they restrict pollinators to just one plant species. Physiological differences are also expected to constrain to only a limited extent.

These are interesting and challenging arguments, though they are still open to question. The identification of biases in both directions in the existing literature does not show that they are of equal strength: showing that generalisation is *in fact* the dominant pattern requires appropriately designed studies. This also applies to the discussion of the extent to which behavioural, morphological and physiological constraints tend towards specialisation or generalisation. Studies by Chittka and others suggest that there are significant differences in the colour preferences of pollinators, and even among bumblebee species, implying at least one limit to generalisation (see Chittka *et al.*, 2001, and Chapter 3). However, the resulting associations may not always be the outcome of selective pressures, but rather be consequences of non-adaptive constraints such as the chemistry of plant pigments (as argued by Waser *et al.*). It also seems likely that there are significant differences in navigational, learning and memory abilities and biases between groups of foragers as diverse as bats, birds and pollen beetles. This must affect their abilities to learn how to access complex floral structures, for example. Finally, it could be argued that Waser *et al.* take an unduly restrictive interpretation of the pollination syndrome concept as the target of their criticisms. According to the concept of pollination syndromes, structural features of a blossom, for example, are expected to set broad limits to the range of pollinators able to efficiently forage from it, not necessarily or even commonly to reduce that range to a single species. The latter extreme case of exclusive one-to-one 'obligate' mutualism is taken to be the paradigm of specialisation in much of Waser *et al.*'s argument, so that generalisation will inevitably appear to be the norm. Interestingly, they acknowledge this, suggesting that the polar contrast between specialisation and generalisation should be abandoned, in favour of recognising these as extreme points on a spectrum. Johnson & Steiner (2000) provide a good review of this issue, and some of the empirical studies bearing on it.

THE ECOLOGICAL CONTEXT: COMMUNITIES, COMPARTMENTS AND LANDSCAPES

Many of the questions posed by our discussion of OFT in Chapter 6 and the idea of pollination syndromes in this chapter are best answered by placing the plant–pollinator interactions in their wider ecological contexts. For example, degrees of specialisation and generalisation in mutualistic systems can only be properly explored through well-designed studies of patterns of interaction in ecological communities, or at larger temporal and spatial scales, as appropriate. The existing literature on, and models of, food webs have provided an important starting point for this (a valuable review is Hall & Raffaelli, 1993). Clearly the insect-mediated pollination systems we have been discussing are a type of food web, bumblebees being almost entirely dependent on nectar and pollen for their nutrition. However, what have come to be called 'pollination webs' are unlike other food webs in several respects. Insects that forage from flowers tend to have a wider range of food sources than do herbivores, and their food sources are restricted in time by the episodic nature and duration of flowering periods (Bronstein, 1995). Most importantly, however, pollination webs differ from most other food webs because there are mutualistic relationships of interdependence between the pollinators and the plants whose flowers feed them. The plants are adapted to attract the animals that feed from their flowers, not to escape from them, as with predators and prey.

Pollination webs: communities and compartments

Jordano (1987), though concerned more with questions about the evolution of mutualistic systems, provided a valuable framework for studying ecological interactions at community level. Co-evolution between pairs of species is quite rare, so the evolution of most mutualisms should be understood as a more diffuse process involving interacting sets of species, commonly relying on 'preadaptations' evolved independently of the association. Also, as the species composition of communities varies from place to place, and the relative abundance of the interacting species can be expected to vary from season to season, the type and direction of selective pressures relevant to the establishment of mutualistic associations will also vary. This is likely to give rise to complex patterns of association within communities. To explore these patterns, Jordano assembled 36 existing studies of pollination systems and 19 seed-dispersal ones. Interactions between species pairs were counted, giving measures of the intensity of interaction and mutual dependency between them, and the overall patterns of interaction across the community. There were general similarities between the pollination and dispersal systems, but with the exception that the increase in the number of interactions with increasing numbers of species in the system was much lower in pollination than in seed-dispersal systems. Ecologists identify an important feature of the patterns of interaction among species in a community as its 'connectance'. This is a measure of the number of *actual* interactions compared with the number of *possible* ones. Low levels of connectance are evidence of mutualisms in the community, which restrict the range of species with which each partner interacts. The number of possible interactions increases in proportion to the number of species in the community, so the lower levels of connectance found by Jordano in the pollination webs indicates a higher degree of specialised interactions in them than in the seed-dispersal systems.

The studies of pollination webs also showed that different, though over-lapping, patterns of connectance existed between different groups of pollinator/plant associations. Overall, the pattern was of a small number of 'nuclei' of strongly interacting species, a much larger number of weakly interacting species, and a variable number of species pairs between which there are no interactions. The subdivision of mutualistic communities into compartments, or modules, within which interactions are more intense than between them, was a particularly significant result. However, complete isolation between compartments was limited by 'minoring' across compartments, as noted in bumblebee foraging by

Heinrich (see Chapter 6). Where strong interactions were observed, these were generally asymmetrical: that is to say, dependence of one partner in a mutualistic relationship tended to be stronger than the reciprocal dependence of the other. In pollination systems, pollinator species tend to be more generalist, and so less dependent on any of the plant species they visit than the plants are upon particular pollinator species. Finally, Jordano concluded that the majority of null interactions in mutualistic communities were the result of non-coincidence of flowering and activity periods of plants and pollinators, respectively. This is relevant to the pattern of 'sequential specialisation', already noted in the social bumblebees, whose reproductive cycle is usually much longer than the flowering period of any one of the plant species that they visit.

So far there are few studies of pollination webs at the level of ecological communities, or still greater spatial scales, designed to investigate the existence and properties of compartments. Fonseca & Ganade (1996) were, however, able to demonstrate the compartmental structure of a rather different mutualistic community of ants and plants in an area of tropical moist forest in Brazil. In this community, the plants showed adaptations that fed and housed the ants, whilst the ants afforded protection from herbivores. Fonseca & Ganade found that groups of related plant species each shared associations with a set of ant species from various lineages. Statistical analysis revealed seven such compartments, consisting of associations between species found elsewhere throughout Central and South America. This suggested that the compartments represented evolved ant/host specialisations, rather than being due to local contingencies of geography or habitat. However, it could be argued that the discovery of such a highly organised community, with strongly differentiated compartments, might be a function of long-term stability peculiar to the 'pristine rainforest' community chosen for the study.

A more recent study by Dicks *et al.* (2002) set out to investigate compartmentalisation of pollination systems in two grassland communities in England. At each site 100 metre transects were walked at regular intervals between 14 May and 16 July, recording both blossoms and their visitors. As far as possible identification was to species level, and all species of Hymenoptera, Lepidoptera, Diptera and Coleoptera above 3 millimetres in length were included. Quadrats were used to assess the abundance of the different flowering plants along each transect. Using a combination of methods of analysing the results, they concluded that the pollination webs in both meadows were, indeed, compartmentalised, with relatively strong interactions between distinct groups of insect pollinators and flower types. To some extent the groups matched what might be expected on the basis of the concept of pollination syndromes, bees and butterflies being associated with pink, purple or yellow flowers with long corolla tubes, and flies grouped with less nectar-rich, open, yellow or white flowers. However, at both sites flies were grouped into two compartments that could not be readily interpreted in terms of pollination syndromes, and some syndromes postulated in the literature were not in evidence. In particular, no separate butterfly compartment was identified and nor did the study reveal distinct long/short-tongued bee compartments, notwithstanding the importance attached to this distinction in the literature on bumblebee foraging patterns, and supported in many observational and experimental studies (such as Fussell & Corbet, 1992*b*, 1993; Stout *et al.*, 1998 and Corbet, 2000).

Had it been possible to measure the relative effectiveness of different visitors as pollinators, the differential rewards offered by each plant species, and, in the case of the bumblebees, to distinguish the sexes and castes, it is possible that more differentiation between compartments might have shown up. However, the study does provide substantial evidence for compartmentalisation of the pollination web studied, and provides some empirical support for the idea of pollination syndromes. One additional finding was the relatively greater generalisation of the plant species, compared with their visitors (that is, the number of insect species visiting each plant species was greater than the number of plant species visited by each insect species, on average). The authors attribute this to the small number of flower species in the community, and this provides one possible explanation for the apparent lack of a distinct long-tongued bee compartment. As Williams (1989*a*) observed, long-tongued bees are constrained to forage from flowers with shorter corolla tubes where deep flowers are absent or in short supply. It may be that in relatively species-poor plant communities, otherwise distinct compartments or syndromes are collapsed into one another by the behavioural strategies of foragers. We might expect this to be particularly true of adaptable and resourceful foragers such as bumblebees, with their considerable learning abilities.

Given the relatively low level of biodiversity in most lowland farmed landscapes, the method of identifying compartments empirically used by Dicks *et al.* (2002) is, as they argue, preferable to assuming hypothetical syndromes. This conclusion is given strong support from one of the few studies comparing the species composition of bumblebee communities in different foraging habitats. Sowig (1989) studied the effects of patch size on the species composition of foraging bumblebees for patches of several flower species. In the case of monk's-hood and comfrey, the longer-tongued species, *B. hortorum* and *B. pascuorum*, predominated in the small patches, whilst the larger patches were visited almost exclusively by the short-tongued species and honey bees. The explanation offered by Sowig was that the longer tongued species foraged more effectively than the shorter tongued species in the smaller patches, whilst the reverse was the case in the larger patches. This was because the shorter tongued species were only able to access nectar from these blossoms by primary and secondary robbing. A much higher proportion of the flowers were robbed in the larger patches, disadvantaging the legitimately foraging long-tongued species in those patches. The resulting pattern of resource partitioning between species implies that in order to study specialisation in plant/pollinator interactions it is necessary to take account of both evolved syndromes and their implications for interspecies competition across different community structures (see Goulson, 2003).

Foraging landscapes

Studies of pollination webs at the level of more-or-less physically discrete communities are likely to be particularly informative about the relationships between flowering plants and those groups of pollinators that fly only short distances within and between patches. However, long-distance foraging, typical of at least some bumblebees, has important implications both for the habitat requirements of the foragers and for the pollination systems and gene-flows in plant populations. For insights into these implications we need to return to studies at the landscape level. This much larger scale of ecological interactions has until relatively recently received little attention from theorists, and has been the subject of rather few systematic studies (Hansson, Fahrig & Merriam, 1995). Research and conservation efforts focused exclusively at the level of individual sites are likely to be ineffective, so both studies and action at landscape scale are a necessary complement to those at community level and smaller spatial scales.

Foragers operating at the landscape scale incur travel and exploration costs, due to the much greater likelihood of fragmentation, isolation, unevenness of reward distribution and the heterogeneity of the discrete ecological communities that may be present in their range. However, they may also be able to exploit a greater range of such communities, have at their disposal a much greater total reward, and be able to take advantage of succession through the seasons of plants flowering in different spatial subdivisions of the range. From the point of view of conservation of both bees and the plants they pollinate, it is important to understand interactions between these variables, and particularly so in those landscapes subject to intensive human activity. These include urban and suburban landscapes, in which domestic gardens, parks and other open spaces, ex-industrial sites and what Shoard (2002) calls 'edgelands' form an interconnected mosaic, as well as, and combined with, agricultural landscapes of various kinds. In large parts of the industrialised world, remaining natural or semi-natural ecosystems rarely persist at landscape scale, and much conservation-oriented research has focused on the way development pressures and agricultural intensification impact on ecosystem stability and biodiversity.

AGRICULTURAL CHANGE AND DISRUPTED MUTUALISMS: PLANTS WITHOUT POLLINATORS?

As we saw in Chapter 1, there has been a sharp decline in bumblebee diversity in lowland south and central England, resulting in local extinctions of several species. This decline was evident from 1960 to the late 1970s, but may have accelerated since then. Similar declines have been noted in parts of France, Germany and Belgium and they are generally attributed to changes in agricultural land management. The role of this and other factors in explaining bumblebee decline will be discussed in Chapter 10, but here the focus is on the wider implications of bumblebee decline for the pollination of both wild and cultivated plants.

The effects of agricultural intensification on biodiversity – including the bumblebees – have been extensively researched. It is generally agreed that both fragmentation of habitats and the overall reduction in size of suitable habitat, widespread consequences of recent agricultural change, have reduced biodiversity. The effects are intensified with increased physical isolation of remaining fragments, and reduction in fragment size (Steffan-Dewenter & Tscharntke, 2002). Various processes may be at work in producing these losses in biodiversity, such as the greater risk of local extinction of small, isolated populations, reduced likelihood of recolonisation of a fragment after local extinction and reduced habitat diversity compared with larger, continuous areas of habitat. For at least some species, the persistence of habitat corridors, such as hedgerows and roadside verges, which link otherwise isolated fragments of suitable habitat, offsets some of these effects. It is also expected that fragmentation will have greater negative effects on more sedentary species than on those species (like at least some bumblebee species) that are able to move between isolated patches of habitat up to considerable distances (Thomas, 2000).

However, attention to the patterns of ecological interactions between groups of species suggests other, less obvious potential consequences of fragmentation. This applies particularly to the mutualistic relationships between pollinators and plants (Steffan-Dewenter & Tscharntke, 2002). Where these relationships are specialised, the disruption caused by fragmentation, especially where plant or pollinators are already scarce, can lead to loss of the plant's reproductive viability due to pollination limitation (that is, reduced seed-set as a result of insufficient levels of pollination, see Corbet *et al.*, 1991; Corbet, 1996, 2000; Richards, 2001). Similarly, where pollinators are relatively specialised, they may suffer from reduced foraging efficiency (Williams, 1988, 1989*b*).

Crops

The disruption of pollinator/plant mutualisms may affect both wild flowers and crop plants adversely (Osborne & Williams, 1996, Kearns *et al.*, 1998; Steffan-Dewenter & Tscharntke, 1999. For the USA see Allen-Wardell *et al.*, 1998). Corbet *et al.*(1991) list 43 crops grown widely in the European Union for which seed-set is dependent on, or enhanced by, bee pollination, and Williams (1996) says that as many as 84 per cent of crop species grown in the EU for food, oil or fodder that have been investigated are dependent on or benefit from insect pollination. Although the role of honey bees in pollination has been most thoroughly researched, it is likely that wild bees, and especially bumblebees, have a particularly important role because of their flower constancy, ability to forage in inclement weather, and access to an exceptionally wide range of blossom types. The pollination services of wild bees have recently acquired a new importance as a result of the impact of the mite *Varroa jacobsoni* on honey bee populations. The decline of honey bees, combined with the decline of bumblebees and other pollinating insects such as butterflies, may have had significant effects on yields of insect-pollinated crops. Unfortunately, the evidence on this is rather fragmentary and limited so far.

Richards (2001) distinguishes several categories of crop plants in relation to their dependence on animal pollinators, and summarises the evidence on the effects of intensification on yield. Most staple crops (wheat, rice, maize, potatoes, yam, cassava) are not dependent on animal pollination. However, there are many other crops that are economically important and are affected by animal pollination – by insects, in particular. Some crop plants, including some *Prunus* species, are entirely dependent on cross-pollination, whilst others show improved seed-set, larger fruit, or hybrid vigour when pollinated by insects. Richards lists cases of reduced yield due to inadequate pollinator service, and these include a number of bumblebee-pollinated crops (Table 7).

Bumblebees are more effective pollinators of red clover than honey bees, and the larger or long-tongued bumblebees are particularly significant in this respect as only they (among bees) can access the nectar of some cultivars (Free, 1993). Lower yields have been reported where bumblebees are not native (New Zealand) or absent because of loss of habitat. Field bean is also effectively pollinated by long-tongued bumblebees, and insect pollination enhances both yield and the vigour of the subsequent generation (Free & Williams, 1976; Corbet *et al.*, 1991). Although short-tongued bumblebees commonly rob field bean, bypassing the pollination mechanism, it seems that this does not reduce yield, possibly because they also forage for pollen. Oil-seed rape is pollinated by a wide spectrum of insects, including several short-tongued bumblebees, most especially *Bombus lapidarius*. Both the quality and uniformity of the crop are improved by insect pollination, as is offspring vigour (Williams *et al.*, 1987, cited in Richards, 2001). Numerous other fruit crops, including grapes, olives, sunflowers, cotton, soya and tomato, benefit from, but are not entirely dependent on, insect pollination. Commercially provided captive colonies of bumblebees (*B. terrestris*, in particular) are now extensively used by commercial growers of tomatoes and other vegetables in glasshouses, where they forage more efficiently than honey bees (Griffiths & Robberts, 1996). The inability of the latter to buzz-forage gives the bumblebees an advantage over them in collecting pollen from tomatoes.

Wild plants

In the absence of commercial pressures, research on the effects of declining pollinator populations on wild flower species has been much less evident. However, there is no reason to expect it to be less significant than it may be for crop plants. Corbet *et al.* (1991) list ten major European families of flowering plants that are pollinated by bees, several of them, such as the Lamiaceae, Scrophulariaceae, and Fabaceae, containing many well-known bumblebee flowers. In the case of specialised mutualisms, where the plant concerned is dependent on cross-pollination, if the key pollinator becomes unreliable, or extinct, extinction of the plant is likely to follow (Osborne & Williams, 1996, Corbet *et al.*, 1991; Corbet, 1997). As far as the more generalised pollination mutualisms are concerned, the fragmentation of habitat and subsequent isolation of remaining subpopulations of a scarce plant may lead to reduced reproduction because of insufficient pollinating visits. Many plants are insect pollinated but are able to reproduce without insect visits. However, these are still likely to suffer in terms of reduced seed-set and loss of vigour in the absence of insect-mediated pollination (Larson & Barrett, 2000). Among pollinators, bumblebees are particularly important in fragmented agricultural landscapes as long-distance foragers that are able to profitably access isolated populations of flowers (Corbet, 2000; Schulke & Waser, 2001).

In some cases, only bumblebees, and particularly the long-tongued species, are able to perform effective pollinator services. Corbet *et al.* (1991) cite the example of black rampion (*Phyteuma nigrum*), an endangered plant in the Netherlands. Its survival depends on pollinating visits by long-tongued bumblebees, particularly

TABLE 7. Examples of poor yield of crop fruits resulting from inadequate pollinator service including seed crops of vegetative produce (reproduced from Richards, 2001, with permission).

CROP SPECIES	POLLINATOR	REPORTED ENVIRONMENTAL CAUSE
Species requiring pollination to set seed		
Elais guineensis	Elaeidobius kamerunicus	Absence of pollinator when crop introduced to Malaysia
Vaccinium spp.	Apis	Shortage of native pollinators
Cucumis melo	Apis	Crops under glass or in tunnels: bees fly upwind in tunnels
Raphanus sativus	Bombus spp.	Distance from pollinator safe sites
Prunus salicina	Apis. Osmia cornuta	Shortage of native pollinators in intensive orchards, Bombus do not pollinate
Trifolium pratense	Bombus hortorum B. pascuorum	Introduced Apis provide inadequate service when long-tongued Bombus not native (NZ) or habitats missing
Medicago sativa	Megachile spp.	Bombus and introduced Apis provide inadequate service; leafcutters rare in intensive agriculture
Averrhoa carambola	Apis cerana Trigona thoracica	Shortage of native Trigona pollinators in intensive orchards
Malus. Pyrus	Apis. Osmia spp.	Shortage of efficient mason bees in intensive orchards; alternative hand-pollination or high hive density expensive
Ficus carica	Blastophaga psenes	Lack of hermaphrodite trees in gardens etc.
Passiflora spp.	Xylocopa. Centris. Eulaema	Absence of suitable nest-sites which can be provided by log piles etc
Durio zihetinus	Bats	Shortage of bats; can be improved by provision of roost sites
Annona spp.	Nitidulid beetles	Shortage of breeding sites e.g. rotting fruit
Theobroma cacao	Ceratopogonid midges	Shortage of breeding sites in pools of water (mosquito risk)
Species in which seed set is increased after animal pollination		
Lycospersicon esculentum	Bombus	Absence of pollinators under glass. Seasonality of Bombus, lack of nectar in tomatoes
Cocos nucifera	Apis. Melipona	Absence of pollinators in plantation monoculture
Actinidia deliciosa	Apis. Bombus	Bombus more effective pollinator and Apis may restrict wind-pollination by removing pollen.
Species in which the quality of seeds or fruits is increased after animal pollination		
Vicia faba	Long-tongued Bombus	Rarity of long-tongued Bombus due to habitat and competition with introduced Apis
Brassica napus	Various	Intensive systems reduce numbers of pollinators
Helianthus annuus	Various	Intensive systems reduce numbers of pollinators
Allium cepa	Apis. calliphorid flies	Seeds raised under glass
Fragaria x ananassa	Apis. Trigona, diptera	Crop raised under glass

EFFECT ON YIELD	REFERENCE
Almost no yield in absence of pollinator	Greathead (1983)
	Syed et al. (1979)
Fruit set increases with proximity to hive	Aras et al. (1996)
Poor pollination reduces set and quality; worst in tunnels at lee end	Dag and Eisikowitch (1995)
Plants in intensive systems set less seed	Steffan-Dewenter and Tscharntke (1999)
Fruit set increases with foraging activity; crop self-incompatible	Calzoni and Speranza (1998)
Long-tongued *Bombus* provide best seed set	Holm (1966), Donovan (1990)
Introductions of leafcutter bees greatly increase seed set	Bohart et al. (1967), Peterson et al. (1992),
Low seed set ascribed to herbicide use	Richards (1996), Benedek (1972)
Introduction of *Apis* increased fruit set	Phoon et al. (1984)
Apis are inefficient pollinators, requiring high hive density	Westerkamp and Gottsberger, (2000)
Non-parthenocarpous females where hermaphrodites absent need introduction of 'caprifigs'	Valdeyron and Lloyd (1979)
Apis and other visitors do not pollinate flowers. Hand-pollination usual in commercial production	Mardan et al. (1991)
Self-incompatible strains will not set fruit except when bat-visited in multiclonal orchards	Vogel and Westerkamp (1991)
Only pollinators; crops usually rely on hand-pollination	Gottsberger (1970)
Pollination usually inadequate and supplemented by hand-pollination	Young (1986)
Tomatoes can set with water etc. but vibration pollination from *Bombus* increases fruit set	Heemert et al. (1990), Ruijter (1997)
Some wind-pollination, but visits by stingless and honey bees increase fruit set	McGregor (1976)
Basically wind-pollinated but in sheltered sites fruit set improved after visits by *Bombus* and *Apis*	Craig and Stewart (1988)
Seed quality improves after cross-pollination; *Apis* not effective pollinator	Free and Williams (1976), Stoddard and Bond (1987)
Seed quality and uniformity and offspring vigour improves after cross-pollination	Williams et al. (1987)
Seed quality and oil yield improves after cross-pollination	Free (1993), Bichee and Sharma (1988)
Offspring yield improves after cross-pollination, greater for bee pollination than blowfly pollination	Van der Meer and Bennekom (1968, 1972)
To maximize 'fruit' size, ten *Apis* visits or 30 *Trigona* visits needed	Kakutani et al. (1993)

B. pascuorum, which can profitably visit plants in isolated patches (see Kwak *et al.*, 1991). However, it is arguable that rare flowers are less likely to be the subject of constancy on the part of the forager, and so they are less likely to receive pollen from a flower of the same species (see Kunin, 1997). Stout *et al.* (1998) reported a study in which 'rare' plants in experimental arrays actually received more visits from bumblebees than more common ones, but they concluded that these were less likely to be effective pollinating visits. Groups of pollinator species (sometimes called guilds) may all forage from one or more shared flower types, so that the insect/pollinator mutualism may not be disrupted by the loss of one member of the guild as its pollination services can be substituted by others.

However, if most of the species in the guild become rare or extinct, then the effect is comparable to the plight of specialist mutualisms. The local extinctions of bumblebee species in lowland England and other parts of Europe leave the guild of long-tongued bumblebees severely depleted, with only *B. hortorum* and the somewhat less long-tongued *B. pascuorum* remaining in many regions (Corbet, 2000). Corbet argues that this raises important issues for priorities in bumblebee conservation. Currently effort is focused on rare species that may already be critically endangered. Higher priority should be given to preserving the long-tongued bumblebee/deep flower compartment whilst its few remaining pollinator components remain relatively widespread, rather than waiting till they, too, become rare. From the point of view of plant conservation, the decline to extinction of plants through pollen limitation may be an insidious and long-term affair, not detected until too late. Individual perennials may be long lived, or reproduce vegetatively for a time, but the population may in the longer term lose genetic diversity, reducing its capacity to colonise new sites or withstand environmental change (Corbet, 1991, 1997; Johnson & Steiner, 2000).

We will return to the task of unpicking the role of environmental change in the diverse patterns of bumblebee decline and survival, and to the various priorities for their conservation, in Chapters 10 and 11.

CHAPTER 8

What Bumblebee is That?

W HEN I FIRST took up the study of bumblebees it was partly because of their attractive and photogenic appearance. But, as an amateur naturalist with other demands on my time, I also thought the bumblebees would be an ideal group to study – not many species, and easy to identify. How wrong I turned out to be! It took a couple of seasons to learn how to recognise the common species in my neighbourhood with reasonable confidence, and then much longer to seek out and learn the jizz of the more localised and scarce species. This chapter is designed with my own learning experiences fresh in my memory. It starts with a beginner's guide, and then moves progressively to the complete key to the British species.

My aim is to enable the reader to identify all the British species with reasonable confidence without the need to kill and dissect them. In part this is because bumblebees have enough enemies without suffering depredations from naturalists who simply want to understand and appreciate them. There is no doubt that much of our current understanding of the wonderful variety and complexity of bumblebee lives has come from scientific research which involved killing many bees. There may also be a justification for killing 'voucher' specimens (preferably males!) if critical identification is needed for conservation purposes: for example, to defend important habitat from developers, or to advise on the management of protected sites. However, there is much to be learned by systematic study of the activities of bumblebees 'in the field'. For this, it is important to be able to distinguish the sexes, castes and species without taking and killing them.

But field identification is by no means easy – and is never *absolutely* reliable. The starting point for all 'bombologists' has to be learning to recognise the typical bumblebee colour patterns: black and yellow bands with variously coloured 'tails', brown or ginger-brown, unbanded, and black with red tails. This is essential, but only the beginning. There are groups of species that share broadly similar colour patterns, and, just to make things even more complicated, some species have several different colour forms. These may be geographical forms, or differences between the sexes or castes, or variations that occur regularly within each population. So for some species it is not enough to recognise the colour pattern. Some back-up clues to identification are necessary. Some of these can be picked out without disturbing the bees. Examples of these traits are presence or absence of corbiculae (pollen baskets) on the hind legs in females, or the much greater length of the antennae in males of some species. Then there are features that require close scrutiny with a hand lens. These include the length and shape of the antennal segments, patterns of distribution of hairs on the legs, and other characteristics. These can nearly always be picked out without killing the bee, by capturing, confining and then releasing it. This procedure has surprisingly little impact on its victims, which often just carry on foraging as if nothing had happened!

Finally, for definitive identification of some species, examination of the genital capsule (males) or microscopic study of minute anatomical details is required. Mostly, this does involve killing the insect, and so should be avoided wherever possible. Some naturalists are less concerned about this than others, but for those who are particularly averse to killing for the sake of their leisure pursuits it is often possible to avoid killing even for definitive identification. Especially in early spring it is common to find the dead bodies of overwintered queens, and road casualties are another source. Another possibility is to learn the signs of heavily parasitised individuals and take these: you might even be saving the lives of other potential hosts! I have a queen of *B. humilis* in my reference collection that was found struggling to climb up a grass stem: she died in my hands a few minutes later, and was presumably heavily parasitised by *Sphaerularia bombi*.

IS IT A BUMBLEBEE?

The first step in studying bumblebees is to learn how to distinguish them from their various lookalikes. As we saw in Chapter 1, several groups of insects are very similar to bumblebees in colour patterns, body shapes and the furriness of their bodies. In Britain the mimics belong to three main groups: moths (order Lepidoptera), true flies (order Diptera) and other bees (Hymenoptera). If we learn the distinctive characteristics of these groups, they can be eliminated from the enquiry. Some of the hover flies are exceptionally close mimics, and the flower bee, *Anthophora plumipes* also looks and behaves very much like a bumblebee. The discussion in Chapter 1 and Figures 7–17 (Chapter 1) should help to separate the bumblebees from their various 'imitators'.

BUMBLEBEE IDENTIFICATION: A BEGINNER'S SEASONAL GUIDE

In most parts of cultivated and urbanised lowland Britain the number of species to be found commonly is very limited. In most places a basic six species of social bumblebees, and a variable number of cuckoos, will be found relatively easily. The rest will be absent, or much harder to find. So a useful way to start is to familiarise yourself with the basic six. Readers who have richer bumblebee habitat close by, or who live in the northern or western uplands, can use the distribution maps and habitat descriptions to define their rather different group of basics. However, for the majority of us, these six species predominate: *Bombus lucorum*, *B. terrestris*, *B. lapidarius*, *B. pratorum*, *B. pascuorum*, and *B. hortorum*.

In southern England some foraging bumblebees can occasionally be found throughout the winter. However, **queens** (Fig. 156) of most of the basic six emerge from hibernation in February or March, though *B. hortorum* is sometimes a little later. This is the best time of year to learn how to distinguish the common species. Nearly all of the individuals you see will be large, clearly marked queens. Most are likely to belong to social species, but in some years and in some districts female cuckoo bumblebees may be quite common. These can be distinguished by the lack of corbiculae on their hind tibiae, which are not shiny, but covered in hair on the outer surface (see Fig. 7, p.12). At this stage it makes sense to concentrate on identifying the social species. The colour patterns of these fall into all three common types: ginger-brown, without bands on the thorax (*B. pascuorum*), black with red 'tail' (*B. lapidarius*), and black-and-yellow banded (*B. pratorum, B. hortorum, B. terrestris, B. lucorum*). *Bombus lucorum* and *B. hortorum* both have white tails, but can be distinguished by the number of yellow bands: *B. hortorum* with two on the thorax, and one at the front of the abdomen, *B. lucorum* with just one on the thorax (collar) and another near the front of the abdomen. *Bombus hortorum* also has a longer face and tongue and is more likely to be seen feeding from flowers with a deep corolla, such as white deadnettle, whilst *B. lucorum* is a frequent visitor to sallow catkins in spring. The queen *B. terrestris* is very similar to *B. lucorum*, but has a buff tail instead of white (and the yellow bands are usually darker or reduced in extent in *B. terrestris*). Finally, *B. pratorum* is like both *B. lucorum* and *B. terrestris*, but

FIG 156. Queens of the six most common and widespread social bumblebees ((a) *Bombus lucorum*, (b) *B. terrestris*, (c) *B. hortorum*, (d) *B. pratorum*, (e) *B. lapidarius* and (f) *B. pascuorum*) together with one of the more common cuckoo bumblebees ((g) *B. vestalis*). (Paintings © Tony Hopkins from Prŷs-Jones & Corbet, 1991.)

has a red tail, rather than white or buff. The buff coloration of the tail of *B. terrestris* is variable, and, in bright specimens, there could be confusion with *B. pratorum*. However, queens of the latter species are usually smaller than those of *B. terrestris*.

Depending on locality and season, the first **workers** of some species may be seen from mid-March onwards. Since in most cases these are just smaller versions of the queens, they should not cause too much confusion. There are just two differences to note. The first is that small workers of *B. pratorum* often have the abdominal yellow band reduced or missing. However, the red tail and single yellow band on the thorax still serve to mark them out from the other species. The second difference concerns workers of *B. terrestris*. Unlike the queens, these generally have white or whitish tails, and often cannot be reliably distinguished from workers of *B. lucorum*. Even experienced observers often pool records of workers of these two species. However, the yellow bands in workers of *B. terrestris* are often darker than those of *B. lucorum*, and there is a narrow brownish transitional zone between the black of the abdomen and the whitish tail. In *B. lucorum* workers there is an abrupt transition from black to pure white.

Males (Fig. 157) and fresh queens of the earliest species begin to appear in early May, and are soon followed by the rest, in May or June. In some species, worn overwintered queens that have not succeeded in establishing a nest may still be seen when the fresh queens begin to emerge. However, from the point of view of identification, it is the appearance of the males that complicates matters. The males have an extra segment on their antennae (13 instead of 12), and the tip of the abdomen is relatively blunt and rounded (pointed in females) (see key figures K.1 and K.2). The males of *B. pratorum* are generally the first of the basic six to appear. The antennae are markedly longer than those of the queens and workers, the yellow on the front of the thorax is much more extensive and they have yellow on their faces. There is a broad yellow band on the abdomen and the tail is red, as in the workers and queens. The males of *B. lapidarius* appear somewhat later, and persist until late summer. They typically have a single yellow band on the thorax (collar), but this is sometimes reduced, and always less extensive than that of *B. pratorum* males. Both *B. lapidarius* and *B. pratorum* males have yellow hairs on the face, but the former usually lack the yellow band on the abdomen. Even when this is present it is much less conspicuous than in *B. pratorum*, and the red tail is more extensive in *lapidarius* males. In general the males of *B. pratorum* appear short and compact, those of *lapidarius* having more elongated abdomens. There might be some risk of confusing male *lapidarius* with workers of *B. pratorum*, especially if the latter lack the abdominal yellow band. However, the presence of the yellow hairs on the face of male *B. lapidarius* is an obvious difference.

FIG 157. Males of (a) *B. pratorum*, (b) *B. lapidarius* and (c) *B. lucorum*. (Paintings © Tony Hopkins from Prŷs-Jones & Corbet, 1991.)

The males of *B. hortorum* have the same colour pattern as the queens and workers (black with three yellow bands, and a white tail). The antennae are relatively long compared with the females, and the tip of the abdomen is blunt. *Bombus terrestris* males are coloured like the queens, though the tail varies in colour between buff and off-white. Although they are like males of other species in having an extra antennal segment, the antennae of male *B. terrestris* are not obviously longer than those of the females. The best way to tell the difference between males and females (workers and queens) of *B. terrestris* is by the shape of the abdomen and by the yellow-ginger coloration of the hairs that fringe the hind tibiae (black in the females). Males of *B. terrestris* do not have yellow hairs on the face, and this serves to distinguish them from males of *B. lucorum*, which usually have a well-defined patch of yellow hairs on the face. The yellow bands on *B. lucorum* males are also usually paler and more extensive – in pale forms much more extensive – and there is often a narrow fringe of yellow hairs on the rear of the thorax (scutellum). The males of *B. pascuorum* are usually to be seen from late May onwards, and they are similar in colour pattern to queens and workers. They have noticeably longer antennae than the females, and also the hind tibiae are narrower and have convex, hairy outer surfaces (flat and shiny in the females).

BEYOND THE 'BASIC SIX': SEPARATING THE LOOKALIKES

So far we have not given ways of identifying the cuckoo bumblebees down to species, and have ignored the scarcer and more localised social species. The systematic way to identify these is to use the complete key given at the end of this chapter. However, this is tedious, and involves eliminating species that do not occur in your area in any case. A short-cut method, which may help to give reliable identifications in the majority of cases, is to distinguish clusters of species which look similar and can be expected to occur in a given locality or habitat. The unfamiliar species in each cluster can be identified by looking for the traits that distinguish them from the relevant member of the basic six, which you have already learned to recognise.

In what follows I have used colour patterns, including the more common variant forms, as the main guide to identification, and avoided using technical terms where possible. However, where colour patterns are not reliable I have tried to include external structural features where these can be observed on freely active bees, or by briefly keeping a bee captive and examining it in the field with a hand lens. In the descriptions given of colour patterns, reference is made to collar and scutellum on the thorax, and to numbered segments of the abdomen. The term **collar** is used here simply to refer to the front part of the thorax. The term **scutellum** has a more precise reference to a distinct structure at the rear of the thorax. Where there are pale or yellow bands on both collar and scutellum, the intervening black area of the thorax is sometimes referred to as the **interalar** band (between the wings). Strictly speaking, the abdomen of the bumblebee has nine or ten segments, but several of these are not visible externally. For ease of reference, my descriptions keep to the convention of numbering the externally visible ones from front to rear (in dorsal view, six in females, seven in males) (Figs 158 & 159).

The length and distribution of hairs on the legs, especially the hind leg, are useful in identifying several species. The **tibia** of the hind leg, and the **metatarsus** (enlarged first segment of the 'foot') are most often distinctive (Fig. 160).

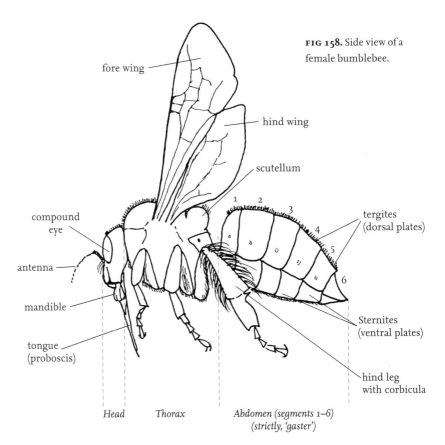

FIG 158. Side view of a female bumblebee.

fore wing

hind wing

scutellum

compound eye

antenna

mandible

tongue (proboscis)

tergites (dorsal plates)

Sternites (ventral plates)

hind leg with corbicula

Head   Thorax   Abdomen (segments 1–6) (strictly, 'gaster')

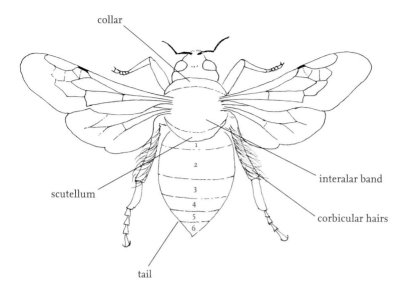

FIG 159. Dorsal view of female bumblebee.

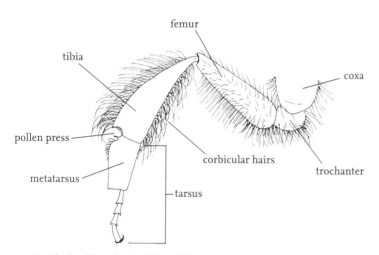

FIG 160. The hind leg of a female bumblebee.

The shapes and relative lengths of the **antennal segments** are useful in separating several species (especially in the males), and these are counted from the **scape** (1) and the **pedicel** (2) to the tip of the **flagellum** (numbered 3–12 in females, 3–13 in males). The shape of the face and some of the facial features are also

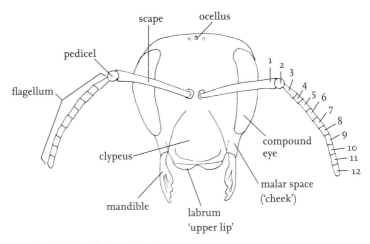

FIG 161. The face of a female bumblebee.

sometimes useful in identification (Fig. 161). The **clypeus** is the front area of the face, below the attachments of the antennae. The **labrum** (upper lip) is a structure between the lower edge of the clypeus and the mouth. The **malar space** is the area at the side of the head, between the lower tip of the compound eye and the attachment of the **mandible** on each side. The structure of the mandibles is sometimes a useful feature for identification.

Most British species can be allocated to one or other of six species-clusters on the basis of colour patterns alone. In most parts of lowland Britain each cluster will have one or more basic species present in local bumblebee communities. This can be used as a standard with which to compare any of the scarcer or more localised species that might be present. Of course, this approach may need to be modified to some extent, depending on where you live. These are the clusters and basics that are likely to be useful in most areas:

1. Ginger-brown, with unbanded thorax. Basic: *B. pascuorum*
2. Yellow band on collar, tail mainly white or buff. Basics: *B. terrestris, B. lucorum*
3. Yellow band on collar and scutellum, tail white or yellow. Basic: *B. hortorum*
4. Yellow band on collar (with or without band on scutellum), tail red. Basics: *B. pratorum*, males of *B. lapidarius*
5. Thorax black, tail red. Basic: *B. lapidarius* (queens and workers)
6. Thorax and abdomen black, with variable amounts of whitish, yellowish or brownish hairs in the tail. No basic: darkened or melanic forms of several species.

Cluster 1: Ginger-brown thorax

Basic: *B. pascuorum*

Other species: *B. muscorum, B. humilis, and B. hypnorum*

Bombus pascuorum has variable amounts of black hair mixed in with the ginger-brown of the abdomen. This may be very extensive, or hardly visible. In northern Britain, pale forms with few or even no black hairs on the abdomen often predominate, but they can also be found in the south. Check with a lens for black hairs on the sides or rear margins of the abdominal segments when in doubt. There are two similar species to *B. pascuorum*, and in mainland Britain neither have black hairs on the abdomen (ignore final segment). *Bombus muscorum* has no black hairs on the dorsal surface of either thorax or abdomen. The hair in the thorax is even in length, giving a 'crew-cut' appearance. This species is very local and increasingly scarce. It inhabits relatively, cool, damp grasslands, and in southern Britain it is mainly coastal. It is more widespread in Scotland. The form *agricolae,* which flies in some Scottish islands, is very distinctive, with black hairs covering legs and the ventral surface of thorax and abdomen. Workers and queens are very easily disturbed while foraging, and fly off rapidly, in contrast to *B. pascuorum*, which is usually unconcerned when approached. The other very similar species in this cluster is *B. humilis*. It tends to inhabit dryer, warmer and more flower-rich grasslands, but in some places flies together with both *B. muscorum* and *B. pascuorum*. Most specimens of *B. humilis* have a few black hairs on the thorax, especially around the wing bases. This is a useful trait to separate it from *B. muscorum*, but, unfortunately, it is not always present. Some authorities list the brown band on the second abdominal segment as a distinguishing feature of *B. humilis*, but unfortunately this is often present in *B. muscorum*, too. In general, *B. humilis* tends to be more placid in behaviour than *B. muscorum*, and its hair is less even (like *B. pascuorum*). It is mainly a southern species in Britain. Without resorting to killing and dissecting specimens it is often difficult to distinguish workers of *B. humilis, B. pascuorum* and *B. muscorum*. The key gives structural characteristics that are reliable, especially for queens and larger workers. **See Key A, couplets 5–9, and Figs K.7 and K.43iv, v & vi.**

Males, which are on the wing in July and August (often in June in the case of *B. pascuorum*), can be distinguished with more confidence. The antennal segments of males of *B. pascuorum, B. muscorum* and *B. humilis* bulge out slightly on the underside (that is, ventrally). These swellings are quite marked in *B. pascuorum* and they are asymmetrical. In both *B. muscorum* and *B. humilis* the swellings are less obvious, and symmetrical (Fig. K.21). This distinction is best seen on segments 7–10 of the antenna, and it is important to get the angle of view exactly right.

However, for definitive identification it is unfortunately necessary to dissect out the genital capsules, which are quite distinctive (Fig. K.45x, xi & xii). Males of all three species have noticeably longer antennae than do the females. **See Key B, couplets 2–7.**

The final species in this cluster is *B. hypnorum*. This is a very recent colonist of Britain, and at the time of writing is very rare and confined to the south. However, it could well become more common, and its possible presence in any area should not be ruled out. In both sexes the thorax is a uniform ginger-brown in colour, with a black abdomen and white tail. Some specimens of *B. pascuorum* have extensive areas of black hairs on the abdomen and could resemble *B. hypnorum*. However, the white tail of the latter is distinctive.

Cluster 2: Collar yellow, scutellum black (or mainly black), tail mainly white or buff (occasionally yellow)

Basics: *B. lucorum*, *B. terrestris*

Other species: *B. soroeensis*, and the cuckoo bumblebees *B. vestalis*, *B. bohemicus* and *B. sylvestris*

As mentioned previously, workers of *B. terrestris* and *B. lucorum* can be difficult to distinguish, but males and queens are fairly distinctive. *Bombus terrestris* is more localised than *B. lucorum* in the north, and in western and northern uplands there is a large form of *B. lucorum*, which has a more extensive yellow collar. This form is known as *magnus*, and is treated as a separate species by some authors. The scarcer members of this cluster include the very localised *B. soroeensis* and three cuckoo bumblebees. Both males and females of *B. terrestris* and *B. lucorum* have flattened and shiny outer surfaces of the hind tibiae. The same is true of *B. soroeensis*. By contrast, all three of the cuckoos have their hind tibiae convex and hairy on their outer surfaces (Fig. K.3). *Bombus soroeensis* is very scarce and localised with a discontinuous distribution in Britain. It occurs on late-flowering, flower-rich calcareous grassland. Queens emerge late from hibernation, and are not usually seen before June. Queens and workers are similar in appearance to *B. lucorum*, but generally smaller. The yellow bands are typically even paler, and the white hairs of the tail are often mixed with ginger ones, especially around the transition between the black and white. A useful characteristic for identifying them in the field is the yellow band on the abdomen. In *B. soroeensis* the yellow band on segment 2 extends forwards onto segment 1 of the abdomen, especially at the sides, but in female *B. lucorum* the yellow is confined to segment 2. This character is fairly easy to pick out in the field and seems to be quite reliable. An alternative feature of the abdominal yellow band is that in *B. soroeensis* it is often broken in the middle by a line of black hairs. However, this feature is not always present, not easy to see, and confusion can be caused because wearing away of the yellow hairs in older workers of *B. lucorum* gives a similar appearance (Fig. K.10). For definitive identification of the females, check the shape of the mandibles (*B. soroeensis* lacks the oblique groove and notch, present in *B. lucorum* – Fig. K.42x & xi). Males of *B. soroeensis* also resemble the males of *B. lucorum*, but the yellow hairs on the face and head are mixed with black, and the tail is commonly suffused with variable amounts of ginger hairs among the white, especially in fresh specimens. The hind metatarsi are narrower than those of *B. lucorum*, and have long hairs on the dorsal edge (mainly very short hairs in *B. lucorum* males) (Fig. K.34). For definitive identification of males, the genital capsules are distinctive (Fig. K.45i & ii).

The three cuckoos in this cluster have the characteristic hairy hind tibiae of the subgenus *Psithyrus* in both sexes. *Bombus vestalis* and *B. bohemicus* both have yellow side-flashes at the leading edge of their white tails. These are present in both sexes and distinguish these species from all others in the cluster. Unfortunately the yellow tends to fade with age, especially on *B. bohemicus*. The third cuckoo is *B. sylvestris*, which lacks the yellow side-flashes. The females of this species have very small, inconspicuous callosities on the ventral surface of the last abdominal segment, and the tip of the abdomen is curled up under the body (Figs K.44iii and K.19). Both *B. bohemicus* and *B. vestalis* females have larger, more conspicuous v-shaped callosities (Fig. K.44v). Males of both *B. vestalis* and *B. bohemicus*, even when their yellow flashes have faded, can be distinguished from *B. sylvestris* by the ginger hairs on the final abdominal segment in the latter (mainly black hairs in both *B. vestalis* and *B. bohemicus*). The typical males in all three species have mainly white tails, though in *B. bohemicus* and *B. sylvestris* there are minority yellow-tailed forms.

The real difficulty comes in separating *B. vestalis* and *B. bohemicus*. Their geographical distributions are rather different, with *B. bohemicus* being more generally distributed and common north and west of a line from South Wales to Yorkshire, *B. vestalis* more common and widespread to the south and east. However, the two species do overlap in many areas. Generally, *B. vestalis* females are larger and more robust, with shorter, more even hair on the thorax. The yellow on the collar of *B. vestalis* is usually golden or brownish, and sometimes reduced, contrasting with the generally paler yellow of the collar in *B. bohemicus*. In *B. vestalis* females there are black hairs mixed in with the yellow on the collar, but in *B. bohemicus* females the hairs on the collar are all yellow. Some authors refer to a difference in the positioning of the callosities on the ventral surface of the final abdominal segment, but this trait is subject to individual variation and is not reliable. The males are rather easier to distinguish. In *B. bohemicus* the yellow collar is paler, more uneven and scruffy looking, compared to the darker yellow and neater, more even appearance of the collar in *B. vestalis*. The yellow side-flashes, even when not faded, are less distinct and less extensive. Confirmation can be achieved by 'tubing' specimens and examining the antennae with a lens. Male *B. bohemicus* have the third and fifth antennal segments roughly equal, but the third is obviously shorter than the fifth in *vestalis* (Fig. K.38). There are also differences in the genital capsules (Fig. K.45xv & xvi).

See Key A (females), couplet 10, then either 15–18, or 24–28; Key B (males), couplet 17 onwards).

Cluster 3: yellow bands on both collar and scutellum, tail white or yellow (the yellow bands on the thorax may be wide, giving the appearance of a yellow thorax with a black median band)

Basic: *B. hortorum*

Other species: *B. jonellus*, *B. ruderatus*, *B. distinguendus*, *B. subterraneus* and the cuckoo bumblebees *B. campestris* and *B. barbutellus*

In both males and females, *B. hortorum* has three yellow bands, two on the thorax, one on the abdomen, and a white tail. *Bombus hortorum* is widespread and often fairly common throughout Britain. It is likely to be present in most local bumblebee communities. Its two closest lookalikes are *B. ruderatus* and *B. jonellus*. Both these species usually have similar patterns of three yellow bands and white tails. The female of *B. jonellus* has a shorter face than the other two (Fig. K.12) and usually has pale or ginger hairs fringing the hind tibiae (black in *B. ruderatus* and *B. hortorum*). Males of *B. jonellus* also have short faces (Fig. K.30), and have yellow hairs on the face (long faces and black facial hair in *B. hortorum* and *B. ruderatus* males). *Bombus jonellus* is frequently, but not exclusively, seen on or close to heaths and moors.

The distinction between *B. hortorum* and *B. ruderatus* is more difficult, especially with workers. Queens of *B. ruderatus* are generally larger than those of *B. hortorum*, and have shorter, more even hairs on the thorax. The width and shade of the yellow collar and scutellum varies in both species (and completely black specimens occur in both species, probably more commonly in *B. ruderatus*), but in *B. hortorum* the yellow band on the scutellum is usually narrower than that on the collar (compare the width of each band in the mid-line). In *B. ruderatus* females the yellow thoracic bands are usually of equal width. Females of both species usually have a yellow band on the first abdominal segment. This is confined to that segment and is often broken in the middle in *B. ruderatus*, but it extends onto segment 2 in *B. hortorum*. The sculpturing on the dorsal surface of the final abdominal segment of *B. ruderatus* is deeper than that on *B. hortorum* (clearer in queens than workers) (Fig. K.15). In males the black band between the collar and scutellum is more clearly defined in *B. ruderatus*, and the yellow scutellum wider in the middle. The angle at which the long hairs fringing the hind tibia project also differs between the two species (Fig. K.32). Finally, the 'beard' on the mandibles is ginger in *B. ruderatus* males, but black in *B. hortorum*. *Bombus ruderatus* appears to have become scarce in Britain, confined to the east Midlands, East Anglia and the Southeast, but may now be increasing. Females of *B. subterraneus* are similar to *B. ruderatus*, but this species is believed to be extinct now in Britain.

Males of *B. lucorum*, especially pale ones, often have some yellow hairs on the scutellum, so might be included in this cluster. They can be readily distinguished from *B. hortorum* and *B. ruderatus* by the shorter, yellow-haired face of *B. lucorum* males (Fig. K.30). *Bombus jonellus* has long hairs on the dorsal edge of the hind metatarsus, whilst in *B. lucorum* these are much shorter (Fig. K.31). Also, the yellow band on the scutellum is as wide as that on the collar in *B. jonellus*, but rarely more than a fringe in *B. lucorum* males.

Two cuckoo bees, *B. campestris* and *B. barbutellus*, are also in this cluster. *Bombus campestris* has a yellow tail in both sexes, compared with the white tails of *B. barbutellus, B. hortorum* and *B. ruderatus*. It is liable to darkening, with completely black specimens not uncommon. *Bombus barbutellus* is similar in colour pattern to the darker forms of *B. hortorum*, but it has a short face, and sparse body hair, especially on the dorsal surface of abdominal segments 1 and 2. *Bombus barbutellus* can be distinguished from *B. jonellus* by the more extensive black area on the abdomen and by the lack of corbiculae (females) and the black face (males) in *B. barbutellus*.

The remaining two members of this cluster are most unlikely to be encountered. Both have yellow or ginger-yellow tails. *Bombus distinguendus* is now confined to some of the Scottish islands, and the far north of the Scottish mainland. In both sexes the abdomen is wholly covered with yellow or ginger-yellow hair, and both have flattened hairless and shiny outer surfaces of the hind tibiae. This species is thus quite different in appearance from *B. campestris* (and also from uncommon forms of *B. bohemicus* and *B. sylvestris* which also have yellow replacing the more typical white on the tail). Males of *B. subterraneus* are quite similar to those of *B. distinguendus*, but, as mentioned above, this species is believed to be extinct now in Britain.

See Key A (females) couplet 10, then 19–23 or 25–31; Key B (males), couplet 17, then 18–22 or 25–28.

Cluster 4: One or two yellow bands on the thorax, tail red

Basics: *B. pratorum*, and males of *B. lapidarius*

Other species: *B. ruderarius*, *B. sylvarum*, *B. soroeensis*, *B. monticola* and the cuckoo bumblebee *B. rupestris* (males)

Both sexes of *B. pratorum* have a yellow band on the thorax and a red tail, but in females the yellow band on the abdomen is often reduced or missing. Males have a wide yellow band on the abdomen, and the band on the collar is also more extensive and continuous with the yellow hair on top of the head and the face. Workers of *B. pratorum* could be confused with males of *B. lapidarius*, but the yellow face of the latter is a simple way to distinguish them. *Bombus ruderarius* is another member of this group that is widespread though increasingly scarce and localised. Females of this species belong to cluster 5, but the males are very variable in colour pattern, and brightly marked ones could be confused with males of *B. pratorum* or *B. lapidarius*.

The most obvious distinguishing feature to separate *B. pratorum* males from males of either *B. lapidarius* or *B. ruderarius* is the much more extensive yellow collar of *B. pratorum*. Also bright specimens of *B. ruderarius* have a yellow band on the scutellum, missing in *B. pratorum*. Distinguishing between males of *B. lapidarius* and *B. ruderarius* in the field can be more difficult. Bright specimens of *B. ruderarius* have a broad yellow band on segment 2 of the abdomen, whereas males of *B. lapidarius* have yellow at most on abdominal segment 1 only. In doubtful cases, close examination of the hind metatarsus can be used to confirm identification: the dorsal edge of this has long hairs in *B. lapidarius*, but both edges have short hairs in *B. ruderarius* (Fig. K.28). This feature is also useful in distinguishing the darker male specimens of *B. ruderarius* from *B. lapidarius* males.

Just to complicate matters further, males of the cuckoo *B. rupestris* also have a broadly similar and variable colour pattern to both *B. lapidarius* and *B. ruderarius*. Since the males of these three species can sometimes be found in the same localities at the same time of year, it is helpful to have some clues to distinguish them in the field, without relying on colour patterns. Males of *B. ruderarius* look short and compact, compared with the more long-bodied shape of *B. lapidarius* and *B. rupestris*. *B. ruderarius* has short hairs on both edges of the hind metatarsus. This structure is also relatively wide and short in *B. ruderarius*. Both *B. lapidarius* and *B. rupestris* have narrow, elongated hind tibiae and metatarsi, with long hairs on the dorsal edge of the latter. In *B. rupestris*, the outer surface of the hind tibia is covered in hair, whereas in *B. lapidarius* the distal half of the hind tibia is flattened and shiny without hairs (Figs K.28 and K.39, and Fig. 162 below).

Even darkened specimens of *B. lapidarius* have yellow hair on the face, unlike
B. rupestris.

---

1. Hind metatarsus broad and with short hair on the dorsal edge – *B. ruderarius*

   Hind metatarsus narrow and with long hairs on the dorsal edge –
   B. rupestris or *B. lapidarius*

2. Hind tibia flattened and outer surface shiny/hairless in lower half –
   B. lapidarius

   Hind tibia convex and outer surface hairy throughout – *B. rupestris*

FIG 162. Quick guide to similar males of three widespread cluster 4 species.

The remaining three members of this cluster are much more localised
and so will not be found in most local bumblebee communities. The first is
B. soroeensis, already featured as a member of cluster 2. Specimens with extensive
ginger hairs in the tail, especially males, could be confused with males of
B. pratorum or *B. ruderarius*. However, the ginger or ginger-red suffusion in the
tail is rarely intense enough, or sufficiently uniform, to cause real difficulty on
close examination. The much more extensive yellow collar of *B. pratorum* males
is a clear back-up feature to distinguish *B. soroeensis* males from that species.
Male *B. soroeensis* can be distinguished from male *ruderarius* by the long hairs
on the dorsal edge of the hind metatarsus (short on both edges in the latter)
(Figs K.24(b) and K.26(a)). In *B. soroeensis* the third segment of the antenna is
equal to or shorter than the fourth. In males of *B. ruderarius* the third is markedly
longer than the fourth (Figs K.25(b) and K.27(a)).

Bombus monticola is a species associated with upland moors, although it is often
found on nearby roadside verges and flowery grassland. There is a prominent
yellow band on the collar, and a yellow fringe on the scutellum. The red tail covers
more than half of the dorsal surface of the abdomen. These features distinguish
B. monticola females from the females of all other species. *Bombus rupestris* males
also have extensive red tails, but differ markedly in other respects. The abdomen
is elongated in *B. rupestris*, compact in *B. monticola*, and *B. monticola* males have
yellow hairs on the face (black in *B. rupestris*). *Bombus monticola* does sometimes
fly in the same localities as *B. lapidarius* and the males of the two species look

superficially similar. On closer inspection, it can be seen that the red on the tail of male *lapidarius* is much less extensive.

Bombus sylvarum is a rare and declining species of flower-rich grasslands, mainly in southern Britain. Compared with the other members of this cluster its colour pattern is rather subdued and lacking in contrasts. It has pale bands on collar and scutellum that almost coalesce at the sides of the thorax. The abdomen is mainly ginger and yellow, with narrow bands of black and an orange-red tail. It lacks the broad bands of black, or contrasting black and yellow, on the abdomen that characterise the other members of this cluster. Workers are small and inconspicuous.

Finally, females of *B. rupestris* usually belong in cluster 5, below, but there is a form (very uncommon in Britain, but more frequent in mainland Europe) that has a faint yellow band on the collar. The large size, darkened wings, large callosities on the underside of the abdomen near the tip, and the lack of corbiculae distinguish it clearly from the other members of this cluster.

See Key A (females), couplet 10, then 12–14 or 24; Key B (males), couplets 9–16.

Cluster 5: Thorax black, unbanded, tail red

Basic: *B. lapidarius* queens and workers

Other species: *B. ruderarius* females and darkened males and the cuckoo bumblebee *B. rupestris* (females)

The basic type here is *B. lapidarius* queens and workers. The queens are large with a glossy black coat, especially when newly emerged. Workers are often very small, and similarly coloured. Both have red tails, which tend to fade to orange-red with age. There are two other species in this cluster: *B. ruderarius* (females, but also dark forms of the males), and the cuckoo *B. rupestris* females. Queens of *B. ruderarius* are generally smaller than those of *B. lapidarius*, and the body is more compact (longer and parallel-sided in *B. lapidarius*) (Fig. K.6). The coat of the queen *B. ruderarius* is also a dull, sooty black, possibly because of the more erect hairs. The most obvious field character, however, is the red-orange corbicular hairs in *B. ruderarius* (black in *B. lapidarius*). This is surprisingly easy to see in living specimens, but is unfortunately not such a reliable feature in workers. The corbicular hairs of worker *B. ruderarius* are usually ginger or ginger-tipped, but faded specimens of *B. lapidarius* also often have pale corbicular hairs. Sometimes, too, the corbicular hairs are discoloured by pollen.

A structural feature that can be seen with a hand lens on captured specimens is the shape of the face. In *B. ruderarius* females the labrum forms an abrupt angle with the clypeus, so that the labrum is hardly visible from the front. In *B. lapidarius* females, the labrum curves back gradually from the clypeus, so that it protrudes below the clypeus in front view (Fig. K.4, and Fig. 161 for anatomical terms). *Bombus ruderarius* females also have a small spine on the mid-metatarsus, absent in *B. lapidarius*, but this is difficult to see, even with microscopic examination (see key A couplet 4, and Fig. K.5(a) & (b)).

Females of *B. rupestris* (a cuckoo of *B. lapidarius*) are quite distinctive, despite sharing a common colour pattern on the body. The wings have a dark, smoky suffusion (clear in *lapidarius* and *ruderarius*) and the body hair is much more sparse, showing the shiny cuticle below (especially on the dorsal surface of abdominal segments 1 and 2). The outer surface of the hind tibia is also covered with dense black hairs, replacing the corbicula of the other two species.

Finally, very dark males of *B. ruderarius* might appear to belong to this cluster, but they usually have some yellow hairs in the collar and segment 2 of the abdomen. Superficially they resemble only workers of *B. ruderarius* and *B. lapidarius* workers in this cluster, but can easily be picked out by the much longer antennae relative to their body size. The shape of the hind metatarsus and the shorter hairs on both edges of it in males of *ruderarius* distinguish them from dark males of both *B. lapidarius* and *B. rupestris* (see Fig. 162 above).

Key A (females), couplets 3 and 4; Key B (males), couplet 34.

Cluster 6: Darkened or melanic forms of various species
Identification has to rely on structural features alone. In males the genital capsule and in females the sting sheath, mandibles and presence or absence of corbiculae will often provide useful guides (use drawings given for use with the key, Figs K.1–K.45). Guides to the identification of a few of the more frequently seen melanic forms are given in the key:

Key A (females), couplets 29–31; Key B (males), couplets 35–37.

GUIDE TO THE COMPREHENSIVE KEY

The key is designed to make possible reliable identification of all the bumblebee species currently known to occur in Britain. One species believed to have become extinct recently – *B. subterraneus* – is also included. However, two species recorded in the distant past (*B. pomorum*, last recorded in 1864, and *B. cullumanus*, not recorded since the 1920s) are not included (see Appendix 1). As recounted elsewhere, the earlier practice of assigning the cuckoo bumblebees to a separate genus has now been abandoned. Following this change in taxonomic understanding,

I have integrated the cuckoos into a general key covering the whole of the newly enlarged *Bombus* genus. In fact, some of the general traits taken to distinguish *Bombus* from *Psithyrus* in the past did not apply without exception, or were often difficult to detect. Reliance on a general contrast between the hind tibiae of male cuckoos and social species, for example, could be misleading. Some social species, such as *B. jonellus*, *B. muscorum* and *B. humilis* have quite hairy outer surfaces to their hind tibiae, and detecting branching on the tibial hairs of the cuckoo males requires high microscopic magnification.

So I hope it will be an advantage not to have to decide at the beginning of the key whether your specimen is or is not a cuckoo bumblebee. However, it is necessary to be able to distinguish males from females. The first couplet should enable you to do this, but there are also some useful preliminary tips. In many species, the males are distinctive in that they have very obviously longer antennae in relation to their body size than do females. This is less clear in a few cases, such as *B. terrestris* and *B. lucorum*. Another useful clue in distinguishing the sexes is that males of many species have yellow faces, in contrast to the black-faced females. These include *B. lapidarius*, *B. lucorum*, *B. jonellus*, *B. pratorum*, *B. monticola* and *B. pratorum*. In some other species, such as *B. ruderarius* and *B. soroeensis*, the males often but do not always have yellow hairs on the face. Of course this does not work for the species in which both males and females have pale hairs on the face (such as *B. pascuorum*, *B. humilis*, *B. muscorum* and others), or for others (such as *B. hortorum* and *B. terrestris*) in which both males and females always have only black hairs on the face.

The characters used in the key are of three main kinds. First, it is expected that colour patterns will be the primary starting point for most readers. Since, as we have seen, there are some species that display considerable variation in colour pattern, the key is designed to work for specimens of all the main colour variants. This means that some species will key out more than once and at different points in the key, depending on which colour variant you have. However, to make the key manageable, some minor variants have been run together, and some very rare forms omitted altogether. This applies particularly to the species that have all black, or melanic, forms. I have included only a small number of these, selected mainly on the basis of my own field experience, as ones likely to be encountered in Britain.

Because colour patterns are variable, and often shared among different species, it is necessary to have more reliable structural characters as a back-up. I have tried to include these for each species, sometimes introducing characters not previously used in any published key. However, the structural characters can themselves be divided into two rough groups: first, macroscopic external features that can be seen on freely active bees, or with a hand lens on captured specimens, and, second, microscopic features and ones needing dissection of dead specimens. Where possible, the key gives external macroscopic features as a back-up to colour patterns for each species. Finally, for definitive identification there are drawings of the genital capsule of the males of each species, as well as sting sheaths and other anatomical characters of females.

Techniques

Free-flying bumblebees can usually be observed at close quarters, as most species are quite placid and not easily disturbed. Even where foraging bees are disturbed by the approach of an observer, they will soon settle down again after a few minutes of quiet observation. To detect finer details of external structures it is often helpful to use a close-focus monocular, or binoculars. To study those traits that require close examination with a hand lens, bees can be harmlessly captured and then released. Standard insect nets can be used to capture them, but this has the disadvantage of disturbing all the bees in range, and risks getting the net caught up in vegetation – especially when target bees are foraging on bramble! A very simple and usually successful method is to wait until the target bee enters a flower to take nectar and quickly place a glass tube over it. The lid can then be replaced as the tube is withdrawn, trapping the bee inside. Usually a bee captured in this way will actively try to get out of the tube, so will need to have its movements restrained if one is to get a clear view of the antennal segments, the structure of the face, or some other small feature. A good way to do this is to press a wad of tissue paper into the tube, gently but firmly trapping the bee against the side of the tube. It can then be viewed through the glass with a hand lens. Specially made tubes with plungers can also be used for this purpose. The bee can next be released back onto its forage plant, whereupon it will either fly off, or merely continue foraging directly. The only risk of harm to the bee is the loss of full pollen loads, though if this happens the detached pollen loads can themselves be an important source of information about the plants being used for pollen collection by the bee.

For those characters that require dissection, there are two main techniques that need to be learned. The genital capsules of males can be exposed by applying gentle pressure on ventral and dorsal surfaces of the final segments of the abdomen with a pair of forceps (Fig. 163).

This can be done only if the insect is recently dead, and still soft. If it has been dead some time and has become rigid, it will need to be 'relaxed' by placing it in a plastic box lined with damp tissue or cotton wool. Specimens should not be left more than 24 hours or there is a risk of mould developing.

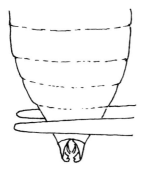

FIG 163. Technique: exposing a male genital capsule.

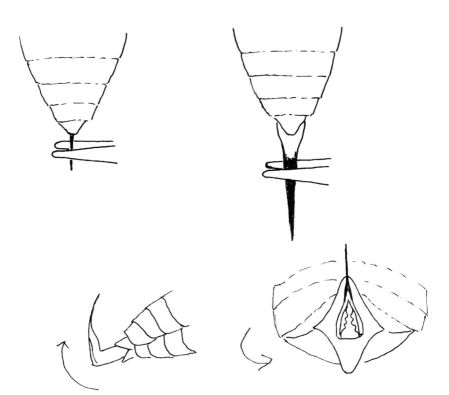

FIG 164. Technique: exposing the female sting sheath.

A slightly more complex technique is required to expose the distinctive features of the sting sheath of females. Unfortunately these are best seen in queens, and so this technique should be used as sparingly as possible. The tip of the sting is grasped with a fine-tipped pair of forceps, and the whole sting pulled back out of its cavity in the abdomen. This involves some tearing of the tissues connecting the base of the sting to the abdomen. The sting can now be bent up, and then forwards over the dorsal surface of the abdomen, exposing the ventral structure of the base of the sting, when viewed from behind. This is the sting sheath, and it takes the form of an arch, with variously shaped and marked inner flaps. Often the sides of the arch have to be stretched apart with forceps or pins to fully view the inner flaps or projections. The sequence is illustrated in Figure 164.

External structures of the bumblebee

In order to make full use of the comprehensive keys, some familiarity with the external structures of the bumblebee will be needed. The brief outline given earlier in this chapter, together with reference to the labelled drawings, Figures 158–161, 165, 166 and 167 should be sufficient for interpreting the key.

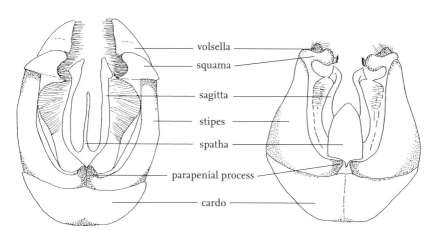

volsella
squama
sagitta
stipes
spatha
parapenial process
cardo

FIG 165. Male genital capsules of (a) *Bombus vestalis* (a cuckoo bumblebee) and (b) *B. terrestris* (a social bumblebee).

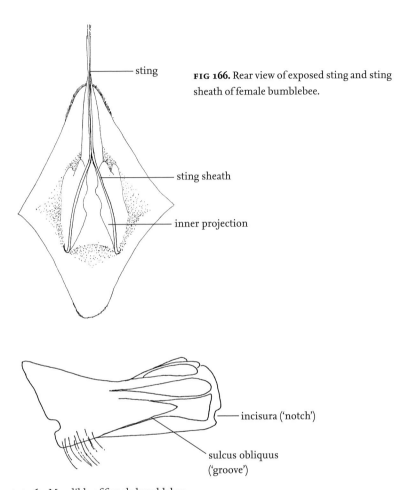

FIG 166. Rear view of exposed sting and sting sheath of female bumblebee.

— sting

— sting sheath

— inner projection

— incisura ('notch')

sulcus obliquus ('groove')

FIG 167. Mandible of female bumblebee.

Key

IF	THEN GO TO
• Antennae with 12 segments *(Fig. K.1(a))*. Abdomen with 6 segments visible from above. Tip of abdomen pointed, and enclosing sting *(Fig. K.2(a))*. ▷ **Female, Key A**	
• Antennae with 13 segments *(Fig. K.1(b))*. Abdomen with 7 segments visible from above. Tip of abdomen rounded, and enclosing genital capsule *(Fig. K.2(b))*. ▷ **Male, Key B**	

Key A. Females

	IF	THEN IT IS ... *or*	THEN GO TO
1	• Thorax black, unbanded.		▷ **2**
	• Thorax mainly ginger-brown or fawn, unbanded (may appear banded in specimens with hair worn from middle of thorax, or with clusters of black hair).		▷ **5**
	• Thorax black with one or two yellow or pale bands (yellow bands may be extensive, giving appearance of yellow thorax with median black band).		▷ **10**
2	• Tail red or ginger-red. Rest of abdomen black.		▷ **3**
	• Tail black, or with variable amounts of white, yellowish or brown hairs only. Rest of abdomen black.		▷ **29**
3	• Lacking corbicula (outer surface of hind tibia covered in short black hairs) *(Fig. K.3(a))*. Wings darkened. Outer edge of mandible oblique *(Fig. K.42i)*.	*rupestris* (formerly rare, but increasing; mainly southern; a cuckoo of *B. lapidarius*)	
	• With corbicula *(Fig. K.3(b))*. Wings not darkened. Outer edge of mandible not as above *(Figs K.42vi to xiii)*.		▷ **4**

IF	THEN IT IS ... *or*	THEN GO TO

4
- Corbicular hairs black (but may be discoloured in old specimens or by pollen grains). Junction of clypeus and labrum not sharply angled (labrum visible from front – *Fig. K.4(a)*). Abdomen relatively long and parallel-sided (especially queens) *(Fig. K.6(a))*. No spine on mid-metatarsus *(Fig. K.5(a))*. Sting sheath with narrow inner projection *(Fig. K.43i)*.

  lapidarius

  (common and widespread)

- Corbicular hairs ginger or ginger-red (queens) or ginger-tipped (workers). Junction of clypeus and labrum sharply angled (labrum not visible from front – *Fig. K.4(b)*). Abdomen oval, tapering to tip *(Fig. K.6(b))*. Short black spine on mid-metatarsus (microscope – among paler bristles, not easy to see) *(Fig. K.5(b))*. Sting sheath with wide inner projection *(Fig. K.43ii)*.

  ruderarius

  (local, patchily distributed and declining)

5
- Tail white. Broad black band on the abdomen (variable amounts of yellow hair on abdominal segment 1, or 1 and 2). Lacking spine on tip of mid-metatarsus. Mandible as in *Fig. K.42vi*, sting sheath as in *Fig. K.43iii*.

  hypnorum

  (a recent colonist of Britain)

- Tail not white. May have no, a few, or a dense band of black hairs on abdomen. May have some or no black hairs on thorax. Small spine on tip of mid-metatarsus *(Fig. K.5c)*. Mandible as in *Fig. K.42vii*.   ▷**6**

6
- Some black hairs on abdominal segments 1–5 (may be extensive, or very few: check sides of segments 3 and 4, and hind margins of segments, using ×10 lens). At least some long corbicular hairs black.   ▷**7**
- No black hairs on abdominal segments 1–5 (check with ×10 lens)

  ▷**8**

7
- Hairs on ventral surface of thorax and abdomen and corbicular hairs all or mostly black. Hairs on sides of abdominal segments arise from tiny bumps (microscope), some fused to make irregular ridges on the cuticle – *Fig. K.7(a)*. Sting sheath as in *Fig. K.43iv*.   *muscorum*

  (form *agricolae*, Scottish islands only)

- Hairs on ventral surface not all or mostly black. Hairs on sides of abdominal segments 3–5 arise from tiny pits (microscope) – *Fig. K.7(b)*. Sting sheath with narrow, simple inner projection *(Fig. K.43v)*.

  pascuorum

  (common and widespread throughout Britain)

IF	THEN IT IS ... *or*	THEN GO TO

8 • Hairs on sides of abdominal segments arise from tiny bumps (microscope), some fused to form irregular ridges on the cuticle – *Fig. K.7(a)*). No black hairs on the thorax. Sting sheath as in *Fig. K.43iv.*

muscorum
(increasingly scarce and local, mainly coastal)

• Hairs on sides of abdominal segments 3–5 arise from tiny pits (microscope – *Fig. K.7(b) or (c)*). May have some black hairs on the thorax.
▷ 9

9 • The pits on the sides of abdominal segments 3 and 4 more sparsely distributed towards the front of each segment, with shiny cuticle between them *(Fig. K.7(b))*. Long corbicular hairs all black, or a mixture of pale and black. Longer hairs on the dorsal edge of the hind metatarsus black. Inner projection of the sting sheath narrow and simple *(Fig. K.43v)*.

pascuorum
(pale forms, more frequent in north)

• The pits at the sides of abdominal segments 3 and 4 are densely and more evenly distributed along the length of the segments, *(Fig. K.7(c))*. In queens, long corbicular hairs pale, with much smaller black ones. Longer hairs on the dorsal edge of the hind metatarsus brown (not black). Inner projection of sting sheath wide and indented *(Fig. K.43vi)*.

humilis
(an increasingly scarce and local southern species, mainly coastal)

N.B. Small workers of *muscorum, humilis* and pale *pascuorum* may be very difficult to distinguish.

10 • With corbicula. Outer edge of mandibles blunt or rounded *(Figs K.42vi to xiii)*. Lacking callosities on ventral surface of last abdominal segment. May or may not have small spine on tip of mid-metatarsus. ▷ 11

• Lacking corbicula (hind tibia not flattened, and outer surface covered in hair). Outer edge of mandibles obliquely angled *(Figs K.42i to v)*. Variously shaped callosities on ventral surface of last abdominal segment *(Fig. K.44)*. Small spine on tip of mid-metatarsus. ▷ 24

11 • Tail red or orange-red. ▷ 12

• Tail buff, yellow, ginger-yellow, white, or white with some ginger hairs.
▷ 15

IF	THEN IT IS ... *or*	THEN GO TO

12 • Thorax with two yellow or pale bands of approximately equal width, one on
the collar, the other on the scutellum.   ▷ **13**

• Thorax with a yellow or pale band (on the collar). Hairs on the scutellum all
black, or with a narrow fringe of yellow.   ▷ **14**

13 • Abdominal segments 1, 2, 4, 5 and 6 with bands of pale hair (ginger-red on tail),
and a band of black hairs on segment 3. Hairs on the face mostly pale. Pale
hairs whitish or greenish-yellow. Small spine on tip of mid-metatarsus
(Fig. K.8(a)). Mandibles with oblique groove but no notch *(Fig. K.42viii)*. Sting
sheath as in *Fig. K.43vii*.   ***sylvarum***
(increasingly scarce and local, mainly
southern)

• Abdominal segments 2 and 3 mainly black-haired. Hairs on the face black.
Pale hairs yellow. Lacking spine on tip of mid-metatarsus *(Fig. K.8(b))*.
Mandibles without distinct oblique groove, but with wide, shallow notch
(Fig. K.42ix). Sting sheath as in *Fig. K.43viii*.
jonellus
(Scottish island forms)

14 • Orange-red tail very extensive, covering abdominal segments 3–5 and much of
segment 2. Scutellum usually with narrow fringe of yellow hairs, but
occasionally all black. Black hairs on abdominal segment 6. Lacking yellow
band on abdomen. Face relatively wide, and clypeus relatively densely
punctured *(Fig. K.9(a))*.   ***monticola***
(increasingly local, and confined to
upland moors and heaths in the north
and south-west)

• Red tail less extensive, covering abdominal segments 5 and 6 (no black hair on
segment 6). Scutellum black. Usually yellow band on abdominal segment 2
(this may be reduced, broken or absent, especially in small workers). Face
narrower. Clypeus relatively sparsely punctured, and shiny around the
middle *(Fig. K.9(b))*.   ***pratorum***
(common and widespread)

15 • Thorax with one yellow band only, on collar (scutellum black). Tail buff, white,
or white with some reddish hairs.   ▷ **16**

• Thorax with two yellow bands; one on collar, the other on the scutellum (the
latter may be a narrow fringe only). Tail white, yellow or ginger-yellow.
▷ **19**

IF	THEN IT IS … *or*	THEN GO TO

16 • Tail buff, or buff-brown. Band on collar golden yellow to brownish (may be reduced and darkened in some individuals). Broad golden-yellow band on abdominal segment 2. Usually a large bee (18 millimetres or more in length). Mandibles with oblique groove and notch *(Fig. K.42x)*. Sting sheath as in *Fig. K.43xii*.

terrestris (queen)

(very common and widespread in England and Wales, but local in Scotland)

• Tail white, orange-red, or white with ginger or ginger-red hairs.

▷ **17**

17 • Yellow band on abdominal segment 2 extends forwards at the sides onto segment 1, and is often (but not always) broken by black hairs in the middle (check this is not due to wear) *(Figs K.10(a) and 10(b))*. Yellow bands pale, especially that on the abdomen. Tail white, often with ginger hairs mixed in. Segment 4 of antenna as wide as or wider than it is long *(Fig. K.11(a))*. Mandibles without oblique groove or notch *(Fig. K.42xi)*. Inner projection of sting sheath simple, similar to that of *B. jonellus (Fig. K.43viii)*.

soroeensis

(very local, on moors and late-flowering grassland)

• No yellow hair on segment 1 of abdomen and yellow band on segment 2 not broken by black hairs in the middle *(Fig. K.10(c))*. Tail white, never with ginger hairs. Segment 4 of antenna longer than it is wide *(Fig. K.11(b))*. Mandibles with oblique groove and notch *(Fig. K.42x)*. Sting sheath as in *Fig. K.43xi or xii*.

▷ **18**

18 • Transition from pure white tail to black of abdomen abrupt. Band on collar and on abdominal segment 2 pale, lemon yellow, rarely reduced or darkened. Sting sheath as in *Fig. K.43xi* (inner projection narrower than in *terrestris*, and, in lateral view, border short and not curved round the base of the sting).

lucorum

(queens and workers)

(very common throughout Britain)

• Narrow brown transitional zone between white or whitish tail and black of the abdomen. Yellow band on collar and on abdominal segment 2 darker, golden or brownish-yellow, and that on the collar sometimes reduced and/or darkened. Sting sheath as in *Fig. K.43xii* (very similar to *lucorum*, but inner projection wider than in *lucorum*, and slight difference in lateral view).

terrestris (workers)

(very common in England and Wales, but local in Scotland)

IF	THEN IT IS ... *or*	THEN GO TO

N.B. It is often difficult or impossible to distinguish reliably between workers of *lucorum* and *terrestris*.

19 • Tail white. Usually with yellow band on abdominal segment 1, or 1 and 2.

▷ **20**

• Tail yellow or ginger-yellow. ▷ **23**

20 • Face short (that is, as wide as it is long – *Fig. K.12(a)*). Hairs on corbicula whitish or ginger, at least towards their tips. Yellow band on abdominal segment 1, or 1 and 2 (often reduced). No spine on tip of mid-metatarsus *(Fig. K.13(a))*. Mandibles without distinct oblique groove, but with wide, shallow notch *(Fig. K.42ix)*. Sting sheath as in *Fig. K.43viii*.

jonellus
mainland form (local but widely distributed; often associated with heaths and coasts)

• Face long, markedly longer than it is wide *(Figs K.12(b) or K.12(c))*. Hairs on corbicula black. Small spine on tip of mid-metatarsus *(Fig. K.13(b))*.

▷ **21**

21 • No yellow band on segment 1 of abdomen. Distinct keel on ventral surface of final abdominal segment *(Fig. K.14(a))*. Mandible as in *Fig. K.42xii* (similar to *distinguendus*).   **subterraneus**
(believed extinct in Britain)

• Usually with yellow band on abdominal segment 1 or 1 and 2. Lacking keel on ventral surface of final abdominal segment (but slightly angled along the median line in the posterior half) *(Fig. K.14(b))*. Darkening and reduction of yellow markings common. Mandible as in *Fig. K.42xiii*.   ▷ **22**

22 • Yellow band on collar wider than that on scutellum. Yellow band on abdominal segment 1 usually extends onto segment 2. Hair on thorax long and uneven (view from side with naked eye or ×10 lens from side). Queens usually smaller than *ruderatus*. Sculpturing on dorsal surface of abdominal segment 6 shallow *(Fig. K.15(a))*. Sting sheath as in *Fig. K.43xiii*.

hortorum
(fairly common and widespread)

IF	THEN IT IS ... *or*	THEN GO TO

• Yellow bands on collar and scutellum of equal width at middle. When present, yellow band on abdominal segment 1 does not extend into segment 2 (at most a few yellow hairs on this segment). Hair on thorax short and even (view from side with naked eye or ×10 lens). Queens usually larger than *hortorum*. Sculpturing on dorsal surface of abdominal segment 6 deeper *(Fig. K.15(b))*. Sting sheath as in *Fig. K.43xiv*.

> **ruderatus**
> (local or rare, mainly south-eastern)

N.B. Small workers of *hortorum* and *ruderatus* may not be distinguishable. Completely black, or strongly darkened specimens may occur in both species, but appear to be more frequent in *ruderatus*.

23

• Abdomen mainly black except for a yellow band on segment 1 and yellow or ginger tail. Hairs on face mostly black. Face as wide as it is long *(Fig. K.16(a))*. No spine on tip of mid-metatarsus *(Fig. K.17(a))*. Mandibles without distinct oblique groove but with wide, shallow notch *(Fig. K.42ix)*.

> **jonellus**
> (Scottish island form)

• Abdomen yellow or ginger-yellow, with a band of brownish hairs on abdominal segment 2. Hairs on the face mostly pale. Face longer than it is wide *(Fig. K.16(b))*. Mid-metatarsus with small spine at tip *(Fig. K.17(b))*. Mandibles with oblique groove and wide shallow notch *(Fig. K.42xii)*.

> **distinguendus**
> (a rare and declining species confined to Scottish islands and north of Scotland)

24

• Tail orange-red, body otherwise black but sometimes with faint yellowish band on collar. Wings darkened. Large callosities on ventral surface of final abdominal segment *(Fig. K.44i)*.

> **rupestris**
> (formerly rare but increasing; a cuckoo of *B. lapidarius*. This colour form is common on the European mainland, but infrequent in Britain)

• Tail white, yellow or white with yellow side-flashes. Thorax usually with one or two yellow bands.   ▷ 25

25   • Tail mainly yellow (abdominal segments 1, 2 and most of 3 black-haired, with yellow-ginger at sides of 3, spreading towards middle in 4 and 5, so that the black of the abdomen extends in a wedge-shape into the mainly yellow-haired segment 5). Wide yellow band on collar, usually with some yellow hairs on scutellum. (The uncommon form reported from western Scotland, *swynnertoni*, has more extensive yellow on both thorax and abdomen). The dorsal surface of abdominal segment 6 is sparsely punctured and shiny towards the middle and the junction with segment 5 *(Fig. K.18(a))*. Callosities on ventral surface of segment 6 as in *Fig. K.44ii*.

campestris

(a cuckoo of *B. pascuorum*, and probably of other carder bumblebees)

• Tail white or white with yellow side-flashes on abdominal segment 3.

▷ 26

26   • Final segments of abdomen tightly curved under the body *(Fig. K.19)*. With v-shaped swelling at rear end of dorsal surface of segment 6 *(Fig. K.18(b))*. Callosities on ventral surface of abdominal segment 6 small and inconspicuous *(Fig. K.44iii)*. Scutellum (mostly) black. Usually some yellow hairs on abdominal segments 1 and 2. Tail white.

sylvestris

(a cuckoo of *B. pratorum*)

• Final segments of abdomen not tightly curved under the body. No swelling at rear end of dorsal surface of segment 6. Callosities on ventral surface of abdominal segment 6 large and conspicuous.   ▷ 27

27   • Dorsal surface of segment 6 dull and densely punctured, with a narrow raised ridge along the mid-line *(Fig. K.18(c))*. Ventral surface of segment 6 with prominent callosities forming a wide, shallow u-shape *(Fig. K.44iv)*. Thorax with wide yellow band on collar, and usually at least a fringe of yellow hairs on the scutellum. Tail white or off-white, lacking yellow side-flashes.

barbutellus

(a cuckoo of *B. hortorum* and probably *B. ruderatus*)

• No median ridge on dorsal surface of abdominal segment 6 *(Fig. K.18(d)* or *K.18(e))*. Callosities on ventral surface of abdominal segment 6 form more acute v-shape *(Fig. K.44v)*. Thorax with yellow band on collar, scutellum usually black. Abdomen black, with white tail and (in fresh specimens) yellow side-flashes on segment 3.   ▷ 28

IF	THEN IT IS ... *or*	THEN GO TO

28 • Collar golden to brownish-yellow, usually with some black hairs mixed in with the yellow. Persistent lemon-yellow side-flashes on abdominal segment 3. Hair on thorax short, dense and even (view from side with ×10 lens). Dorsal surface of segment 6 moderately punctured and shiny. Punctures distributed widely over surface of the segment, except for narrow median shiny area *(Fig. K.18(d))*. Callosities on ventral surface of abdominal segment 6 as in *Fig. K.44v* (not consistently different from *bohemicus*).

> ***vestalis***
> (a cuckoo of *B. terrestris*; common and widespread, with more southerly distribution)

• Collar pale yellow, with no black hairs mixed in. Pale yellow side-flashes on abdominal segment 3, often fading to white in older specimens. Hair on thorax more uneven (view from side with ×10 lens). Dorsal surface of segment 6 sparsely punctured and very shiny, punctures mostly at sides of the segment *(Fig. K.18(e))*. Callosities on ventral surface of segment 6 as in *Fig. K.44v* (as *vestalis*).

> ***bohemicus***
> (a cuckoo of *B. lucorum*; has a more northerly distribution)

29 • Lacking corbicula.   ▷ **30**
   • With corbicula.   ▷ **31**

30 • Hind tibia covered with black hair. Antennal segment 3 not greatly elongated (shorter than 4+5 – *Fig. K.20(a)*). Callosities on ventral surface of abdominal segment 6 form wide v-shape as in *Fig. K.44ii*. (other melanic cuckoos may key out here. Check against key figures).

> ***campestris***
> (cuckoo of *B. pascuorum* and probably other carder bumblebees; a minority melanic form)

• Hind tibia and metatarsus covered with long yellow-orange hairs. Antennal segment 3 greatly elongated (longer than 4+5+6 – *Fig. K.20(b)*). Lacking callosities on ventral surface of abdominal segment 6.

> ***Anthophora plumipes*** (female)
> (a common bumblebee lookalike)

IF	THEN IT IS ... *or*	THEN GO TO

31 • Face as in *Fig. K.12(b)*. Hair on thorax uneven in length (view from side with naked eye or ×10 lens). Sculpturing on dorsal surface of abdominal segment 6 shallow *(Fig. K.15(a))*. Sting sheath as *K.43xiii*. See couplet

▷ **22.**

hortorum
(melanic form)

• Face as in *Fig. K.12(c)*. Hair on thorax of even length (view from side with naked eye or ×10 lens). Sculpturing on dorsal surface of abdominal segment 6 deeper *(Fig. K.15(b))*. Sting sheath as *K.43xiv*. See couplet

▷ **22.**

ruderatus
(relatively frequent melanic form)

N.B. Separation of melanic forms of *ruderatus* and *hortorum* is difficult, especially with small workers.

Key B. Males

IF	THEN IT IS ... or	THEN GO TO

1 • Thorax ginger-brown or fawn, unbanded (may appear banded in specimens with hair worn from middle of the thorax). ▷ **2**

• Thorax black, with yellow band on collar, or on both collar and scutellum. (yellow bands may be extensive, giving appearance of yellow with a median black band). ▷ **8**

• Thorax black, unbanded. Tail black, red or with some whitish or yellowish hairs (rest of abdomen black, or mainly black). ▷ **33**

2 • Thorax ginger-brown with black hairs around the centre, not forming a band. Abdomen mainly ginger-brown. Antennal segments more-or-less parallel-sided, not swollen ventrally. Genital capsule as in *Fig. K45xix*: volsella prominent, pale and broadly triangular in shape.

> **campestris**
> (an uncommon form, *swynnertoni*, reported from western Scotland; a cuckoo of *B. pascuorum*, and probably other carder bumblebees)

• Not as above (thorax with mostly ginger or ginger-brown hairs, any black ones not concentrated round the centre). Volsella smaller and darker, partially concealed by squama. ▷ **3**

3 • Abdomen black with white tail. Thorax without black hairs. Genital capsule as in *Fig. K.45vi* (sagitta hooked inwards).

> **hypnorum**
> (a recent colonist of Britain)

• Abdomen ginger-brown, with or without black hairs. Tail not white. Thorax mainly ginger; may have some black hairs, but not forming a band. Genital capsule: sagitta either straight or barbed towards the tip, not inwardly hooked. ▷ **4**

4 • Hairs on ventral surface of thorax and abdomen, and hairs on legs and head mostly black (may have some yellow hairs on face). Antennal segments with slight symmetrical swellings ventrally *(Fig. K.21(b))*. Genital capsule as in *Fig. K.45xii*: sagitta with barbed tip, volsella with blunt tip and inner edge with pointed, inwardly projecting tooth, and squama with long, pointed inner projection.

> **muscorum**
> (form *agricolae*, Scottish islands only)

IF	THEN IT IS … or	THEN GO TO

• Ventral surface of thorax and abdomen and legs with pale hairs, or mixed pale and black.   ▷ 5

5   • Abdomen with some black hairs on segments 1–6. These may be very extensive, or very few in number and inconspicuous (check rear edges and sides of segments with ×10 lens). Antennal segments (especially 7–10) with marked asymmetrical swellings ventrally, and segment 4 approximately as wide as it is long *(Fig. K.21(a))*. Long hairs on edges of hind tibia mostly black, and outer surface with extensive shiny, sparsely haired area *(Fig. K.22(a))*. Genital capsule as in *Fig. K.45x*: sagitta without barbed tip.

pascuorum
(common and widespread throughout Britain)

• Abdomen without black hairs on segments 1–6.

6   • Antennal segments (esp. 7–10) with asymmetrical ventral swellings, and segment 4 as wide as it is long *(Fig. K.21(a))*. Outer surface of hind tibia with extensive shiny, sparsely haired area *(Fig. K.22(a))*. Genital capsule: sagitta without barbed tip *(Fig. K.45x)*.

pascuorum
(pale forms, more frequent in north)

• Antennal segments with slight, symmetrical swellings (especially segments 7–10), and segment 4 slightly longer than it is wide *(Fig. K.21(b))*. Shiny, sparsely haired area on outer surface of hind tibia smaller, close to distal tip *(Fig. K.22(b))*. Genital capsule: sagitta with barbed tip *(Fig. K.45xi or K.45xii)*.   ▷ 7

7   • No black hairs on the thorax (check with ×10 lens, especially near the wing bases). Genital capsule: tip of volsella rounded, squama with narrowly pointed inner projection *(Fig. K.45xii)*.

muscorum
(mainland form; increasingly scarce and local, mainly coastal)

• Usually some black hairs on the thorax (may be very few and inconspicuous – check near the wing bases with ×10 lens). Genital capsule: tip of volsella pointed and long, squama with wide inner projection *(Fig. K.45xi)*.

humilis
(increasingly scarce and local, a mainly coastal southern species)

IF	THEN IT IS ... *or*	THEN GO TO

8   • Tail red or ginger-red.   ▷**9**

      • Tail not red, but buff, yellow, ginger-brown, white, white with variable amounts of ginger hairs, or white with yellow side-flashes.

          ▷**17**

9   • Red or ginger-red tail extensive: red or ginger-red hairs on abdominal segments 2–7 or 3–7.   ▷**10**

      • Red or orange-red tail less extensive (no red or ginger-red on segments 2 or 3).

          ▷**11**

10   • Hind tibia flattened, outer surface shiny and only sparsely hairy (*Fig. K.23(a)*). Yellow hairs on face and top of head. Abdominal segments 3–7 with red hair, segment 2 with a mixture of red and black. Thorax with wide yellow band on collar, and fringe of yellow hairs on scutellum. Compact body shape (abdomen approximately as wide as long). Genital capsule as in *Fig. K.45v*: volsella small and inconspicuous, partly hidden by squama. Sagitta curled inwards at tip, and with a spine below (view from side).

          monticola

          (increasingly local and confined to upland moors and heaths in the north and south-west)

      • Hind tibia elongated and outer surface covered with dense hair (*Fig. K.23(b)*). Hairs on face black. Colour pattern variable: red tail may extend forwards to sides of segment 2, and yellow bands on collar, scutellum and abdominal segment 1 may be faint and/or reduced. Elongated body shape (abdomen longer than wide). Genital capsule as in *Fig. K.45xvii*: volsella prominent, triangular and pale. Sagitta barbed, not curled inwards.

          rupestris

          (formerly rare, but increasing; mainly southern; a cuckoo of *B. lapidarius*)

11   • Abdominal segment 2, or both 1 and 2, predominantly yellow-haired.

          ▷**12**

      • Abdominal segments 1 and 2 black (may have some yellow hairs mixed with the black).   ▷**16**

12   • Thorax with yellow band on the collar only (may be some yellow hairs on scutellum, but not forming a yellow band).   ▷**13**

      • Thorax with pale or yellow bands on both collar and scutellum.

          ▷**14**

13 • Yellow on thorax extensive, covering approximately anterior half of the dorsal surface. Hair on face and head mainly yellow. Hair on thorax long and uneven. Hind metatarsus relatively wide at base *(Fig. K.24(a))*. Antennal segment 3 long, approximately equal to 5 (3 plus 4 clearly longer than 5) *(Fig.25(a))*. Black band on abdomen looks wide compared to red tail (abdominal segments 1 and 2 yellow, 3, 4 and part of 5 black, and remainder of 5, 6 and 7 orange-red). Genital capsule as in *Fig. K.45iv*: sagitta curled inwards at tip, squama and volsella relatively small. (on Orkney, local form of *jonellus* may key out here. See couplet 14 and compare genital capsules *(Figs K.45iii and K.45iv))*.   **pratorum**
(common and widespread)

• Yellow band on collar less extensive than in *pratorum*, covering approximately one third of the dorsal surface of the thorax. Yellow hairs on the head and face mixed with more black than in *pratorum*. Hair on thorax more even, giving neater appearance. Ginger or ginger-red hairs on the tail usually mixed with white ones, especially towards the tip. Hind metatarsus narrow at base *(Fig. K.24(b))*. Antennal segment 3 much shorter than 5 (3 plus 4 approximately equal to 5) *(Fig. K.25(b))*. Black band on abdomen looks narrow compared to red tail (abdominal segments 1 and 2 yellow, 3 and part of 4 black, the rest orange-red to white). Genital capsule as in *Fig. K.45ii*: sagitta barbed and bent outwards at tip, squama long and narrow, volsella more prominent than in *pratorum*.   **soroeensis**
(red-tailed form, may be more frequent in southern populations; the species is local, on moors in north, and on late-flowering grassland, declining in south)

14 • Hair on dorsal edge of hind metatarsus short (longest shorter than the width of the metatarsus) *(Fig. K.26(a) or K.26(b))*. Asymmetrical swellings on ventral surface of antennal segments (view segments 7–10) *(Fig. K.27(a))*
▷ 15

• Hair on dorsal edge of hind metatarsus long (longest longer than the width of the metatarsus) *(Fig. K.26(c))*. Ventral surface of antennal segments not swollen *(Fig. K27(c))*.   **jonellus**
(local form, Scottish islands)

15 • Abdomen with broad black band on segment 3 contrasting strongly with ginger-red tail. (Abdominal segments 1 and 2 often with yellow band that may be faint and/or reduced). Hairs on side of thorax black in rear half. Hind metatarsus relatively broad and narrowing slightly towards the outer end *(Fig. K.26(a))*. Antennal segment 3 markedly longer than 4 *(Fig. K.27(a))*. Genital capsule as in *Fig. K.45ix*: similar to *sylvarum*, but middle tooth of volsella narrowly truncate at tip, and the lower one longer and narrower than in *sylvarum*.

ruderarius

(pale forms; local and patchily distributed)

• Abdomen with narrow fringes of black hair on segments 3 and 4, mixed with pale yellow or ginger, not contrasting strongly with ginger tail. Hairs on side of thorax pale, continuous with collar and scutellum. Hind metatarsus narrow and parallel-sided *(Fig. K.26(b))*. Antennal segment 3 equal to or only slightly longer than 4 *(Fig. K.27(b))*. Genital capsule as in *Fig. K.45xiii*: similar to *ruderarius*, but middle tooth of volsella broadly truncate with extended terminal point, and lower tooth broader than in *ruderarius*.

sylvarum

(increasingly scarce and local; mainly southern)

16 • Hind metatarsus relatively long and narrow, with long hairs on dorsal edge (longer than the width of the metatarsus) *(Fig. K.28(a))*. Antennal segments parallel-sided, and 3 as long as 5 *(Fig. K.29(a))*. Yellow hairs on face, and yellow band on collar. Sometimes also some yellow hairs on scutellum and abdominal segment 1 (not 2). Yellow may be faint and/or reduced in darker specimens. Genital capsule as in *Fig. K.45viii*: sagitta with pointed barbs, volsella small and without inwardly projecting teeth.

lapidarius

(common and widespread)

• Hind metatarsus relatively broad, with short hairs on both edges (much shorter than the width of the metatarsus) *(Fig. K.28(b))*. Antennal segments with asymmetrical swellings ventrally (especially 7–10), and segment 3 shorter than 5 *(Fig. K.29(b))*. Head, thorax and segments 1–3 of abdomen mostly black, but often some yellow hairs on abdominal segment 2. Genital capsule as in *Fig. K.45ix*: sagitta with rounded tip, volsella relatively large, and with inwardly projecting teeth.

ruderarius

(darker forms; the species is local and patchily distributed, declining)

IF	THEN IT IS ... *or*	THEN GO TO

17 • Hind tibia with flattened, shiny, more-or-less hairless area on outer surface.
    ▷ 18
    • Hind tibia strongly convex and covered with hair.   ▷ 26

18 • Tail white, off-white to buff, or white with ginger hairs.   ▷ 19
    • Tail (and much of rest of abdomen) yellow or ginger-yellow. Thorax with yellow or ginger-yellow bands on both collar and scutellum.
    ▷ 25

19 • Thorax with yellow bands on both collar and scutellum.   ▷ 20

    • Thorax with yellow band on collar only (may be some yellow hairs among the black on the scutellum, but not forming a yellow band).   ▷ 23

20 • Face short *(Fig. K.30(a) or K.30(b))* and with yellow hairs.   ▷ 21
    • Face long *(Fig. K.30(c))* and black (without yellow hairs).   ▷ 22

21 • Yellow band on scutellum extensive. Hind tibia only slightly flattened on outer surface, and with sparse hairs. Hind tibia and metatarsus relatively long and narrow, and hind metatarsus with long hairs on dorsal edge (longer than the width of the metatarsus) *(Fig. K.31(a))*. Abdominal segments 1 and 2 yellow. Genital capsule as in *Fig. K.45iii*: sagitta curled inwards, no inner projection on squama.   *jonellus*
    (mainland form; local but widely distributed; often associated with heaths and coasts)

    • Yellow band on scutellum usually a narrow fringe. Hind tibia strongly flattened on outer surface, with extensive shiny and hairless area. Hind tibia and metatarsus relatively broad, with short hairs on metatarsus (much shorter than the width of the metatarsus) *(Fig. K.31(b))*. Abdominal segments 1 and 2 yellow. Sometimes yellow more extensive. Genital capsule as in *Fig. K.45i*: sagitta barbed and curved outwards at tip, pointed inner projection on squama.   *lucorum*
    (pale form; very common throughout Britain)

IF	THEN IT IS ... *or*	THEN GO TO

22

• Yellow band on scutellum usually narrower than collar, and boundary between black and yellow areas on thorax not clearly defined. Fringe of long hairs on the mandibles usually black. Hair on thorax uneven (view from side with naked eye or ×10 lens). Long hairs on dorsal edge of hind tibia project approximately at right angles to it *(Fig. K.32(a))*. Genital capsule as in *Fig. K.45vii*: similar to *ruderatus*.   **hortorum**
(fairly common and widespread)

• Yellow band on scutellum wide at the middle (as wide as collar), with a straight and clearly defined boundary between it and the black interalar band Fringe of long hairs on the mandibles usually ginger, at least towards their tips. Hair on the thorax relatively short and even (view from side with naked eye or ×10 lens). Hairs on dorsal edge of hind tibia project at markedly acute angle near to the base and are shorter than those of *hortorum (Fig. K.32(b))*. Genital capsule as in *Fig. K.45vii*: similar to *hortorum*.

ruderatus
(local or rare, mainly south-eastern)

N.B. Both species have strongly darkened forms in which the yellow bands are absent (see couplet **36**), but *hortorum* also has intermediate forms in which the yellow bands are reduced.

23

• Long hairs on edges of hind tibia mostly black. Antennal segment 3 equal to or slightly shorter than 4 *(Fig. K.33(a))*. Hind tibia convex with shiny outer surface and with sparse covering of short hairs. Hind metatarsus narrow at base, widening gradually and with long hairs on dorsal edge (longer than the width of the metatarsus) *(Fig. K.34(a))*. Face black or with some yellow hairs mixed with black. Collar and abdominal segments 1 and 2 pale yellow, and tail all white, or with ginger-red transitional zone. Genital capsule as in *Fig. K.45ii*: elongated squama without inner projection.

soroeensis
(very local, on moors in north and late-flowering grassland in south, declining)

• Long hairs on edges of hind tibia mostly pale (yellow or ginger-yellow). Antennal segment 3 markedly longer than 4 *(Fig. K.33(b))*. Hind tibia with shiny flattened area on outer surface hairless for at least distal half of its length. Hind metatarsus wider at base and abruptly widening, without long hairs on dorsal edge *(Fig. K.34(b))*. Face black or yellow, tail white or whitish-buff. Never with ginger hairs in tail. Genital capsule as in *Fig. K.45i*: squama not elongated and with pointed inner projection.   ▷ **24**

IF	THEN IT IS ... *or*	THEN GO TO

24 • Face yellow. Pale yellow band on collar, and often fringe of scattered yellow hairs on scutellum. Pale yellow band on abdominal segment 2. Tail white. Genital capsule as in *Fig. K.45i*: similar to *terrestris* except for difference in shape of squama (outer margin strongly curved out to a point).

lucorum
(dark form; very common throughout Britain)

• Face black. Thorax with yellow collar (sometimes darker, golden yellow than in typical *lucorum*), and no yellow hairs on scutellum. Yellow band on abdominal segment 2 usually darker than in *lucorum*. Tail usually off-white, and often buff, or with a transitional buff zone. Genital capsule as in *Fig. K.45i*: similar to *lucorum* except for difference in shape of squama (outer margin less strongly curved, forming more obtuse angle with inner edge).

terrestris
(very common in England and Wales, but scarce in Scotland)

N.B. *Bombus lucorum* and *B. terrestris* are 'sibling' species, with few differences in colour pattern to distinguish them. The character in the genitalia is subject to some individual variation, but the contrast is generally valid. The character in the volsella given by Alford (1975) is unreliable.

25 • Abdominal segments 1–6 yellow, with a few black hairs on segment 7 only. Hairs on face yellow. Yellow on segment 2 often brownish. Genital capsule as *Fig. K.45xiv*: very similar to *subterraneus*, except for smaller side projection of sagitta.

distinguendus
(a rare species confined to Scottish islands and north Scotland)

• At least some black hairs on abdominal segments 1–6 (check sides of segment 2). Hairs on face mostly black. Genital capsule as in *Fig. K45xiv*: see enlarged detail.

subterraneus
(now believed to be extinct in Britain)

26 • Face and abdominal segments 1 and 2 mainly yellow. Hind tibia narrow but with shiny area on outer surface, only sparsely hairy *(Fig. K.35(a))*. Hair on abdomen dense. Genital capsule as in *Fig. K.45iii*: tip of sagitta inwardly curled, volsella small and inconspicuous. Thorax with bright yellow bands on collar and scutellum. Tail white or, in Scottish islands, yellow to ginger-red.

jonellus
(local but widely distributed; often associated with heaths and coasts)

IF	THEN IT IS ... *or*	THEN GO TO

• Face and abdominal segment 2 black. Hind tibia densely hairy over most of the outer surface (though sometimes with small shiny and hairless area at distal end) *(Fig. K.35(b) or (c))*. Hair on abdomen less dense, especially on dorsal surface of abdominal segments 1 and 2. Genital capsule with conspicuous volsella: pale and wide, roughly triangular, or long and narrow, darker *(sylvestris) (Figs K.45xv – xx)*. ▷ **27**

27 • Tail yellow, or a mixture of black and yellow. ▷ **28**
• Tail white, white with yellow side-flashes, or white tipped with ginger. ▷ **30**

28 • A tuft of long black hair on each side of the ventral surface of the last abdominal segment *(Fig. K.36)*. Thorax with yellow on both collar and scutellum. Abdominal segments 3–6 yellow or a mixture of yellow and black. Genital capsule as in *Fig. K.45xix*.

campestris
(pale forms; a cuckoo of *B. pascuorum* and probably other carder bumblebees)

• Sides of ventral surface of last abdominal segment without tufts of long black hair. Thorax with yellow band on collar only (may be a few yellow hairs mixed with the black on scutellum). Abdominal segments 4–6 yellow. ▷ **29**

29 • Yellow or ginger hairs on dorsal surface of last abdominal segment. Genital capsule as in *Fig. K.45xx* (volsella elongated and narrow).

sylvestris
(infrequent colour form, more common in the north)

• Black hairs on dorsal surface of last abdominal segment. Genital capsule as in *Fig. K.45xvi* (volsella broad and roughly triangular).

bohemicus
(infrequent colour form, mainly northern)

30 • Tail white, or white tipped with ginger. Lacking yellow side-flashes. ▷ **31**
• Tail white with yellow side-flashes on segment 3 of abdomen (anterior edge of white tail). ▷ **32**

IF	THEN IT IS ... *or*	THEN GO TO

31 • Thorax with pale yellow bands on collar and scutellum. Abdominal
segments 6 and 7 with mostly black hairs (may be some white ones on 6).
Raised mound on each side of ventral surface of last abdominal segment
(Fig. K.37(a)). Genital capsule as in *Fig. K.45xviii*: volsella rounded at distal
end.

> **barbutellus**
> (a cuckoo of *B. hortorum* and
> probably *B. ruderatus*)

• Thorax with yellow band on collar only (may be a few yellow hairs mixed with
the black one on scutellum, but not forming a band). Abdominal segments
6 and 7 with ginger hairs. Lacking raised mounds on ventral surface of last
abdominal segment *(Fig. K.37(b))*. Genital capsule as in *Fig. K.45xx*: volsella
elongated and narrow, with oblique tip. (if hair on abdominal segments
6 and 7 is black, and volsella broadly triangular, go to couplet 32).

> **sylvestris**
> (a cuckoo of *B. pratorum*)

32 • Antennal segment 3 markedly shorter than 5 *(Fig. K.38(a))*. Band on collar
golden yellow, no yellow on scutellum. Hair on thorax relatively dense and
even (view thorax from side with naked eye or ×10 lens). Abdominal segment
3 with lemon yellow hairs at the sides, shading to whitish in the middle (a
persistent character, but fading in very old specimens). Genital capsule as in
Fig. K.45xv: similar to *bohemicus*, but note differently shaped squama.

> **vestalis**
> (a cuckoo of *B. terrestris*)

• Antennal segment 3 approximately as long as 5 *(Fig. K.38(b))*. Thorax with
bright lemon yellow band on collar (often sparse yellow hairs on scutellum,
but not forming band). Hair on thorax uneven in length, and less dense
(view from side with naked eye or ×10 lens). Abdominal segment 3 with pale
yellow hairs at the sides, often faded and inconspicuous. Genital capsule as
in *Fig. K.45xvi*.

> **bohemicus**
> (a cuckoo of *B. lucorum*)

33 • Tail red or orange-red. ▷ **34**

• Tail all black or with some white, yellow or brown hair. ▷ **35**

IF	THEN IT IS … *or*	THEN GO TO

34   Hind tibia relatively long and narrow, outer surface dull and densely covered with hair. Hind metatarsus relatively long and narrow, with long hairs on dorsal edge (much longer than width of the metatarsus) *(Fig. K.39(a))*. Antennal segments parallel-sided *(Fig. K.40(a))*. Genital capsule as in *Fig. K.45xvii*: volsella rounded at tip, and lacking inwardly projecting teeth.

         rupestris
         (dark forms; formerly rare, but increasing currently; a cuckoo of *B. lapidarius*)

   • Hind tibia relatively short and broad, outer surface sparsely hairy, and shiny towards the tip. Hind metatarsus relatively short and broad with short hairs on dorsal edge (shorter than width of the metatarsus) *(Fig. K.39(b))*. Antennal segments with asymmetrical ventral swellings (especially segments 7–10) *(Fig. K.40(b))*. Genital capsule as in *Fig. K.45ix*: volsella pointed at the tip, and with inwardly projecting teeth.

         ruderarius
         (dark forms; a local and patchily distributed species, declining)

35   • Hind tibia with extensive flattened shiny and hairless outer surface, fringed by long hairs *(Fig. K32(a) or K32(b))*. Coat relatively dense. Face long *(see Fig. K.30(c))*.

         ▷ **36**

   • Hind tibia with outer surface convex and mostly covered with hair *(Fig. K.35(b) or (c))*. Coat less dense (most obvious on segments 1 and 2 of abdomen). Face short *(see Fig. K.41)*.   ▷ **37**

36   • Fringe of longer hairs on the mandibles usually black. Hair on the thorax uneven (view from side with naked eye or ×10 lens). Long hairs near to the base of the dorsal edge of hind tibia project approximately at right angles *(Fig. K.32(a))*. Genital capsule as in *Fig. K.45vii* (very similar to *ruderatus*).

         hortorum
         (fairly common and widespread)

   • Fringe of longer hairs on the mandibles usually ginger, at least towards the tips of the hairs. Hair on thorax relatively short and even (view from side with naked eye or ×10 lens). Long hairs near to the base of the dorsal edge of the hind tibia, shorter than in *hortorum*, and project at an acute angle *(Fig. K.32(b))*. Genital capsule as in *Fig. K.45vii* (very similar to *hortorum*).

         ruderatus
         (local or rare, mainly south-eastern)

37   • A tuft of long black hair on each side of ventral surface of last abdominal segment *(Fig. K.36)*. Outer surface of hind tibia entirely covered with hair, lacking shiny, hairless area *(Fig. K.35(b))*. Genital capsule as in *Fig. K.45xix*: volsella broadly triangular.

campestris

(a cuckoo of *B. pascuorum*)

• Lacking tufts of long black hair on ventral surface of last abdominal segment. Outer surface of hind tibia mostly covered with hair, but with small shiny hairless area towards the tip *(Fig. K.35(c))*. Genital capsule as in *Fig. K.45xx*: volsella long and narrow.   *sylvestris*

(a cuckoo of *B. pratorum*)

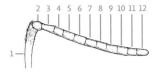

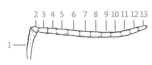

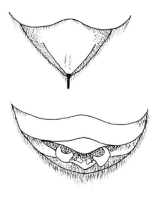

◁ **FIG K.1** Antenna of:
  (a) female, and
  (b) male bumblebees

▷ **FIG K.2** Ventral view of tip of
  abdomen of bumblebees:
  (a) female (with tip of sting
  exposed), and
  (b) male (with genital
  capsule partly exposed)

◁ **FIG K.3** Hind tibia and
  tarsus of:
  (a) *B. rupestris* female, and
  (b) a social bumblebee
  female, showing corbicula

▷ **FIG K.4** Faces of:
  (a) *B. lapidarius*, and
  (b) *B. ruderarius* females,
  front and side views,
  showing shape of the
  labrum

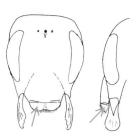

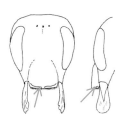

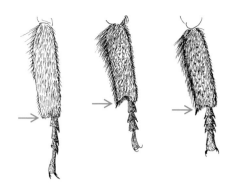

◁ **FIG K.5** Mid-tarsus of:
(a) *B. lapidarius,*
(b) *B. ruderarius* and
(c) *B. pascuorum* (*muscorum*
and *humilis* similar) females,
showing absence or
presence of spine on the
metatarsus

◁ **FIG K.6** Body shapes of:
(a) *B. lapidarius* and
(b) *B. ruderarius* females

◁ **FIG K.7** Sides of abdominal
segments 3 and 4 of:
(a) *B. muscorum,*
(b) *B. pascuorum* and
(c) *B. humilis* females

▷ **FIG K.8** Mid-tarsus of:
(a) *B. sylvarum,*
(b) *B. jonellus* females,
showing presence
or absence of spine on
metatarsus

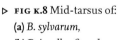

▷ **FIG K.9** Face of:
(a) *B. monticola* and
(b) *B. pratorum* females,
showing punctuations
on the clypeus.

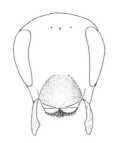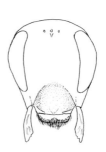

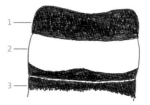

△ **FIG K.10** Abdominal
segments 1 and 2 of:
(a & b) *B. soroeensis*
(c) *B. terrestris/lucorum*
females

▽ **FIG K.11** Antenna of:
(a) *B. soroeensis* and
(b) *B. terrestris/lucorum*
females, showing shape of
segment 4.

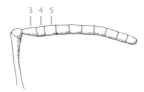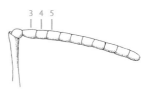

◁ **FIG K.12** Face of:
(a) *B. jonellus,*
(b) *B. hortorum* and
(c) *B. ruderatus* females.

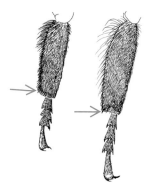

◁ **FIG K.13** Mid-tarsus of:
(a) *B. jonellus*,
(b) *B. hortorum* (as *B. ruderatus*) females, showing absence or presence of spine on metatarsus

▷ **FIG K.14** Ventral view of final abdominal segment of:
(a) *B. subterraneus*,
(b) *B. hortorum* (as *B. ruderatus*) females

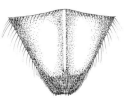 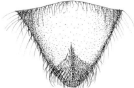

◁ **FIG K.15** Dorsal surface of final abdominal segment of:
(a) *B. hortorum* and
(b) *B. ruderatus* females, showing sculpturing of cuticle

▷ **FIG K.16** Faces of:
(a) *B. jonellus* and
(b) *B. distinguendus* females

 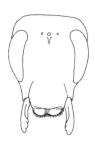

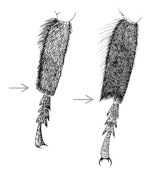

◁ **FIG K.17** Mid-tarsus of:
(a) *B. jonellus* and
(b) *B. distinguendus* females,
showing absence or
presence of spine on
metatarsus

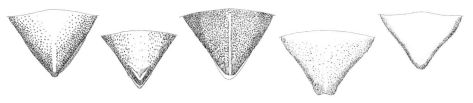

△ **FIG K.18** Dorsal surface of
final abdominal segment of:
(a) *B. campestris,*
(b) *B. sylvestris,*
(c) *B. barbutellus,*
(d) *B. vestalis* and
(e) *B. bohemicus* females

◁ **FIG K.19** Side view of
B. sylvestris female

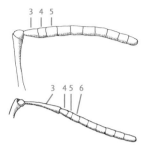

◁ **FIG K.20** Antenna of:
(a) *B. campestris* and
(b) *A. plumipes*, females

▷ **FIG K.21** Antenna of:
(a) *B. pascuorum* and
(b) *B. muscorum/humilis*
males, showing shape
of segment 4 and ventral
swellings

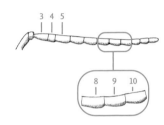

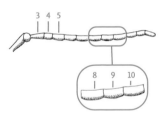

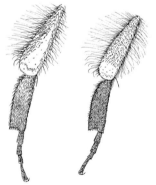

◁ **FIG K.22** Hind tibia and
tarsus of:
(a) *B. pascuorum* and
(b) *B. muscorum/humilis*
males, showing distribution
of hairs on outer surface of
tibia

◁ **FIG K.23** Hind tibia and
tarsus of:
(**a**) *B. monticola* and
(**b**) *B. rupestris* males,
showing shapes of segments
and distribution of hairs

▷ **FIG K.24** Hind tibia and
tarsus of:
(**a**) *B. pratorum* and
(**b**) *B. soroeensis* males
showing shape of
metatarsus

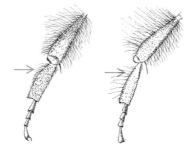

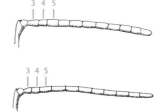

◁ **FIG K.25** Antenna of:
(**a**) *B. pratorum* and
(**b**) *B. soroeensis* males
showing relative lengths of
segments 3, 4 and 5

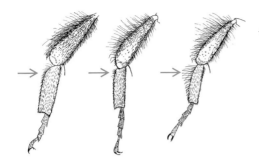

◁ **FIG K.26** Hind tibia and
tarsus of:
(a) *B. ruderarius*,
(b) *B. sylvarum* and
(c) *B. jonellus* males, showing
shapes of segments and
distribution of hairs

▷ **FIG K.27** Antenna of:
(a) *B. ruderarius*,
(b) *B. sylvarum* and
(c) *B. jonellus* males

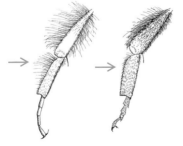

◁ **FIG K.28** Hind tibia and
tarsus of
(a) *B. lapidarius* and
(b) *B. ruderarius* males,
showing shapes of segments
and distribution of hairs

▷ **FIG K.29** Antenna of:
(a) *B. lapidarius* and
(b) *B. ruderarius* males,
showing shapes of segments
3–5 and the slight
asymmetrical ventral
swellings in ruderarius

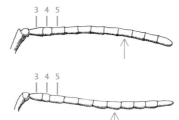

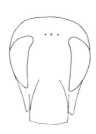

◁ **FIG K.30** Faces of:
(a) *B. jonellus,*
(b) *B. lucorum,*
(c) *B. hortorum*
(as *B. ruderatus*) males.

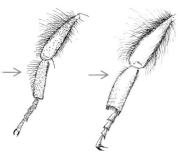

◁ **FIG K.31** Hind tibia and
tarsus of:
(a) *B. jonellus* and
(b) *B. lucorum* males.

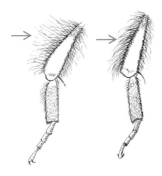

◁ **FIG K.32** Hind tibia and tarsus of:
(a) *B. hortorum* and
(b) *B. ruderatus* males

▷ **FIG K.33** Antenna of:
(a) *B. soroeensis* and
(b) *B. lucorum/terrestris*
males showing relative
lengths of segments 3 and 4

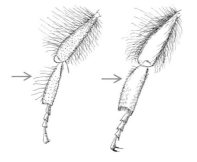

◁ **FIG K.34** Hind tibia and tarsus of:
(a) *B. soroeensis* and
(b) *B. lucorum/terrestris* males

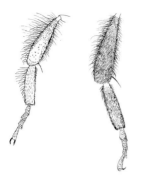

◁ **FIG K.35** Hind tibia and tarsus of:
(a) *B. jonellus,*
(b) *B. campestris* and
(c) *B. sylvestris* males

▷ **FIG K.36** Ventral surface of hind abdominal segment of *B. campestris* male, showing lateral tufts of long hairs

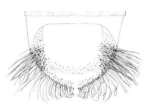

◁ **FIG K.37** Ventral surface of final abdominal segment of:
(a) *B. barbutellus* and
(b) *B. sylvestris* males

▷ **FIG K.38** Antenna of:
(a) *B. vestalis* and
(b) *B. bohemicus* males, showing relative lengths of segments 3 and 5

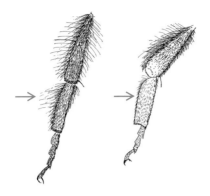

◁ **FIG K.39** Hind tibia and
tarsus of:
(a) *B. rupestris* and
(b) *B. ruderarius* males

▷ **FIG K.40** Antenna of
(a) *B. rupestris* and
(b) *B. ruderarius* males,
showing relative lengths
of segments 3 and 5
and ventral swellings of
segments in *B. ruderarius*

◁ **FIG K.41** Face of male
cuckoo bumblebee

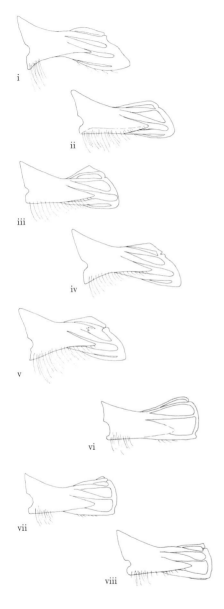

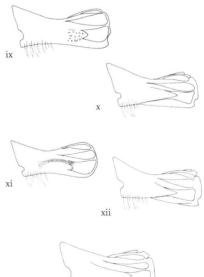

FIG K.42 mandibles of female *Bombus* species:

i. *B. rupestris*
ii. *B. campestris*
iii. *B. sylvestris*
iv. *B. barbutellus*
v. *B. vestalis* (as *B. bohemicus*)
vi. *B. hypnorum*
vii. *B. pascuorum*
viii. *B. sylvarum* (as *B. ruderarius*)
ix. *B. jonellus*
x. *B. terrestris* (as *B. lucorum*)
xi. *B. soroeensis*
xii. *B. distinguendus*
    (as *B. subterraneus*)
xiii. *B. hortorum* (as *B. ruderatus*)

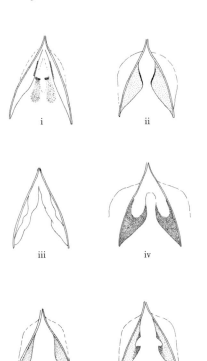

FIG K.43 sting sheaths of female
Bombus species:

i.   *B. lapidarius*
ii.   *B. ruderarius*
iii. *B. hypnorum*
iv.   *B. muscorum*
v.   *B. pascuorum*
vi.   *B. humilis*
vii. *B. sylvarum*
viii. *B. jonellus*
ix.   *B. monticola*
x.   *B. pratorum*
xi.   *B. lucorum* (with lateral view)
xii. *B. terrestris* (with lateral view)
xiii. *B. hortorum*
xiv. *B. ruderatus*

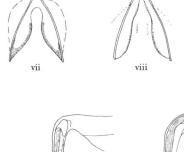

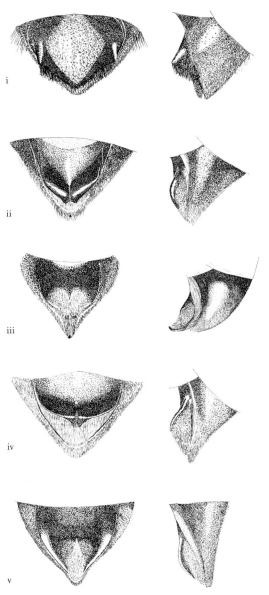

FIG K.44 callosities on ventral surface of final abdominal segment of female cuckoo bumblebees:
i.   *B. rupestris*
ii. *B. campestris*
iii. *B. sylvestris*
iv. *B. barbutellus*
v.   *B. vestalis/bohemicus*

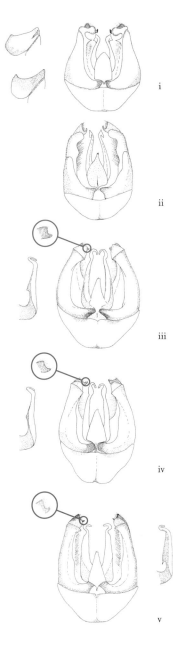

FIG K.45 Genital capsules of male *Bombus* species:

i: *B. terrestris/lucorum* (with rear view of squama of *terrestris* (top) and lucorum (*bottom*)

ii: *B. soroeensis*

iii: *B. jonellus* (and lateral view of sagitta)

iv: *B. pratorum* (and lateral view of sagitta)

v: *B. monticola* (and lateral view of sagitta)

vi: *B. hypnorum* (and lateral view of sagitta)

vii: *B. hortorum* and *B. ruderatus*

viii: *B. lapidarius*

ix: *B. ruderarius*

x: *B. pascuorum*

xi: *B. humilis*

xii: *B. muscorum*

xiii: *B. sylvarum*

xiv: *B. distinguendus* and *B. subterraneus* (ringed)

xv: *B. vestalis*

xvi: *B. bohemicus*

xvii: *B. rupestris*

xviii: *B. barbutellus*

xix: *B. campestris*

xx: *B. sylvestris*

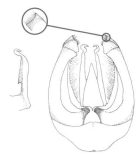

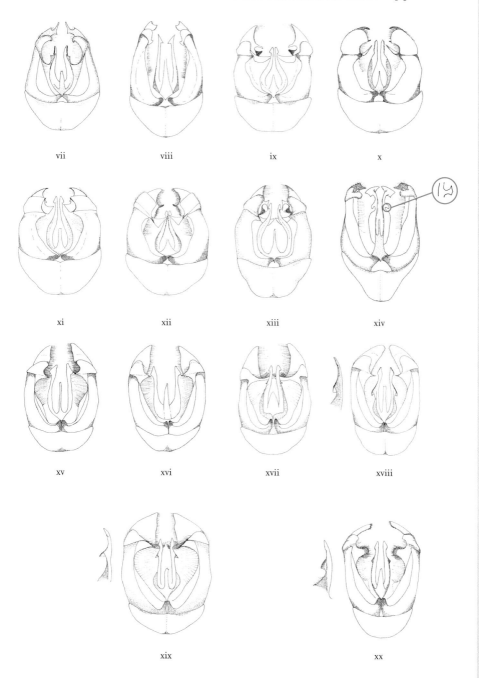

vii viii ix x

xi xii xiii xiv

xv xvi xvii xviii

xix xx

CHAPTER 9

The British Species

A TOTAL OF 25 species of bumblebee has been recorded in Britain. Of these, one, *Bombus pomorum*, has not been recorded in Britain since 1864. Another, *B. cullumanus*, has not been recorded for several decades and is almost certainly extinct. These two species are not dealt with in this chapter, but relegated to Appendix 1. A further species, *B. subterraneus*, is also now believed to be extinct in Britain, but its probable extinction was so recent that it was decided to include it here.

Bumblebees are a relatively homogeneous group of insects in terms of their structural features, and there has been a long history of disagreement about how to group the various species into a taxonomic order. One early classification was provided by Krüger (1917). This established a division between the *Odontobombus* and *Anodontobombus* group. The females of the former have a small spine on the outer tip of the mid-metatarsus, which is lacking in the *Anodontobombus*. The division also correlates with a difference in the structure of the male genitalia. Other subdivisions have sometimes been elevated to the status of proposed genera, but until recently the most widely accepted system has been to group all the social species into a single genus: *Bombus*. The cuckoo bumblebees were generally assigned to a second, closely related genus: *Psithyrus*. Within the genus *Bombus* a number of more-or-less clearly defined subgenera have been distinguished, mainly on the basis of structural characteristics. The currently occurring British species are included in seven of these: *Thoracobombus, Megabombus, Kallobombus, Subterraneobombus, Pyrobombus, Bombus* (in a narrow sense), and *Melanobombus*. The extinct species *B. cullumanus* and *B. pomorum* were included in two further subgenera: *Cullumanobombus* and *Rhodobombus*, respectively. The consolidation of this set of subdivisions by Richards (1968) has generally been followed by subsequent authors. However, systematic analysis of structural variations within the whole group, including *Psithyrus,* led Williams (1994) to argue for the inclusion of *Psithyrus* as a subgenus within the wider genus *Bombus.* This change has been generally accepted.

Research using modern techniques of chemical and molecular analysis has produced new evidence about the phylogenetic relationships between the bumblebee species, as well as helping to clear up controversies about the specific status of some closely related forms (for example, Svensson, 1979*a*). In some cases these newer studies have produced results that seem inconsistent with patterns of affinity established on the basis of structural features. However, the broad pattern of allocation of the British species to subgenera seems reasonably secure, and the taxonomic grouping presented by Williams in his annotated checklist of 1998 will be followed here. However, the sequence of subgenera, and the order of individual species in their subgenus is adjusted so as to place similar-looking species close together where this is feasible, as an aid to identification.

There is continuing disagreement about the status of some taxa, and here, again, a compromise has been adopted. The *Bombus lucorum* complex includes at least three forms that are given specific status by many authors: *B. lucorum* in the strict sense, *B. magnus,* and *B. cryptarum.* I have included these forms under *B. lucorum,* with some discussion of the forms *magnus* and *cryptarum* under 'variation'. The separation of *B. hortorum* and *B. ruderatus* has also been to some extent controversial, but the combination of recent ecological study and molecular evidence confirm its validity (see Ellis *et al.,* 2005). Accordingly, the two taxa are treated as distinct species here.

A point needs to be made about the use of English language names for bumblebees. Few of these are in common use, but previous authors have invented them, and more recently a few have become more widely used to popularise bumblebees in the context of efforts at conservation. Throughout this book I have given prominence to scientific names, but in this chapter I have also given the English names of some species. However, some of the English names given by authors such as Sladen (1912) and Step (1932) are rather misleading and I have omitted these, relying instead solely on the scientific names for these species.

Finally, a word about the distribution maps. Although recording effort in recent years has been intensified, especially for the more scarce species, the current maps still, to some extent, reflect the distribution of recorders! Gaps for many of the common and widespread species do not necessarily imply absence of the bee. Yellow dots show recordings from 1800–1969, and the green dots show those from 1970 to the present day.

SUBGENUS BOMBUS (in the strict sense)

Bombus lucorum (Linnaeus)

White-tailed bumblebee

Bombus lucorum is best regarded as a species complex, including the forms
B. magnus and *B. cryptarum*, which are sometimes recognised as distinct species.

FIGS A–D. *Bombus lucorum* queen; *B. lucorum* male (pale form);
B. lucorum male (dark form); *B. lucorum*, face of male
showing yellow hairs.

E

F

FIGS E–G. *B. lucorum* worker;
B. lucorum queen (form *magnus*); *B. lucorum*
worker with pollen loads (form *magnus*).

G

Description

QUEENS are large (length 18–22 mm, wingspan over 36 mm), but usually slightly
smaller than queens of *B. terrestris*, except for larger forms referable to *B. magnus*
(see below). The colour pattern is predominantly black, with a single yellow band
(collar) at the front of the thorax, and another on the second abdominal segment.
The tail is white. The yellow bands are generally of a pale lemon shade. The face is
as wide as it is long, and the tongue is relatively short. WORKERS are similar to the
queens, but generally considerably smaller, though variable in size. MALES show
considerable normal variation. All forms to be found in Britain have yellow hairs
on the face. Darker forms have a similar colour pattern to the females, except for
the yellow on the face. Paler forms are more extensively yellow, with wider pale
yellow bands on the collar and abdomen (often including at least the first as well
as the second abdominal segment) and a fringe of yellow hairs on the scutellum.

Variation

In upland areas of northern Britain, Wales and south-west England the form known as *magnus* is found, often flying together with typical *lucorum*. Females of *magnus* have the yellow collar extended down the sides of the thorax, well below the wing bases, and the band is wider. The tail in freshly emerged specimens is sometimes described as pinkish, yellowish or brownish-white (for example, Alford), and queens are held to be larger than those of *lucorum*. Some authors (for example, Alford; Prŷs-Jones & Corbet; von Hagen & Aichhorn and Macdonald, 1999), as well as many field naturalists, regard *magnus* as a distinct species. Against this, Williams provides an analysis of specimens allocated to both taxa which shows that the usual characters relied on to separate them either overlap or are linked by intermediate forms. *Bombus cryptarum* is another closely related form that is generally treated as a distinct species by European authors. Although 'typical' individuals can be distinguished, particularly in the queens, the high levels of individual variation in colour patterns and structural features makes confident discrimination between these three groups difficult. However, chemical analyses of enzymes and pheromone secretions have tended to confirm the specific status of the three forms, as has a recent study of mitochondrial DNA (Pamilo *et al.*; Bertsch; Pedersen). Unfortunately there has been little examination of the relationship of British populations of these groups to those from the European mainland, and there is still no consensus about their taxonomic status. More research, especially using modern techniques of molecular analysis, is clearly needed.

Similar species

Bombus terrestris, *B. soroeensis*, and the cuckoo bumblebees *B. vestalis*, *B. bohemicus* and *B. sylvestris*. For distinguishing features see Chapter 8, cluster 2 and the key.

Distribution

Bombus lucorum is very widely distributed throughout Britain, including the north of Scotland, the Western Isles and Orkney. Only form *magnus* occurs on Shetland.

Colony cycle

Queens of this species are among the earliest to emerge from hibernation in the spring, typically in mid-March in southern Britain. Depending on weather conditions, they may be seen prospecting for nest sites from that time on through April and, less commonly, into May. When engaged in this, they fly close to the ground, systematically investigating the contours of areas of rough, tussocky grass or other rank vegetation, often in the vicinity of scrub. Other characteristic sites explored include crevices in a garden rockery, bare patches among nettle beds, the edge of woodland rides, roadside verges and overgrown gardens. Less commonly they investigate short, sheep-grazed turf, flying 5–10 centimetres above the ground. During this period the queens may also be observed with full pollen loads on the hind legs, signifying that a nest has already been established. The nests are usually below ground, in holes, and often in disused nests of small mammals, using finely shredded grass, mosses or leaf litter as nesting material. They also sometimes make their nests in abandoned mouse nests under garden sheds and outhouses.

The first workers appear from mid-April to mid-May, depending on locality and season, and numbers build up through June and July. The first males and daughter queens appear from late May or early June onwards. Like *B. terrestris*, *B. lucorum* is a complex species, in which queen-dominance is maintained partly by pheromonal communication. Queens can control the timing of the switch to production of males and daughter queens. Some colonies produce males early in the season, while others produce mainly daughter queens later. *Bombus lucorum* is a pollen storer (see Chapters 2 & 3). At maturity the number of workers in a nest can be very large – as many as 400. Researchers in Switzerland found a significant correlation between early nest establishment, size of the colony at maturity, and reproductive success (that is, numbers of males and daughter queens produced). About half of the colonies produced no sexual generation.

The males indulge in patrolling flights, often in numbers, and typically fly low down along field boundaries or other linear features. They have been observed to stop more frequently than males of *B. terrestris*, and to scent-mark grasses.

As with most other species, mating is not commonly observed, but the extraordinary event of a male *B. lapidarius* mating with a female *B. lucorum* was noted in Essex in 1994, and a mating pair of *B. lucorum* on the ground with a male *B. lapidarius* attached to the *B. lucorum* queen was observed in 2004 (see Fig. 62).

Most colonies die out by late August, but observations of workers collecting pollen in September, followed by sightings of daughter queens well into October, suggest that second broods may be reared in some years in southern England. Persistence of small numbers of foraging workers through the winter months is puzzling, and it is unclear whether these represent a subsequent colony cycle, or an extended life span of earlier colonies, perhaps by replacement of the foundress queen.

In northern Scotland colonies develop more slowly, with numbers of males not peaking until August and September, and both males and workers being seen until mid-October. *Bombus magnus* reportedly emerges from hibernation later than *B. lucorum*.

Foraging behaviour

Small numbers of winter-foraging bees seen in southern England have been foraging exclusively on garden flowers and shrubs. Overwintered queens initially forage to meet their own requirement, but after nest initiation turn to collecting pollen. Both queens and workers visit a wide range of wild and cultivated flowers, and are able to rob deep flowers of their nectar by biting holes in the corolla with their strong mandibles (see Chapter 6). Workers buzz-forage from *Hypericum*, and probably other flowers, causing the anthers to release pollen by vibrations of the appropriate frequency (see Chapter 6). Rapid trampling over the anthers of bramble is also used to shake pollen onto their coats. Workers of this species are known to forage at considerable distances from their nests, and are able to adapt to fragmented urban and agricultural landscapes. In northern Scotland it is estimated that overwintered queens are dependent on garden flowers for at least a month after emergence from hibernation.

Bombus lucorum foraging patterns. Plants in **bold** are garden plants, and (p) signifies recorded pollen source. Some observers aggregate workers of *B. lucorum* and *B. terrestris*, and these records have been included under *B. terrestris*.

QUEEN — winter: ***Japonica, Fuchsia, Hebe, Erica***
spring: sallows, **Prunus** spp., ground ivy, white (p) and red deadnettles, ***Japonica, Rhododendron,* rosemary, crocus, *Mahonia,* laurel (p), flowering currant, roses,** bluebells.

WORKERS — spring: comfrey, mallow, common vetch, red deadnettle, **broom, *Ceanothus,* wallflower, *Rhododendron,*** field bean.
summer: ***Ceanothus, Campanula, Hebe,* lavender, snowberry, tamarisk, privet, *Buddleia,* sage, *Fuchsia* (p), *Hypericum* (p),** bramble (p), red bartsia (p)
Fabaceae (trefoils, vetches, clovers, lupins and broom), Asteraceae (various thistles and knapweed) and Lamiaceae (hedgewoundwort, black horehound (p), thyme, wood sage) buttercups, iris, viper's bugloss, bell heather, ling, ivy (p).

DAUGHTER QUEENS — bramble, comfreys, Asteraceae (thistles and knapweeds), scabious **honeysuckle, *Hebe,* lavender, *Lavatera, Linaria, Buddleia, Sedum,* Michaelmas daisy.**

MALES   **Ceanothus, Hebe,** lavender, **Lavatera, roses, Rhododendron,**
thyme, Campanula, Asteraceae (thistles, greater burdock,
knapweed, ragwort), Fabaceae (clovers, tufted vetch), Lamiaceae
(marsh woundwort, thyme), purple toadflax, viper's bugloss,
bramble, bell heather, ling.

Predators and parasites

Bombus lucorum is the main recorded host species of the cuckoo bumblebee,
B. bohemicus. Thirty per cent of colonies of *B. lucorum* were invaded by this
cuckoo in Müller & Schmid-Hempel's study. Cumber found very high levels of
infestation of overwintered queens of this species by the nematode *Sphaerularia*
bombi. Overall, 69 per cent were infected, with proportions infected increasing
with time, as healthy queens established their nests and disappeared from view.
He also recorded nest parasitism by the tachinid fly, *Brachicoma devia.* Müller &
Schmid-Hempel recorded high levels of infestation of workers by conopid flies
(*Sicus ferrugineus* and *Physocephala rufipes*) from late June onwards. *Bombus lucorum*
is also listed as host to the scuttle fly *Megaselia giraudi* and significant numbers are
taken by crab spiders while foraging (see Figs 80–81). There is also a report of
predation on queens by great tits, which were probably collecting them from
cracks in the bark of a tree where they were spending the nights after hibernation.
Later in the year they are among the species whose eviscerated carcasses can be
found in considerable numbers under trees – presumably victims of predation
by birds (probably great or blue tits).

Habitat and conservation

Bombus lucorum is a woodland edge species found in a wide variety of habitats,
including roadside and motorway verges, remaining hedgerows, woodland rides,
river banks, urban and suburban parks, gardens and open spaces as well as
marginal habitat on farmland. It is common and does not appear to be threatened.
For more details see Chapter 11.

Sources: Alford, 1975; Baker, 1996; Bertsch, 1997; Brian, 1951; Cumber, 1949; Disney, 2002; Else, pers.
comm.; Forster Johnson, 2002; Fussell & Corbet, 1991, 1992; Macdonald, 1998, 1999, pers. comm.;
Müller & Schmid-Hempel, 1992; Nisbet, in press; Pamilo et al., 1997; Pedersen, 2002; Prŷs-Jones &
Corbet, 1991; von Hagen & Aichhorn, 2003; Williams, 2000; own obs.

Bombus terrestris (Linnaeus)

Buff-tailed bumblebee

FIGS A–D. *Bombus terrestris* queen; *B. terrestris* male;
B. terrestris male (rare black form);
B. terrestris worker (nectar robbing).

Description

QUEENS are usually very large (length 20 mm or more, wingspan over 40 mm). As with *B. lucorum*, the coat is mainly black, with two yellow bands: one on the collar, the other on the second abdominal segment. These are usually of a duller hue than in *B. lucorum*, tending to a golden or even brownish-yellow. The abdominal yellow band is narrowed in some specimens, and the yellow band on the collar is often very narrow and dark. The tail is typically buff, but is sometimes only slightly off-white, or may be pale brown. The face is as wide as it is long and the tongue is relatively short. WORKERS are much smaller than the queens, but are similarly coloured except for the tail. This is usually white, or whitish, with a narrow brownish transitional zone between the tail and the black of the abdomen. MALES are very similar in appearance to the queens, though usually somewhat smaller. The tail varies from slightly off-white to pale buff in colour. The hairs on the face are black. The hind tibiae are flattened with a shiny hairless outer surface, and fringed with ginger-yellow hairs that shade to yellow towards the tip (this character is an easy way to distinguish males from daughter queens).

Variation

Darkening of the yellow bands (especially that on the collar) and of the tail is quite common. All-black specimens of the male are occasionally seen. The release of specimens from imported commercial colonies is resulting in the appearance of unusual colour forms in some areas.

Similar species

Bombus lucorum, *B. soroeensis* and the cuckoo bumblebees *B. vestalis*, *B. bohemicus* and *B. sylvestris*. For distinguishing features see Chapter 8, cluster 2 and the key.

Distribution

Bombus terrestris is very common and widespread throughout England and Wales. Prior to 1973 it was fairly widespread in southern Scotland, with sporadic records further north. However, since 1990 it has become more firmly established in northern Scotland, in Grampian and in coastal areas around the Moray Firth in the Highland region.

Colony cycle

In England, queens of this species are by far the most frequently observed in early spring as they alternate between foraging, sunning themselves on warm days, and prospecting for nest sites. They engage in this activity soon after emerging from hibernation (as early as late February, later in the north). They fly very close to the ground, systematically 'contouring' areas of tussocky long grass, often close to nettle beds, hedges or scrub. Occasionally they will disappear into deep vegetation to explore the ground under tussocks or nettles, presumably searching for abandoned mammal nests, only to reappear a few seconds or minutes later to continue the search. Sometimes as long as 10–15 minutes will be taken to explore a given search area, before the insect flies up and away to continue the search elsewhere. Usually areas of rough grassland are chosen, but queens can also be seen prospecting the inner banks of sea walls, river and canal banks, in overgrown gardens, under old hedgerows, in woodland glades and also more exposed sites, such as old walls and bare banks of ditches, as well as over bare earth in woodland. *Bombus terrestris* will occasionally nest elsewhere, such as in barns and outhouses, or among ivy on old walls. Prospecting for nest sites can still be observed as late as late May in some years.

Nests are usually underground, and approached by way of a long, downward-sloping tunnel. The comb is dark brown, untidy, and frequently covered by a wax-pollen canopy. *Bombus terrestris* is a pollen storer, and large quantities of pollen are stored by workers in tall wax cylinders. Although pollen collection by queens in spring suggests that nests are established early, numbers build up very slowly, with few workers appearing before mid-May. However, the eventual size of the *B. terrestris* colony is large, with several hundred workers at its peak.

Bombus terrestris, like *B. lucorum*, is a complex species, in which the queen uses pheromones as well as behavioural cues to maintain its dominance over the workers, and control the timing of reproductive events in the nest. At first the queen lays an average of two eggs in each of three to eight cells. She rears the resulting larvae herself, and subsequently lays more eggs in cells placed on the cocoons once the first batch have pupated. She then goes on to lay increasing numbers of eggs in subsequent days, resulting in a build-up of workers, at first slow, but increasing rapidly later on. As with *B. lucorum*, some colonies switch to production of (mainly male) sexuals early in the season, while others switch later, producing mainly daughter queens. This may go some way to explaining the prolonged period during which both males and daughter queens can be seen. However, it seems increasingly likely that *B. terrestris*, like *B. lucorum*, can complete two colony cycles in a single year in the south. More details about the colony cycle can be found in Chapters 2 and 3.

Guard bees are posted in the tunnel leading to the nest entrance, and there is a general alarm reaction when the colony is disturbed. As noted by Sladen, the workers 'defend the nest bravely when it is disturbed, hovering around it for some time ready to sting anything that approaches'. The first males and daughter queens appear in late May or early June, and male patrolling behaviour has been observed at various times of day between mid-July and mid-August. Various patrol routes may be used, such as field-boundary hedges and ditches. The approach sites may be from 5–10 metres apart and some are visited by all the males patrolling a route, others by only some of them. Sometimes several males will arrive at an approach site together. Approach sites may be high points in a hedge, or hollows. Most colonies break up by late August or early September, but, as with *B. lucorum*, there is evidence of continued colony activity, albeit in very small numbers, through the winter in southern England.

There are a few records of hibernation sites: three queens were disturbed from the soil at the beginning of September by a gardener digging up a nettle patch. The patch was situated close to, and on the northern side of, a pile of grass-cuttings some 1.5 metres high (Heywood). Edwards reported two found in late October, in holes that had been excavated in a rotten *Cupressus* stump. They were 7 and 15 centimetres below ground, and in chambers made of compressed wood chewings, and another in a mud cell in an old stream-bed.

Colony development is later in northern Scotland, but colonies break up no later than in England (Macdonald).

Foraging behaviour

Sometimes winter-active bees are observed in January and later sunning themselves on warm days, in flight, or feeding from both wild and cultivated flowers. Queens have been observed inside crocus flowers as these opened in early morning, indicating that this is where they spent the nights (Down). During the early spring when few herbaceous species are flowering, early-flowering shrubs play a very important role for *B. terrestris* which is less attracted to the early deadnettles than are longer-tongued species such as *B. hortorum* and *B. pascuorum*. Ground flora in woodland is also important, with often a surprisingly frequent traffic of bumblebees passing through even quite dense woodland in spring.

Sladen has an amusing description of foraging workers of this species on blackberry 'the numerous stamens of which seem to irritate them, for they shake their wings and buzz impatiently as they rifle each blossom'. This is presumably a description of the now well-understood phenomenon of buzz-foraging, which serves to detach pollen from the anthers. Like *B. lucorum* workers, they frequently bite holes in the corollae of deep flowers and remove nectar without brushing against the anthers. However, workers may collect pollen legitimately and nectar rob from flowers of the same species in a single foraging episode (for example, on comfrey, own obs.). *Bombus terrestris* workers are pollinators of agricultural crops such as borage and oil-seed rape and are widely used in horticulture, most notably in greenhouse cultivation of tomatoes.

Bombus terrestris foraging patterns. Plants in **bold** are garden plants, and (p) signifies a recorded pollen source (in the case of workers, aggregated with *B. lucorum*).

QUEEN
winter: ***Begonia*, daffodil, crocus, stinking hellebore,** ground ivy, red deadnettle.
spring: sallow catkins, cherry, blackthorn, gorse, broom, ***Hebe*, flowering currant, winter-flowering honeysuckle, *Mahonia*, *Erica*, *Rhododendron*, *Teucrium fruticans*, rosemary,** bluebell.

WORKERS
winter: ***Hebe*, winter-flowering honeysuckle, winter box, *Mahonia*, *Erica*, *Fuchsia*.**
spring: broom (p), gorse (p), white (p) and red deadnettles, common vetch, comfrey (p), ***Ceanothus*.**
summer: various thistles, field scabious (p), purple loosestrife (p), hog weed (p), woundworts, black horehound, comfrey, viper's bugloss, purple toadflax, bittersweet, dandelion, borage, oil-seed rape (p), bird's-foot trefoil (p), red clover (p), white clover (p), tree lupin (p), restharrow, bramble (p), rose, ***Antirrhinum*,** hoary plantain (p), common poppy (p), **lavender, sage, marigold, marjoram, *Hebe*, snowberry, privet, *Buddleia*.**
autumn: ragwort, bristly ox-tongue, white deadnettle (p), ivy (p), restharrows, bird's-foot trefoils, **snowberry.**

DAUGHTER QUEENS
bramble, dogwood, mallow, clovers, burdock, thistles, ragworts, viper's bugloss, black horehound, ***Rhododendron*, *Antirrhinum*,** field scabious, ***Echinacea*, *Sedum*** and **marigold.**

MALES
common and tufted vetch, bramble, viper's bugloss, marsh woundwort, chives, *Rhododendron*, lavender, thistles, knapweed, burdock, bristly ox-tongue, ragworts, **marigold, Michaelmas daisy.**

One study comparing colonies in suburban gardens with others in agricultural land reported 23 pollen types in pollen loads, with a greater diversity being used by garden foragers than those foraging in agricultural land. Some individual workers were constant to a single pollen source, while others had up to seven pollen types in their corbiculae. Another study of pollen loads reported that 36 per cent were mixed, but others were overwhelmingly composed of pollen of borage or red clover. In all, pollen from 17 flower species was collected. Another study of pollen loads pooled those collected from *B. lucorum* and *B. terrestris*. Twenty-nine of these were collected from returning workers at the nest. Most contained pollen of one species only, and the mixed loads were still dominated by a single species. Almost one third of the pollen loads were composed entirely of bramble pollen.

Predators and parasites
The very common cuckoo bumblebee *B. vestalis* uses *B. terrestris* as its main host. Although *B. vestalis* is currently by far the commonest cuckoo bumblebee, *terrestris* remains abundant. Nests in suburban gardens may be especially vulnerable to infestation by the wax moth (see Chapter 5). In Cumber's study, 31 per cent of overwintered queens were infected with *Shaerularia bombi*, but conopid fly infestation was found in only one dissected worker. The parasitic fly *Brachicoma devia* was recorded from *B. terrestris* nests, as many as 100 cocoons having been destroyed in one. *Bombus terrestris* is also recorded as host of the scuttle fly *Megaselia giraudi* (Disney) and is very susceptible to the protozoan parasite *Crithidia bombi*. Although this is generally considered relatively mild in its effects, there is evidence that infected queens are less likely to establish nests, and that colonies with high levels of infection have lower chances of reaching maturity. *Crithidia* infestation may be one reason why only a small minority of nests produce daughter queens and so are disproportionately responsible for the continuation of a local population from one year to the next. Different genetic strains of the parasite may thus alternate with different family lineages of *Bombus terrestris* from year-to-year (Schmid-Hempel). Pinchen reports a nest of this species destroyed by a badger. Eviscerated bodies of *B. terrestris* workers are among those frequently found under lime trees in early summer, presumably the victims of predation by birds (probably blue or great tits).

Habitat and conservation
Like *B. lucorum*, this species occurs in a wide variety of habitats, including marginal uncultivated land on farms, roadside verges and remaining hedges (especially where these are bordered by ditches), woodland rides, river banks, sea

walls, gardens, parks and public open spaces, and ruderal habitat associated with former industrial sites. It appears not to be threatened. For more detail see Chapter 11.

Sources: Carvell, pers. comm.; Corbet & Tiley, 2000; Cumber, 1949; Disney, 2002; Down, pers. comm.; Duchateau & Velthuis, 1988; Edwards, 1991, pers. comm.; Else, pers. comm.; Goulson et al., 2002; Heywood, pers. comm.; Macdonald, 2001; Pinchen, 2003; Schmid-Hempel, 2001; Sladen, 1912; own obs.

SUBGENUS KALLOBOMBUS Dalla Torre

Bombus soroeensis (Fabricius)

A

B

C

D

FIGS A–D. *Bombus soroeensis* large worker; *B. soroeensis* male
(note the extensive ginger hairs in the tail); *B. soroeensis* worker
with pollen loads; *B. soroeensis* male (white-tailed form).

Description

QUEENS are relatively small (average length 16 mm, wingspan 30 mm), with two pale yellow bands, one on the collar, the other on abdominal segment 2. The latter band usually extends forwards onto segment 1, especially at the sides. This character is particularly distinctive when present. The yellow abdominal band is also often broken in the middle by black hairs, but this is difficult to see without capturing the insect, and confusion with worn specimens of *B. lucorum* is possible. The tail is white, or white with variable amounts of ginger hair. The face is slightly longer than it is wide, and the tongue is of medium length. The mandibles lack both oblique groove and notch (Fig. K.42xi). WORKERS resemble the queens in colour and structure, but are often very small. MALES (length 14 mm, wingspan 26 mm) have a yellow collar, which extends down the sides and under the thorax, encircling the head, as viewed from the front. There are usually yellow hairs mixed with the black on the face and top of the head. The yellow band on the abdomen is wide, and extends over segment 2 and most of 1. In some specimens the tail is pure white, but there are usually some ginger hairs in the tail, and sometimes the ginger is predominant. The hind metatarsus is narrow at the base and widens gradually (Fig. K.24(b)).

Variation

The species is relatively constant in coloration except for the amount of ginger hairs in the tail, and the form of the yellow abdominal band. In northern Scotland, white-tailed forms of the female predominate. Melanic forms (distinguished as a subspecies by some authors, for example, Pedersen) are common in some parts of Europe, but have not been reported from Britain.

Similar species

Bombus terrestris, *B. lucorum* and the cuckoo bumblebees *B. vestalis*, *B. bohemicus* and *B. sylvestris*. For distinguishing features see Chapter 8, cluster 2 and the key.

Distribution

This species was always very thinly but widely distributed in Britain. However, there is strong evidence of a marked decline in southern Britain in recent decades, with an apparent loss of almost all populations in the English midlands, south and south-east by 1960. Scattered populations remained in Scotland and the north of England, west Wales, the south-western peninsula, and the area around Dungeness in Kent (where it had been lost by the early 1980s, but has subsequently reappeared). *Bombus soroeensis* may be under-recorded because of its similarity to *B. lucorum*, and it is encouraging that systematic searches by Macdonald have revealed its widespread presence on moorland across northern Scotland. It is now found all over the Highlands including Skye and smaller Scottish islands. However, the loss and fragmentation of flower-rich downland in lowland southern Britain suggests that the species remains very vulnerable here. This is also the position elsewhere in Europe.

Colony cycle

The queens are very late emerging from hibernation, from late May onwards in the south. Nests are established from mid-June to late July. A variety of locations have been reported, and these are usually underground. Mature nests are medium-sized, with between 80 and 150 workers reported (average 100). The first workers appear in July, with the first males emerging in late July, but becoming more frequent in August and September. Daughter queens have been observed in August and September. Males and workers continue to fly until late October. In northern Scotland the cycle is even later, with males on the wing from September to early November.

G. Else reports a sighting of males flying in a straight line parallel to a footpath, circling around the dead heads of umbellifers (and himself). Presumably this is an example of male patrolling behaviour.

Foraging behaviour

On southern grasslands, small-flowered legumes, red clover and various bell-flowers are important pollen sources according to locality and date. In Scottish moorland, various *Erica* species, bramble and raspberry are important. Late forage is provided by devil's-bit scabious in many localities, north and south.

Foraging workers are very wary, and are apt to fly up to an intruder, and then make off with a very swift, high flight. They are able to forage at low temperatures (for example, 1°C, Macdonald).

Bombus soroeensis foraging patterns. Plants in **bold** are cultivated plants, and (p) signifies a reported pollen source.

QUEENS	early summer: red clover, white clover, bell heather, bramble raspberry, bird's-foot trefoil. autumn: devil's-bit scabious.
WORKERS	summer: red clover(p), bird's-foot trefoil (p), sainfoin (p), melilot (p), meadow vetchling (p), red bartsia(p), clustered bellflower (p),

harebell (p), bramble (p), spear thistle (p), field scabious (p), lesser scabious, black knapweed, greater knapweed, bell heather, cross-leaved heath, ling, **shrubby cinquefoil** and **borage**.
autumn: devil's-bit scabious, harebell.

MALES   ling, bell heather, cross-leaved heath, devil's-bit scabious.

Predators and parasites
Parasitised by *Sphaerularia bombi*, otherwise unknown.

Habitat and conservation
Three main habitats are used by this species: extensive, flower-rich, late-flowering grasslands, forest edge and open moorland. It appears secure in Scotland, but has declined markedly in England and is in need of conservation measures. For a detailed discussion, see Chapters 10 and 11.

Sources: Banaszac, 1995; Edwards, 2002; Else, 2000; Goulson & Darvill, 2003; IBRA/ITE, 1980; Lundberg & Svensson, 1975; Macdonald 2000a; Nisbet, 2005; Pinchen, 2003, 2004; von Hagen & Aichhorn, 2003; own obs.

SUBGENUS PYROBOMBUS Dalla Torre
Bombus jonellus (Kirby)

FIGS A–D. *Bombus jonellus* queen; *B. jonellus* male;
B. jonellus queen showing short face; *B. jonellus* male,
showing yellow hairs on the face.

E   F

FIGS E–F. *B. jonellus* queen (darkened form); *B. jonellus* worker.

Description

QUEENS are medium-sized (average length 17 mm, average wingspan 29 mm – relatively short in relation to body length), somewhat smaller than queens of *B. hortorum*, which they closely resemble. The face is black, sometimes with yellow hairs on the top of the head. The thorax is black, with yellow bands on both collar and scutellum. The abdomen is black with a yellow band on segment 1, sometimes also on segment 2, and the tail is white. The face is short (length and width about equal), the tongue is short, and the hairs on the corbiculae usually pale or ginger in colour. WORKERS are similar, but smaller. MALES are similarly coloured, but have more extensive areas of yellow. The yellow collar extends down the sides and under the thorax and there is a wide yellow band on both abdominal segments 1 and 2. There is a prominent tuft of yellow hairs on the face, and the antennae are long relative to the body size.

Variation

The yellow bands on the thorax and abdomen of females are subject to reduction and darkening. Populations on offshore islands differ slightly from the main-land forms and are considered to be subspecies by some authors. These include: *monapiae, vogtii* and *hebridensis*. In these forms there are variations in the width of the yellow collar, and the white tail is suffused with buffish or yellow coloration. The corbicular hairs are black, or black with red tips. In one form found on Orkney and the Western Isles the males have reddish tails and are very difficult to distinguish from males of *B. pratorum* (not so far recorded from there).

Similar species

Bombus hortorum, *B. ruderatus* and the cuckoo bumblebee *B. barbutellus*. For distinguishing features see Chapter 8, cluster 3 and the key.

Distribution

In Britain, this species is widespread but local, with strong populations in the north and west, and further concentrations in the south-east (Hampshire, Surrey, Sussex and Kent) and East Anglia (especially the Brecks and heaths of Suffolk and Norfolk). It is widespread on the northern Scottish mainland (Macdonald), and the ginger-yellow tailed form, *B. vogtii* Richards, is present on the Orkney and Shetland Islands (Else). The similar *hebridensis* occurs on the Outer Hebrides (Else), and form *monapiae* occurs on the Isle of Man.

Williams includes this species in his 'widespread local' category. However, owing to the ease with which it may be confused with *B. hortorum*, it may well have been overlooked in some areas. In Scotland it is widely distributed in the north and in the Western Isles, Orkney and Shetland.

Colony cycle

In southern Britain the colony cycle is short, and the species commonly rears two broods in a season. Queens emerge from hibernation in late March or early April. They are unspecific in their choice of nest sites, using both under-ground and above-ground locations. Reported locations include a squirrel's nest, discarded bird's and mammal nests and the rafters of an old workshop. In northern Sweden the species nests among dwarf shrubs and willows in low alpine habitats, where it also uses old rodent nests. Workers can be seen from late April onwards, and mature nests are reported to have from 50–120 workers. Fresh queens and males of the first brood emerge in June or July, and workers, males and queens continue to be observed into mid-September. *Bombus jonellus* is a pollen storer.

On heather moorland in Scotland queens emerge from hibernation some-what later, and do not become common until mid-June. Workers begin to appear in early June, and numbers build up slowly to a peak in late September. The males fly from August until early October. There is no evidence of double broods in the northern range, but there are considerable variations in flight periods according to altitude and local climate.

Male patrolling behaviour was studied in northern Sweden by Svensson. Patrolling males flew at tree-top level, approaching marked twigs with a zigzag flight, and flying rapidly between approach places. Relatively isolated trees were used for marking, and leaves or twigs close to the tops of the trees were selected.

One mating was observed: a queen settled on wood cranesbill, with three males climbing on her back, in meadow and heath birch forest surroundings.

Foraging behaviour

Bombus jonellus foraging patterns. Plants in **bold** are garden plants, and (p) signifies a recorded pollen source.

QUEENS	sallow, white clover, red clover, daisy, dandelion, common vetch, bird's-foot trefoil, meadow vetchling, eye-bright, ***Rhododendron***, bell heather, ling, spear thistle, creeping thistle, devil's-bit scabious.
WORKERS	cowberry, bell heather, ling, white clover, red clover (p), gorse (p), bird's-foot trefoil (p), melilot, viper's bugloss (p), ***Antirrhinum*** (p), bramble (p), purple loosestrife (p), thyme, wood sage, **lungwort**, red bartsia, hawkbit, ragwort, teasel, devil's-bit scabious.
MALES	bell heather, ling, ragwort, cowberry, devil's-bit scabious, cross-leaved heath, white clover.

Bombus jonellus is also frequent visitor to gardens. Pollen loads collected by Pinchen from workers returning to a nest at Dungeness included several plant species, but individual loads were wholly or almost wholly composed of pollen from one species. The evidence so far suggests that *B. jonellus* visits a wide variety of flowers for nectar, pollen or both, but that individual workers are remarkably flower constant.

Predators and parasites

There is circumstantial evidence that the cuckoo bumblebee, *B. sylvestris,* may sometimes invade nests of *B. jonellus* as well as its more typical host, the closely related *B. pratorum. Sphaerularia bombi* has been reported from *B. jonellus* queens.

Habitat and conservation

Bombus jonellus is closely associated with heathland and moorland, but also coastal habitats. However, it is not confined to them. It seems likely that the shrubby character of heathland vegetation provides preferred nesting habitat. In Scotland

B. jonellus has two quite distinct habitats: heather moorland and machair grassland. It is abundant on the moorland, and apparently flies later there. In addition to its lowland heath habitats in southern Britain, it also occurs at low density on some grassland sites in southern England (for example, Salisbury Plain and Kent and Essex coasts). See Chapter 10 for further details.

Sources: Alford, 1975; Else, 2002, 2003; Fraser, 1947; Lundberg & Svensson, 1975; Macdonald, 2000b; Nisbet, 2004a; Pinchen, 2003; Sladen, 1912; Svensson, 1979b; Svensson & Lundberg, 1977; von Hagen & Aichhorn, 2003; Williams, 1989a; own obs.

Bombus pratorum (Linnaeus)

Early-nesting bumblebee

A

B

C

D

FIGS A–D. *Bombus pratorum* queen; *B. pratorum* male;
B. pratorum worker (note reduced yellow band on the abdomen);
B. pratorum worker robbing nectar from comfrey.

FIG E. *B. pratorum* queen (darkened form).

E

Description

QUEENS are relatively small (average length 16 mm, wingspan 30 mm). They have
a yellow band on the collar, and another on abdominal segment 2. The latter
band is often constricted in the middle, and occasionally absent. The tail is
rust-red and confined to abdominal segments 5 and 6. The tongue is short.
WORKERS are very variable in size, some being very tiny indeed. They resemble
the queens in colour pattern, but the abdominal yellow band is often reduced
or missing.

MALES have a wide yellow collar (usually covering approximately the frontal
half of the thorax), which extends down the sides of the thorax and under it, so
encircling the head as viewed from the front. The hairs on the top of the head and
face are mostly yellow. There is a wide yellow band on abdominal segments 1 and 2,
followed by a black band and a rust-red tail. The antennae are relatively long in
relation to the body. The face is short (as wide as it is long).

Variation

The yellow bands on the thorax and abdomen of females are often darkened
and/or reduced in extent. This is particularly true of the band on abdominal
segment 2, which may be constricted, broken in the middle, or entirely absent.
The red on the tail is also subject to reduction in extent, and may be quite
inconspicuous in some dark individuals. The red tail of the males tends to fade
with age, and is sometimes whitish in old specimens.

Similar species

Bombus lapidarius (males), *B. ruderarius* (males), *B. soroeensis*, *B. sylvarum*, *B. monticola* and the cuckoo bumblebee *B. rupestris* (males). For distinguishing features see Chapter 8, cluster 4 and the key.

Distribution

This is a 'mainland ubiquitous' species, common and widespread throughout Britain, though less common in the north, especially north-west Scotland, and absent from Orkney, Shetland and the Western Isles of Scotland (except Skye). It is a little less frequently observed than other common species, but this may be due to the smaller size of mature colonies, and the shorter flight period (when second broods are sparse or absent).

Colony cycle

The queens of *B. pratorum* are among the earliest to emerge from hibernation, occasionally as early as February in southern England, but more usually in mid-March. They are less often seen prospecting for nest sites than other common species, but search low over tussocky grassland, as well as exploring cracks and hollows in rockeries and overgrown corners of gardens. Like those of *B. jonellus*, queens of this species make their nests in a variety of places. These may be underground, in old mammal nests, in disused birds' nests, in roof spaces of buildings, in trees, hedges or shrubs, frequently in sheltered corners of gardens. According to the survey conducted by Fussell & Corbet they are more often at or above ground level than below. The first workers appear between late March and late April, depending on season and locality. Colonies reach maturity very rapidly, probably within two months of the establishment of the nest and the maximum number of workers at maturity is thought to be fewer than 100. Males and daughter queens appear during May and continue to late June in most years. There is often a partial second brood, with males and/or daughter queens emerging in August and September. In other years, no *B. pratorum* are seen after the end of June. The conditions that favour attempts at a second colony cycle are unknown. Occasional sightings of workers in October and queens in late October are consistent with the possibility of even a third cycle in some years.

In northern Scotland there is generally just one colony cycle each year, with workers often not seen until mid-May, and males not until early July. There, colonies persist into early September (Macdonald). *Bombus pratorum* is a pollen storer.

In nests studied by Williams, more than half of *B. pratorum* workers were found in nests where they had not been born, and continued to forage, incubate brood and carry out other tasks in their adopted nests. Also non-natal queens were found in some nests, possibly attempting to establish a second generation in a declining nest. Males indulge in patrolling behaviour, often several together following a fixed route. They approach lower branches of trees or other higher features.

Foraging behaviour

Bombus pratorum foraging patterns: Plants in **bold** are garden plants, and (p) signifies a recorded pollen source.

QUEENS — spring: sallow, **Christmas rose, *Bergenia, Mahonia, Viburnum, Erica* cultivars, flowering currant,** *Ceanothus,* **Geranium cultivars, *Hebe*, lungwort, rosemary**, red deadnettle, white deadnettle (p), ground ivy, yellow archangel, apple, blackthorn, chickweed, dandelion.
summer: **globe thistle,** *Hypericum* and many other cultivated shrubs and herbs, prickly ox-tongue, hound's-tongue, bird's-foot trefoil, common vetch, white clover, bramble.

WORKERS — spring: *Mahonia* (p), ***Geranium* cultivars** (p), *Ceanothus* (p), ***Cotoneaster, Erica carnea,* japonica (*Chaenomeles speciosa*), *Rhododendron, Weigela*, raspberry, gooseberry**, comfrey, broom, common vetch, white deadnettle, red deadnettle, bugle, ground ivy, green alkanet, horse chestnut.
summer: **snowberry, roses, honeysuckle,** *Hebe, Valerian,* comfrey (p), ***Geranium* cultivars**, bramble (p), mallows, hawthorn, hound's-tongue, viper's bugloss, purple toadflax, iris, herb Robert, wild mignonette, buttercup, meadow vetchling, white clover, bird's-foot trefoil, melilot, white deadnettle (p), red deadnettle (p), black horehound, marsh woundwort, thistles, knapweed, hawkbits, red bartsia (p), sycamore (p).

MALES — ***Geranium* cultivars, *Cotoneaster*, snowberry, bellflowers, *Valerian*, sage, raspberry, corncockle, lavender, tamarisk, *Rhododendron*, garden catmint, *Hebe, Antirrhinum*,** bramble, mallows, green alkanet, comfrey, hound's-tongue, buttercup, purple toadflax, vetches and clovers, white deadnettle, bugle, ground ivy, marsh woundwort, thyme, thistles, burdocks, ragwort.

Overwintered queens forage quite unsystematically in gardens, nectaring opportunistically on a wide variety of flowers.

Workers of *B. pratorum* often make use of holes bored in the corolla of comfrey flowers (presumably by *B. terrestris* or *B. lucorum*) to rob nectar, but they can also forage 'legitimately' by reaching into the mouth of the corolla tube with their head and thorax. They are agile foragers, and frequently visit flowers that hang downwards (Prŷs-Jones & Corbet). When there is a second generation, workers make particular use of late-flowering garden shrubs such as snowberry.

Predators and parasites

Bombus pratorum is the main host species for the common cuckoo bumblebee *B. sylvestris*. More than a quarter of the queens tested by Cumber were parasitised by *Sphaerophoria bombi*, and nests of *B. pratorum* were parasitised by the tachinid fly *Brachicoma devia*. As an early nester, *Bombus pratorum* seems to be less subject than other species to attack by conopid flies.

Habitat and conservation

Bombus pratorum is a very common and widespread species that may be found in many different habitats: open woodland, meadows and pasture, upland moors and heathland, coastal grazing marshes, roadside verges and railway banks as well as urban and suburban habitats. It is particularly common in gardens, rough ground and public open spaces in urban areas. However, it appears to be less capable of surviving in intensively farmed areas than other common species such as *B. lucorum* and *B. terrestris*. It appears to be a generalist both in its choice of nest sites and in its use of forage plants, so that management regimes in parks, gardens and public open spaces can relatively easily meet its requirements. One critical condition is abundance of suitable early-flowering plants, such as deadnettles, sallows, *Prunus* species, and flowering currant for overwintered queens from their emergence through to the rearing of the first cohort of workers. Another is the presence of undisturbed hedges, bushes and neglected corners for nesting habitat. The loss to development or overmanagement of public open spaces, waste ground, neglected allotment sites and so-called 'brownfield' sites must pose a significant threat to this species.

Sources: Cumber, 1949; Frankum, 2003; Fussell & Corbet, 1992; Macdonald, pers. comm.; Nisbet, 2005; Prŷs-Jones & Corbet, 1991; Sladen, 1912; Williams, 1997; own obs.

Bombus monticola Smith

This species was formerly referred to as *B. lapponicus*, but it is now known that the British population belongs to *B. monticola* (see Svensson).

A

B

C

D

FIGS A–D. *Bombus monticola* queen; *B. monticola* male; *B. monticola* male (ventral view); *B. monticola* worker with pollen loads.

FIG E. *B. monticola* worker entering its nest.

E

Description

QUEENS are relatively small (average length 16 mm, wingspan 32 mm), with a compact, rounded appearance. The thorax is black, with a lemon yellow band on the collar and a narrow fringe of yellow hairs on the scutellum. The abdomen has mainly black hairs on segment 1, and the front half of segment 2. The final abdominal segment has short black hairs, but the rest of the abdomen is covered in reddish to yellow hairs. These have a deep, rich red tint towards the middle and front of the abdomen, and shade through orange to yellow at the sides and rear. There are often some yellow hairs on the top of the head, and usually just a few mixed with the black on the face. The hairs on the legs are black. The head is as wide as it is long, and the tongue is relatively short. WORKERS are similar to the queens, but smaller.

MALES, too, are similar in colour pattern, but they have distinct patches of yellow hair on the top of the head and on the face, and some pale hairs mixed with the long black ones on the hind tibia. The yellow band on the collar is extended down the sides of the thorax to the ventral surface. The antennae are long relative to the body.

Variation

Apart from darkening of the yellow bands in some specimens (Nisbet, pers. comm.), the colour pattern in Britain is constant.

Similar species

Bombus pratorum, B. lapidarius (males), *B. ruderarius* (males) and the cuckoo bumblebee *B. rupestris* (males). For distinguishing features see Chapter 8, cluster 4.

Distribution

Bombus monticola is confined to upland moors and nearby habitats. The main populations are in mainland Scotland, North Yorkshire Moors, the Peak District, Welsh uplands, and Dartmoor and Exmoor in the south-west of England.

Colony cycle

In England, queens emerge from hibernation in April, and can still be observed until late May. It seems likely that nests are established from late April through May. The nests are usually constructed in old mammal nests underground, though disused birds' nests have also been recorded, as has another in a natural cavity beneath a boulder. Nests studied by Yalden were from 10–60 centimetres below ground. Sites chosen for nests seem to be exclusively on moorland (though not far from moorland-edge habitats), and with dense above-ground cover made up of ericaceous shrubs, including bilberry, and mosses. The first workers appear in mid-May and during May, June and July numbers increase to a peak of 50–120 in a colony. There are reports of males as early as June and July, but the main emergence of males and daughter queens is usually from the beginning of August. Males and foraging workers continue to be seen until mid-September.

In the Scottish Highlands the species flies later. Queens usually emerge from hibernation in May, with workers following in June and males from mid-August. Males continue to be seen until early or mid-October.

Daughter queens have been observed both leaving and re-entering the nest. *Bombus monticola* is a pollen storer.

Foraging behaviour

Pioneering work by Yalden established the sequence of pollen sources used by *B. monticola* at selected sites in the Peak District by analysing pollen samples taken from workers returning to the nest and the husks of pollen left in larval meconia (waste left by the larva when it pupates). This demonstrated that workers leave the moorland to forage on nearby grassland during the gap between the flowering of bilberry and the later-flowering heathers. Her work also illustrated the extent of observer-bias when pollen samples are collected from foraging workers on abundant or showy flowers. The bees clearly seek out preferred forage sources even where these are scarce or inconspicuous. Subsequent studies in Dartmoor, the Scottish Highlands and the Peak District have broadly confirmed the pattern established by Yalden. Pollen loads frequently contain pollen of only one species, or a mixture of just two or three species, indicating a high degree of flower constancy on the part of workers in their search for pollen. So far, evidence suggests that nest-founding queens select bilberry pollen to prime their nests and rear the first brood, even where other pollen sources (such as the sallow) are abundant. However, large aggregations of overwintered queens can sometimes be seen nectaring at isolated clumps of sallow.

Bombus monticola foraging patterns. (p) signifies a recorded pollen source.

QUEENS	spring: sallow, bilberry (p), bird's-foot trefoil (p), white clover summer: bell heather, white clover, devil's-bit scabious.
WORKERS	spring: bilberry (p), gorse (p), cowberry (p). summer: gorse (p), bird's-foot trefoil (p), white clover (p), red clover (p), bell heather (p), ling (p), bilberry (second flowering), raspberry (p), devil's-bit scabious (p), meadowsweet (p), cinquefoil (p), self-heal, bramble, dandelion, chickweed, marsh thistle, bramble, *Rhododendron*, honeydew.
MALES	bell heather, thyme, white clover, buttercup, ragwort, devil's-bit scabious.

Workers observed on Dartmoor foraged exclusively for nectar after overnight poor weather, but switched to collecting pollen later in the day. Workers were also observed to rob bell heather flowers for nectar by feeding from holes bored in the side of the corolla. Nisbet's observation of workers drinking honeydew is also of interest.

Predators and parasites

There is some circumstantial evidence that the cuckoo bumblebee *B. sylvestris* may sometimes invade nests of this species as well as its more usual host, *B. pratorum* (which is very closely related to *B. monticola*).

One nest discovered on Dartmoor had been the subject of an attack by a mammalian predator (probably a fox), as the shrubs covering the entrance had been torn apart. However, the attack had failed, as workers as well as both males and daughter queens were seen emerging.

Habitat and conservation

Recent studies suggest that *B. monticola* is declining rapidly, and it is the subject of an English Nature Species Recovery project. It is threatened by habitat loss in much of its former territory. Scottish populations are generally regarded as safer than those in England, but *B. monticola* is very local and declining in East and West Ross (Nisbet, pers. comm.). It is regarded as a montane species (up to 2,700 metres) in mainland Europe and in Britain is confined to upland moors in the north and west (up to 900 metres in Scotland). In the northern part of its range, where the flowering periods of its moorland forage plants are more concentrated, *B. monticola* may be able to forage continuously on the moorland throughout the colony cycle. It appears to be a cold-adapted species, which is often the most abundant species in spring above 650 metres on Cairngorm (Nisbet, pers. comm.). However, further south, there is a gap between the flowering period of bilberry, which seems to be essential at least in the initial stages of colony growth, and the flowering of other Ericaceae on the moorland. During this period the workers leave the moorland to forage in nearby grassland, where they use mainly Fabaceae pollen. See Chapters 10 and 11 for further discussion.

Sources: Edwards, 2002; Macdonald pers. comm.; Nisbet, 2004b, pers. comm.; Pinchen & Edwards, 2000; Pinchen & Wright, 2001; Svensson, 1979a; von Hagen & Aichhorn, 2003; Yalden, 1982; own obs.

Bombus hypnorum (Linnaeus)

This is a newly established species in Britain (Goulson & Williams).

A   B

FIGS A–B. *Bombus hypnorum* queen; *B. hypnorum* male.

Description
QUEENS are relatively large, with a ginger-brown, unbanded thorax, mainly black abdomen and a white tail. There are usually yellow hairs at least on the sides of abdominal segment 1, and sometimes an extensive covering of yellow on segments 1 and 2. The head is slightly longer than it is wide, and the tongue relatively short. WORKERS are similar to the queens, but smaller. MALES, too, have a similar general colour pattern, but they have yellow hairs mixed with black on the face.

Variation
Some continental forms have more extensive ginger-yellow on the abdomen, but so far too few specimens have been observed to determine the range of variation in the British population.

Similar species

Bombus pascuorum, *B. humilis* and *B. muscorum*. The white tail in *B. hypnorum* distinguishes it from all three similar species. For other distinguishing features see Chapter 8, cluster 1 and the key.

Distribution

First recorded in Britain on 17 July 2001 near the village of Landford, Wiltshire, on the northern fringe of the New Forest, but subsequently observed at a number of sites in south and south-east England. In mainland Europe it is very widely distributed as far north as the Arctic Circle.

Colony cycle

In mainland Europe queens emerge in late March and can be seen foraging and searching for nest sites until the end of April. Løken reports nest-site searching along house walls in Scandinavia, with queens investigating dark objects as if searching for holes. The nests are built in various locations, as with its relative *B. pratorum*. Sites chosen are usually above ground, in holes in trees or walls, birds' nest boxes, abandoned birds' nests and within buildings. Workers emerge in mid-April, and continue to the middle of August. Mature colonies are relatively large, compared with those of its close relatives, with as many as 150 workers or more (von Hagen & Aichhorn say up to 400). Males and daughter queens fly from the end of May or early June through to the end of August. In Scandinavia the flight periods are somewhat later and more extended: workers fly from late April, and the first males are seen late in June. Colonies persist to late September.

Bombus hypnorum is a pollen storer.

Foraging behaviour

In mainland Europe the queens forage in urban parks and gardens on a wide range of cultivated flowers, with a particular preference for *Rhododendron*. Cherry blossom and grape hyacinth are also visited frequently. In northern montane habitats it forages from *Vaccinium* species.

Predators and parasites

None of the cuckoo bumblebees specialises in *B. hypnorum* as its host, though there is a record of a nest occupied by *B. barbutellus* (more usual host *B. hortorum*).

Habitat and conservation

In mainland Europe *B. hypnorum* is closely associated with human settlements. It is often common, flying with *B. terrestris*, *B. lucorum* and other common species in parks and gardens. It also inhabits upland heath and woodland, especially in its northern range. There seems to be no reason why, having gained a foothold in Britain, *B. hypnorum* might not spread more widely to become an established member of the local fauna.

Sources: Goulson & Williams, 2001; Løken, 1973; Løken, 1984; von Hagen & Aichhorn, 2003; own obs.

SUBGENUS MEGABOMBUS Dalla Torre

Bombus hortorum (Linnaeus)

Garden bumblebee

A

B

C

D

FIGS A–D. *Bombus hortorum* queen; *B. hortorum* male; *B. hortorum* queen, showing long face; *B. hortorum* male (note long hairs on hind tibia).

Description

QUEENS are variable in size, usually somewhat smaller than *B. lucorum* and
B. terrestris (length 19–22 mm, wingspan 35–38 mm). The ground colour of the coat
is black, with a yellow band on the collar, another, narrower one on the scutellum,
and a third on abdominal segments 1 and 2. The tail is white, and the coat relatively
long and uneven. In typical specimens, the yellow is bright, similar in hue to the
yellow bands on *B. lucorum*. The corbicular hairs are black. The face is markedly
elongated, a feature which immediately distinguishes this from all other common
species (see Fig. K.12), and the tongue is long. WORKERS are variable in size, the
larger ones overlapping the smaller queens. Their colour pattern is the same as
that of the queens. MALES also are similar in colour pattern. The hairs on the
face are black. The 'beard' on the mandibles is black. The long hairs on the edge
of the hind tibia are mostly black, and project out approximately at right angles
to the leg (Fig. K.32a).

Variation

In some specimens the band on the abdomen is reduced, and may be broken in
the middle. Darkened forms, in which the thoracic yellow bands are greatly
reduced and the abdominal one more-or-less absent, are relatively common.
Strongly darkened males are occasionally seen.

Similar species

Bombus ruderatus, B. jonellus, B. subterraneus and the cuckoo bumblebee
B. barbutellus. For distinguishing features see Chapter 8, cluster 3 and the key.

Distribution

Bombus hortorum is a 'mainland ubiquitous' species, being widespread through
England, Wales and throughout Scotland and the Isles. Because this species has
a shorter season than other common species, and also a relatively small number
of workers per nest, it is probably somewhat under-recorded.

Colony cycle

The first queens may be observed from late March onwards, but in some years
overwintered queens may be seen foraging as late as the end of May. The queens
establish their nests soon after emerging from hibernation, and are observed with
pollen loads from early April. Pinchen reports nest-site prospecting by several
overwintered queens on a badger's sett, where they systematically investigated
small holes in the complex. Nests have been found among rank grasses, teasels
and nettles in a south-west-facing flood bank, under a sheet of tin, and in a

sparrow's nest about 20 feet above the ground. Sladen states that the nests of this species are generally underground, with a short entrance tunnel, but in Fussell & Corbet's survey only about half the nests were below ground. They were commonly in situations exposed to sunlight.

The first workers are usually in evidence from late April or early May. According to Sladen, relatively few workers ('seldom … more than 100 workers') are produced in each nest, whilst von Hagen and Aichhorn estimate from 50–120. *Bombus hortorum* has a short colony cycle, consistent with the relatively small number of workers per nest at maturity. The first males usually appear in late May or early June, but depending on the season they can be seen as early as early May, or not until late June. Males, daughter queens and workers can be seen until mid-July in most years.

In favourable seasons and localities there may be a partial second brood, with males, workers and queens seen as late as September. Sightings of daughter queens with pollen loads in August are consistent with nest establishment, although it is now recognised that daughter queens may forage for their colony of origin.

Darwin's account of the patrolling behaviour of male *B. hortorum* in his own garden was recounted in Chapter 2. A more recent description is given by Fussell & Corbet who recorded bees visiting patches of bare earth and crevices at the base of tree trunks on their patrols. The bees appeared to be following different routes, but these intersected at the approach sites. As many as eight males in an hour visited a particular spot, and individuals made repeated visits (at measured intervals varying from eight minutes to over one hour), at least one of them still patrolling some six days after first being marked.

Owing to the slower development of colonies in northern Scotland it is unlikely that double broods are successfully completed there.

Bombus hortorum is a pocket maker.

Foraging behaviour

Bombus hortorum is a long-tongued species that forages mainly from deep flowers, including, as its vernacular name implies, many garden varieties.

Bombus hortorum foraging patterns. Plants in **bold** are garden plants, and (p) signifies a recorded pollen source.

QUEENS	spring: white deadnettle (p), red deadnettle, bugle, ground ivy, primrose, bluebell (p), common vetch, comfrey, apple, ***Aquilegia,***

Ceanothus, Aubrieta, **daffodil, pansy, flowering currant.**
summer: various vetches and clovers (p), black horehound,
woundworts, hemp-nettles, yellow toadflax, comfrey, red
campion, teasel, thistles and garden flowers such as **foxglove** (p),
Antirrhinum, **honeysuckle** (p).

WORKERS   spring: white deadnettle (p), bugle, ground ivy, common vetch,
red clover, white clover, comfrey (p)
summer: white deadnettle (p), tufted vetch, bush vetch, iris,
viper's bugloss, black horehound, woundworts, self-heal,
foxglove, red bartsia, knapweeds, thistles, honeysuckle,
lavender, garden catmint, greater bindweed (p), devil's-bit
scabious, **monk's-hood, marjoram,** *Phlomis,* **sage, lungwort,**
Rhododendron, **garden catmint,** *Fuchsia*

MALES   various Lamiaceae and Fabaceae as well as comfrey, Himalayan
balsam, ***Delphinium,*** red campion, foxglove, mallow, bramble,
teasels, thistles, knapweed.

When foraging from white deadnettle the queens start with the lowest whorl
of flowers, and work their way round it, either clockwise or anticlockwise. They
forage from several plants before taking shelter under vegetation to brush pollen
onto their corbiculae. They frequently rest for some minutes before starting on
another foraging bout. Foxgloves in both woods and gardens are also commonly
visited, and are a key forage plant in northern Scotland (Macdonald, pers. comm.).
The bees completely disappear into the long corolla tubes, and subsequently
retreat (usually covered in pollen) rear-end first. Flowers of greater bindweed are
accessed by the bees clambering down the cluster of anthers and style and using
them as a platform from which they probe the nectar stores at the base of the
funnel-shaped corolla. This results in a dusting of pollen on the legs and ventral
surface of the bee.

Bombus hortorum shows a distinct, but not exclusive, preference for deep,
usually zygomorphic flowers – often in the Lamiaceae and Fabaceae. Of eight
pollen loads collected from foraging workers at Dungeness, five contained red
clover pollen only, while another contained 50 per cent each of red clover and a
Vicia species. Pollen remains from larval meconia in nests excavated by Brian in
Scotland confirm the importance of red clover, which comprised 74 per cent by
volume, and white clover (10 per cent).

I have one very detailed report of three successive episodes of a *B. hortorum* queen 'licking up' bird droppings from leaves (Heywood). In Macdonald's view, *B. hortorum* in the Highlands would lose about 50 days at the beginning of its cycle in the absence of the exotic forage provided by gardens.

Predators and parasites

Bombus hortorum is the main recorded host of the cuckoo bumblebee *B. barbutellus*. *Sphaerularia bombi* has been reported from *B. hortorum* queens, and Cumber found high levels of infestation by the tachinid fly *Brachicoma devia* (64 pupae in one nest). He also found some degree of infestation of workers by conopids (4 infested workers out of 31 dissected). Edwards observed several individuals of the conopid *Physocephala rufipes* emerging from an old nest of *B. hortorum*, indicating that workers parasitised by this conopid return to the nest (compare Schmid-Hempel & Müller).

Habitat and conservation

Bombus hortorum is probably a woodland species, but it is frequently to be seen in urban and suburban habitats including urban parks, private gardens, public open spaces, cemeteries, allotments, roadside verges and hedgerows, as well as (less frequently) marginal habitat in farmland. It is a significant pollinator of field bean. As one of only two long-tongued species that remains widespread its conservation may be important for the pollination of some agricultural crops and also of more specialised wild flower species (Corbet). Although *B. hortorum* is a frequent visitor to urban parks and domestic gardens, it appears to be the least common of the 'basic six' in these habitats (see, for example, Chapman's study of urban sites across London).

In general, *B. hortorum* may be already suffering some decline, and its conservation deserves attention. See Chapters 10 and 11.

Sources: Brian, 1951; Chapman, 2004; Corbet, 2000; Cumber, 1949; Darwin (tr. Freeman, 1965); Edwards pers. comm.; Frankum, 2003; Fussell & Corbet, 1992a, b, c; Heywood, pers. comm.; Macdonald, 1998, pers. comm.; Nisbet, in press; Pinchen, 2003; Prŷs-Jones & Corbet, 1991; Schmid-Hempel & Müller, 1991; Sladen, 1912; von Hagen & Aichhorn, 2003; personal observation.

Bombus ruderatus (Fabricius)

FIGS A–D. *Bombus ruderatus* queen; *B. ruderatus* male (note hairs on hind tibia); *B. ruderatus* queen, showing short, even hair on thorax; *B. ruderatus* worker.

FIG E. *B. ruderatus* black male (note ginger hairs on the mandibles).

E

Description

QUEENS are usually very large (length 23 mm, wingspan 40 mm), comparable in size with queens of *B. terrestris* and *B. lapidarius*. In general appearance they resemble large *B. hortorum* queens. However, the yellow bands on the thorax are often less bright, and narrower. The yellow band on the scutellum is usually equal in width to that on the collar. The yellow band on the abdomen is confined to segment 1 and is commonly broken in the middle, or entirely absent. The tail is usually rather dull and off-white. The coat is short and even, particularly on the thorax. The head is longer than it is wide (Fig. K.12). WORKERS are similar to the queens, though smaller. MALES have a similar pattern of three yellow bands and a whitish tail. The yellow band on the scutellum is as wide as, or wider than, that on the collar, and the boundary between it and the black interalar band is straight and clearly defined. The longer hairs fringing the mandibles are usually ginger. The hind tibia is flattened and shiny on the outer surface, and the long hairs on the edges project at an acute angle (Fig. K.32(b)).

Variation

As in *B. hortorum*, there is considerable individual variation in the width of the yellow banding on the thorax in females. Also the yellow band on the abdomen is often reduced, broken or absent. Darkened forms of the female grade into fully melanic forms. In males, the yellow bands appear to be more constant, without intermediate forms between the typical and melanic forms. Sladen reports nests containing all black individuals, and others with varying proportions of all the colour forms.

Similar species

Bombus hortorum, B. jonellus, B. subterraneus and the cuckoo bumblebee
B. barbutellus. For distinguishing features see Chapter 8, cluster 3 and the key.
See also Falk, 2004 and Edwards, 2004.

Distribution

Sladen reported the species 'very common' in England, though less abundant
in Scotland. There is some doubt about subsequent accounts of its distribution,
owing to absence of agreed characters for field identification. However, there
is general agreement that it has declined significantly, and it now appears to
be localised in south and south-east England. Searches by Williams, Falk and
Edwards in the Nene and Ouse Washes in East Anglia and in Warwickshire
have confirmed the continuing existence of several populations. Subsequent
discoveries by Benton, Carvell, Else, Falk, Harvey and others have added Bedfordshire, Cambridgeshire, Essex, Oxfordshire, north Norfolk and Warwickshire to
the list. It had earlier been recorded in north Kent by Roberts.

Colony cycle

Emergence from hibernation in these localities is approximately a week later
than *B. hortorum* queens, but there are occasional earlier sightings. Saunders states
that it nests underground, often in the old burrows of small mammals. Sladen
also reports it as nesting underground, often with a long entrance hole, but admits
to having 'very seldom' found nests of this species. However, he does report one
in a mole's nest, and von Hagen & Aichhorn say that nests are predominantly
underground and are adapted from abandoned mouse nests. The first workers
appear in mid-May, and mature colonies are held to be more prolific than those
of *B. hortorum*. However, ones excavated by Sladen contained no more than
100 workers.

In recent years, males and daughter queens have been seen from mid-June to
early July onwards in south-east England and East Anglia. This contrasts markedly
with von Hagen & Aichhorn, who give much later dates for both the emergence
of daughter queens and males (mid-August to mid-October) and the break-up
of colonies (end of September) in Germany. More research is needed for us to
establish typical flight periods for successful colonies in Britain.

Male patrolling behaviour is, as with other species, likely to vary according
to local vegetation structure. According to Sladen, the males follow one another,
flying high among the foliage, whereas Williams observed them at Dungeness
patrolling low over broom bushes.

Bombus ruderatus is a pocket maker.

Foraging behaviour

Like *B. hortorum, B. ruderatus* is a long-tongued species that visits deep flowers.

Bombus ruderatus foraging patterns. Plants in **bold** are garden plants, and (p) signifies a recorded pollen source.

QUEENS	spring: red deadnettle (p), white deadnettle, foxglove. summer: red clover, large-flowered hemp-nettle, ***Petunia*, busy Lizzie.**
WORKERS	spring: iris (p), comfrey (p). summer: marsh woundwort (p), red clover (p), large-flowered hemp-nettle, bramble, black horehound (p).
MALES	red clover, sulphur clover, large-flowered hemp-nettle, creeping thistle.

Other plants mentioned in the literature include toadflax, white clover, field bean, motherwort and rosebay willowherb. Red clover is widely reported as a favoured forage source and conservation plantings of agricultural red clover have resulted in records from numerous sites in several south-eastern counties (Carvell). *Bombus ruderatus* was successfully introduced to New Zealand in 1885, where its foraging behaviour has recently been studied. There, as in Britain, red clover is its main pollen source (76 per cent of pollen collecting visits). It also collects pollen from perforated St John's-wort (7.9 per cent), viper's bugloss (7.1 per cent) and bird's-foot trefoil (6.3 per cent), whilst viper's bugloss and red clover were the most frequently visited nectar sources (Goulson & Hanley).

Predators and parasites

Bombus ruderatus is probably an alternative host to *B. hortorum* for the cuckoo *B. barbutellus.*

Habitat and conservation

This is considered to be one of the rarest British species, with a small number of known established populations in the east midlands and East Anglia. It is also reported to be declining in much of the rest of Europe. However, there are very recent signs of a possible recovery. It is the subject of a UK BAP.

Remaining populations occupy three main habitat types: flower-rich unimproved grassland and marshes within flood banks along river valleys in East Anglia; sea walls and associated grazing marshes and farmland; and farms with planted conservation strips rich in red clover. The strongest populations appear to be in the first habitat type, but results from conservation plantings in farmland are also encouraging. See Chapters 10 and 11 for further discussion.

Sources: Alford, 1975; Archer, 1998; Carvell, pers. comm.; Day, 1979; Edwards, 1998, 2002, 2004, pers. comm.; Ellis, Knight & Goulson, 2005; Else, pers. comm.; Falk, 1991, 2004; Goulson & Hanley, 2004; Goulson et al., 2005; Løken, 1973; Saunders, 1898; Sladen, 1912; UK Biodiversity Steering Group, 1995; von Hagen & Aichhorn, 2003; Williams, 1989; own obs.

SUBGENUS MELANOBOMBUS Dalla Torre

Bombus lapidarius (Linnaeus)

Red-tailed bumblebee

A

B

C

D

FIGS A–D. *Bombus lapidarius* queen; *B. lapidarius* male;
Face of *B. lapidarius* queen; *B. lapidarius* male (dark form).

Description

QUEENS are large (length 22 mm, wingspan 38 mm), and black with a red tail. The hairs on the thorax and abdomen are relatively short and even, giving a rather velvety appearance (especially when they are freshly emerged). The corbicular hairs are black. The abdomen is relatively long and parallel-sided (Fig. K.6(a)). The face is slightly longer than it is wide, and the tongue is short to medium in length. The labrum projects down below the clypeus in front view (Fig. K.4(a)). WORKERS are similarly coloured, but smaller – sometimes very tiny indeed. MALES are quite variable in coloration. The most common form is black with a single yellow band on the collar, a tuft of yellow hairs on the face, and a reddish tail. Often there are yellow hairs mixed in with the black on the scutellum (hind edge of the thorax), but these do not form a clearly distinct band. Individuals may show varying degrees of darkening, with the yellow collar significantly reduced. In such specimens, the tail is often a dull yellow/orange. The hind metatarsus is elongated, with long hairs on the dorsal edge (longer than the width of the metatarsus) (Fig. K.28(a)).

Variation

There is little variation in the females. Even in darkened forms of the male there are generally some yellow hairs on the face.

Similar species

Bombus ruderarius, B. monticola, B. pratorum and the cuckoo bumblebee B. rupestris.
For distinguishing characteristics see Chapter 8, cluster 5 for lookalikes of queen and worker B. lapidarius. For distinction from lookalikes of B. lapidarius males, see Chapter 8, cluster 4. Also see key.

Distribution

Formerly B. lapidarius was widely distributed throughout England and Wales, but with very limited Scottish distribution, along the east coast to a little north of Dundee, and the islands of Coll and Tiree. However, during the 1990s, significant expansions of its range in Scotland have been recorded, both along the east coast of the Highland region, and in Grampian, and this expansion in Scotland is continuing (Macdonald).

Colony cycle

Queens of this species usually emerge from hibernation during March, but may be seen as early as mid-February (later, mid-April, in Scotland). They may be observed searching for nest sites through April to mid-May. Their behaviour in this is similar to that of many other species, flying very low over grassland, or the ground in scrub and light woodland. Unlike other species, however, they also prospect for nest sites in close-cut turf, investigating areas of bare earth and small hollows, often quartering an area as small as 20 square metres for several minutes before flying off. Areas of rabbit-grazed turf are also investigated, and queens will disappear down rabbit holes for several minutes before reappearing and continuing the search. According to Alford, nests are established in 'all manner of sheltered places, both above and below ground', but the survey conducted by Fussell & Corbet indicated that nest sites used by this species are generally underground. Also, they were reported to nest more frequently than other species in soil close to brick, concrete, stone or bare earth, possibly benefiting from heat-reservoir effects in their chosen nest locations. My own observations of both nest-site prospecting activity by queens, and of actual nest sites all indicated below-ground sites, usually in holes in ditch banks, woodland edge, grassland or (commonly) on inner banks of sea walls. Several sites were holes in bare earth, one in a hole 1.5–2 centimetres in diameter in soil below mowed turf, another on a west-facing grassy bank.

Sladen states that the comb is particularly neat and clean, and that wax is produced in great quantities. The comb is usually covered by a wax-pollen canopy.

The first workers are seen from early to mid-May, but their numbers build very slowly to a peak of up to 300 in July and August.

Young queens are usually first seen in June, as are the males. The latter patrol regular routes, usually between early July and late August. Along sea walls, they patrol stretches as much as 100 metres in length, sometimes 'contouring' or stopping momentarily at the tips of the tallest plants (common reeds, or seed-heads of 'escaped' oil-seed rape). Here they walk over leaves or tips of twigs, presumably replenishing their scent marks. They fly at 1–2 metres above ground level between approach places, with from five to more than 20 individuals following one another along the route. I have only once seen a daughter queen approach such a route, but no mating was observed. Fussell & Corbet describe routes along a strip of grass in a field of wheat stubble, along a field boundary and along the top of an exposed bank. Here, too, the approach places visited on the route were the tallest landmarks – the tallest bushes, seed-heads of hogweed and of cocksfoot grass in the case of the grass strip.

Mating pairs of *B. lapidarius* are seen more frequently than other species. Pairs are sometimes seen on the ground in short turf, or by paths. The queen's sting is extended, but curved over her back, while the male clings onto her back and curves the tip of his abdomen to insert his genital capsule into an opening in her abdomen, ventral to the sting. The male makes periodic rapid movements with his legs during the lengthy process. Occasionally mating pairs can be seen at flower-heads, with the queen continuing to forage as if unaware of the diminutive male on her back.

In general, colonies are in decline by the end of August, with some individual workers and males continuing to forage into early or mid-September.

Queens hibernate underground in loose soil, and considerable numbers can be seen in early spring close together along a ditch bank or hedgerow, where they have spent the previous winter.

Bombus lapidarius is a pollen storer.

Foraging behaviour

After hibernation queens spend a considerable time apparently 'grounded' in cool weather, or sunning themselves when conditions permit. They are particularly attracted to dandelions, unlike most other species, and forage from bluebells in woodland. *Bombus lapidarius* is a very adaptable forager, taking pollen from a wide range of deep flowers, especially smaller Fabaceae, but also from open, dish-shaped blossoms such as buttercup and cinquefoil. Workers observed foraging from an extensive patch of the latter flower performed a rapid 'twirl' on each flower before moving on to the next. They periodically stopped to scrape pollen onto their corbiculae. It seems likely that the twirl functions to release pollen from the anthers. Pollen loads analysed by Pinchen from Martin Down and Dungeness were predominantly composed of pollen from a small number of Fabaceae (horseshoe vetch, bird's-foot trefoil and red clover), but with other families represented (poppy and bramble). The uniform composition of these loads suggests that individual workers tend to be flower constant when foraging for pollen.

Bombus lapidarius foraging patterns. Plants in **bold** are garden plants, and (p) signifies a recorded pollen source.

Queens	spring: sallow, dandelion, common vetch, broom (p), gorse (p), apple, green alkanet, red deadnettle (p), white deadnettle, blackthorn, ground ivy, bluebell, **flowering currant, *Hebe*, crocus, *Mahonia*, *Berberis*, *Erica* cultivars** and oil-seed rape. summer: black horehound, self-heal, thyme, woundworts, vetches, mallow, bramble, purple loosestrife, teasel, burdocks, thistles, knapweed, bristly ox-tongue, *Hebe*, *Lavatera*, **busy Lizzy, sage, *Sedum*, *Caryopteris*.**

WORKERS spring: broom, creeping buttercup, white deadnettle, chickweed, bird's-foot trefoil, common vetch, green alkanet, thrift.
summer: bird's-foot trefoils (p), common vetch, red (p), white (p), subterranean and sea (p) clovers, hairy tare, common tare, melilot, tufted vetch (p), dyer's greenweed, tree lupin (p), grass vetchling, spiny restharrow (p), horseshoe vetch, knapweeds, burdock, thistles, ragwort, greater burdock, cat's ears, hawkweed, golden samphire, bristly ox-tongue, mallow (p), perforated St John's wort (p), bramble (p), creeping cinquefoil (p), sea lavender, greater bindweed, teasel, field poppy (p), bell heather, willowherb, comfrey, viper's bugloss, black horehound, marsh woundwort, buttercup, **wallflower, chive, sage, lavender,** *Laburnum, Hebe, Ceanothus,* **tamarisk,** *Aster, Lavatera,* **borage,** field bean.

MALES black horehound, thyme, self-heal, woundworts, clovers, bird's-foot trefoils, melilot, common vetch, tufted vetch, viper's bugloss, Himalayan balsam, bell heather, mallow, purple loosestrife, bramble, thistles, knapweeds, burdocks, ragworts, bristly ox-tongue, field and devil's-bit scabious, **marjoram,** *Lavatera, Hebe, Dahlia,* **busy Lizzie,** *Aster.*

When disturbed, foraging workers of *B. lapidarius* often fly up to investigate an intruder, and even follow for some distance before making off at speed.

Predators and parasites

This species is the host of the cuckoo bumblebee, *B. rupestris*. Cumber recorded low levels of infestation of overwintered queens with *Sphaerularia bombi,* and relatively low levels of infestation of workers by conopids later in the season. He also reported *B. lapidarius* nests as among those infested by the tachinid fly *Brachicoma devia.*

Nests that have been subject of attacks by large, mammalian predators, probably badgers, are sometimes seen. Also, workers of this species are among those whose eviscerated bodies can often be found under trees – presumably victims of predation by blue or great tits.

Habitat and conservation

Like other common species, *B. lapidarius* is found in a wide range of both cultivated and uncultivated habitats: gardens, public parks and open spaces, open woodland, golf courses, coastal marshes and hedgerows. It is a highly adaptable species, and will even nest and forage in areas of close-cut or grazed turf.

Sources: Alford, 1975; Cumber, 1949; Fussell & Corbet, 1992; ITE/IBRA, 1980, Macdonald, 2000, pers. comm.; Pinchen, 2003, 2004; Sladen, 1912; own obs.

SUBGENUS THORACOBOMBUS Dalla Torre

Bombus ruderarius (Müller)

Red-shanked carder bumblebee

A

B

C

D

FIGS A–D. *Bombus ruderarius* queen; *B. ruderarius* male (pale form);
B. ruderarius male (dark form); *B. ruderarius* worker.

Description

QUEENS are relatively small (length 17 mm, wingspan 32 mm), and the coat is black except for a red tail. The corbicular hairs are mainly ginger or ginger-red (but may be black at the base). The abdomen is compact and oval in shape (Fig. K.6(b)). The face is longer than it is wide and the tongue is relatively long. The labrum forms a marked angle with the lower edge of the clypeus, so that the labrum is hardly visible from the front (Fig. K.4(b)). WORKERS are similarly coloured, but smaller. The corbicular hairs may be darker, and ginger-red only towards the outer tip. MALES are quite variable in colour pattern. Dark forms look quite similar to the workers, with indistinct clusters of yellow-brown hairs mixed in with the black on the collar and scutellum, black abdomen, and red tail. In pale forms, there are wide greenish-yellow bands on the collar and scutellum (of more-or-less equal width), and a wide band of similar colour on segments 1 and 2 of the abdomen. Segment 3 of the abdomen is black, and the tail red. The antennae are long relative to the body. The hairs on the dorsal edge of the hind metatarsus are short (less than the width of the metatarsus) (Fig. K.26(a)).

Variation

As described above, there is considerable individual variation among the males in the extent of the yellow markings. However, these are never very bright, and usually a dull greenish-yellow. The colour of the tail in both sexes is variable, and often faded to a rusty ginger.

Similar species

Bombus lapidarius, B. monticola, B. pratorum, B. sylvarum, B. soroeensis and the cuckoo bumblebee *B. rupestris*. For distinguishing features see Chapter 8, cluster 5 for lookalikes of *B. ruderarius* females and darkened forms of the male. For distinction from lookalikes of pale forms of male *B. ruderarius*, see Chapter 8, cluster 4. For definitive identification see the key.

Distribution

Sladen regarded this as a widely distributed species, 'common in many places'. Because of the possibility of confusion with the superficially similar *B. lapidarius*, it is difficult to be certain of either its former or present distribution. However, it seems likely that this species was formerly common in the south and east of England, with more scattered records further north, in Wales and the south-west, in western Scotland and some of the Western Isles. It seems that *B. ruderarius* has declined rapidly in the last 15 or 20 years, with recent confirmed records concentrated in south-eastern England, parts of East Anglia, and the English midlands. It persists along the southern coastal districts of Wales, and on Coll and Tiree in the Inner Hebrides, where it is well established.

Colony cycle

In England, queens emerge from hibernation a little later than the commoner species, at the beginning of April, or later. The queens begin prospecting for nest sites soon after emerging from hibernation. They search for nest sites by 'contouring' areas of rough, tussocky grassland, especially in the vicinity of shrubs. Queens with pollen loads are seen from early April onwards. While some queens have already established nests during April, others may still be observed prospecting for nest sites as late as mid-May. The nest is constructed of grass clippings and moss on or just under the ground, among tall vegetation. An old mouse or vole nest is often used as a foundation (Edwards & Philp). According to Sladen, the first batch of cocoons in the nest are always eight in number, and symmetrically arranged. The workers first appear at the end of April, and may be observed foraging through the spring and summer, with males and daughter queens emerging from early July onwards. The colonies break up by late July or August.

At maturity a nest may have from 50–100 workers.

Bombus ruderarius is a pocket maker.

Foraging behaviour

In urban sites, white deadnettle seems to be the main pollen source for over-wintered queens. Foraging on this plant is very systematic beginning with the lower whorls of flowers, and progressively moving upwards before moving on to the next plant until each plant in a patch has been visited. They are less easy to approach than most other species, and when disturbed often fly round the intruder, before flying off at a considerable height.

Bombus ruderarius foraging patterns. (p) signifies a recorded pollen source.

Queens	spring: white (p) and red deadnettles, common vetch, red clover, purple milk vetch (p), hound's-tongue. summer: bird's-foot trefoils (and presumably other legumes).
Workers	white (p) and red deadnettles, comfrey, red and white clover, bird's-foot trefoil, mallow, bramble, viper's bugloss,

dyer's greenweed, melilot, black horehound (p), hound's-tongue, purple milk vetch (p).

MALES   teasel, knapweed, tufted vetch, white clover, knapweed, spear and cotton thistles.

Predators and parasites

Cumber found 19 pupae of the conopid fly *Physocephala rufipes* in a nest of this species and also recorded it as a host of the tachinid fly *Brachicoma devia*. He also recorded a nest destroyed by an infestation of the wax moth *Aphomia sociella*. The cuckoo bumblebee *Bombus campestris* has been recorded as a nest parasite of *B. ruderarius* in Germany (Westrich).

Habitat and conservation

Bombus ruderarius is regarded by Edwards & Williams as a species of open ground, and several of its currently known populations survive on flower-rich grasslands, such as the machair of the Inner Hebrides and Salisbury Plain. However, it also frequents heath and open woodland in the East Anglian brecks, and some urban and suburban habitats, particularly the complex of flood defences, mineral extraction sites and ex-industrial land in East London and along the lower Thames estuary. In many of these sites it is found together with some or all of the other threatened carder bumblebees. More research is urgently required, and it is the subject of an English Nature Species Recovery Project. See Chapters 10 and 11 for more a more detailed discussion.

Sources: Cumber, 1949; Edwards pers. comm.; Edwards & Philp, 1999; Edwards & Williams, 2004; Macdonald pers. comm.; Sladen, 1912; Westrich, 1989; Williams, 1989, pers. comm.; own obs.

Bombus pascuorum (Scopoli)

Common carder bumblebee

FIGS A–D. *Bombus pascuorum* queen; *B. pascuorum* male;
B. pascuorum male (dark specimen); *B. pascuorum* worker with
pollen loads.

FIG E. *B. pascuorum* male
(pale, northern form).

E

Description

QUEENS are rather small (length approximately 17 mm, wingspan 32 mm). They are variable in colour pattern, with relatively long and uneven coats. There are usually tufts of ginger-yellow hair on the head and face. The thorax is uniformly ginger-coloured, lacking the contrasting bands of many other species, though there are often black hairs mixed with the ginger, especially around the front margin. The abdomen is ginger, usually mixed with variable amounts of black hairs. The longer hairs on the dorsal edge of the hind metatarsus are mostly black. The face is longer than it is wide, and the tongue is also relatively long. WORKERS are very variable in size, some being very tiny indeed, others overlapping small queens. Colour pattern and other features are generally similar to the queens. MALES are also similar in colour pattern. However, the black hairs on the abdomen often form narrow bands across the segments (commonly segments 2, 3 and 4), rather than being concentrated at the sides as they frequently are in females. The hairs on the face are yellow, mixed with some black ones. The head is longer than it is wide. The antennal segments have asymmetrical ventral swellings (especially segments 8 to 10 – Fig. K.21(a)).

Variation

The main variation is in the amount and distribution of black hairs on the thorax and abdomen. There are named subspecies linked to geographical distributions (for example, *septentrionalis* Vogt in Scotland and northern England, and *vulgo* (Harris) in central and southern England), but it is generally accepted that local populations may include the full range of individual variation. In one common pale form, the pale hairs predominate on each segment of the abdomen, but there are concentrations of black hairs at the sides of segments 2–5. In somewhat darker forms, these extend across the abdomen, giving the impression of narrow dark bands. In the darkest forms, segments 2 and 3 of the abdomen may be mostly black, with a rust-brown tail. At the opposite extreme, some individuals have no black hairs on the abdomen (most frequently in northern mainland Britain, and also in the Channel Islands (form *flavidus* Krüger, 1931)). The ground colour, too, is variable, especially among males, ginger- or grey-brown in some specimens, yellowish in others.

Similar species
Bombus humilis, *B. muscorum* and *B. hypnorum*. For distinguishing features see Chapter 8, cluster 1 and the key.

Distribution
Bombus pascuorum is a 'mainland ubiquitous' species that remains common, often abundant throughout the British Isles. It is a recent arrival in Orkney, but is not recorded from the Outer Hebrides.

Colony cycle
In England, queens emerge from hibernation a little later than *B. lucorum*, *B. terrestris* and *B. pratorum*, in late March or early April. During April, queens alternate between foraging and prospecting for nest sites. In the latter mode they fly low over rough tussocky grassland, or in rank vegetation around shrubs and hedge banks, often in gardens, stopping occasionally to explore a potential site before flying off again. They sometimes spend long periods crawling through and around grass tussocks, presumably searching at close quarters by scent. They spend the night nestled into moss or leaf litter in rough grassland prior to the establishment of their nests. These are usually constructed at or slightly below ground level and the survey organised by Fussell & Corbet confirmed the preference of this species for unmown and tussocky grassland, often near hedges or shrubs, for its nest sites. The workers first appear during late April, or the beginning of May, and are observed foraging actively right through the spring and summer into October.

    Bombus pascuorum, like the other carder bumblebees, constructs a nest out of mosses or other vegetation, woven together among tussocks of grass. Shuckard described the workers biting off filaments of moss, forming them into pellets, and passing them back along chains of workers to the nest. Studies by Brian showed that egg batches were laid on cocoons of developing workers in numbers that ensured there would be sufficient workers from the developing broods to nourish their successors. She also noted very high rates of mortality (30–40 per cent), especially at late larval and early pupal stages. In this species, the peak number of workers per nest is reputed to be between 100 and 200, though Brian noted 250 larval cells in one nest she examined.

High failure rates of more than 50 per cent of nests have been recorded, but in those that do reach maturity, males emerge first (from late May onwards) followed by a mixture of males and daughter queens (during June), and finally queens only. *Bombus pascuorum*, like the other carder bumblebees, is a pocket maker, in which there is competition among larvae for food. This is held to explain the divergence in size among workers. According to Free and Butler the switch from production of workers to males and daughter queens results from a change in feeding regime to one in which the workers supplement the diet of the larvae with regurgitated pollen and nectar.

Some authors consider *B. pascuorum* to have a long colony cycle, with no evidence of a second brood. However, sexual adults are observed from June through to early November, with active workers observed until at least early October. Observations of males and daughter queens (including instances of the latter with pollen loads in late September) over a period of some four months are consistent with double broods, although other explanations are possible. It may be that there are considerable differences within a population in the date at which nests are initiated, or that some colonies simply take much longer to mature than others. Colonies of this species are among the last to break up in the autumn.

In northern Scotland, queens emerge later, from mid- to late April, with workers following on from mid-June. Males appear at the end of July or early August, but colonies break up by mid-October. In the colder Central Highlands, nest-founding and subsequent development is delayed by some two weeks, but colonies still break up by mid-October (Nisbet).

Foraging behaviour

Overwintered queens are particularly attracted to white deadnettle and early garden flowers, and are significant pollinators of fruit trees.

Bombus pascuorum shows a strong preference for flowers with deep corollae, such comfrey, thistles and knapweed, and most commonly bilateral, zygomorphic ones, such as the Fabaceae, Scrophulariaceae, and Lamiaceae. Later in the season, foraging attention tends to shift from the Fabaceae to the later flowering Lamiaceae and Asteraceae, and to garden flowers. *Bombus pascuorum* workers show great ingenuity in accessing complex and exotic flower morphologies. For example, their novel way of accessing the nectaries of *Tricyrtis* involves using the external surfaces of the corolla as a platform while they insert their probosces between the petals.

Bombus pascuorum foraging patterns. Plants in **bold** are garden plants, and (p) signifies a recorded pollen source.

QUEENS	spring: sallow, white deadnettle (p), red deadnettle, ground ivy, bugle, yellow archangel, common vetch, gorse, comfrey, blackthorn, horse chestnut, dandelion, creeping buttercup, red campion, green alkanet, bluebell, **wallflower, flowering currant, apple, cherry,** *Mahonia,* **Jasmine,** *Berberis, Dicentra, Rhododendron, Weigela, Geranium* **cultivars, periwinkle,** *Erica* **cultivars, periwinkle,** *Aubrieta,* **lilac, rosemary.** summer/autumn: black horehound, white deadnettle, marsh and hedge woundworts, red and white clovers, restharrows, bird's-foot trefoils, common toadflax, foxglove, greater willowherb, Himalayan balsam, **garden catmint,** *Caryopteris, Sedum,* **Michaelmas daisy.**
WORKERS	spring: sallow, white deadnettle (p), bugle, ground ivy, common vetch, red clover (p), broom, green alkanet, comfrey (p), **wallflower, sage,** *Rhododendron,* **rosemary,** *Geranium* **cultivars (p).** summer: hedge and marsh woundworts (p), white deadnettle (p), wood sage, black horehound (p), lesser calamint, water mint, self-heal, bird's-foot trefoils (p), common, tufted (p), and bush vetches, white (p), red (p) and sea clovers, meadow vetchling (p), grass vetchling, spiny restharrow (p), field scabious, burdocks, thistles (p), knapweed, water figwort, purple toadflax, creeping cinquefoil, bramble (p), raspberry, viper's bugloss, hound's-tongue, comfreys, buttercup, bittersweet, iris, bell heather, herb Robert, mallow (p), mignonette (p), **comfrey cultivars,** *Geranium* **cultivars, sage, lilac, foxglove,** *Lavatera,* **snowberry,** *Rhododendron,* **lavenders,** *Hypericum, Antirrhinum,* **garden catmint.** late summer/autumn: black horehound, white deadnettle, self-heal, marsh woundwort (p), common calamint, goat's rue, bird's-foot trefoils (p), meadow vetchling, Himalayan balsam,

red bartsia (p), common toadflax (p), devil's-bit scabious (p), greater bindweed, greater willowherb, bramble (p), **Hibiscus, Perovskia, Caryopteris, Tricyrtis,** marjoram, garden catmint, **Verbena, Mentha** cultivars and **Michaelmas daisy.**

MALES   bittersweet, bramble, water mint, greater bindweed, common toadflax, black horehound, self-heal, white deadnettle, ling, greater willowherb, burdocks, thistles, knapweeds, ragworts, field scabious, devil's-bit scabious, **lavenders, Geranium** cultivars, **Verbena,** garden catmint, **Caryopteris, Michaelmas daisy.**

Although *B. pascuorum* is a highly adaptable forager, visiting a very wide range of flower species, the available evidence from pollen loads suggests rather narrower specialisation in its pollen gathering to a few species of Fabaceae (red and white clovers, bird's-foot trefoils, meadow vetchling). However, observation of foraging activity suggests that some Lamiaceae and Scrophulariaceae are also important, especially early and late in the year (Brian, Carvell, Pinchen, own obs.).

The colony cycle of *B. pascuorum* is significantly shorter in northern Scotland than in southern and central counties of England, and even then colonies depend on the availability of exotic forage plants in gardens both early and late in the season, with colonies persisting for as much as 30 days after the end of their wild forage sources (Macdonald).

Predators and parasites

Bombus pascuorum is the usual host of the cuckoo bumblebee *B. campestris.* Twenty-five per cent of overwintered queens were found by Cumber to be parasitised by *Sphaerularia bombi,* and later in the year high levels of infestation (13 of 81 dissected) of workers by conopids. Some of these were reared to the adult stage, and turned out to be *Physocephala rufipes.* Like those of other surface nesting species, *B. pascuorum* nests are vulnerable to attacks from large mammals, such as badgers, and, possibly, foxes. One nest discovered on the seaward side of flood defences on the Essex coast had been exposed and damaged, presumably by a large mammalian predator, but workers were still actively scurrying in and out of the nest, while others were carrying out repairs bypassing nesting material back through their legs as described by Shuckard.

Habitat and conservation

In contrast to the other carder bumblebees, *B. pascuorum* remains common and widespread. Edwards & Williams view it as a woodland edge species that has successfully colonised urban and suburban parks, gardens and waste ground. For a more detailed discussion see Chapters 10 and 11.

Sources: Brian, 1951a, b, 1952; Carvell, pers. comm.; Edwards pers. comm.; Edwards & Williams, 2004; Frankum, 2003; Free & Butler, 1959; Fussell & Corbet, 1992; Macdonald, 1998 and pers. comm.; Nisbet, 2005; Pinchen, 2003, 2004; von Hagen & Aichhorn, 2003; Shuckard, 1866; own obs.

Bombus humilis Illiger

A

B

C

D

FIGS A–D. *Bombus humilis* queen; *B. humilis* male;
B. humilis worker (note black hairs on the thorax);
B. humilis queen (note the brown band on the abdomen).

FIG E. *B. humilis* queen, showing tongue.

E

Description

QUEENS (length 17 mm, wingspan 30 mm) are very similar in appearance to pale
queens of *B. pascuorum*. The thorax is yellow-ginger and unbanded, usually with
a small number of black hairs mixed in. In some specimens the black hairs are
very few indeed, and occasionally they are absent. When present, black hairs are
generally close to the wing bases. The dominant coloration of the abdominal
hairs is also yellow-ginger, but there is usually a rather indistinct band of darker
brownish coloration across segment 2. Sometimes there are similarly coloured,
but narrower bands on segments 3 and 4. There are tufts of yellow hair on the head
and face. There are no black hairs on abdominal segments 1–5. The longer hairs
on the dorsal edge of the hind metatarsus are ginger-brown (not black). The face is
longer than it is wide, and the tongue is relatively long. WORKERS are similar to
the queens, but usually smaller. MALES are also very similar in colour pattern, and
approximately the same size as the workers. The antennae are long relative to the
body size. There are no black hairs on segments 1–6 of the abdomen, and there are
usually (but not always) some black hairs mixed with the ginger or ginger-yellow
of the thorax. The hairs on the face are yellow mixed with some black. The head is
longer than it is wide. The antennal segments have slight, symmetrical ventral
swellings (Fig. K.21(b)).

Variation

In Britain, this is mainly in the presence and extent of black hairs on the thorax,
though these are rarely very numerous. In continental Europe, melanic or partially
melanic forms are more common than in Britain. The ground colour varies from

a rich ginger-brown (especially on the thorax) to pale greyish-yellow. To some extent this may be the result of fading in older specimens.

Similar species
Bombus pascuorum, *B. muscorum* and *B. hypnorum*. For distinguishing features see Chapter 8, cluster 1 and the key.

Distribution
According to Sladen, *B. humilis* was 'not rare' in the Dover district, and it probably occurred throughout the south and east, having been taken 'not uncommonly' in Suffolk, Cambridgeshire, Sussex, Oxfordshire, Hampshire and Devonshire. Because of early taxonomic confusion and the similarity of this species to *B. muscorum*, there is some doubt about past summaries of its distribution, but there is little doubt that it has suffered serious decline in recent decades. Recent survey work conducted by the UK Bumblebee Working Group has clarified the current status of *B. humilis*, identifying populations along the south coast and in the south-west peninsula of England, South and West Wales, the eastern Thames estuary, and at a small number of inland sites, most notably Salisbury Plain.

Colony cycle
The queens emerge late from hibernation, usually from mid-May onwards, but in favourable weather as early as mid-April. During May and early June queens alternate between foraging, when many may be seen together in favourable localities, and prospecting for nest sites. They fly low over open grassland, investigating tussocks as they do so, in a similar manner to *B. muscorum*. Like other carder bumblebees, *B. humilis* nests on the ground (though occasionally also in burrows, Else, pers. comm.), usually in open grassland. Optimal nesting habitat for this species is a tall but open vegetation structure, allowing the warmth of the sun to penetrate to the base of the grass stems, and with a litter layer of dead grass and/or mosses. These materials are woven into the nest cover, and it is thought that this must be open to the sun. Nest-construction is initially carried out by the founding queen, but subsequently taken over by the workers. Within a suitable habitat, nesting density is estimated to be relatively high – from one to five nests per square kilometre.

Workers appear from late May onwards, and their numbers increase quite slowly, peaking at probably no more than 40–50 in a colony at maturity during August.

Occasionally daughter queens are seen as early as the end of June, but more typically they emerge from mid-July through August. Males are more commonly observed from early August until the latter half of September.

Wet spring weather can delay nest initiation, with overwintered queens still foraging as late as 28 July in 2001.

Bombus humilis, like other carder bumblebees, is a pocket maker.

There is little evidence on mate location or on hibernation, but it is thought that queens overwinter dug into moss or leaf litter in the grassland.

Foraging behaviour

A long-tongued species, *B. humilis* shows a strong preference for deep flowers in the Fabaceae, Lamiaceae and Scrophulariaceae. This is especially true of pollen collection, with loads analysed so far containing a preponderance of pollen from a small range of Fabaceae (red clover, bird's-foot trefoil and various vetches). However, individual workers show rather less flower constancy in their pollen collecting than other close relatives (such as *B. sylvarum*), with a majority of loads containing two or more pollen species. In East London, Chapman recorded *B. humilis* visiting 38 flower species, and showing no preferences for wild over cultivated plants.

Bombus humilis foraging patterns. Plants in **bold** are garden plants and (p) signifies a recorded pollen source.

QUEENS	spring/early summer: white deadnettle, dandelion, red clover, meadow clary, sage, alkanet, bladder senna, bird's-foot trefoils, fodder vetch, broad-leaved everlasting pea, common vetch, tufted vetch, fodder vetch, red and white clovers, black horehound. Late summer: white deadnettle, common vetch, red clover, bird's-foot trefoil.
WORKERS	red clover (p), white clover (p), bird's-foot trefoils (p), tufted vetch (p), kidney vetch (p), meadow vetchling (p), lucerne, restharrows, wild basil (p), goat's rue (p), mignonette, viper's bugloss (p), bramble, dewberry, creeping thistle, spear thistle (p), musk thistle, knapweed, greater knapweed, field scabious, small scabious, sea holly, teasel, red bartsia (p), marsh

woundwort (p), black horehound, *Perovskia atriplicifolia,*
Nepeta sibirica, lavender, *Lythrum virgatum.*

MALES   black horehound, red bartsia, ragwort, spear thistle, knapweed,
coneflower, cornflower, lavender, garden catmint.

Workers often repeatedly follow a regular route from one flower patch to
another (traplining). In patches of plants with flower spikes (for example, goat's
rue) they tend to move rapidly among the flower spikes, often approaching, then
passing by several before foraging briefly at one or two florets before moving on,
presumably a response to short-lived scent marks (see Chapter 6). They do not
show the 'bottom up' pattern of movement on the inflorescences often taken as
typical in the general literature.

Pinchen timed pollen- and nectar-collecting workers at Dungeness, finding
that gathering a full pollen load takes much longer (commonly from one to two
hours) than a nectar collecting trip (half to three-quarters of an hour), though
there were considerable variations as between different individual workers
and dates.

Predators and parasites

Bombus humilis is recorded as a host of *Sphaerularia bombi*, and Cumber found
pupae of the conopid fly *Physocephala rufipes* in a nest of *B. humilis.* The larvae of
the syrphid fly *Volucella bombylans* are common commensals in the nest debris of
B. humilis and other carder bumblebees, and Cumber reports the fly *Brachicoma
devia* from *Bombus humilis* nests. As with other surface-nesting carder bumblebees,
predation on nests by badgers is a significant threat. Løken also gives *B. humilis* as
an alternative host to the cuckoo bumblebee *B. campestris* (more typically a nest
parasite of *B. pascuorum*).

Habitat and conservation

This species is the subject of a UK BAP, though it remains relatively frequent
where its habitat has so far survived intense development pressure and agricultural intensification. There is some very recent evidence of a possible expansion
of range in the south-east.

Bombus humilis thrives in large areas of dry, flower-rich grassland, with a
continuous source of nectar and pollen throughout its flight period. Abundance of
deep flowers such as the Lamiaceae, Fabaceae and Scrophulariaceae is important,
as is the vegetation structure: tall but open grassland, with moss or leaf litter.

Availability of suitable forage late in the year is particularly significant. For a more detailed discussion see Chapters 10 and 11.

Sources: Carvell, 2000, 2001; Chapman, 2004; Cumber, 1949; Edwards, 1998, 1999, 2000a, b, 2002; Goulson & Darvill, 2003, Harvey, 2000; Løken, 1984; Pinchen, 2003, 2004; Sladen, 1912; Williams, 1989 and own obs.

Bombus muscorum (Linnaeus)

A

B

C

D

FIGS A–D. *Bombus muscorum* worker; *B. muscorum* male;
B. muscorum male, showing tongue; *B. muscorum* worker
with pollen loads.

FIG E. *B. muscorum*, worker of the form
agricolae (Hebrides).

E

Description (mainland forms)

QUEENS are larger (length 19 mm, wingspan 35 mm) than those of *B. pascuorum*
and *B. humilis*, but are very similar in general appearance. The ground-colour on
the thorax and abdomen is ginger, often with a darker brown but indistinct band
on segment 2 of the abdomen. In mainland forms there are no black hairs mixed
with the ginger on the thorax or on segments 1–5 of the abdomen. There are tufts
of yellow-ginger hair on the face and top of the head. Usually the longer hairs on
the dorsal edge of the hind metatarsus are black (as in *B. pascuorum* – ginger-brown
in *B. humilis*). The hair on the thorax is very even in length, giving a neat, 'crew cut'
appearance. The head is longer than it is wide, and the tongue is relatively long.
WORKERS are very similar to the queens, but smaller. MALES, again, are similar in
appearance, and roughly of the same size as the workers. There are no black hairs
on the thorax or segments 1–6 of the abdomen. The face has yellow hair, mixed
with some black. The antennal segments have a slight, symmetrical ventral
swelling (Fig. K.21(b)).

Variation

There are several named subspecies in Britain. These differ mainly in the amount
and distribution of black hairs on the legs and ventral surfaces. The most
distinctive form is subspecies *agricolae* Baker (previously referred to as *smithianus*),
which occurs in the Hebrides and Shetland Islands. In these females the face, the
underside of the body, and the legs are black. The males are similar, but usually
with some yellow hairs on the face. On the mainland, northern populations are
said to be longer haired, and to have more black hairs on the mid- and hind femora
and corbiculae in the queens. The form *orcadensis* Richards, which occurs on the

Orkney Islands, appears not to differ significantly from *pallidus* Evans, the northern mainland form (Else, 2002). These are said to have 'a darker, redder tint to the thorax' than the typical English form, *sladeni* Vogt (Alford). However, as with *B. pascuorum*, there is a considerable range of variation in the ginger ground-colour within populations.

Similar species

Bombus pascuorum, *B. humilis* and *B. hypnorum*. For distinguishing features see Chapter 8, cluster 1 and the key.

Distribution

According to Sladen this species was not abundant, but was widespread throughout Britain, being more common in Scotland and Ireland than in England. There is some evidence of decline in recent decades, but the species has always been very localised inland in central southern England and the Midlands. Its rather sparse distribution in England and Wales since 1960 is primarily coastal. In Scotland there are more inland as well as coastal localities. It also occurs on the Isle of Man, the western Scottish islands, and the Orkneys and Shetlands.

Colony cycle

In southern England the queens do not usually emerge from hibernation until May, although an unseasonable spell of warm weather can trigger an early appearance. They may be seen prospecting for nest sites through May until early June. When engaged in this activity they fly low down over rough grassland, investigating grass tussocks in a systematic way, sometimes crawling through or over them. Having investigated an area, they fly off high into the distance, presumably to search a new area (Pinchen, own obs.). Like other carder bumble-bees, *B. muscorum* builds its nest on or near the surface of the ground, using dead grasses or moss from the litter layer as materials. Sometimes a disused birds' nest may be used. Materials are raked together to form or repair the nest. Various sites are used, most often among long grass, but often with the top of the nest exposed to the sun (as with *B. humilis*). Other reported locations include the edge of a ditch in dense grass and in sparse vegetation on shingle (Pinchen).
The first workers appear in late May or early June, and numbers build up through June to a peak in July. However, even at maturity, the number of workers in a nest is small, estimated at fewer than 100, and probably much less.

Workers of this species are reputedly quite fierce in the defence of their nests. Sladen describes the response of colonies shown to him by farm labourers: '… as soon as I disturbed the nests, the workers flew round my head in a most menacing manner; they also had the disagreeable trick of persisting in doing this, following me wherever I went for a minute or two'.

Occasional males may appear by the end of June, but they are most frequent from the second week in July and through August in most years. Daughter queens are less often seen, but fly from the beginning of August into September. The males gather at nest entrances in early morning, in anticipation of the emergence of daughter queens (Edwards, pers. comm.). Colonies break up in late August or early September in most years.

There is little evidence concerning the hibernation sites of queens, though it seems likely that they bury themselves in mosses or leaf litter in open grassland.

Bombus muscorum is a pocket maker.

Foraging behaviour

Few suitable forage sources are available on marshes and sea walls before the queens emerge from hibernation. In some localities there is a restricted range of forage plants even later in the season, but this is compensated by abundance of a small number of favoured species, such as clovers, bird's-foot trefoils and tufted vetch.

Bombus muscorum foraging patterns. (p) signifies a recorded pollen source.

QUEENS	spring: red deadnettle, red clover, white clover, common vetch summer: red clover, tufted vetch, prickly ox-tongue.
WORKERS	bird's-foot trefoils (p), common vetch, tufted vetch (p), meadow vetchling (p), spiny restharrow (p), red (p), white (p), zigzag and sea clovers, black horehound, purple toadflax (p), bramble (p), slender, creeping and spear (p) thistles, sea aster, hoary ragwort, prickly ox-tongue.
MALES	narrow-leaved bird's-foot trefoil, tufted vetch, red, white and strawberry clover, creeping thistle, spear thistle, knapweed, teasel.

Workers of *B. muscorum* are much more irritable than those of other species. If approached while foraging they fly off well in advance of the observer, and quickly disappear out of sight. They frequently forage alongside workers of *B. lapidarius* on coastal grazing marshes and sea walls, but are more restive than the latter species, probing fewer florets per flowerhead of clover, and moving on from patch to patch more quickly. Unlike the workers, the males forage lazily and are easy to approach.

On the Hebridean machair, *agricolae* forages from red clover and knapweed, and continues to forage in cold and wet weather, when other species have long since taken cover. Inland in Scotland *B. muscorum* is associated with cross-leaved heath on wet moorland (Macdonald).

Predators and parasites

Lundberg & Svensson list *B. muscorum* among the hosts of the nematode, *Sphaerularia bombi*. The cuckoo bumblebee *B. campestris*, whose usual host is *B. pascuorum*, may also invade the nests of *B. muscorum*, but this is yet to be confirmed. Pinchen reports finding two nests at Dungeness, both opened and destroyed by badgers. It could be that a history of vulnerability to large mammals might explain the evolution of the aggressive mode of nest-defence described by Sladen (although this is not encountered by all observers – Edwards, pers. comm.).

Habitat and conservation

Like *B. humilis*, this is an increasingly scarce species with a scattered but mainly coastal distribution in Britain. It requires tall, open grassland with mosses or leaf litter for nesting, and presence of its menu of forage plants. It has become a primarily coastal species in England and Wales, where it survives on extended linear habitats such as sea walls and flood defences. Unlike *B. humilis*, *B. muscorum* favours damp, cool grasslands, or more northerly aspects where populations of the two species overlap.

In Scotland it inhabits machair and similar coastal grassland, and wet moors inland.

Bombus muscorum is the subject of an English Nature Species Recovery Project. See Chapters 10 and 11 for a more detailed discussion.

Sources: Alford, 1912; Baker, 1996; Carvell, pers. comm.; Edwards, 2002a, b, pers. comm.; Else, 2002 and pers. comm.; Lundberg & Svensson, 1975; Macdonald, pers. comm.; Pinchen, 2003; Sladen, 1912; own obs.

Bombus sylvarum (Linnaeus)

Shrill carder bumblebee

A

B

C

D

FIGS A–D. *Bombus sylvarum* queen; *B. sylvarum* male;
B. sylvarum worker with pollen loads;
B. sylvarum queen, showing tongue.

Description

QUEENS are relatively small (length approximately 17 mm, wingspan 30 mm), and inconspicuous. There are pale hairs on the face and head. The thorax is black, with whitish or greenish-yellow bands on the collar and scutellum, and mostly pale hairs on the sides. The first and second segments of the abdomen have mostly pale yellowish or ginger hairs, and there are variable amounts of black hair mixed with pale on segments 3 and 4. The tail is mainly ginger or reddish. The face is slightly longer than it is wide, and the tongue is relatively long. WORKERS resemble the queens in coloration and patterning, but are often very small. MALES are similarly coloured, but the yellow hairs on the face are more extensive, covering the clypeus.

Variation

In some parts of continental Europe melanic specimens are relatively frequent. A rare form occasionally found in Britain is black, with an orange-red tail (Mortimer).

Similar species

Bombus ruderarius (males), *B. pratorum* (males), *B. lapidarius* (males), *B. soroeensis* and the cuckoo bumblebee *B. rupestris* (males). For distinguishing features see Chapter 8, cluster 4 and the key.

Distribution

Formerly *B. sylvarum* was widespread but local through most of southern and south-central England, and along the southern coast of Wales. Further north it had a more scattered distribution up to the Scottish border region. Sladen noted that the species was then 'widely distributed in England and Ireland, and common in a good many places'. Falk gives references evidencing local abundance in several counties (Glamorganshire, Bedfordshire, Gloucestershire, Cambridgeshire and Devon) during the first half of the twentieth century. However, subsequent decline has been very rapid. Critical analysis of the available data for the 1980 *Atlas*, and intensive searches under the auspices of the UK Bumblebee Working Group, have yielded the estimate of a 90 per cent decline between the pre-1970 confirmed distribution and the results of intensive searches in the period 1990–2001, and a 75 per cent decline between the periods 1970–90 and 1990–2001 (Edwards, 2001).

There are currently known populations along the Thames estuary in south Essex and north Kent, Salisbury Plain and the Somerset Levels, in England, and in South and south-west Wales (Pembrokeshire, Glamorgan and Gwent). The likelihood of surviving populations so far undiscovered seems fairly small.

Colony cycle

The queens emerge from hibernation late in the season, usually in the latter part of May, and can be seen until mid-June (occasionally into July). They alternate between foraging and prospecting for nesting sites. One queen is described as having a 'swinging flight' over grassland, occasionally landing on a tuft of slightly longer vegetation, exploring the ground around it and digging into a mossy hump before flying off (Edwards, 1998). Early in the season queens are frequently encountered in flight, there is circumstantial evidence that queens disperse over considerable distances at this time of year prior to nest-founding.

As with other carder bumblebees, the nests are generally on the ground in a slight hollow, or slightly underground (though Sladen reports often finding them underground, with a short tunnel). Dead litter is required for nesting materials, and it seems that, unlike *B. humilis*, this species does not need its nests to be exposed to the sun. It may, therefore, nest in denser grassland than *B. humilis*, and use old vole runs (Edwards, 1998). A nest studied by Claire Carvell confirms these general points. It was situated on the surface, in relatively tall grassland, slightly oriented to the south and open to the sun. It was almost certainly based on an old mouse nest, and consisted of mosses wound into a ball, with an entrance hole at the side. There was a tunnel through the grass next to the entrance which was the route taken by house-bees when clearing material from the nest.

The first workers appear in late June, and their numbers increase through July and August, tailing off during the first part of September. According to von Hagen & Aichhorn, mature nests have from 80–150 individuals, but Carvell's study and other evidence suggests that they are usually less populous than this – probably with typically fewer than 50 workers.

Where the species thrives, males are often numerous in August and the first half of September, and commonly forage alongside workers. There is one report of male patrolling behaviour: over 100 seen in an hour, patrolling a line of reeds along a ditch (on 18 September, north Kent, Edwards, 2001).

Little or nothing is known about hibernation sites, although daughter queens investigating tussocky grassland in late summer are likely to be searching for suitable hibernation sites.

Like the other carder bumblebees, *B. sylvarum* is a pocket maker.

Foraging behaviour

Bombus sylvarum workers forage from a very wide range of flower species, but analysis of pollen loads suggests that their choice of species for pollen collection is much narrower: mainly a small number of species of Fabaceae, Lamiaceae, Scrophulariacea, together with smaller quantities of Asteraceae. Of 107 loads analysed, 63 per cent contained Fabaceae (more than half of that made up of clovers), 11 per cent Lamiaceae, and 28 per cent Scrophulariaceae (probably red bartsia in the main). Pollen from Asteraceae was present in 14 per cent of samples.

Bombus sylvarum foraging patterns. Plants in **bold** are garden plants, and (p) signifies a recorded pollen source.

QUEENS	spring: red clover, white clover, bladder senna, everlasting sweet pea, fodder vetch, common vetch. summer: red clover, red bartsia, **coneflower (*Echinacea purpurea*)**
WORKERS	bird's-foot trefoils (p), red and white clovers (p), hare's-foot clover, sainfoin, lucerne, restharrow, white, ribbed and tall melilots, tufted vetch, black horehound (p), wild basil, self-heal, white deadnettle, marsh woundwort, thyme, yellow-rattle, viper's bugloss, red bartsia (p), hawkbit, creeping, spear, musk and carline thistles, black and greater knapweeds, bristly ox-tongue, sea holly, teasel, field scabious, devil's-bit scabious, bramble, dewberry, rosebay willowherb, eyebright, ***Escallonia*, Russian sage**.
MALES	red bartsia, knapweed, **Russian sage.**

Shortage of forage sources late in the year may be a limiting condition for *B. sylvarum*. In many sites red bartsia is intensively used in late summer, but in others late-flowering clovers and bird's-foot trefoils are used. In some sites, the workers forage from red bartsia growing along uncut margins of the tracks. Here the bartsia flowers favoured by *B. sylvarum* workers (and males) are almost obscured by surrounding and overtopping rank vegetation, so the bees have to be searched-for as they weave their way inconspicuously among a 'jungle' of rank grasses, knapweeds and thistles. One useful way of locating *B. sylvarum* workers is by the shrill buzz they emit when they fly from flower to flower on a foraging trip. On longer flights between patches or en route to or from the nest they are silent.

At the nest observed by Carvell, one instance was recorded of a house-bee being fed by a returning forager. Twenty-one foragers were marked, and their collecting trips timed. These varied from 45 minutes to two hours. Pollen collectors took longer in the nest to detach their loads and re-emerge for the next trip. Some foragers marked at the beginning of the study period were still foraging at the end, two weeks later.

Predators and parasites
Not known.

Habitat and conservation
This species has declined alarmingly in recent decades, and is now a national priority BAP species, but there are very recent signs of what may be a recovery in south-eastern England.

Edwards (1998) suggests that *B. sylvarum* was possibly associated with hedgerows and headlands in the days of small mixed farms. Some of the remaining British populations occur in comparable conditions: tall, but open grasslands, herb-rich, and in early stages in the succession of disturbed grassland to scrub. This is true of the mosaic of habitats along the Thames estuary, although the favourable conditions are not the product of farming practices. The other well-studied populations of *B. sylvarum* occupy very large areas of unimproved, flower-rich grassland, with very different management histories, but surprisingly comparable outcomes. Here, a variety of grazing practices and sporadic disturbance by heavy vehicles has maintained habitats that provide both the densely floristic grassland, and tall, open sward with leaf litter that *B. sylvarum* requires for foraging and nesting. *Bombus sylvarum* completes its colony cycle late in the season, from mid-August well into September. Intrusive management operations such as grass cutting and grazing should be avoided before late September. Winter grazing maintains favourable foraging habitat, but rotational grazing on larger sites may produce a variety of successional stages that meet both nesting and foraging requirements. See Chapters 10 and 11 for further discussion.

Sources: Carvell, 2000; Edwards, 1998, 1999, 2000, 2001, 2002, Falk, 1991, Harvey, 1999b, 2000; Mortimer, 1922; Philp, 1998, Philp & Edwards, 2001; Sladen, 1912; von Hagen & Aichhorn, 2003; Boyd & Boyd, 2000; Williams, 1989a; own obs.

SUBGENUS **SUBTERRANEOBOMBUS** Vogt

Bombus distinguendus Morawitz

Great yellow bumblebee

A

B

C

FIGS A–C. *Bombus distinguendus* worker;
B. distinguendus male; *B. distinguendus* male,
showing all-yellow abdomen.

Description

QUEENS are large (length 20 mm, wingspan over 40 mm), and yellow or brownish-yellow, with a black interalar band on the thorax. The face has some yellow hairs, mixed with black. The yellow bands on the collar and scutellum are both wide, and that on the collar extends down the sides of the thorax. The hair on the thorax is of even length, giving a neat appearance. The hairs on segments 1 and 2 of the abdomen form a darker, brownish band, and the rest of the abdomen is yellow (except for some shorter black hairs on the final segment). The face is long, and the tongue is relatively long. WORKERS are similar but smaller, though late in the colony cycle they approach the size of the queens. MALES are approximately the same size as workers, and similar in colour pattern. The hairs on the face are mainly yellow, and cover the clypeus.

Variation

There is only slight variation in the shade of yellow, otherwise the species is very uniform.

Similar species

Bombus pascuorum, *B. humilis* and *B. muscorum*. The black band on the thorax in *B. distinguendus* separates it from these species, but confusion can arise where thoracic hair has been worn away in specimens of the latter group and the black cuticle is exposed. This can easily be checked. *Bombus subterraneus* (males) and the cuckoo bumblebee *B. campestris* (pale forms of the males are also similar). For distinguishing features see Chapter 8, cluster 3 and the key.

Distribution

Bombus distinguendus has a generally northern distribution across Europe and Asia. Although it formerly had a scattered distribution throughout Britain, it was always more concentrated in the north. Current estimates, based on a critical review of data presented in the 1980 *Atlas* and intensive recording efforts since 1990, suggest a decline in distribution of more than 50 per cent since the 1970–90 period, and more than 80 per cent compared with the pre-1970 recording period. The species is now known to occur on the Inner and Outer Hebrides, the Orkneys and the extreme north of mainland Scotland. A thinly distributed metapopulation persists on the mainland, with some five 'nuclei'. It is thought probable that these can interchange with those on Orkney (Macdonald, pers. comm., and genetic evidence).

Colony cycle

Queens emerge late from hibernation, occasionally being seen as early as mid-May, but more frequently flying from the second week in June. They initially forage for nectar, but subsequently turn to searching for suitable nest sites. In this, they fly with a characteristic side-to-side swinging motion, some 10–20 centimetres above ground level. They typically search over areas some 200 square metres, where the grasses have been winter-grazed, leaving a tussocky structure, with the sides of tussocks exposed to the sun. However, they have also been observed searching in short, rabbit-grazed turf, and among stands of marram grass on the crest of dunes. They investigate new and old rabbit holes and other cavities under grass tussocks. There is evidence also of an association with old mouse nests – particularly those of the wood mouse. There are several reports of more than one queen entering and leaving the same hole, suggesting that there is competition for nest sites (or, just possibly, multiple occupation of the same burrow or complex).

One nest discovered down a rabbit hole was a ball of grass and mosses. The occupying queen gave a warning buzz and came to the entrance of the burrow in response to disturbance. Other nests have been located in similar situations, including three among tussocky grass along the edge of a field drain in machair habitat. Nesting density is estimated at no more than one or two nests per square kilometre, even in high-quality habitat.

Workers appear from mid-July onwards, and reach peak numbers of only 40 or so rather quickly (Hughes), with males emerging by the second week in August and daughter queens following on one or two weeks later. Males have been observed gathering round nest entrances more then ten days before the appearance of daughter queens. According to observations by Neill (in Edwards, 1999) the males stood guard around a nest entrance, occasionally going away and returning, and occasionally interacting with emerging workers, for several days. They were also observed to mark and patrol sheltered routes among knapweed, ragwort and other tall vegetation. Eventually, when the daughter queens emerged, they were fought for by the males (now up to seven in number). One successful mating was recorded on that occasion.

Colonies die out by late August or early September.

Very little is known about hibernation sites, but it is supposed that after mating, the daughter queens dig into deep plant litter or soil under tussocks. There is evidence from the distribution of queens immediately after emergence from hibernation that they favour the grass tussocks on the dune systems that bound many of their favoured coastal localities.

Bombus distinguendus is a pocket maker.

Foraging behaviour

Red clover is a dominant plant in the machair grassland community and is the main forage plant visited by queens, males and workers of *B. distinguendus* until it is replaced by black knapweed in mid-August.

Bombus distinguendus foraging patterns. (p) signifies a recorded pollen source.

QUEENS	spring: bird's-foot trefoil, red clover, white clover, tufted vetch, kidney vetch, yellow-rattle, chives. summer: red clover, black knapweed.
WORKERS	red clover (p), black knapweed (p), hogweed (p), wild carrot (p), catsear (p), perennial sow-thistle (p), marsh thistle (p), white clover (p), devil's-bit scabious (p), harebell (p).
MALES	red clover, black knapweed

Analysis of pollen loads confirms the dominance of red clover and knapweed, with 71 per cent of a sample of 73 loads comprising clover pollen, and 15 per cent knapweed. However, only a minority of loads contain one pollen species only, with up to four species in some loads.

Marking of individual workers has provided evidence that the foraging range of a colony is likely to be at least 1 square kilometre, with workers being recaptured at distances of up to 500 metres.

Both *B. distinguendus* and *B. muscorum agricolae* forage on a closely similar range of flowers (90 per cent coincidence – Edwards, 1998), and share the close association with red clover, followed by knapweed. However, the foraging behaviour of the two species shows significant differences. *Bombus distinguendus* rarely forages except when the sun is shining, whereas *B. muscorum agricolae* continues to feed in cold, overcast conditions, even in light rain.

Predators and parasites

Vulnerable to mammalian predation, but otherwise unknown.

Habitat and conservation

Now a rare species confined to Scottish Islands and the north of the Scottish mainland, and the subject of a BAP.

So far the available evidence suggests that *B. distinguendus* has rather different habitat requirements for nesting and foraging. Nesting habitat seems to be tussocky grassland and dunes, which harbour small mammal populations, perhaps mostly rabbit or wood mouse (possibly voles on the mainland). These conditions may be produced by low-density grazing, or by succession from previous arable farming strips. Fencing off previously grazed areas seems to produce suitable conditions. Favourable foraging habitat is extensive flower-rich grassland, characterised by abundance of bird's-foot trefoil, white clover and other legumes in June, followed by red clover and then knapweed in mid- to late summer. On the machair these conditions are produced by traditional crofting, which combines winter-grazing of sheep and/or cattle on large areas with rotational cultivation of arable strips. The latter yield the most suitable forage by the third year of fallow, or later. As with other species, very large areas of suitable habitat are required to sustain viable populations.

The principal reasons for decline of *B. distinguendus* have been intensification of arable cultivation, loss of flower-rich meadows and confinement of sheep in fenced fields, especially if summer grazing is allowed. Surviving populations on the Scottish islands and northern mainland fringe continue to be threatened by these pressures, and by more intensive management of grassland for silage. There is some overlap between the habitat conditions favourable to corncrakes and those required by *B. distinguendus*, and it is argued (Edwards, 1998) that management favourable to *B. distinguendus* would also benefit the corncrake (though not necessarily the reverse).

Although most attention has been focused on the appropriate management of extensive areas of foraging habitat, the evidence of dual occupation of nest sites by queens suggests that a limiting factor for *B. distinguendus* at least on its quality machair habitats might be shortage of nest sites.

Recent studies of relict mainland populations of *B. distinguendus* (Macdonald in Edwards, 1999) provide limited grounds for optimism. Although reproductive populations even on the larger islands are probably small, there is evidence of gene flow between Orkney and mainland populations. With appropriate conservation measures it may be that more extensive habitat and larger sub-populations could be encouraged on the mainland. Another reason for guarded optimism is the discovery of *B. distinguendus* on cliff-top habitat, and at very low densities inland on the mainland, utilising a rather different range of forage sources, including pollen collection from marsh thistle. Observations of *B. distinguendus* foraging from conservation margins in farmed land in the

Orkneys gives reason to hope that appropriate agri-environmental measures can benefit this species. See also Chapter 10.

Sources: Edwards, 1997, 1998, 1999, 2000b, 2001a, b, pers. comm.; Falk, 1991; Hughes, 1998; IBRA/ITE, 1980; Macdonald, 1998, pers. comm.; Taylor, 2000; own obs.

Bombus subterraneus (Linnaeus)

Description

QUEENS are large with a short coat, especially on the front segments of the abdomen. The face is long. There are two yellow bands on the thorax, but these are often reduced and the one on the scutellum may be reduced to a few brown hairs. The abdomen is black (often with a fringe of whitish or brownish hairs on the posterior margins of segments 1–3), with a white or dingy white tail. There is a keel on the ventral surface of the final abdominal segment (Fig. K.14(a)). WORKERS are similar to the queens, though smaller. They may entirely lack pale hairs on the scutellum.

MALES have wide pale yellow bands on the collar and scutellum, whilst the abdomen has alternating bands of black and greenish or brownish-yellow. The extent of the black on the abdomen is variable.

Variation

In both sexes, there are lighter and darker forms, with more-or-less extensive yellow markings.

Similar species

Bombus ruderatus, *B. hortorum*, *B. distinguendus* and the cuckoo bumblebees *B. barbutellus* and *B. campestris*. For distinguishing features see Chapter 8, cluster 3 and the key.

Distribution

According to Sladen it was abundant in the Deal and Dover districts in most years. He also considered it common in Suffolk and many localities in southern and eastern England. However, the species suffered a dramatic decline such that by the 1970s it was present in only 22 10-kilometre squares (1980 *Atlas*), with a marked concentration in the Dungeness area. Despite intensive searches, there have been no sightings of this species in Britain since the mid-1980s. It seems very likely that *B. subterraneus* is now extinct in Britain.

Colony cycle

According to Sladen the queens emerge late from hibernation (from early June, according to Williams's observations at Dungeness). Sladen says this species has 'little skill in wax-building' and the larvae are often imperfectly covered. The nest apparently has a 'disagreeable odour', and is usually underground. Queens are said to hibernate in tunnels excavated in banks or other sheltered situations. The first brood of workers is very large, but the numbers in a mature nest are comparatively small, with males and daughter queens emerging quite soon after the establishment of the colony, from late July. As with *B. distinguendus*, males locate young queens by gathering around the nest site and waiting for them to emerge (Alford).

Bombus subterraneus is a pocket maker.

Foraging behaviour

As a long-tongued species, it favours deep flowers such as the Lamiaceae, Fabaceae (especially clovers) and honeysuckle. Teasel was apparently much visited at Dungeness.

Bombus subterraneus was introduced to New Zealand towards the end of the nineteenth century, and still survives there. Goulson & Hanley indicate that workers there have a very narrow range of pollen sources: mainly red clover, together with smaller amounts of bird's-foot trefoil and perforated St John's-wort. Both queens and workers visited mainly viper's bugloss for nectar, with red clover also important for workers.

Predators and parasites

Not known.

Habitat and conservation

Bombus subterraneus was included as a UK BAP species, but it appears this designation came too late to save it as a British species.

Falk says that *B. subterraneus* favours a large variety of open, flower-rich situations, including shingle, dunes and saltmarshes on the coast, and a variety of grassland types inland. It seems to particularly favour dry locations (Williams, 1988), and large areas of suitable habitat seem to be necessary. The few remaining populations in New Zealand are along the margins of man-made lakes in areas of dry, often sheep-grazed land, and some appear to be threatened, as in Britain and large parts of Europe, by agricultural intensification. While the New Zealand populations remain, there is the possibility that British-derived stock might be reintroduced. However, as Goulson points out, this would be unlikely to succeed unless the causes of its presumed extinction in Britain were understood and reversed.

Sources: Alford, 1975; Edwards, 1998; Falk, 1991; Goulson & Hanley, 2004; IBRA/ITE, 1980; Sladen, 1912; Williams, 1988, 1989.

SUBGENUS PSITHYRUS Lepeletier

Bombus vestalis
(Geoffroy in Fourcroy)

This is a cuckoo in the nests of *B. terrestris*, and is currently the most common of the cuckoo bumblebees in southern Britain.

A

B

C

FIGS A–C. *Bombus vestalis* female; *B. vestalis* male; *B. vestalis* female, showing face and tongue.

Description

FEMALES are often large (length 19 mm, wingspan 37 mm), approaching the size of their host species. The colour pattern is mainly black, with a single golden or brownish-yellow band on the collar. There are usually black hairs mixed with the yellow on the collar. Segments 1 and 2 of the abdomen are black. Segment 3 is also mainly black, but has a fringe of yellowish hairs, which is broken in the middle. The hairs on segment 4 are mainly white, and those on segment 5 mainly black, with tufts of paler hair at the sides. The wings are slightly darkened, with a ginger-brown suffusion. The hair is dense and even in length on the thorax, but more sparse on segments 1 and 2 of the abdomen. As with other cuckoo bumblebees, there is no corbicula on the hind tibia, which is convex and densely covered in short hairs. The ventral surface of the final abdominal segment has callosities that form an acute v-shape (Fig. K.44v). There is no worker caste. MALES are generally similar to females in colour and pattern, but smaller. The face is black, and the antennae long relative to the body. Antennal segment 5 is much longer than 3 and segment 4 is wider than it is long (segment 5 approximately equal in length to 3 plus 4) (Fig. K.38(a)). The hind tibia has a dense covering of black hair on the outer surface.

Variation

In females, the collar is subject to darkening and reduction in extent. This is also true of males, which may also have yellow hairs on segment 1 of the abdomen.

Similar species

Bombus bohemicus, *B. sylvestris*, *B. terrestris*, *B. lucorum* and *B. soroeensis*. For distinguishing features see Chapter 8, cluster 2 and the key.

Distribution

Sladen declared *B. vestalis* to be very common in south and east England, wherever its host, *B. terrestris* was abundant. This is still true. The species is more locally distributed north and west of a line from the Wash to the Bristol Channel, and so far it reaches no further north than County Durham.

Life history

Females of *B. vestalis* emerge early from hibernation, as soon as, or a little after, the host queens appear. After a period spent mainly foraging, they commence prospecting for nests of their host species, *B. terrestris*. Their behaviour when engaged in this activity closely resembles that of *B. terrestris* queens themselves when prospecting for suitable nest sites. According to Sladen, successful usurpation by *B. vestalis* females always results in the death of the host queen, and this view is supported by the results of artificial introductions of *B. vestalis* females into three nests of *B. terrestris* by Frehn & Schwammberger. The queens were killed between six hours and six days after the introduction of the cuckoo, but in two of the colonies the host workers still managed to produce male offspring. In the other colony, the cuckoo successfully suppressed the reproduction of host workers, and produced male progeny of its own.

However, Fisher's observation of two artificial introductions of *B. vestalis* females into *B. terrestris* nests told a different story. In each case the intruder was attacked by the host queen and her first-brood workers. In one nest the cuckoo permanently left, but in the other, aggressive behaviour had subsided after one hour and both host queen and cuckoo cohabited for approximately a further two weeks, when the host queen was found dead. The cuckoo began to eject host larvae and eat their eggs within a day of being introduced, and began to lay its own eggs some five days later. It dominated the host queen and workers by mauling and pushing them. However, some host brood were spared, and 25 worker and 19 males survived to adulthood. Meanwhile, the cuckoo incubated both its own and host cocoons, and 14 *vestalis* males were produced. The death of the host queen coincided with renewed attacks on the cuckoo and its brood by host workers. Attempts by the cuckoo to reassert its dominance and protect its brood failed and she died some 46 days after the initial usurpation.

The artificiality of the introduction makes it difficult to generalise from these cases. However, the cohabitation of the host queen and cuckoo over a prolonged period, the successful reproduction of both, and the loss of dominance on the part of the cuckoo coinciding with the death of the host queen present a rather more complex picture of host/parasite relationships than commonly assumed. It is possible that the conflicting evidence from the available studies could be explained in terms of the age and number of host workers as well as the vigour of the female cuckoo at the point of introduction. In all cases the entry of the cuckoo provoked an aggressive response from the host bees. Sladen's reports of more advanced and populous nests of *B. terrestris* suggest that these successfully fight off and kill intruding female *B. vestalis*.

The fresh males and females of *B. vestalis* emerge in late May or early June, more-or-less simultaneously with the appearance of the sexual forms of the host species. After emerging from the nest, the males exhibit patrolling behaviour similar to many other species. They sometimes congregate in considerable numbers, and follow one another in a rapid flight along a constant route over tree canopies or hedgerows (for example, eight to ten individuals 'contouring' the canopy of a small sycamore and an adjacent line of *Hebe* shrubs at Frinton-on-Sea,

Essex in early July 1999). Alternatively they may be observed patrolling singly over low vegetation. Occasionally they take a break from this activity to pay brief visits to flowers. Fussell & Corbet report a rather different pattern in which males patrolled a general area rather than specific approach places, and they observed an attempt at mating on the ground by one of the males in a repeatedly patrolled area of recently cut grass.

Fresh females and males continue to forage until late August, after which date the females have entered hibernation.

Foraging behaviour

Overwintered queens alternate between foraging on a variety of spring flowers and prospecting for nests. As a short-tongued species its apparent preference for deep flowers is surprising. Males are particularly frequent on white clover. Foraging behaviour, as with other cuckoos, is rather lazy and unhurried.

Bombus vestalis foraging patterns. Plants in **bold** are garden plants.

FEMALES	spring: sallow, blackthorn, dandelion, red and white deadnettles, bluebell, ground ivy, common and tufted vetches, crab apple, horse chestnut, **bay, *Prunus* species, periwinkle, rosemary, *Valerian, Rhododendron.*** summer: red and white clover, tufted vetch, ground ivy, knapweed, ***Sedum.***
MALES	tufted vetch, narrow-leaved bird's-foot trefoil, clovers (especially white clover), green alkanet, viper's bugloss, comfrey, hogweed, buttercup, hedge woundwort, thyme, black horehound, bramble, spear, marsh and creeping thistles, knapweeds, lesser burdock, teasel, field and devil's-bit scabious, ***Hebe, Lavatera, lavender, snowberry.***

Habitat and conservation

Bombus vestalis is currently abundant in southern and eastern England, with a similar, but more southerly, distribution to its host. So long as *B. terrestris* remains common, it seems likely that *B. vestalis* will maintain its status, albeit within a smaller geographical range in Britain.

Sources: Fisher, 1988; Frehn & Schwammberger, 2001; Fussell & Corbet, 1992; Sladen, 1912; own obs.

Bombus bohemicus (Seidl)

This species is a cuckoo in the nests of *B. lucorum.*

A

B

C

FIGS A–C. *Bombus bohemicus* female;
B. bohemicus male; *B. bohemicus* male,
showing sparse hairs on the abdomen.

Description

FEMALES are generally slightly smaller (length 18 mm) than those of *B. vestalis*, which they closely resemble. There is a pale yellow band on the collar, which normally lacks intermixed black hairs. The rest of the thorax and abdomen is black, except for pale yellow side-flashes on segment 3 of the abdomen and the white tail (segments 4 and 5). The yellow side-flashes are inconspicuous, and subject to fading with age. The face is rounded, and the tongue short. The hair on the thorax is uneven in length. As with other cuckoo bumblebees there is no corbicula. The outer surface of the hind tibia is densely covered with hair. The ventral surface of the final abdominal segment has callosities that form an acute v-shape (similar to *B. vestalis* – Fig. K.44v). MALES are similarly coloured, but much smaller. The hair on the thorax is relatively long and uneven, giving a 'scruffy' appearance. There is usually some yellow hair on segment 1 of the abdomen. The hairs on the final abdominal segment are mostly black (some white ones towards the side of the segment). Antennal segment 3 is approximately equal in length to 5 (Fig. K.38(b)). The hind tibia has long black hairs on both edges, and has a dense covering of shorter hairs on the outer surface.

Variation

There is very little recorded variation. However, in northern Scotland some males have bright yellow replacing the white tail.

Similar species

Bombus vestalis, B. sylvestris, B. terrestris, B. lucorum and *B. soroeensis*. For distinguishing features see Chapter 8, cluster 2 and the key.

Distribution

Sladen found only one specimen in east Kent, and none on his excursions elsewhere in the south-east. He therefore presumed it to be rare in south-eastern England. This remains true today, but it is widespread and often common in parts of northern Britain and the south-western peninsula. It also has a well-established population on the East Anglian brecks.

Life history

The females emerge from hibernation in April, and may be seen foraging or searching for *B. lucorum* nests through May. Females are assumed to enter the nests of the host species early in the colony cycle of the latter, when the first brood of workers have emerged, and there is further brood undergoing development. Fisher introduced *B. bohemicus* females into freely foraging early-stage colonies of

B. lucorum, but in most cases the cuckoo refused to remain in the host nest, despite the host bees' apparent lack of response. One cuckoo that did remain experienced no aggressive response from the hosts, but proceeded to assert its own dominance by grabbing and mauling the host bees – especially the incumbent queen. After four days in the nest, the cuckoo began ejecting host larvae from their brood cells, and eating host eggs. However, some host brood were left and the queen also laid eggs subsequent to the entry of the cuckoo. After a further four days the female cuckoo began laying eggs in wax cells she constructed from destroyed cells and storage pots originally made by the hosts. The resulting larvae were fed by both the cuckoo female and the host workers by regurgitating food from stores in the nest. Meanwhile, the complement of host workers rose from 8 to 28, and 20 host males reached adulthood.

However, the host queen eventually lost her dominance over the workers and this coincided with destruction of all the cuckoo brood by the host workers. Efforts of the cuckoo to protect her brood by pushing host workers away and buzzing loudly failed. Both the cuckoo and host bees died soon after.

The failure of the hosts to react aggressively to the intruder is confirmed by Müller & Schmid-Hempel's observations on naturally parasitised *B. lucorum* nests in Switzerland. Ten out of the 36 nests they studied were invaded by *B. bohemicus* females, and most of these were subject to more than one invasion (after the initial invader had been removed by the researchers). Although the cuckoos were present in the nests for up to three days prior to removal, the incumbent queens were not killed.

Several features of Fisher's study are of interest. First, the cuckoo female contributed to the nurture of her own brood, contrary to common assumptions. Second, the host queen succeeded in reproducing despite the presence of the cuckoo. Third, and most intriguing, is the apparent relationship between the loss of dominance by the host queen and the destruction of the cuckoo's brood. This raises the speculative question of whether the cuckoo depends in some way on the host queen's continued dominance in the nest. Since *B. lucorum* is a complex species in which chemical signals play a part in the queen's dominance over the workers, one possibility is that the cuckoo's control over host workers has to be mediated by way of its control over the host queen.

The males and fresh females emerge from late June onwards, and males may be seen until late September.

Foraging behaviour

Bombus bohemicus foraging patterns. Plants in **bold** are garden plants.

FEMALES sallow, dandelion, white clover, bilberry, sycamore, raspberry, **Centaurea montana,** bistort, bugle, **Thymus polytrichus, cotoneaster, Erica cultivars.**

MALES field scabious, devil's-bit scabious, thyme, marsh, creeping and cotton thistles, knapweed, bramble, ling, rosebay willowherb, **lavender, masterwort.**

Habitat and conservation

The population of *B. bohemicus* is presumed to be dependent on that of its host species.

Sources: Alford, 1975; Edwards, 2002; Fisher, 1998; Macdonald, 1998, pers. comm.; Müller & Schmid-Hempel, 1992; Nisbet, 2005; own obs.

Bombus rupestris (Fabricius)

This species is a cuckoo in the nests of *B. lapidarius*.

A

B

C

FIGS A–C. *Bombus rupestris* female; *B. rupestris* male; *B. rupestris* male (dark form).

Description

FEMALES are large and long-bodied (length 22 mm). They resemble queens of
B. lapidarius in colour pattern. The thorax and segments 1–3 of the abdomen are
black, and the tail is red. The wings are suffused dark brown, and the coat is short
and thin, especially on abdominal segments 1 and 2. The face is rounded, and
the tongue of medium length. There is no corbicula on the hind tibia, the outer
surface of which is densely covered with black hairs. The callosities on the ventral
surface of the final abdominal segment are very distinctive: they are particularly
large and prominent (Fig. K.44i). MALES are smaller and somewhat variable in
colour pattern. As in the females, the dominant colour of the coat is black, and
the tail (abdominal segments 4– 7) is red. The facial hairs are black, and there are
variable pale whitish or yellowish bands on the collar, scutellum and the first
abdominal segment. Antennal segment 4 is as wide as, or wider than, it is long,
and 5 is longer than 3 (Fig. K.40(a)). The hind tibia is long and narrow, with long
ginger hairs on both edges, and a dense covering of shorter hairs on the outer
surface. The hind metatarsus is also long and narrow with long hairs (longer
than the width of the metatarsus) on the dorsal edge (Fig. K.23(b)).

Variation

On mainland Europe, females with more-or-less distinct yellow bands on the
collar and scutellum are quite frequent. This form also occurs rarely in Britain,
but many females have a few yellow hairs mixed with the black on the collar. The
pale yellowish or whitish bands on the thorax and abdomen of the male are rarely
well defined, and subject to reduction. The band on abdominal segment 1 is often
reduced to tufts of pale hair at the sides of the segment. The red hairs on the tail
in males fade with age to orange and finally to whitish. Wholly black specimens
are known but are rare.

Similar species

Bombus lapidarius, *B. ruderarius*, *B. monticola* and *B. pratorum*. For distinction
between female *B. rupestris* and its lookalikes (*B. lapidarius* and *B. ruderarius*)
see Chapter 8, cluster 5 and the key. For male *B. rupestris* and its lookalikes see
Chapter 8, cluster 4 and the key.

Distribution

According to Sladen it was then 'to be found in most places where its host is
abundant' and was particularly common in parts of Suffolk and Norfolk. In his
account, it was plentiful in east Kent. By the 1960s serious decline had set in, with
the species still present only in extreme south-east England and south-west Wales.

However, by the mid-1990s a recovery was evidently under way, and Philp was able to report increasing abundance, especially on some chalk grassland sites. This recovery has been maintained, but the distribution remains strongly skewed to south-central and south-eastern England, with scattered records further north to the Scottish border. Like other cuckoo bumblebees it is likely that *B. rupestris* is under-recorded.

Life history

Sladen states that this is the latest of the cuckoo females to emerge from hibernation in the spring, though there are recent records of them from mid-April onwards. The overwintered females seek out nests of *B. lapidarius* in May and June. Sladen's observations suggest that queens of *B. lapidarius* and their cuckoos do not cohabit for long, and that successful usurpation always results in the death of the host queen. In one natural invasion he observed, two, and on one occasion three, *B. rupestris* females entered the nest, but only one remained. The cuckoo and the host queen cohabited with no sign of aggression for ten days, but then both host queen and three workers were found dead outside the nest. Sladen's inference is that conflict arises when, after a period of living off the food reserves in the nest, the cuckoo is ready to lay its eggs. He did not know of a parasitised colony in which the host succeeded in reproducing.

The new generation of males and females emerges in July or August, the females going into hibernation before the end of August, whilst the males continue into mid-September.

According to Sladen, *B. rupestris* parasitised from 20–40 per cent of *B. lapidarius* nests in east Kent. In mainland Europe, *B. rupestris* has been reported as usurping nests of *B. sylvarum* and *B. pascuorum* in addition to its usual host (Løken).

Foraging behaviour

Bombus rupestris foraging patterns. Plants in **bold** are garden plants.

FEMALES	spring: sallow, ox-eye daisy.
	summer: field scabious, spear thistle, ***Lavatera* and other garden flowers**.
MALES	marsh thistle, spear thistle, knapweed.

Habitat and conservation

Fluctuations in the distribution and abundance of *B. rupestris* are not obviously connected to the fortunes of the host species. Its former scarcity and recent recovery are presumably due to some other cause, possibly climatic.

Sources: Falk, 1991; IBRA/ITE, 1980; Løken, 1984; Philp, 1997; Sladen, 1912; own obs.

Bombus barbutellus (Kirby)

This is a cuckoo in the nests of *B. hortorum*.

A   B

FIGS A–B. *Bombus barbutellus* female; *B. barbutellus* male.

Description

FEMALES are medium-sized (length 17 mm). There is a yellow band on the collar, extending forwards on the top of the head (where the yellow hairs are mixed with black). There is a fringe of yellow hairs on the scutellum, and usually an indistinct band of sparse yellow hairs on the first abdominal segment. Abdominal segments 2 and 3 are black, and there is an off-white tail (segments 4 and 5). The coat is short and thin, especially on segments 1–3 of the abdomen, so that the shiny abdominal plates show through – this is especially so in older, worn specimens after hibernation. As with other cuckoo bumblebees, there is no corbicula. The callosities on the ventral surface of the final abdominal segment form a conspicuous wide u-shape (Fig. K.44iv). MALES are very similar in colour and pattern to the females, but smaller. In some individuals, the yellow hair on the scutellum is more extensive and evident. The tail is whitish, but with black hair on the final segment. The facial hairs are black. Antennal segment 3 is markedly shorter than 5. The ventral surface of the final abdominal segment has a raised mound on each side (Fig. K.37(a)).

Variation
Little reported, apart from minor differences in the distribution and amount of yellow.

Similar species
Bombus hortorum, B. ruderatus, B. subterraneus, B. jonellus and *B. campestris*. For distinguishing features see Chapter 8, cluster 3 and the key.

Distribution
Sladen found *B. barbutellus* widespread but not very common – less so, interestingly, than *B. rupestris*. There is a scattered distribution across the British Isles, with most records clustered in south-east and south-west England, west Wales and East Anglia. It occurs on Coll and Tiree in the Inner Hebrides, but is absent from the other Scottish islands and from the Highland region.

Life history
Post-hibernation females are on the wing from mid-April, a little later than queens of the host species. They alternate between foraging and searching for established nests of *B. hortorum*. In this activity they fly very low in and around patches of rough vegetation in hedge banks or ditches, settling frequently to explore holes and hollows. They examine small areas very intensely and systematically, then flying off if they are unsuccessful. It may be that they, like other cuckoo females, are attracted by scent trails of their host species. It is unclear whether the similarity in colour and pattern of the coat to that of *B. hortorum* is a significant factor in their establishing themselves in the host nests, and there are no detailed accounts of the interactions between *B. barbutellus* and its hosts within the nest. Sladen reports one parasitised *B. hortorum* nest that he excavated. It contained 49 *B. hortorum* workers, and the dead body of the host queen, together with 16 fresh *B. barbutellus* females and two males. Among the remaining brood were five cocoons of male *B. hortorum*, suggesting the possibility of successful host reproduction.

Males are most commonly seen in June and July, but continue to fly until the end of August in some years. Fresh females are also mostly seen in June and July. The flight periods of this species thus correspond closely with those of the

host species, but it is unclear whether they can complete two cycles in a season.
Bombus barbutellus possibly also colonises *B. ruderatus* nests.

Foraging behaviour

Bombus barbutellus foraging patterns. Plants in **bold** are garden plants.

FEMALES	spring: white deadnettle, bush vetch.
	summer: tufted vetch, spear thistle, creeping thistle.
MALES	bramble, thistles, knapweed, **lavender, honeysuckle cultivars**

Habitat and conservation
Conservation of *B. barbutellus* would appear to be dependent on the status of its host species (for discussion of which, see Chapters 10 & 11).

Sources: IBRA/ITE, 1980; Macdonald, pers. comm.; Sladen, 1912; own obs.

Bombus campestris (Panzer)

This species is a cuckoo of *B. pascuorum,* and possibly of other closely related species.

FIGS A–D. *Bombus campestris* female; *B. campestris* male (pale form); *B. campestris* male (black form); *B. campestris* male (intermediate form).

FIG E. *B. campestris* female (dark form).

E

Description

FEMALES are medium-sized (length 17 mm). The coat is very thin on the dorsal surface of the abdomen, especially on segments 1 and 2, giving a very worn appearance, even in quite fresh specimens. There is a dull, golden yellow band on the collar (and sometimes some yellow hairs on the top of the head). The rest of the thorax is black, sometimes with an indistinct fringe of paler hairs on the scutellum. Segments 1 and 2 of the abdomen are very thinly coated with black hair, whilst segments 3–5 are black in the middle, progressively encroached from the sides by yellow. There is no corbicula. The callosities on the ventral surface of the final abdominal segment are prominent, and form a wide v-shape (Fig. K.44ii). MALES are very variable in colour and pattern, ranging from pale to completely black. Intermediate, darkened forms are common. In pale specimens the head and thorax are black, but with yellow hairs on top of the head, a wide pale whitish-yellow collar, and long pale hairs on the scutellum. The first segment of the abdomen has a thin coat of black hair in the middle, and tufts of pale hairs at the sides. Segment 2 is thinly coated with black hairs and has a yellowish fringe along the rear edge. Segments 3–6 are predominantly pale yellow (often with a central line of black hairs). Darkened forms are black except for an indistinct narrow pale band on the collar and yellow hairs at the sides of segments 4– 6 of the abdomen. All forms have a tuft of long, curved black hair sprouting from each side of a median groove on the ventral surface of the final abdominal segment (Fig. K.36).

Variation

Both males and females are subject to darkening and reduction of the yellow markings. Fully melanic forms are relatively frequent. In parts of western

Scotland, form *swynnertoni* has more extensive yellow markings in the female, the thorax being mainly pale whitish-yellow, with a few black hairs in the middle. Abdominal segments 1 and 2 have fringes of yellow hairs, and the tail is mainly yellow as in the typical forms. Males have a more distinct patch of black hairs on the thorax, whilst the abdomen is mainly yellow, with variable amounts and distributions of black hairs.

Similar species

Bombus barbutellus, B. distinguendus, B. subterraneus and *B. jonellus hebridensis.* For distinguishing features see Chapter 8, cluster 3 and the key.

Distribution

Sladen considered *B. campestris* widespread and common in some places in the British Isles, but noted it was seldom seen in the Dover district. It is currently widespread in England and Wales, becoming more scattered in the Midlands and northwards. In Scotland it is much more localised, mainly southern and coastal, but occasionally occurring as a vagrant in the Highlands. There is some evidence that it may have declined recently, but as with other cuckoo species, there are considerable local variations and seasonal fluctuations in abundance.

Life history

The females emerge from hibernation during April, but are not often seen.

Fisher introduced a female of *B. campestris* into an observation nest of *B. pascuorum* containing a queen and 32 workers. The workers attacked the intruder, forming a ball round it and attempting to sting it. Seven workers were killed, but the parasite was also killed. A second cuckoo was introduced, and this, too, was attacked by the host workers. Interestingly, the host queen withdrew to the nest entrance during hostilities and did not attack the intruder herself. Fisher was finally able to overcome resistance of the host colony only by temporarily withdrawing all workers and later reintroducing five of them. After this, hosts and parasite cohabited for 33 days before conflict was resumed. For eight days after being introduced the cuckoo was quiescent, but then began to eject host larvae and eat their eggs. This change of behaviour coincided with the parasite making egg cells out of wax obtained from destroyed host cells and nectar pots, and laying its own eggs. There was no evidence of direct dominance behaviour on the part of the cuckoo, and it co-operated with host workers (whose numbers it allowed to grow to a peak of 45) in tending its brood. Both the cuckoo female and host workers took pollen from pockets in the larval cells and fed it to the larvae by regurgitation through holes bitten into the cell walls. Sometimes the cuckoo would bite the holes, and the host workers would feed its larvae through them. Eventually workers became aggressive towards the cuckoo and expelled it from the nest, while the host queen continued in residence. In all, 16 males of the host species were reared and ten males and three females of *B. campestris*.

It seems likely that the successful defence of the nest from the first introductions was a consequence of the large cohort of host workers. Presumably usurpations under natural conditions would typically affect nests at an earlier stage of colony development. However, the exclusive role of workers in combat makes sense in terms of the crucial importance of the queen to the reproductive success of the colony. As with detailed observations of other cuckoo/host interactions, the common view that the cuckoo plays no part in the rearing of its brood is challenged, as is the earlier view that the invader invariably kills the host queen.

Males and fresh females emerge from mid-May onwards, rather earlier than the corresponding sexual generation of the host species, but as with the host, there are also late sightings of both males and females of *B. campestris* (in August and September). Taken together with some circumstantial evidence supporting double-broodedness of *B. pascuorum*, this raises the fascinating question whether *B. campestris* may not also go through two reproductive cycles in some years. The alternative is that they have a remarkably long flight period, from mid-May through to September.

In mainland Europe, there are reports of *B. campestris* parasitising the nests of *B. humilis* and *B. pratorum* in addition to its usual host.

Foraging behaviour

Bombus campestris foraging patterns.

FEMALES	spring: green alkanet, red clover, dandelion, germander speedwell. summer: marsh thistle, ground ivy, devil's-bit scabious.
MALES	green alkanet, bramble, thistles, knapweed, devil's-bit scabious.

Habitat and conservation
Bombus campestris is widespread within the geographical range of its host, but with a more strongly southern bias. Within its range, it appears to be far more localised

than its ubiquitous host, which suggests that some other factors, as yet unknown, must affect its reproductive success – possibly, as Fisher's work indicates, the host species is effective at defending its nests from attack. It has been most frequently recorded in open, flowery areas on urban fringes, often in or near woodland. Although the host species remains abundant, *B. campestris* appears to have declined rapidly in some areas recently.

Sources: Fisher, 1988; IBRA/ITE, 1980; Macdonald, pers. comm.; Richards, 1936; Sladen, 1912; own obs.

Bombus sylvestris (Lepeletier)

This species parasitises nests of the very common and widespread B. *pratorum*, and probably other closely related species.

A

B

C

FIGS A–C. *Bombus sylvestris* female; B. *sylvestris* male (note ginger tip to the abdomen); B. *sylvestris* female, showing the shape of the face.

Description

FEMALES are small (length 15 mm). The main colour of the coat is black, with a wide yellow band on the collar, and a whitish tail. There are sometimes a few pale hairs mixed in with the black on the top of the head and on the scutellum. Some specimens also have an indistinct fringe of pale hairs on segment 1 of the abdomen. The head is rounded and the tongue relatively short. The tip of the abdomen is curled up under the body, and the callosities on the underside of the final segment are small and inconspicuous (see Figs K.19 and K.44iii). MALES are generally very similar, but smaller. The whitish tail generally gives way to a narrow band of black and then to a fringe of pale yellowish or ginger hairs on the final abdominal segment. The facial hair is black. Antennal segments 3 and 5 are approximately equal in length.

Variation

There is little reported variation in the species, except for the occasional completely melanic form of the male. In northern Scotland some males have bright yellow instead of white tails. Very occasionally the ginger-yellow hairs on the final abdominal segment of the males are replaced by black.

Similar species

Bombus vestalis, B. bohemicus, B. terrestris, B. lucorum and *B. soroeensis*. For distinguishing features see Chapter 8, cluster 2 and the key.

Distribution

The distribution of *B. sylvestris* in Britain coincides closely with that of its main host species, *B. pratorum*. Like that species it is very widespread throughout the country, but records are much more thinly scattered. Like other cuckoo species it is probably under-recorded.

Life history

Females are sometimes seen as early as late March, but more typically are on the wing from mid-April onwards. *Bombus sylvestris* is a nest parasite of the early-nesting *B. pratorum*, but there is some evidence that it also invades the nests of *B. monticola* and *B. jonellus*, both close relatives of *B. pratorum*. Both Hoffer and Küpper & Schwammberger report that *B. sylvestris* cohabits with its host queen, and that both host and cuckoo succeed in reproducing. Males and fresh females emerge from the end of May onwards. Occasional late records are consistent with the possibility that *B. sylvestris* is able, like its host, to pass through two reproductive cycles in one year.

Apparently in Germany *B. sylvestris* is also recorded as a nest parasite of *B. lucorum, B. terrestris, B. hypnorum* and *B. hortorum.*

Foraging behaviour

Bombus sylvestris foraging patterns. Plants in **bold** are garden plants.

QUEENS	spring: sallow, white deadnettle, dandelion, horse chestnut, crab apple, ***Mahonia*, bay,** oil-seed rape. summer: marsh thistle, bramble**, lavender.**
MALES	green alkanet, bramble, white clover, bird's-foot trefoil, hound's-tongue, meadow cranesbill, knapweed, viper's bugloss, thyme, bugle, buttercup, mallow, thistles, knapweed. Scotland: devil's-bit scabious, creeping thistle, **globe thistle**.

Habitat and conservation

It possibly occurs wherever the host species is common, and seems not to be threatened.

Sources: Hoffer, 1889; Küpper & Schwammberger, 1993; Macdonald, pers. comm.; Nisbet 2005; Sladen, 1912; von Hagen & Aichhorn, 2003; own obs.

CHAPTER 10

Agricultural Change and Bumblebee Decline: Explaining the Patterns

BUMBLEBEE HABITAT

MOST OF THE PUBLISHED research on the habitat requirements of bumblebees has concentrated on the availability of adequate supplies of accessible nectar. Bumblebees have been regarded as good research subjects for testing general theoretical hypotheses about foraging behaviour. Also, of course, foraging is the most openly accessible aspect of bumblebee behaviour, and foraging for nectar, in particular, lends itself to the sort of quantitative study that is highly regarded in the academic literature. More recently it has become widely recognised that pollen, sometimes from a narrow range of flower species, is of great importance to colony development. However, no matter how important it is for the colony to be supplied with sufficient and appropriate food, this is not the only requirement that has to be met for it to succeed. Paul Westrich (in Matheson *et al.*, 1996; see also Westrich, 1989) has distinguished four 'partial habitats' for bees, including bumblebees. These are habitats suitable for nesting, foraging, mating and hibernating. One and the same physical area may support all four activities, but even if it does so, it will be different features of the site that are used for each one. Alternatively, the partial habitats may be at some distance from each other. This is particularly likely to be true for insects such as bumblebees that are powerful fliers, and it is now known that workers of at least some species of bumblebee fly long distances – up to 2 kilometres or more – between the nest and foraging patches.

The social bumblebee species differ significantly from one another in their habitat requirements, but there are some aspects common to all. All species are dependent on flower-rich partial habitats for foraging. These have to be within the foraging range of the nests of the species concerned, though, as we have seen, this may be considerably further than was once believed. Pollen is a particularly important resource for queens after their winter hibernation and for larval development throughout the colony cycle. Some species appear to be relatively selective in the menu of plants from which they collect pollen. Adequate supplies of both pollen and nectar must be available continuously through the colony cycle, as bumblebees do not store large quantities of food in their nests, as do honey bees. All species require suitable nesting sites. Many species, including both surface and underground nesters, make use of abandoned nests of small mammals. We do not have reliable evidence on the extent to which particular species may be dependent on this, or on whether there are associations between bumblebee species and particular mammal species. However, on the assumption that many bumblebee species are 'nest adapters' rather than 'nest builders', their nesting habitat will be closely related to the various habitat requirements of the mice, voles and shrews whose abandoned nests are used. These include rough, tussocky grass verges and hedge banks, woodland rides, undisturbed corners in parks and gardens and open meadowland. In some cases additional nesting materials, in the shape of leaf litter or mosses, are needed.

Less is known about the partial habitats required for hibernation of the queens, but north-facing banks, woodland floor, loose soil in gardens, stone walls and rotten tree stumps are among the known sites for the commoner species. Queens of most species bury themselves a few centimetres into the ground, or dig into mosses or leaf litter, so the surface structure has to be loose enough to make this possible. Once buried, they form a cell of compacted soil, which may offer some protection from waterlogging (Edwards, pers. comm.). The aspect chosen (generally north-facing) will be such as to avoid premature emergence by the queens as a result of warming of the soil in early spring. Queens of some species hibernate in considerable numbers at a single site, and often numbers of queens of several species will hibernate in the same area (Sladen, 1912; Skovgaard, 1936; Edwards, 1991; M. Heywood, pers. comm.). Mating habitat mainly concerns the patrolling behaviour of males. In this they make use of a variety of structural features, with a degree of species-specific consistency in flight levels, and the sort of feature that is scent-marked. However, these patterns are very variable, depending on the nature of the local habitat. So long as there are at least some structural features, it seems unlikely that the partial habitat required for patrolling and mating is critical for most species.

A consequence of bumblebee sociality is that the effective reproductive population is a function of the numbers of successful nests, not the number of individual insects. For a colony to rear males and daughter queens successfully, the nutritional requirements of the successive cohorts of non-reproductive workers, and the material and energy demands of nest maintenance have to be met by the local environment. Other things being equal, this means that the effective reproductive population of bumblebees will be much more thinly distributed than is the case for non-social species. Genetically viable populations therefore require very extensive areas of suitable habitat: conservation of bumblebees has to be effective at the landscape scale.

SURVIVAL AND DECLINE

As we saw in Chapter 1, only six species of the social bumblebees remain common and widespread throughout Britain. Declines in five others (*B. humilis, B. rupestris, B. sylvarum, B. subterraneus* and *B. ruderatus*) were so severe that they were singled out for action in the UK Biodiversity Action Plan of 1994. Largely as a result of subsequent research stimulated or carried out by the UK BAP Bumblebee Working Group, evidence has come to light that at least a further four species – *B. monticola, B. muscorum, B. ruderarius* and *B. soroeensis* – may also be in serious decline. It seems that support came too late for *B. subterraneus* as it is now considered extinct in Britain.

For effective conservation measures to be worked out, the first priority is to get a clearer picture of the patterns of decline, and deeper understanding of their causes. Some widespread environmental changes such as urban expansion and agricultural intensification over the past five or six decades have probably affected populations of all bumblebee species, along with much of the rest of Britain's wildlife. But it is already clear that these changes have had very different impacts on different species: a few remain common and widespread, one has become extinct and the rest have undergone a variety of different patterns of decline. So the challenge of trying to explain the patterns of decline will necessarily involve focused exploration of the interactions between various aspects of environmental change and ecologically significant features of each bumblebee species: morphology, physiology, foraging range and preferences, nesting and hibernating habitat, powers of dispersal and others. The aim will be to identify particular points of vulnerability or adaptability that may help to explain how well or badly each species is coping.

This task is already well under way, and there are several important contributions. Understandably, attention has focused on the social species on the assumption that the status of the cuckoos is largely dependent on the strength of the populations of their host species. This may be a justified assumption, but there is a case to be made for more research attention to be devoted to the requirements of the cuckoos. However, here we will be concerned with just 16 social species (including the recently extinguished *B. subterraneus*, but not the recently arrived *B. hypnorum*).

Several hypotheses have been advanced to explain the dramatic changes in bumblebee distribution that were highlighted in the 1980 *Atlas*, and have been confirmed or updated by subsequent field work. I have space here to give only a rather simplified account of these, and the reader is recommended to consult the original articles. Paul Williams's research and publications through the latter half of the 1980s offered an explanation in terms of a 'marginal mosaic' model (Williams, 1985*a*, 1986, 1989*a*, 1989*b*). If each bumblebee species has its own optimal climatic range within which it forages most efficiently, we would expect those species close to the edge of their range to flourish only in the most reward-ing habitats. Williams suggests that the combination of a period of climatic cooling together with agricultural intensification would have resulted in local extinctions and the fragmentation of populations of those species close to the edge of their climatic range in Britain. This model accounted particularly well for the decline of the southern local species, and gained support from Williams's further work on the relationship between tongue length and the depth of available flowers at two contrasting sites. The evidence suggested the bees were foraging less efficiently at the less rewarding site, which lacked the localised species. Corbet *et al.* (1995) shared Williams's emphasis on tongue length and climatic tolerances in relation to floral rewards (see Figs 168–171).

Subsequent research on distribution patterns as well as foraging behaviour has led to renewed discussion of how to explain the varied patterns of decline, geographical retreat as well as stability shown by the different species. We can distinguish three main approaches, though none claims to offer a complete explanation, and the differences between them are, to a considerable extent, matters of emphasis. Goulson *et al.* (2005) put the focus on foraging behaviour, and make use of their own data on the pollen preferences of the different species. This suggests that an important factor explaining the decline of some species is their relative specialisation to flowers of certain groups (mainly the pea family) as sources of pollen. Agricultural intensification has affected this group of bees most severely in reducing the availability of this group of plants. Williams (2005) raises both methodological and empirical questions about this explanation, and offers further evidence from international distribution patterns in support of his own emphasis on ecological and climatic tolerances in the face of agricultural intensification: species at the edge of their range, or those with a narrow range, are the ones most vulnerable to environmental deterioration. Edwards & Williams

FIG 168. *Bombus hortorum,* showing very long tongue.

FIG 169. *Bombus sylvarum,* showing long tongue.

FIG 170. Queen *Bombus lapidarius*, showing medium-length tongue.

FIG 171. *Bombus pratorum*, a short-tongued species.

(2004) put the emphasis directly on habitat, and the way habitat change has differentially affected the various British species. They divide the species into two groups: those that are associated with woodland edge, and species of open ground (heath or grassland species) (Table 8). The woodland edge species have earlier forage, establish their nests early, and readily inhabit domestic gardens as a substitute for woodland edge. The species of open ground establish their nests later, and have been affected much more severely by agricultural intensification (and development pressures).

TABLE 8. The British species of bumblebee, grouped by habitat association, with data on biology and conservation status (reproduced from Edwards & Williams, 2004, with permission).

Group 1 Garden/woodland-edge species, widespread, often frequent in gardens.

B. hortorum	long-tongued, nesting underground or at surface
B. hypnorum	short-tongued, nesting underground, at surface or above ground (new to Britain)
B. lapidarius	mid-tongued, underground-nesting
B. lucorum	short-tongued, underground-nesting
B. pascuorum	long-tongued, surface-nesting
B. pratorum	short-tongued, nesting underground, at surface or above ground
B. terrestris	short-tongued, underground-nesting

Intermediate

B. jonellus	short-tongued, nesting underground, at surface or above ground. It is regularly double-brooded in the south, with early-emerging queens. It is also typical of open heathland and moorland habitats, where queens are late-emerging. In the north, the queens are late-emergers only. In Britain, it is one of the commonest bumblebees of open moorland.

Group 2 Open-ground species associated with flower-rich grasslands, rarely found in gardens unless adjacent to other suitable habitat. All are declining, some more than others. One is recently extinct in Britain. Similar declines throughout Europe. Declines are most marked in the areas of most intensive agriculture (excluding heavily wooded areas, which are in any case unsuitable).

B. distinguendus	long-tongued, underground-nesting, now north-west Scotland only (BAP priority species)
B. humilis	long-tongued, surface-nesting, now southern England and Wales only, largely coastal (BAP priority species)

B. monticola	short-tongued, underground- or surface-nesting. Upland species associated with tall moorland vegetation, especially bilberry areas, but also uses legume pollen (Species Recovery Programme = SRP. Will be put forward for inclusion in BAP at next review)
B. muscorum	long-tongued, surface-nesting, largely northern and coastal (SRP)
B. ruderarius	long-tongued, surface-nesting, largely southern (SRP)
B. ruderatus	long-tongued, underground-nesting, southern (BAP priority species)
B. soroeensis	mid-tongued, underground-nesting, Biology unclear but associated with extensive flowery grasslands and moorland throughout Britain (SRP).
B. sylvarum	long-tongued, underground- or surface-nesting, southern. On verge of extinction in Britain. (BAP priority species)
B. subterraneus	long-tongued, underground-nesting, southern. Extinct in Britain in the past 15 years

Group 3 Social parasites (cuckoos). All are associated with at least one widespread species, although most will attack some of the scarce species when possible. Formerly considered to be a separate genus, *Psithyrus*. All widespread, although populations do have regional differences and numbers fluctuate year by year and over longer time-scales. There are no data on relationship with the density of host populations.

B. barbutellus, B. bohemicus, B. campestris, B. rupestris, B. sylvestris, B. vestalis

As Table 9 shows, some of the causal factors mentioned do correlate quite well with what is known about changes in distribution and abundance. However, none of them seems capable by itself of explaining all the changes. It seems likely, as most participants to the discussion accept, that some combination of several factors is at work.

The meshing of a range of environmental changes together with specific features of the mode of life of each bumblebee species might offer illumination, and at least open up questions for future research.

A POSSIBLE SYNTHESIS?

Our next step is to synthesise these ideas, together with some others, into a more comprehensive framework for analysing the complex patterns of bumblebee survival and decline. There is little doubt that agricultural intensification has been the main overall determinant of bumblebee decline, but this is too abstract to provide much in the way of specific guidance for conservation measures. We need

TABLE 9. Principal factors used by various authors to explain patterns of stability and decline among British social bumblebees since 1960. Numbers refer to the number of species in each category. Species named may belong to both groups or to neither, and '?' implies insufficient evidence currently available.

	STATUS CHANGE SINCE 1960	STABLE	DECLINED/EXTINCT
LARVAL FEEDING REGIME	pocket makers	2	7
	pollen storers	5	1
HABITAT	open ground	(B. jonellus)	8 (+ B. ruderarius)
	woodland edge	6 (+ B. jonellus)	(B. ruderarius)
TIMING	early nest-founding	7	3
	late nest-founding	0	6
TONGUE LENGTH	medium/long	2	7
	short	5	2
FORAGING BEHAVIOUR	pollen specialist	2 (+ B. pascuorum?)	7 (+ B. ruderarius?)
	pollen generalist	4 (+ B. pascuorum?)	1 (+ B. ruderarius?)
CLIMATIC LIMITS	edge of range in Britain	2	5
	centre of range in Britain	5	4

to understand patterns of agricultural intensification in more detail, but also to relate them to other environmental changes, patterns of development, industrial development and decline as well as the legacy of past policies for environmental conservation. It seems clear from the above discussion that no single cause is at work, and that both understanding the complex interactions involved and devising suitable conservation strategies will require a multidimensional approach. We will need to understand the dynamics of environmental change in more detail, but also to match these against specific features of the mode of life of each affected species. It is important to include both declining and currently common species in the analysis. This is partly because, as argued by Corbet (2000) and Rasmont (1995), the long-tongued bee compartment may already be undergoing subliminal decline. The risk is that the vulnerability of this compartment, including two bumblebee species still regarded as common, will be noticed only when it is too late, or much more difficult to save it. Also, however, the common species should be included because understanding why some species seem to be still holding their own may shed light on why others manifestly are not. Finally, because climatic limitation of the geographical range of some species has been suggested as one condition affecting bumblebee decline, international comparisons – especially with the mainland of Europe – are of particular value.

The proposed approach is to draw up a list of key features of bumblebee ecology, behaviour and biology, exploring the diversity among species with respect to each feature. The resulting patterns of similarity and diversity can then be matched up with a detailed account of the environmental changes that have occurred over the past half-century to see if they shed light on the observed patterns of change in bumblebee abundance and distribution.

Unfortunately, this is not so easy! Despite the recent explosion of interest in bumblebee behaviour and ecology, many potentially important questions remain unanswered. There is considerable unevenness in our knowledge of the various species, and the ecology of no species is fully understood. As we saw in chapter 5, there are good grounds for thinking that predation and parasitism have significant effects on bumblebee population dynamics and local assemblages, but there is little quantitative evidence about these for any British species. Similarly, little is known about the distances and frequency of dispersal between local populations of any species. Some species, such as *B. terrestris* and *B. lucorum*, have been the subjects of intensive research for many years, while others, such as *B. sylvarum*, *B. humilis* and *B. distinguendus*, have been closely studied more intensively only since the mid-1990s. Still others, including both common and widespread species such as *B. pratorum* and *B. hortorum*, and declining species such as *B. ruderarius*, are only now beginning to attract attention. Even for the more thoroughly researched species, there are many obstacles to the discovery of potentially important aspects of their ecology and reproductive behaviour. The most obvious of these is the difficulty of finding nests, and particularly of finding nests at a sufficiently early stage in colony development to monitor the whole sequence of events. Much valuable information has been gathered from captive colonies, or colonies artificially placed outside, but the mere fact of the artificiality limits the questions that can be answered by these methods. Also, it is very difficult to establish nests of most species in captivity.

The evidence we have about the past and current status of bumblebee populations, too, has its limitations. First, there are the mainly anecdotal accounts of the pioneer bombologists – notably in the British context, F. W. L. Sladen. These are, admittedly, qualitative only, but they still have great value. Second, we have the data presented in the 1980 *Atlas*. These are divided into two sets according to date order: pre-1960, and 1960 onwards. The latter, however, take us up to the mid-1970s only. Subsequent attempts to check the sources of data used in compiling these maps have revealed significant limitations. At the level of fine detail, therefore, these maps are unreliable, though it seems likely that in terms of large-scale patterns of distribution, as well as the scale of change between the two periods, the *Atlas* is a fairly reliable guide. It is, in any case, all we have to go on! Subsequent work carried out by the UK Bees, Wasps and Ants Recording Society and Bumblebee Working Group (Edwards & Telfer, 2001, 2002; various BWARS Newsletters) has edited the data for earlier periods, and updated our knowledge of the distribution of a number of species. It seems likely that we now have close to full information about the current distribution of several species: in particular *B. sylvarum, B. humilis* and *B. distinguendus*.

THE ENVIRONMENTAL CHALLENGES

Apart from short-term climatic fluctuations, the main environmental changes that have confronted our bumblebee populations have been caused, intentionally or not, by human activity. If we confine our attention to the period from the Second World War onwards, the fortunes of bumblebees, along with those of other groups of animals and plants, have been shaped by four main fields of human activity:

1. Shifts in patterns of human habitation, themselves strongly influenced by the system of town and country planning set up just after the War.
2. Agricultural change, affecting the 80 per cent of the British land surface under agricultural management, and itself strongly influenced by both the framework of government policy and the planning system.
3. The changing structure, geographical distribution and decline of manufacturing industry, along with mineral extraction and the transport, energy and water supply, sewage and waste-disposal infrastructures associated with it.
4. Government policy on wildlife and landscape conservation, and public access to the countryside.

AGRICULTURAL CHANGE AND THE PLANNING SYSTEM

A sharp division between urban and rural life has been a recurrent theme in British culture, dating back to the early days of industrialism and urban expansion, and perhaps best known in Blake's famous images of 'dark satanic mills' contrasting with 'England's green and pleasant land'. During the twentieth century, influential writers of the interwar years praised the stability, order and tranquillity of rural life against the supposed immorality, squalor and disorder of the urban environment, with its threatening multitudes. These cultural influences fed into an elite demand to protect the aesthetic and moral integrity of the countryside from urban expansion. This, in turn, was one powerful motivation for a post-war planning system, the main aim of which was to give local authorities power to resist urban development in the countryside. The zoning of green belts around urban settlements was one outcome of the use of these powers, but another was the leeway it gave for radical changes to take place in the countryside itself, as we shall see.

The second major aim of the new planning system was to protect the farming industry. The exigencies of war exposed the vulnerability of Britain's dependence on imports for much of its food and timber needs. In response, war committees in each area were set up to preside over the mechanisation of farming, the provision of fertiliser and the ploughing up of grassland for cereal production. In the post-war period, the legacy of the wartime need to maximise food production and achieve food self-sufficiency persisted to shape both planning and agricultural policy. Agricultural land, especially in the most productive areas, was to be protected against urban expansion, and, in a set of assumptions sometimes referred to as 'agricultural fundamentalism', it was supposed that the farming community could be relied on to preserve the aesthetic and moral values of the wider countryside. In other words, protecting the farming industry was, at the same time, protecting the countryside. Accordingly, changes in agricultural land use were defined as changes in land 'management' only, and exempted from the rigours of the planning system.

Unrestrained by planning controls, agricultural change amounting to a 'second agricultural revolution' took place over a period of some 30 years, and remained largely unchallenged until the mid-1970s. The policies that drove the changes were promulgated by a narrow policy community comprising the main farming unions and the Ministry of Agriculture Fisheries and Food (MAFF). Under this regime the intensification of agricultural production through mechanisation, application of artificial fertilisers and pesticides, increased field sizes, drainage of wetlands and bringing marginal land into cultivation was promoted by generous handouts of public money. After British entry into the European Union (then the EEC) in 1973, these policies, and the grant-aid that went with them, were reinforced and complemented by the Common Agricultural Policy (CAP).

Over this period, large commercial farms increasingly displaced smaller, family farms, which had often relied on more traditional agricultural methods. At the same time, an earlier pattern of integrated mixed farming gave way to a mainly specialised arable farming landscape in eastern Britain, with grazing regimes persisting in the west, and on the uplands (Coppock, 1971; Stoate, 1996). Grasslands had been lost on a large scale during the war, and they continued to be lost, especially in eastern England, with widespread conversion to arable cultivation. Such grasslands as remained were now subjected to new forms of intensive management. Less nutritious grass species were replaced by more productive varieties such as timothy, cocksfoot and rye-grass that responded well to the application of nitrogenous fertilisers. This allowed for greater grazing densities on permanent grassland, and prolonged the outdoor grazing season. At the same time, a government-sponsored shift from hay meadows to silage production for winter cattle feed eventually took off, and reached its peak in the 1970s. Silage production also involved more productive grass species, fertiliser use, and earlier and more frequent cutting. One review estimates that 90 per cent of Britain's unimproved grasslands were lost between the 1930s and 1980s, either to arable conversion, or to these more intensive forms of grassland management (Fuller, 1987). The resulting swards were short and even, eliminating the tussocky structure of unimproved pasture, and were species-poor, compared with the floristic riches of the older hay meadows (Figs 172 & 173).

Some areas of grassland escaped the general pattern of 'improvement', either for financial reasons where farming was already economically marginal, or because

FIG 172. Unimproved flower-rich grassland, a flood-meadow.

FIG 173. 'Improved' lowland sheep-pasture. Note the close-grazed, uniform turf.

of the intractability of the terrain. Some of the steeper slopes of the southern downland fell into this category, but much of the more accessible land was converted to arable, whilst the loss of both sheep and rabbit grazing (following the introduction of myxomatosis in 1954) allowed succession to scrub to take place on many of the remaining unimproved fragments (Figs 174 & 175).

Meanwhile, especially in lowland, eastern England, cereal production was transformed by a combination of larger farming units; new, high-yielding crop varieties; increased use of artificial fertiliser and pesticide; and mechanisation. This new, industrialised farming system required a more uniform landscape structure with larger fields and ease of movement for vehicles. The new technologies also made possible – while grant-aid made profitable – the bringing of previously marginal land into cultivation. Wetlands were drained, hedges were removed to increase land in cultivation as well as to assist mechanisation, and small farm woodlands were grubbed out (Fig. 176). Where hedgerows and field margins were retained, their value as wildlife habitat was degraded by a combination of lack of management and insensitive mechanical cutting. Over time, field margins and hedgerows lost their mix of perennial plant species to pesticide drift, and the invasion of herbicide-resistant annual grasses.

Initially, Britain's entry into the European Community intensified the 'productivism' of UK agricultural policy, as the CAP continued to encourage intensification of farm production through its price support mechanism and

FIG 174. Remnant of flower-rich downland on a steep slope, South Downs.

FIG 175. Former downland, now under intensive arable cultivation.

FIG 176. Arable monoculture in north-west Essex.

generous grant-aid. However, as we shall see, this framework of farm support soon fell victim to its own success.

Industrial growth and decline

A further pattern of change in human activity in the post-war period has been the economic boom of the 1950s, 1960s and early 1970s, followed by severe decline in manufacturing industry since that time. Large-scale changes in patterns of development of associated infrastructures, such as port facilities, road, rail and air transport, waste disposal systems and energy supply have followed on. The implications of these changes for wildlife conservation are little understood and hardly ever systematically researched, but they are likely to be considerable. One obvious point is that the industrialisation of agriculture itself could only take place in the context of technical innovation and expansion in the 'agribusiness' sector of manufacturing industry. But quarries, mines and industrial plant as well as infrastructural developments both replace the habitats that previously occupied the locations where they are built, and also provide new habitat niches (Mabey, 1973). Depending on the quality of the habitat they destroy, there may be conservation gains as well as losses. Many industrial plants occupy only a small part of the parcel of land on which they are built, as firms allow for possible future expansion, and much depends on how that land is managed. Urban zoning for industrial and trading estates, often located in what Shoard calls 'edgelands' (2002), frequently involves setting land aside from agricultural or building development for long periods before it is taken up. Infrastructures such as roads, flood defences, railway tracks, sewage works and waste tips often support extensive, flower-rich and diverse mosaics of grassland habitat, unaffected by agricultural intensification. Still more significantly, in periods or areas of significant industrial decline, ex-industrial sites can develop very rich communities of animals and plants. As we shall see, such habitats have provided crucial refuges for some of our most threatened bumblebees and other invertebrate species (Harvey, 2000), but these habitats, too, are very vulnerable to development pressures (Figs 177 & 178).

Defending nature?

Along with the new planning system, the framework for nature conservation was also established in the immediate aftermath of the Second World War. The legislation set up the Nature Conservancy (later Nature Conservancy Council) as an independent advisory body to government, with powers to designate for special protection sites important for wildlife conservation (Sites of Special Scientific Interest – sssIs) and to establish National Nature Reserves. The legislation also

FIG 177. Mill Wood Pit, a 'brownfield' site in south Essex, formerly habitat for a rich community of aculeates, including scarce carder bumblebees (photograph by Peter Harvey).

FIG 178. New housing estate on the Mill Wood Pit site (photograph by Peter Harvey).

provided for the setting up of National Parks, where conservation of ecological and landscape values would play a role alongside public access, agricultural and economic interests in shaping land-use decisions (Fig. 179).

Initially the National Parks were mainly located in upland areas, in any case less threatened by agricultural intensification. For most of the lowland farmed

FIG 179. Walking in the Lake District National Park.

landscape, nature conservation objectives were to be met by a combination of sssi designations and a network of local and national nature reserves. By the mid-1980s the ncc had designated some 6,000 sssis, covering 8 per cent of Britain (ncc, 1987), but both the sssis and nature reserves consisted mostly of small 'islands' of habitat, widely dispersed in the agricultural landscapes. Except where farmers themselves were concerned to preserve wildlife habitat – and luckily quite a few were – most of the remaining lowland farmed landscape was left to unrestrained and grant-aided intensification, with attendant massive habitat loss.

THEME AND VARIATIONS

It was not until the beginning of the 1980s, that alarm about bumblebee decline was first registered. Here we explore the dimensions of variation between bumblebee species in their biology and mode of life, to see whether this sheds light on why some of them might have been more vulnerable to specific environmental changes than others.

So what dimensions of interspecies variation might be relevant to explaining the patterns of extinction, decline and survival among the British bumblebee fauna in the face of the environmental changes just outlined? Table 9 summarises six such sources of variation, reduced to simple binary oppositions, which have figured in recent discussions of this question. There is no doubt that a more qualified discussion of each would be worthwhile, but is beyond the scope of this chapter. However, the growing body of research on bumblebees is beginning to reveal other dimensions of variation between them, and we might speculate that yet more aspects of bumblebee modes of life, about which little is so far known, might also be significant.

The following is a provisional list of the dimensions along which bumblebee species may vary in ways that might affect their ability to withstand environmental change.

1. Nesting behaviour
Pocket maker/pollen storer
Simple species/complex species (Brian, 1980, and see Chapter 2)
Underground nests/surface nests/various
• if on surface: open habitat/under cover
Dependent on disused mammal nests/not dependent on disused mammal nests
• if dependent on disused mammal nests, does it matter which species of mammal?

Builds nest/adapts nest
Colony size: small/medium/large
Woodland edge/open grassland/heath and moorland

2. Foraging

Bee morphology:
Tongue length: long/medium/short
Physiological adaptation
- lower temperature threshold: low/high
- upper temperature threshold: low/high

Flower preferences
Nectar visits: generalist/specialist
Pollen collection: generalist/specialist
Foraging distance
- long-distance/medium/doorstep (this might significantly affect ability to cope with habitat fragmentation)

3. Mating habitat

This is highly adaptable and variable, but it is possible that loss of landscape features may lead to hybrid mating by undermining spatial separation of male patrolling routes (see Chapter 2). Clustering of nest sites through fragmentation of habitat could lead to inbreeding and production of infertile diploid males.

4. Hibernating habitat

Since it is believed that the death rate among hibernating queens is high, it seems likely that this plays a significant part in the overall success or failure of local populations. Infection by *Sphaerularia*, waterlogging and ploughing are among the risks that might affect species differently. Unfortunately there are few records of hibernation habitat for the scarcer species.

5. Seasonality

Colony cycle: short/medium/long
Nest-foundation: early/late
Colony dispersal: early/mid-season/late
Overall length of season: short/medium/long
Species with short cycles may have fewer problems with disrupted seasonal sequences of forage plants. Early nest-founders may benefit in competition for suitable nest sites. Late-dispersing species may suffer from shortage of late-flowering forage plants. Species capable of second broods may be able to

compensate for poor colony success rates in first broods. Some species with short to medium colony cycles have long seasons, resulting in co-presence of males and daughter queens for long periods of two months or more. The significance of this for overall reproductive success should be researched.

6. Enemies

Species-specific vulnerability to
- cuckoo nest parasites
- predators (birds, mammals, spiders, wax moth etc.)
- parasitoids (conopid flies)
- parasites (*Sphaerularia, Nosema,* etc.)
- micro-pathogens

(see discussion in Chapter 5)

7. Population structure and density

Nesting density: high/low
Dispersal distances of daughter queens: close/distant
(that is, effective metapopulation: ability to discover and colonise new habitat, maintain genetic diversity of local populations, and recolonise after local extinctions).

8. Geographical range

Species close to northern edge of range in Britain/species at centre of range
(= cool-/warm-adapted species?)

Table 10 gives the conservation status of British social bumblebees, together with a selection of factors that might help in explaining the patterns of stability or decline. The first seven species listed appear to have a relatively stable distribution in Britain. They have not suffered the dramatic declines in range and distribution evidenced by the other nine. However, population declines may well be taking place among the supposedly common species, but not showing up in the form of reduced geographical distribution. Since the reproductive unit in the social bumblebees is not the individual bee, but rather the colony, a reliable census of populations is virtually impossible for the social bumblebees. This would require some comprehensive method of locating and counting nests: something no one has yet been able to devise (but see discussion below of important new genetic research reported in Chapman *et al.*, 2003). A small number of species have been studied in detail, and for these there exists good evidence on such aspects as foraging range, colony size and organisation. However, for the majority of species there is little reliable information. For reasons outlined above, there are methodological limitations in the data about preferences for pollen sources, so judgements about degrees of specialisation in pollen gathering are very much open to question. In sum, much of the information given in the table is little better than informed guesswork, and much potentially important information is simply missing.

With these and other limitations acknowledged, the table may still be used as a provisional source of testable ideas to explain the changing pattern of bumblebee distributions in Britain. One striking pattern is shown by three species of carder bumblebees, *B. muscorum*, *B. humilis* and *B. sylvarum*. All three have declined significantly in recent decades, though the pattern of decline shows some differences. All three are late nest-founders, have long colony cycles, nest in open grassland on the surface, are long-tongued and are relative pollen specialists (primarily Fabaceae, Lamiaceae and Scrophulariaceae). There is evidence that all three also typically have small colonies, perhaps of no more than 50 workers at maturity. On this assumption, nesting densities are probably rather high where habitat is favourable, since workers of all three species are sometimes very numerous.

TABLE 10. *Overleaf* – Biology, ecology and conservation status of British social bumblebees. All data and judgements given should be treated as highly provisional and potentially controversial. It should also be remembered that there is considerable variation among colonies of each species, and also variation from season to season, and locality to locality. Tongue lengths given follow Edwards & Williams, 2004. Early nesting species are ones that begin to establish nests in March and April, 'early +' signifies the later species in this group, beginning to establish nests from mid-April onwards. Late nest-founders are species that do not establish their nests until May or later, and very late ones (*soroeensis*) not until June. These dates apply mainly to southern England, and may be later further north ('s', 'n'). A short colony cycle is one that takes from two to two and a half months from nest establishment to the appearance of daughter queens. A medium colony cycle is approximately three months, and more than three months is counted as long. Some species have short or medium length colony cycles but long seasons, with males and daughter queens observed for up to three months after the first daughter queens emerge. Pollen preference judgements are based on Williams, 2005, Goulson *et al.*, 2005, UK Bumblebee Working Group and personal observation. Descriptions of the status of species prior to 1960 are based on Williams, 1982, and change to 1980 on the IBRA/ITE Atlas, 1980. Current status is estimated from BWARS and UK Bumblebee Working Group recording and own observation. '?' indicates that this value is unknown. '?' against a given value indicates that some evidence is available, but it may be weak or comparative information for other species may be absent.

TABLE 10.

	LUCORUM	TERRESTRIS	LAPIDARIUS	PASCUORUM
Pocket maker/ pollen storer	pollen storer	pollen storer	pollen storer	pocket maker
Simple/complex	complex	complex	complex?	simple
Nest position	below ground	below ground	below ground	various – usually above ground
Colony size	large	large	large	medium
Nesting habitat	woodland edge/ urban	woodland edge/ urban	woodland edge/ urban	woodland edge/ urban
Tongue length	short	short	short/medium	long
Pollen preferences	general	general	general	general? mainly deep flowers
Foraging range	large	large	large?	medium – large
Colony cycle	short – medium	short – medium	medium	medium
Early or late nesting	early	early	early	early
Colony dispersal	medium	medium	medium	late
Length of season	long	long	long	very long
Nesting density	?	medium?	?	high?
Dispersal ability	good	good	good	good
Geographical range	central	northern edge	northern edge	central
Status before 1960	mainland ubiquitous	mainland ubiquitous, but local in north	mainland ubiquitous, but local in north	mainland ubiquitous
Change 1960 to 1980	unchanged	unchanged	unchanged	unchanged
Current trends	stable	northerly expansion	northerly expansion	stable

PRATORUM	HORTORUM	JONELLUS	RUDERATUS
pollen storer	pocket maker	pollen storer	pocket maker
simple	?	simple?	?
various	below ground	various	below ground
small	medium	small	large
woodland edge/ urban	woodland edge/ urban	heath/moors, etc.	open
short	very long	short	long
general	Fabaceae, Lamiaceae	Ericaceae, Fabaceae	Fabaceae/Lamiaceae
medium – large?	large?	?	large?
short	short	short?	medium
early	early +	early (s) or late (n)	early +
early (late 2nd generation)	early (late 2nd generation)	late	medium
short (long if two generations)	short (long if two generations)	varies n/s	medium
?	?	?	?
good	good?	?	good?
central	central	central	northern edge
mainland ubiquitous	mainland ubiquitous	widespread local	southern local
unchanged	unchanged?	unchanged?	strong decline
stable	possibly declining?	stable?	recovery?

TABLE 10. *(Table 10. continued)*

	RUDERARIUS	MUSCORUM	HUMILIS	SYLVARUM
Pocket maker/ pollen storer	pocket maker	pocket maker	pocket maker	pocket maker
Simple/complex	simple	simple	simple	simple
Nest position	surface	surface	surface	surface
Colony size	small	small	small	small
Nesting habitat	open/scrub edge	open	open	open/scrub edge
Tongue length	long	long	long	long
Pollen preferences	?	Fabaceae/ Asteraceae	Fabaceae/ Lamiaceae	Fabaceae/ Lamiaceae/Scroph.
Foraging range	?	?	?	?
Colony cycle	medium	short	long	long
Early or late nesting	early +	late	late	late
Colony dispersal	medium	medium	late	late
Length of season	medium	medium	medium	medium
Nesting density	?	?	high?	high?
Dispersal ability	?	good?	good?	good?
Geographical range	northern edge	central	northern edge	northern edge
Status before 1960	southern local	widespread local	southern local	southern local
Change 1960 to 1980	stable?	decline inland?	strong decline	strong decline
Current trends	declining	declining?	stable or recovering?	declining (possible local recovery?)

DISTING'DUS	SUBT'ANEUS	SOROEENSIS	MONTICOLA
pocket maker	pocket maker	neither	pollen storer
?	?	?	simple?
below ground	below ground	below ground	various
medium?	?	medium?	medium?
open	open	open	open
long	long	short/medium	short
Fabaceae/ Asteraceae	Fabaceae	general?	Ericaceae/Fabaceae
?	?	?	medium?
medium	?	medium	long
late	?	very late	early
late	late?	very late	medium
medium	?	medium	medium
?	?	?	?
?	?	?	?
central	northern edge	central	central
widespread local	southern local	widespread local	widespread local
strong decline	strong decline	strong decline	stable?
declining	extinct	declining in south	declining

However, only two of this group are close to the northern edge of their geographical range in Britain. *Bombus muscorum* has strong, but mainly coastal populations in northern Scotland and the Isles, and is present through Scandinavia to 67°N (see Williams, 1988, and 2005 for a more sophisticated discussion on whether a species is close the edge of its range in Britain).

All three species share a common feature in their decline: abandonment of most of their former localities in lowland southern England and the Midlands (Williams's 'central impoverished zone'). In the two 'edge-of-range' species, isolated populations remain only where substantial mosaics of flower-rich grasslands have escaped agricultural intensification, in southern England and South Wales. Edwards estimates that neither species survives where the area of suitable habitat is less than 10 square kilometres in extent. These conditions appear to be satisfied in the Somerset Levels, extensive military training areas on Salisbury Plain and South Wales, and, of particular interest, in the eastern fringes of London and along the lower Thames estuary. Here a complex of ex-industrial sites, old mineral workings, remnant grazing marshes, disused waste tips and flood defences combines with favourable climatic conditions and well-drained sandy soils to support strong populations of these species as part of an outstanding assemblage of invertebrate species.

Bombus sylvarum and *B. humilis*, as late-season, relatively specialised pollen foragers that nest on the surface in flower-rich grasslands are particularly vulnerable to both the main aspects of the agricultural intensification that took place in the post-war period. The expansion of arable cultivation that took place during and after the Second World War entailed the loss of large areas of permanent grassland. This would have had drastic effects on suitable grassland for these species, both eliminating and fragmenting their habitats. But the more intensive management of remaining areas of grassland devoted to animal husbandry would also have been unfavourable to both species. The 'improved' grasslands, with their short, even sward would not provide either species' nesting requirements, and colonies would, in any case, be eliminated by the early onset and frequency of cutting for silage. The drastic reduction in flora, and particularly the species of the older hay meadows that are preferred by these species would also deprive them of foraging habitat.

Outside the more extensive mosaics that still hold populations of *B. sylvarum* and *B. humilis*, small fragments of flower-rich grasslands remain, often as nature reserves or specially managed components of country parks, but these are often cut in early or mid-summer. This eliminates bumblebee forage just as the later bumblebee nests are approaching maturity, and probably also directly destroys nests in the cutting process. In any case, many such fragments appear too small to sustain viable populations of these species, or too distant from extant populations for colonisation to incorporate them as satellites in a larger metapopulation (Fig. 180).

Bombus muscorum, the third species in this group, differs in that it is not at the edge of its range in Britain. It has also disappeared from the 'central impoverished zone' identified by Williams, but the available evidence suggests it never did have much of a presence there. This suggests that there are probably quite small differences in habitat requirement or physiological adaptation within this group of species that account for their different, but overlapping, patterns of distribution even prior to recent agricultural changes. However, the dominant factor in the decline of all three has been the loss of sufficiently large areas of appropriately managed grasslands rich in the limited menu of deep flowers on which they depend, and offering the right vegetation structure for their nesting requirements.

In *B. muscorum*, the pattern of retreat is distinctive. Such evidence as we have suggests that its former distribution was biased towards coastal districts, as well as, in the southern part of its range, damper and cooler low-lying grasslands. The same is true of its Scandinavian distribution. A review of coastal grassland loss in south and south-east England between 1938 and 1981 revealed a pattern comparable to the losses suffered in Britain as a whole (Williams & Hall, 1987). Almost all of these grassland losses have been to arable cultivation, with very

FIG 180. A disused railway cutting, now a small remnant of chalk grassland in the midst of intensive arable cultivation.

rapid change during the Second World War, and another acceleration in the 1970s following EC entry. The coastal grazing marshes of Kent and East Essex that formerly held strong populations of all four of our declining carder bumblebees were particularly hard-hit, although the timing of losses differed, and the percentage losses were higher in east Essex than either Romney or north Kent (Figs 181 & 182, Table 11).

Both *B. humilis* and *B. sylvarum* have been lost from the coastal marshes of north-east Essex, but *B. muscorum* still survives here on sea walls and the few remaining areas of grazing marsh. In the rest of England, *B. muscorum* now has an almost entirely coastal distribution, but with a greater spread of inland localities

FIG 181. The loss and fragmentation of coastal grassland in east Essex, 1938–81. Areas of coastal grassland are shown in black (reproduced from Williams & Hall, 1987, with permission).

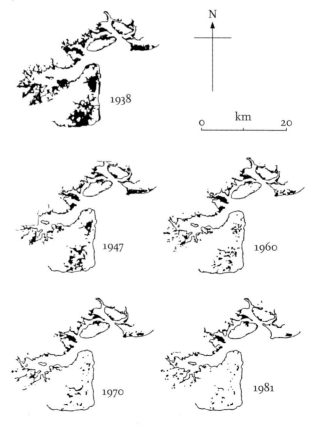

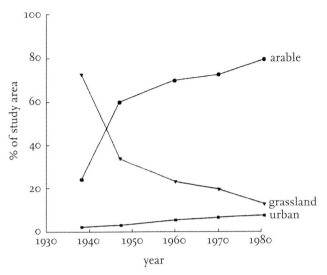

FIG 182. Changes in the areas of three land-use categories in east Essex, 1938–81. Note the rapid shift from grassland to arable during the period of the Second World War, with the same trend continued more gradually subsequently. Note, also, the relatively slight increase in urban settlement in the area up to 1981 (reproduced from Williams & Hall, 1987, with permission).

in Scotland and the Scottish Islands. Inland in Scotland it is associated with wet moors and with cross-leaved heath as a principal forage plant (Macdonald, pers. comm.). Workers of *B. muscorum* in northern Scotland will forage during cold and wet weather when other species remain torpid or return to their nests, suggesting that *B. muscorum* (or, perhaps, its northern populations?) may be a cold-adapted species. Its continued presence along extensive stretches of coast-line may be explained partly by the cooler and damper climatic conditions often present there, and partly by the linear grasslands offered by sea defences, relict grazing marshes, sea cliffs and dune systems (Figs 183 & 184). Both *B. muscorum* and *B. humilis* have predominantly coastal distributions, and, compared with *B. sylvarum*, it seems that they are more capable of surviving on narrow strips of habitat that are often provided in their coastal haunts. *Bombus muscorum* and *B. humilis* also forage in long-grass habitats where their forage flowers are relatively dispersed, whereas *B. sylvarum* seems to require patches of floristically rich grassland. This difference shows up in pollen loads, which are often mixed in *B. muscorum* and *B. humilis* but usually composed of or dominated by one flower species in *B. sylvarum*.

TABLE 11. Land-use statistics for the east Essex study area, 1938–81 (from Williams & Hall, 1987). Figures for each category are given in hectares. The figures in parentheses are percentages of the total study area.

	1938	1947	1960	1970	1981
Arable	3,816	8,918	11,120	11,588	12,718
	(24)	(56)	(70)	(72)	(79)
Grazing marsh	2,600	2,841	1,830	1,185	1,077
	(16)	(18)	(11)	(7)	(7)
Pasture	9,149	2,542	1,972	2,088	1,006
	(57)	(16)	(12)	(13)	(6)
Total grassland	**11,749**	**5,383**	**3,802**	**3,273**	**2,083**
	(73)	**(34)**	**(23)**	**(20)**	**(13)**
Urban	279	316	867	1,019	1,093
	(2)	(2)	(5)	(6)	(7)
Woodland	89	90	101	92	86
	(0.5)	(0.5)	(0.6)	(0.6)	(0.5)
Orchards and allotments	67	93	110	28	20
	(0.4)	(0.6)	(0.7)	(0.2)	(0.1)
Unsurveyed	—	1,200	—	—	—
		(7.5)			
Total	**16,000**	**16,000**	**16,000**	**16,000**	**16,000**

These small differences may go some way to explaining the more catastrophic decline of *B. sylvarum*, compared with the other two species. It could also be that there are differences among the three in their capacity to deal with habitat fragmentation. The distance from the nest at which foragers can work profitably is one factor that would be relevant to this. Another is the distances over which daughter queens disperse prior to hibernation and nest-founding the following season. There is so far no reliable test of the foraging range of any of these species. Such indirect evidence as exists is equivocal. An instructive case is the relationship between a complex of nature reserves and a country park situated in south Essex, only 3–4 kilometres from the nearest sites known to be occupied by *B. sylvarum* and *B. humilis*. Significant areas of potentially suitable habitat are present in this complex, but the bees appear to be absent. However, Chapman (2004) found scattered populations of *B. humilis* in 12 sites in east London, a few kilometres west of the known Thames estuary populations. Very small numbers of *B. sylvarum*

FIG 183. Coastal habitat of *Bombus muscorum* in late May. Note the dispersed flowers of common vetch, an important forage source for the queens as they emerge from hibernation at this time.

FIG 184. *Bombus muscorum* habitat in July, with white clover and bird's-foot trefoil.

were also found. In her study at Castlemartin, Carvell also found *B. sylvarum* workers foraging on patches of suitable habitat on farms 3 and 4 kilometres from the core population. Small, scattered populations of *B. sylvarum* have also been discovered up to 20km from their Thames estuary strongholds. In *B. muscorum*, scattered breeding populations occur along the Essex coast, for example, some of them separated by up to 5 kilometres of coastal development. Occasional local extinctions and recolonisations suggest that there is at least some exchange between these populations (own obs.). Daughter queens of *B. humilis, B. muscorum* and *B. sylvarum* have all been observed at distances up to 30 kilometres from the nearest known breeding sites (Edwards, pers. comm.).

So the limited evidence currently available suggests that all three species are able to sustain metapopulations over wide areas, despite significant habitat fragmentation. It may be that *B. sylvarum* is less able to deal with floristic impoverishment in its grassland habitat, and it may also be that it needs large, unfragmented areas of habitat to sustain its core populations. More evidence on nesting densities, foraging range and the genetic structure of surviving populations is urgently needed in the face of continuing habitat loss.

Two other carder bumblebees (usually classified together in the subgenus *Thoracobombus*) share many features with these three, but they have fared very differently in the face of recent environmental changes. These are *B. ruderarius* and *B. pascuorum*. *Bombus pascuorum* is one of the six species that remain common and widespread. Like the other carder bumblebees it is relatively long-tongued, and favours deep flowers, especially Fabaceae and Lamiaceae, although it seems to be less specialised in its pollen-gathering than the declining carder species. It usually nests on or above the ground, and the length of the colony cycle is medium (about three months). However, it differs from the three declining species just discussed in several respects. First, overwintered queens establish their nests much earlier, and it can be included in the 'woodland edge' group distinguished by Edwards & Williams (2004). Second, workers have a substantial foraging range. There is evidence that this is less than that of *B. terrestris* and *B. lucorum* (Darvill *et al.*, 2004; Chapman *et al.*, 2003), but at least of the order of 300 metres. The foraging range of the other carder bumblebees is unknown, but if it turns out to be significantly less this may be a partial explanation of their decline in the face of habitat fragmentation. Third, *B. pascuorum* has a very long season, from mid- or late March through to October, or even November in some years. It is unclear whether this is a result of 'staggered' nest-founding in spring, variable rates of colony growth, or double broods. It may be a combination of all three (as a simple species it is unlikely to have the option of early and late-switching, as in *B. lucorum* and *B. terrestris* (see Chapters 2 & 3)). However, one consequence of the long season is that males and daughter queens can be seen for some four months after the first daughter queens emerge. This distinctive pattern may be adaptive in giving prolonged opportunities for mating, and also buffer local populations against spells of adverse weather or seasonally concentrated parasite attacks (see Chapter 5). Like *B. muscorum*, but unlike *B. humilis* and *B. sylvarum*, it is not close to the edge of its climatic range in Britain, and is ubiquitous as far north as 70° in Scandinavia.

It seems likely that this combination of characteristics accounts for the continued abundance of *B. pascuorum*, alone among the carder bumblebees. Woodland has declined less than other semi-natural habitats in the face of agricultural intensification, and widespread conversion to conifer plantation may not have affected *B. pascuorum* so adversely as, for example, some woodland butterflies. Wide open rides and large areas of clear-fell may still provide sufficient foraging, nesting and hibernating sites (Fig. 185). The farmed countryside has almost certainly become less favourable to *B. pascuorum*, with the loss of orchards, hedgerows, uncropped field edges and other marginal features. However, these losses have not been so devastating as those affecting the species of permanent grassland. Many thousands of kilometres of hedgerow remain, while the edges of tracks and roadside verges also continue to provide foraging, nesting and hibernating habitat (Fig. 186). In recent years, agricultural set-aside, especially

FIG 185. Foxgloves in a woodland clearing, favoured forage sources for *Bombus pascuorum* and *B. hortorum*.

FIG 186. A roadside verge and hedgerow with bramble, toadflax and mallow.

where this is maintained for more than one year (Corbet, 1995), has offered some compensation for habitat losses suffered elsewhere in the farmed landscape. Key sources of forage in early spring, such as sallow, white and red deadnettle are often abundant in these marginal habitats, and later in the year black horehound and bramble are important pollen sources, with white deadnettle reappearing from late July (Fig. 187). These forage plants are supplemented for relatively short periods by crops such as field bean, which is also used by *B. pascuorum*.

However, it is likely that the continued success of *B. pascuorum* is due more especially to its ability to colonise urban and suburban habitats. Here, footpath margins, lightly managed public open spaces, ex-industrial sites as well as parks and domestic gardens form a mosaic of habitats that sustain large populations of *B. pascuorum*, along with the other common species (Fig. 188). Its ability to move between marginal urban habitats and gardens, aided by its relatively extensive foraging range (estimated at 500 metres or more), enable it to obtain a continuous supply of forage throughout its long season. Compared with the carder bumble-bees of open grasslands, the more varied and often well-hidden nest sites chosen by *B. pascuorum* are less vulnerable to destruction by intrusive management regimes (Fussell & Corbet, 1992a). Both *B. humilis* and *B. sylvarum* can, but much more rarely, sustain urban populations. They appear to be dependent on ex-industrial sites, cemeteries, urban nature reserves and unmanaged wasteland. Populations of *B. humilis* in east London studied by Chapman (2004) occupied

FIG 187. A *Bombus pascuorum* worker foraging from white deadnettle, a common plant of urban waste ground and hedgerows.

FIG 188. An urban open space, habitat for *Bombus pascuorum* and other common species.

such habitats rather than formal parks or gardens. However, this is not due to any inability to forage from garden varieties. Chapman included loosestrife, Russian sage and lavender in her long list of forage plants used by urban *B. humilis*, and use was made of a similar group of cultivated varieties by *B. humilis* in a formal garden adjacent to nesting habitat at Pitsea (Fig. 189) (own obs.). It may be that the more exacting nesting requirements of *B. sylvarum* and *B. humilis* limit their ability to thrive in most urban environments.

Bombus ruderarius is yet another of the carder bumblebees that appears to have suffered a marked decline in recent decades. Detailed research on this species is lacking, but it seems to share many characteristics with the other declining species. It is relatively long-tongued, a relatively specialised pollen forager, and it nests on the surface of the ground. The colony size is probably small, and the colony cycle of medium length. According to earlier authors it was once common and widespread (for example, Sladen, 1912; Morley, 1899; Saunders, 1896; Step, 1932). The 1980 *Atlas* shows extensive loss of ground in northern England, and in Scandinavia its distribution is mainly southern. Despite the survival of a strong population on the machair of the Hebrides, it seems appropriate to include *B. ruderarius* in the list of southern species close to the edge of their climatic range in Britain. Unlike the other declining carder bumblebees, *B. ruderarius* queens establish their nests relatively early in the season – but usually in April, a little later than the suite of common and widespread species.

Although Edwards & Williams include *B. ruderarius* in their list of species of open ground this is rather problematic. This species certainly is found in

FIG 189. A male *Bombus humilis* on *Echinacea* in an urban garden.

such localities, but queens usually emerge from hibernation and establish their nests somewhat earlier than is typical of that group of species. It also occurs in ex-industrial, warm coastal and estuarine habitats along with *B. humilis* and *B. sylvarum*, and is to be found together with *B. pascuorum* on open woodland rides and edges, as well as hedgerows, urban and suburban habitats. Here, however, its foraging for pollen seems much more restricted than is the case with *B. pascuorum*. The latter forages on a wide range of garden herbs and shrubs, including those such as rosemary, sage, cat-mint, bugle, yellow archangel that belong to the same families as its wild flower preferences, but it also forages for both nectar and pollen on a wide variety of other cultivated flowers such as *Mahonia, Fuchsia, Tricyrtis* and *Delphinium*. Urban *B. ruderarius*, by contrast, is rarely reported as visiting garden flowers. A narrow range of labiates and legumes (white and red deadnettle, black horehound, clovers and bird's-foot trefoil) in overgrown gardens, allotments, river banks, roadside verges, uncultivated development land and the margins of sports fields constitute their main forage sources in these habitats. These comments, however, are rather subjective, as *B. ruderarius* workers are not easy to distinguish from those of *B. lapidarius* in the field, and the sheer scarcity of *B. ruderarius* might account for the rarity of reports of its foraging from garden flowers.

More research is needed, but my current impression is that the decline of *B. ruderarius* is currently taking the form of a general loss of abundance and increasing localisation, rather than a loss of geographical range. Unless successful conservation measures are taken, this may be the prelude to the breaking up of metapopulations and accelerated decline (see Williams, 1988). Unlike *B. humilis* and *B. sylvarum*, *B. ruderarius* seems not to be common anywhere. Rural populations have presumably been lost through the combination of the loss of much permanent grassland and intensified management of what remains, as with the other declining carder bumblebees. However, the apparent decline in urban and suburban habitats requires a different explanation, particularly as its relative *B. pascuorum* thrives in the urban environment. Like the other carders, urban *B. ruderarius* seems to favour ex-industrial sites, wasteland, and other marginal or lightly managed spaces, rather than domestic gardens or formal parks (Fig. 190). This might be particularly problematic for the species in the face of the loss of informal, lightly managed open spaces. A combination of 'infill' development and the obsession with uniform close-mowing of green spaces in towns eliminates both nesting and foraging sites (Fig. 191). Its slightly later nest-founding might also disadvantage it if there is competition between it and *B. pascuorum* for nest sites. The relationship between these two species in urban environments would be a valuable research topic.

FIG 190. An urban open space with grass heathland and scrub, habitat for 12 *Bombus* species.

FIG 191. An urban open space with close cut turf, and early mechanical clearance of rank vegetation on the slope, eliminating bumblebee nesting and foraging habitat.

Table 10 also illustrates an interesting comparison among three of the longest-tongued species: *B. hortorum*, *B. subterraneus* and *B. ruderatus*. All three share many biological and lifestyle features. They are predominantly underground nesting, with a rather narrow range of pollen sources, favouring deep flowers for both pollen and nectar. All three are believed to have large colony sizes (though not as large as *B. terrestris* and *B. lucorum*). However, the three species have fared very differently in the face of the environmental changes of recent decades in Britain. *Bombus ruderatus* seems to have declined dramatically. Sladen thought it very common, and Step (1932) considered it 'common throughout England'. So far as is currently known, it remains locally common only in a small number of very distinctive sites in East Anglia, and has a small, very thinly distributed population in parts of south-eastern England. *Bombus subterraneus* had already declined to a very few sites in the extreme south-east by the time of the surveys for the 1980 *Atlas* and is now believed to be extinct in Britain. Meanwhile *B. hortorum* remains very widespread and apparently common.

In *B. ruderatus* and *B. subterraneus*, habitat loss is likely to have been the most important cause of decline. Both are near to the edge of their geographical range in Britain, but both are also sharply declining further south in Europe (for example, Westrich, 1989; Banaszak, 1995; Kosiov, 1995; Rasmont & Mersch, 1988; von Hagen & Aichhorn, 2003; Edwards, 2001*a*). All three species were introduced into New Zealand, and a recent study of the populations that still survive there by Goulson confirmed the dependence of them all on collecting pollen from a narrow range of deep flowers. This was particularly true of *B. subterraneus*, which used only red clover, St John's-wort and bird's-foot trefoil. In New Zealand the remaining populations of *B. ruderatus* also showed a strong preference for red clover as a source of both pollen and nectar. The British populations, too, use red clover where it is available, but the East Anglian river valley populations use red and white deadnettle, yellow iris and comfrey early in the season, moving on to later-flowering labiates such as black horehound, marsh woundwort or large-flowered hemp-nettle.

The former distribution of both species was broadly south-eastern in England. This, together with the association with both labiates and agricultural legumes in *B. ruderatus*, suggests the possibility that these species thrived in the mixed and arable farming landscapes that were characteristic of this part of Britain. Less intensively managed arable farmland, hedgerows, track sides, river banks and other marginal habitats would have provided underground nesting sites, as well as harbouring deep-flowered forage of such habitats, such as the deadnettles, black horehound, woundworts and comfrey. These latter may have supplemented the clovers and other agricultural legumes that featured in the crop rotations of mixed and arable farms prior to the fertiliser- and fungicide-aided shift to continuous cereal production. Although both species used to occur on the grazing marshes of Kent and Essex, it seems likely that permanent flower-rich grasslands are not essential to their survival as they are in the case of the surface-nesting carder bumblebees. Currently it seems that *B. ruderatus* survives best in a few remaining damp lowland river valleys, where its menu of deep flowers provides abundant forage through the relatively long colony cycle (Fig. 192). However, small, sparse, and fluctuating populations do survive in more intensively agricultural areas, and that they survive at all in such areas suggests that they are able to forage at sufficient distances to cope with fragmentation of forage sites, as well as having considerable powers of dispersal. There is recent evidence that the species responds positively to conservation sowings of agricultural legumes in arable landscapes (Fig. 193) (for example, Meek *et al.*, 2004).

This leaves us with the puzzle that *B. hortorum*, similar in so many respects to both *B. ruderatus* and *B. subterraneus*, remains common and widespread. *Bombus hortorum* queens emerge from hibernation a little earlier than those of *B. ruderatus*, and also have a shorter colony cycle. Since they are therefore less dependent on late-flowering forage species, the problems of maintaining a continuous supply of appropriate forage through the nest cycle will be correspondingly less pressing. The partial second brood may also help to build up populations in favourable

FIG 192. River valley habitat of *Bombus ruderatus* in East Anglia. Note the abundance of marsh woundwort.

FIG 193. A wide cereal field margin sown with a clover-dominated wild flower mix where *Bombus ruderatus* has been recorded. Half the margin was cut in late June to extend the flowering period (photograph by Claire Carvell).

seasons and localities. Also, unlike either *B. subterraneus* or *B. ruderatus*, *B. hortorum* is not close to the northern edge of its range in Britain. However, as with *B. pascuorum*, it seems that an important condition of its survival is its ability to benefit from urban and suburban gardens. Here it forages from a very wide range of deep garden flowers, such as sage, broad-leaved everlasting pea, lavender, *Antirrhinum*, honeysuckle and foxglove, but also makes use of lightly managed urban open spaces, roadside verges, abandoned allotments and the like. Chapman's (2004) study of urban habitats in London revealed *B. hortorum*'s strong preference for foraging in gardens, as against commons and wasteland (Figs 194 & 195). However, it is not clear whether gardens supply all the habitat requirements of *B. hortorum*. It may be that the combination of development and unsympathetic management of open spaces in the towns, with habitat loss in the farmed landscape is leading to a decline in this species, albeit a less dramatic one than is evident with *B. ruderatus* and *B. subterraneus*. In Chapman's survey it was much less frequently encountered, and appeared to have a more restricted distribution in London than the other common and widespread species. More than other common species, it seems particularly closely associated with woodland (Fig. 196).

FIG 194. Suburban gardens, valuable foraging habitat for *Bombus hortorum* and other common bumblebees. These gardens are within range of the open space pictured in Fig. 190.

FIG 195. *Bombus hortorum* foraging from *Delphinium* in an urban garden.

FIG 196. Woodland with bluebells, a popular forage plant for *Bombus hortorum* and several other common bumblebee species in spring.

Yet another declining, long-tongued species, closely related to *B. subterraneus*, is *B. distinguendus*. It too has a narrow menu of deep flowers, of which red clover is a very important component as a pollen source. Queens emerge from hibernation late and make their nests underground. The colonies do not reach maturity until August. *Bombus distinguendus* appears to be in rapid decline throughout its European range. According to Sladen (1912) it was always rare and local in southern Britain. Unlike *B. subterraneus* and *B. ruderatus*, which have retreated to the south-east, *B. distinguendus* has entirely disappeared from England and Wales, continuing to exist only on the north coast of Scotland and some of the Scottish islands. It is tempting to interpret this pattern of decline in terms of climate, supposing *B. distinguendus* to be a cold-adapted species. Its global distribution certainly is more northerly than its close relative *B. subterraneus*, and it is not close to the northern limit of its distribution even in its remaining Scottish localities (it is recorded up to approximately 67°N in Sweden). However, it occurs, or used to occur, further south in lowland mainland Europe (Amiet, 1996; von Hagen & Aichhorn, 2003; Banaszak, 1995; Westrich, 1989), and it does not forage in inclement weather (contrasting with *B. muscorum* in the Scottish Isles, own obs.). As it appears to have been rare even before the environmental changes of recent decades, it is probable that it has particularly stringent habitat requirements.

The combination of vegetation structure and the distinctive plant community of the coastal and machair habitat it now occupies provide conditions unlikely ever to have been widespread in southern Britain (Fig. 197). Such highly localised and isolated populations as there were would have been especially vulnerable to the agricultural intensification that has affected the other declining species. This, indeed, seems to be the main continuing threat to its populations in the Scottish islands (Edwards, 2001b). Its climatic range would have been significant in that it could maintain northern populations in regions less subject to intensification, an 'option' not available to similarly affected species close to their northern limits.

Bombus soroeensis is another species generally considered to be in steep decline, but its general similarity to B. lucorum makes it difficult to interpret maps of its distribution. It is possible that it has sometimes been mistaken for the latter species, and so been under-recorded. On the other hand, Sladen thought it rare and local, and the evidence of the 1980 Atlas suggests it always was a very localised species in central and southern England, with near-complete abandonment of this area by the mid-1970s. Current evidence suggests that it survives in a few of the remaining extensive areas of flower-rich grassland in south-west England and Wales, but that its stronghold is in northern Scotland. In some respects it is comparable with the declining carder bumblebees – notably B. muscorum. It is associated with flower-rich grasslands, is late to establish its nest, and has

FIG 197. Machair habitat for Bombus distinguendus, B. muscorum agricolae and B. ruderarius, Inner Hebrides.

FIG 198. Calcareous grassland on Salisbury Plain, habitat of *Bombus soroeensis* and other scarce bumblebees. Note the abundance of melilot.

a medium-length colony cycle. Like *B. muscorum,* it is not close to its northern limit in Britain. Unlike the carder bumblebees, it usually nests underground. It is short to medium-tongued and its menu of forage plants is different from theirs, though overlapping.

Edwards & Williams include *B. soroeensis* in their list of species of open ground (Fig. 198). The southern British populations appear to be confined to remaining extensive areas of unimproved grassland, and in northern Scotland it is associated with moorland and heaths. However, in other parts of Europe it is also regarded as a species of woodland edge (for example, von Hagen & Aichhorn, 2003). In southern Britain, the queens and workers forage for pollen mainly from small-flowered Fabaceae, such as melilot and sainfoin, during the earlier part of the colony cycle (Fig. 199). Queens establish their nests very late in the season, and the long colony cycle leads to peak numbers of workers and the emergence of daughter queens and males as late as mid-September. By this time, pollen is taken mainly from devil's-bit scabious and red bartsia, with bellflowers and various scabious species also visited by both males and females (Edwards, 2002; Pinchen, 2004; Goulson & Darvill, 2003; own obs.). The requirement for extensive late-flowering grassland may well be an important factor that has limited the distribution of the species in southern Britain. Northern Scotland seems to be the current stronghold of *B. soroeensis* in Britain, and there is no evidence of decline

FIG 199. A worker *Bombus soroeensis* collecting pollen from melilot.

there. In the north, *B. soroeensis* frequents heaths and moors (where its main forage plants are ling and other heathers, bramble and raspberry), as well as gardens and woodland edge habitat. The colony cycle is even later starting and ending (Macdonald, 2000a).

Although, as we have seen, many of our declining species are long-tongued species of open, flower-rich grasslands, this is not the whole story. *Bombus soroeensis* is a short to medium-tongued species, and *B. monticola*, a short-tongued species associated with western and northern uplands, is also currently giving rise to concern among conservationists. Here, the evidence suggests marked decline, with increasing localisation, rather than large-scale reduction in its British range. This species has always been closely associated with upland heaths and moors in northern and western Britain, where its principal spring pollen source is bilberry (Figs 200 & 201). Recent research confirms the importance of bilberry, particularly for the early stages of colony foundation by the overwintered queens, but in many locations there is a seasonal gap between the end of the bilberry flowering period and the flowering of other moorland species, especially bell heather, but also cross-leaved heath and ling. Accordingly, *B. monticola* workers leave the moorland to forage from flowers such as red and white clover, bird's-foot trefoil and meadowsweet (Figs 202 & 203). In many of its localities, then, *B. monticola* is a moorland-edge species that depends on flower-rich grasslands adjacent to the moors to ensure continuity of suitable forage throughout its

FIG 200. Habitat of *Bombus monticola* on Dartmoor in April. Here queens forage from sallow until the bilberry comes fully into flower.

FIG 201. Bilberry flowers, in May the main forage source of nest-founding queen *Bombus monticola*.

FIG 202. Dartmoor habitat of *Bombus monticola* in July. Note the flowering bell heather and sheep-grazed valley floor with white clover.

FIG 203. Peak District moorland, showing 'improved' sheep pastures adjacent to the moors.

long colony cycle. In many areas its decline and local extinction may be the result of loss of hay meadows and 'improvement' of sheep pasture adjacent to the moors (Fig. 204). On the moorland itself, evidence that workers forage more intensively on early-succession areas suggests that the pattern of moorland management has an important role. Winter grazing by sheep suppresses flowering of the bilberry, whilst with lack of management later-succession moorland is less rich in forage sources.

There is little evidence of decline in the case of *B. jonellus*, our other species of heath and moorland. This species is short-tongued, and rather specialist in its use of forage plants. In northern Britain it is a widespread species of moorland, often sharing localities with *B. monticola*. In the north, the queens establish their colonies very late in the season, with worker numbers reaching their peak in late August and September. In southern Britain, *B. jonellus* nests early, and is typically double-brooded. It is associated with lowland heaths, but despite loss of lowland heath to urbanisation it does not appear to be greatly threatened (Fig. 205). It is often found away from heathland, and commonly visits domestic gardens.

So there is no single pattern of decline shared by our threatened species, and probably no single cause. However, some degree of generalisation is possible. Several of the surface-nesting carder bumblebees, together with *B. soroeensis* and

FIG 204. A *Bombus monticola* worker foraging from white clover, off the moor, in July.

FIG 205. Building development on lowland heath, Dorset.

B. distinguendus, have been lost from all, or almost all, of their southern and central lowland habitats as a result of the massive loss of flower-rich grasslands and inappropriate management of many of those that remain. As late-nesting species they all depend on the availability of suitable flowers for forage late in the season – through August and (for some species) also September – but their foraging habitat is also threatened by succession to rank grassland and scrub in the absence of management. Some of these species, probably with the addition of *B. ruderatus* and *B. subterraneus,* may have thrived in the context of an earlier pattern of mixed farming, in which agricultural legumes, particularly red clover, were grown extensively as part of crop rotation. Loss of both types of habitat as a result of increasing industrialisation of agriculture has led to the northward retreat of species not close to the northern limit of their geographical range. Southern species in this group are now reduced to isolated relict populations in a few areas where, for historical or other reasons, agricultural intensification has been less severe – on the Somerset Levels, some military training areas, and the unique mosaic of ex-industrial sites, flood defences, waste tips, grazing marshes and quarries along the Thames estuary.

In general, the species that appear to have declined least are those Edwards & Williams classify as 'woodland edge' species. These species, *B. terrestris, B. lucorum, B. lapidarius, B. pratorum, B. hortorum* and *B. pascuorum,* comprise the short list of 'ubiquitous' species not currently thought to be in danger. For these species it seems that urban wasteland and ex-industrial sites as well as domestic gardens, lightly managed open spaces, parks and cemeteries offer effective substitutes for woodland edge habitat, and buffer their populations from the deleterious effects of loss of farm woodland, hedgerow removal and intensive cultivation of former marginal land. In fact, however, several of these species remain capable of coping with the new farmed landscapes, too. The four short- (or short-medium) tongued species in the list are generalist foragers, both for pollen and nectar, and several of them – possibly all – are long-distance foragers. They are thus well adapted to deal with fragmentation of foraging patches, and can also benefit from short-term abundance of food sources in the form of agricultural crops such as field bean and oil-seed rape, so long as there are enough remaining marginal foraging habitats to give them continuity of resources through the colony cycle (Fussell & Corbet, 1991). *Bombus lapidarius* is one of the very few bumblebees that forages extensively on the buttercups that survive in 'improved' grazing regimes. The remaining hedge banks, roadside verges, field margins and green lanes are important habitats for small mammals such as field voles and wood mice (Bellamy *et al.*, 2000), and so provide a continuing supply of possible nest sites.

The two long-tongued members of this group share many characteristics with certain of the declining species – *B. hortorum* with *B. ruderatus* and *B. subterraneus*; *B. pascuorum* with the other carders. The key difference seems to be their ability to exploit, as woodland edge species, urban and suburban settings. Again, however, both common species are able to maintain populations – albeit presumably significantly reduced – in the farmed landscape. It may be that they have longer foraging distances, or better powers of dispersal, that enable them to cope with the greater distances between fragmented foraging patches and suitable nesting sites imposed by the newer farmed landscapes. In the rural setting, too, there is evidence that domestic gardens may play an important role for these more resilient and adaptable species (Osborne *et al.*, 1999).

One of the most damaging effects of agricultural intensification on the populations of most bumblebee species is likely to have been disruption in the continuity of available and appropriate forage plants throughout their colony cycle. Many of the studies by academic researchers have been limited by their own resources to time-limited 'snapshots' of foraging activity and so provide little insight into this. In Essex, forage plants used by the sexes and castes of each bumblebee species through its seasonal cycle were noted over a 15-year period (Benton, 2000). Even for the common species, queens recently emerged from hibernation had a very narrow range of wild forage plants, among which sallows and red and white deadnettle were predominant, along with blackthorn and early woodland flowers, especially bluebell. Both queens and early cohorts of workers were able to supplement this narrow menu with garden flowers, especially early-flowering shrubs such as *Mahonia*, flowering current and *Berberis*. The scarce and localised species, including *B. muscorum*, *B. humilis* and *B. sylvarum*, were confined to an even narrower range of species at the beginning of the colony cycle, despite the tendency of their queens to emerge from hibernation later than those of the common species. These species also suffered, even on land managed for conservation, by cutting regimes that eliminated forage sources before the nests reached maturity. As we saw above, *B. monticola* is also threatened by a disruption in the continuity of its forage sources (Pinchen & Edwards, 2000; Pinchen & Wright, 2001).

Though we are now much closer to understanding the main causes of the alarming patterns of decline that have taken place in recent decades, it remains to be seen whether this can be translated into practical action. In Chapter 11 we will consider some of the shifts in agricultural and planning policy that have taken place since the mid-1980s, and explore some of the opportunities this has created for bumblebee conservation. Finally, some possible avenues of further research will be suggested.

Back from the Brink?
Bumblebee Conservation

PRESSURE FOR CHANGE

NOW THAT ALARM BELLS have been both rung and heard, and most of our declining species have attracted the attention of official bodies, academic researchers and amateur naturalists, the question remains: what is to be done? Some things have been done already, and there is a growing body of careful research to provide us with important information on how 'target' species are responding to a range of conservation efforts. But to understand both the successes in the conservation of bumblebees and the limitations of current approaches, we need not only to keep in mind the social and economic trends that led to current patterns of survival and decline, but also to take into account the significant changes that have taken place in both the planning and agricultural policy framework since the beginning of the 1980s.

By the 1970s, the 'second agricultural revolution' and the political framework that promoted it were already coming under sustained criticism. Concern was being expressed by voluntary organisations, academics, and some parliamentarians about a wide range of environmental, health and socio-economic consequences of the new farming techniques.

Through the 1960s and 1970s, especially, farming provided fewer rural employment opportunities, and the composition of rural communities, especially in the more populated south-eastern and central lowlands of England, was rapidly changing. The new rural population was less identified with the farming interest, and began to voice demands for a more pluralistic approach to the countryside. Many village residents were now ex-urbanites, continuing to work in town or city, but hoping for an idyllic leisure spent walking through unspoilt countryside, enjoying the peace and tranquillity of a 'green and pleasant land' (Fig. 206). The county Naturalists' Trusts (later Wildlife Trusts) recruited many tens of thousands as members and volunteer workers, while the Council for the Protection of Rural England, National Trust and more specialised groups such as the Royal Society for the Protection of Birds massively expanded their memberships and thus their political influence.

These newly emergent or revitalised social movements and voluntary organisations had agriculture, landscape conservation, wildlife and food health as their main concerns, but their growth coincided with the rise of a wider environmental movement campaigning on global issues, energy conservation, industrial pollution and poverty. The rapid growth of international organisations such as Friends of the Earth and Greenpeace, as well as electoral successes of Green parties in several European countries, ensured that a wide raft of environmental concerns took centre stage in the national policy debate from the beginning of the 1980s. However, it is unclear whether agricultural and planning regimes would have given way to these new external pressures without a major new economic challenge. The very success of the drive to increase agricultural productivity was now generating its own contradictions: the combination of grant-aided intensification and state support for food prices had produced a massive gap between food production and demand. Huge agricultural surpluses

FIG 206. Road protesters' graffiti, Epping Forest.

had to be stored at great cost, or dumped on world markets, undermining the delicately balanced food systems of poorer countries. In addition, some 70 per cent of the EU budget was devoted to subsidising the production of these food surpluses, generating a financial crisis for the EU itself.

Above all, it was the demand to develop a policy response to this crisis of overproduction that opened up the agricultural policy community to alternative voices. By the mid-1980s, official policy, as expressed in the 1986 Agriculture Act, included at least lip service to a wider public interest in access to the farmed countryside for leisure, to the need for a more diverse rural economy, and even for wildlife conservation to be included as a policy objective, albeit under the continuing priority of agricultural 'stability and efficiency'. Already in the early 1980s the Government's own statutory advisory bodies, the Countryside Commission and the Nature Conservancy Council, were voicing the concerns of a wider conservation movement that the 1981 Wildlife and Countryside Act was too limited to defend threatened wildlife and landscapes from the ravages of agricultural intensification. The limitations of this approach were by now evident. Nature Conservancy Council reports told of high annual rates of destruction of SSSIs which it was powerless to prevent, whilst pesticide drift, fertiliser runoff and lowered water tables in surrounding agricultural land degraded both SSSIs and nature reserves. At the same time, the requirement of many species for large areas of habitat began to be recognised, and pressure increased for a shift away from preserving small islands of biodiversity in favour of change at the level of the wider countryside.

Public outcry at the failure of the existing framework of support for conservation to defend threatened grazing marshes in the Norfolk Broads triggered a significant shift in UK and subsequently European policy. This enabled the 1986 Act to provide for the designation of 'Environmentally Sensitive Areas'. This designation allowed for voluntary agreements under which farmers would be subsidised for maintaining or converting to traditional farming practices, with the aim of preserving or enhancing existing wildlife habitat, landscape or archaeo-logical values. Six ESAs were designated initially, with a further six in 1988, and subsequent additions amounted to a total of 43 at the time of writing. Several of the initial ESAs were upland areas of northern England and Wales, where the main priority was to maintain the livelihoods of low income small farmers and prevent environmental loss from the abandonment of marginal upland farms. ESAs in lowland southern and central England included wetlands and river systems as well as remaining areas of flower-rich grassland and lowland heath that still retained landscape or wildlife value. These included, among others, the South Downs and Somerset Levels and Moors.

Strong pressures and powerful arguments for extending this approach to reconciling agriculture and environment in the wider countryside were, however, resisted, and the dominant policy response to agricultural overproduction was to pay farmers for taking land out of production. Initially, 'set-aside' was simply a response to the problem of surpluses, and the required management regimes generally ran counter to nature conservation objectives. Later, however, longer-term set-aside, farm woodland, stewardship and other voluntary schemes combined environmental objectives with lowered production targets (Fig. 207).

Pressures for change have continued into the 1990s, fuelled by recurrent food health scares, disquiet about new agricultural technologies, and high profile exposures of the abuse suffered by many farm animals in intensive regimes. These pressures have resulted in significant shifts in patterns of consumer demand, as well as provoking institutional and policy shifts. Health and ethical concerns have led to large increases in vegetarianism and escalating demand for organic produce. At the same time, in an attempt to integrate agricultural and environmental briefs, a new Department of State, DEFRA, was formed by means of a reorganisation of the former DOE and MAFF, while monitoring and enforcement of food standards was allocated to a new body, independent of the producer interests that had been entrenched in MAFF. A range of environmental functions previously dispersed over several public bodies were integrated in the newly created Environment Agency.

A renewed impetus for wildlife protection came with the 1992 'Earth Summit' conference in Rio. As we saw in Chapter 1, the Convention on Biodiversity agreed at the summit resulted in the writing of UK BAPs, covering both selected species and threatened natural and semi-natural habitats. In accordance with another of the Rio agreements, Agenda 21, much of the responsibility for implementing these plans was devolved to local authorities. However, the early 1990s saw initiatives at national level to shift at least some of the grant-aid to agriculture towards environmental goals. In 1991 a 'Countryside Stewardship Scheme' was introduced to cover agricultural land in England not already included in ESA designation. Similar schemes were also introduced in Scotland, Wales and the north of Ireland. Other, smaller schemes included more targeted habitat projects and some land adjacent to watercourses (Table 12). Meanwhile, and of potentially greater long-term significance, pressure to radically reform the CAP at EU level continues.

With up to 17 years' experience of the ESA approach, and some 10–12 years of the Countryside Stewardship and related schemes, a considerable body of evidence is now being put together on their contribution to biodiversity conservation. Most of the systematic monitoring of progress has, appropriately

FIG 207. Poppies and thistles in agricultural set-aside.

TABLE 12. UK agri-environment schemes with potential to contribute to the conservation of lowland semi-natural grassland (reproduced from Critchley *et al.* 2003, with permission).

COUNTRY	SCHEME	YEAR FIRST INTRODUCED	COVERAGE
England	Environmentally Sensitive Areas (ESAS)	1987	Twenty-two designated areas
	Countryside Stewardship Scheme (CSS)	1991	Countrywide outside ESAS
	Habitat Scheme	1994	Former set-aside land countrywide (1997)[a]; land adjacent to watercourses in 5 designated areas (1999)[a]
Northern Ireland	Environmentally Sensitive Areas (ESAS)	1993	Five designated areas
	Countryside Management Scheme (CMS)	1999	Countrywide outside ESAS
Scotland	Environmentally Sensitive Areas (ESAS)	1987	Ten designated areas (2000)[a]
	Countryside Premium Scheme (CPS)	1999	Countrywide outside ESAS (2000)[a]
	Rural Stewardship Scheme (RSS)	2001	Countrywide; replaces ESAS & CPS
Wales	Environmentally Sensitive Areas (ESAS)	1987	Six designated areas (1999)[a]
	Tir Cymen	1992	Three designated pilot areas (1999)[a]
	Habitat Scheme	1994	Countrywide outside ESAS (1999)[a]
	Tir Gofal	1999	Countrywide; replaces ESAS, Habitat Scheme and Tir Cymen

[a] Closed to new applicants.

enough, been botanical, with some more focused attention given to birds and butterflies. Much of this research has indirect relevance to bumblebees, given what we now know about their foraging and other requirements, but important research has also been conducted under the auspices of the UK BAP Bumblebee Working Group, drawing funding from various sources including voluntary organisations, English Nature's Species Recovery Programme and also agri-environmental schemes such as Countryside Stewardship.

So there is now at least some evidence on which to base a provisional evaluation of the implications of the current policy framework for our bumblebee fauna. This will be presented in terms of the characteristic habitats affected by the major policy areas:

1. Large-scale grassland habitats taken out of the main dynamics of agricultural intensification by military occupation.
2. Land covered by ESA designations.
3. Agricultural land covered by agri-environmental schemes.
4. Urban and suburban land, including ex-industrial landscapes.

MILITARY PROTECTION

Two large grassland areas under M.o.D. control have been the subjects of careful research as a result of the discovery by Working Group surveys (Edwards, 1997, 1998, 2000b) of strong populations of BAP and other threatened bumblebee species. These are the Salisbury Plain tank training area, and the Castlemartin Ranges, on the South Wales coast close to Pembroke. At both sites, commercial pressures are less intense, and there has been a long-standing conservation input into management regimes. Ongoing survey work and management advice under the auspices of Mike Edwards and the UK Bumblebee Working Group at both sites is yielding valuable insights into the conservation of several of our rarest bees of calcareous grassland: *Bombus soroeensis* and all four of the threatened carder bumblebees. One published outcome of the research at Salisbury Plain suggests that grassland grazed by cattle during the winter months provides the most attractive foraging areas for the more common bumblebees, but that *B. humilis* is more often found foraging on track edges, where the ground has been disturbed by vehicles, and also on reverting former arable land (Carvell, 2002). Grassland that had been grazed by cattle two or more years previously was less attractive to foraging bumblebees than recently grazed areas, suggesting the appropriateness of a rotational grazing regime. Summer grazing by cattle, and especially by sheep, is deleterious, as it eliminates bumblebee forage and destroys nests. Sheep preferentially graze flowerheads, produce a shorter, more even vegetation structure, and so in general they are much less suitable than cattle for maintaining bumblebee habitat (Figs 208 & 209). Although few nests of the rarer species have been studied, it seems clear that a tall, open grassland structure, with a ground cover of mosses or leaf litter for nesting material is important for both *B. humilis* and *B. sylvarum* (Fig. 210).

These conclusions were reinforced at Castlemartin, where hard grazing during the winter keeps scrub and bracken from encroaching on flower-rich grasslands, and favours the tall, open vegetation structure and continuous abundance of suitable forage plants through the season required by both *B. humilis* and *B. sylvarum* (Fig. 211) (Carvell, 2000). Loss of bumblebee foraging and nesting habitat as a result of grass-cutting during the colony cycle was demonstrated at Castlemartin and at another large grassland reserve (Kenfig) in South Wales. Where this occurs in the context of very extensive mosaics of habitat at different successional stages it may not be disastrous. However, on less extensive sites, with smaller, more vulnerable populations of the scarce species, it is particularly important to avoid grazing or large-scale management operations between May and September.

These studies have confirmed the selectivity of both *B. sylvarum* and *B. humilis* in their use of forage plants, though with some variation between the sites because

FIG 208. Dune slack at Kenfig NNR showing the effect of summer sheep grazing on previously flower-rich dune grassland (photograph by Claire Carvell).

FIG 209. Flowering stems of red clover showing the effects of sheep grazing (photograph by Claire Carvell).

FIG 210. Location of a *Bombus sylvarum* nest in tall but open grassland habitat on Castlemartin Range (photograph by Claire Carvell).

FIG 211. Flower-rich mesotrophic grassland on Castlemartin Range, Pembrokeshire, where extensive winter cattle grazing promotes a succession of bumblebee forage plants (photograph by Claire Carvell).

of their different mix of available flower species. As elsewhere, species of Fabaceae (particularly bird's-foot trefoils, clovers and melilot), Lamiaceae (particularly woundworts), Scrophulariaceae (red bartsia and yellow-rattle) and Asteraceae (knapweed) were particularly favoured. The studies also show that where suitable habitat is maintained both *B. humilis* and *B. sylvarum* can be abundant. At Castlemartin, *B. sylvarum* represented more than 15 per cent of sightings on regular 'bee walks', with only *B. lucorum* and *B. terrestris* seen more frequently. *Bombus humilis* was present in similarly high numbers at Kenfig. Such evidence as exists suggests that these species have small colony sizes, so sightings of such high numbers of workers indicates high nesting densities where habitat is suitable.

Both Salisbury Plain and Castlemartin include very large areas of flower-rich grassland, under a number of different management regimes. The Plain is the largest area of unimproved calcareous grassland in north-western Europe, while the Castlemartin range occupies an area of 2,381 hectares, 62 per cent of which is unimproved grassland. Carvell's research suggested that at Castlemartin *B. sylvarum* ranged over some 32 square kilometres. Habitat mosaics on this scale are capable of supporting large, viable populations of the scarce grassland species, with late-succession areas favouring small mammal populations and associated nesting habitat for the surface-nesting carder bumblebees, and winter-grazed areas, especially, providing abundant forage through the full colony cycle. Interestingly, although loss of large areas of unimproved grassland over most of the lowland agricultural landscape probably accounts for the steep declines in our four grassland carder bumblebees, these studies suggest that their habitat requirements are not identical. *Bombus humilis* and *B. sylvarum* appeared to be using different foraging habitat on Salisbury Plain. While *B. sylvarum* was much more abundant on Castlemartin ranges during the period of study than *B. humilis*, the positions were reversed at Kenfig. *Bombus ruderarius* appears not to have been present at Castlemartin, but was at Kenfig. It occurs in very small numbers on Salisbury Plain, where *B. muscorum* and *B. humilis* both occur, together with *B. sylvarum* and *B. soroeensis* (Fig. 212).

Finally, an interesting indicator for future conservation policy is that Carvell found at least some evidence of *B. sylvarum* on smaller areas of habitat up to 4 kilometres from the ranges, suggesting that the species is able to establish 'satellite' colonies away from its core population. *Bombus humilis*, too, appeared to be more widely distributed in coastal South Wales. It may be that both species are able to cope with a degree of habitat fragmentation so long as they retain local strongholds of sufficient size and habitat quality. This may be of particular significance for attempts to conserve populations in ex-industrial and suburban landscapes.

FIG 212. Grassland habitat of scarce carder bumblebees on Salisbury Plain, showing vehicle tracks. Occasional disturbance promotes colonisation of valuable bumblebee forage plants.

POLITICAL DESIGNATION:
THE 'ENVIRONMENTALLY SENSITIVE AREAS'

There is some hope that what is now understood about the habitat requirements of our threatened carder bumblebees may inform land management in the few other remaining British localities for them. The designation of some areas with remnants of more traditionally farmed semi-natural habitats as 'Environmentally Sensitive Areas' provides for grant-aided conservation management. The Somerset Levels and Moors have ESA designation, and retain populations of several of the scarce carder bumblebees. The area is relatively remote, and much of the land is susceptible to winter flooding, so that more intensive farming has been inhibited. Peat cutting is a major economic activity here, and constitutes a serious threat to grassland habitats. However, *B. sylvarum*, in particular, forages on the edges of the drove-ways used for vehicular access, where some of its favoured forage plants (such as red bartsia and white clover) thrive on occasional disturbance of the soil. Recent survey work has established that *B. sylvarum* is found in an area some 30 square kilometres in extent. *Bombus humilis* does not appear to occur here, but *B. ruderarius* and *B. muscorum* do. This is one of the few remaining inland localities for *B. muscorum*, and confirms its reputation for preferring damper grassland habitats (Boyd, 1999; Boyd & Boyd, 2000; 2001a, 2001b, 2002). Other lowland ESAs include the East Anglian brecklands and the South Downs. Although the latter once had large expanses of flower-rich calcareous grassland, suitable bumblebee habitat is now much reduced and fragmented. However, it is possible that downland restoration may permit the successful reintroduction of lost species. The Brecklands include vast tracts of coniferous forest, as well as large areas of lowland heather heath and dry unimproved grassland (Fig. 213). Their bumblebee fauna is not well studied, but the cuckoo bumblebee *B. bohemicus*, more usually a species of northern and western Britain, is relatively common here. There is also a strong and widely distributed population of the carder bumblebee *B. ruderarius*, offering potential for future research on this rapidly declining species.

Upland ESAs include the Derbyshire Peak District and, in the south-west, Dartmoor and Exmoor. Farming in these upland areas is often economically marginal, and grant-aid is available to maintain farm incomes as well as to achieve specified environmental objectives. In the main, payments are aimed at enabling low-intensity traditional forms of land management to remain viable so as to retain landscape values as well as wildlife habitat. In these areas, where *B. monticola* is the main focus for bumblebee conservation, there are contradictory threats.

FIG 213. Lowland heather heath, grassland and conifer forest, Breckland ESA, Suffolk.

Farming support mechanisms have in some areas led to overgrazing and loss of flower-rich grasslands, whereas in others abandonment of grazing has led to the spread of bracken and scrub on the open moorland (English Nature, 2003; Everett, 2004. See also Chapter 10, Figs 200–204).

Evidence collected so far suggests *B. monticola* thrives where there is a mosaic of open moorland habitats, with foraging concentrated on earlier succession patches of *Erica* species, or on hay meadows or other grassland habitats adjacent to the moor (Fig. 214). This has implications for management of both moorland itself, and upland hay meadows where these still survive. Rotational burning is a widely used management system for moorland, but its effects on wildlife are complex and vary considerably from site to site (Tucker, 2004). Loss or intensification of upland hay meadows is a particularly serious threat. Studies in the Peak District National Park, a significant stronghold for *B. monticola*, show a dramatic loss or decline in flower-rich hay meadows of some 76 per cent between the mid-1980s and the mid-1990s, with a further 25 per cent loss of the remainder in the two or three years up to 1998. This was despite the availability of grant-aid from three sources for farmers to enter into voluntary agreements. A combination of high land values and the failure of grant-aid to fully compensate farmers are held responsible for the continued alarming loss of this crucial habitat component (Buckingham *et al.*, 1999). It is even argued by some that the effects of standardised and prescriptive agri-environmental schemes on remote and upland

FIG 214. Entrance to a nest of *Bombus monticola*, Dartmoor.

farming systems can actually reduce biodiversity (Bignal *et al.*, 2001), although it may be that these schemes are now applied with more attention to particular local conditions and objectives (Critchley *et al.*, 2003).

BUMBLEBEE SURVIVAL IN AGRICULTURAL LANDSCAPES

Outside the military training areas, ESAs, National Parks and other areas where conservation is an acknowledged objective, habitat for bumblebees and other wildlife in the agricultural landscape has been largely reduced to marginal, uncultivated patches. As we have seen, several of our 'ubiquitous' bumblebee species have continued to survive despite the habitat degradation and fragmentation brought about by intensification. How do they do it? Clearly some species do it better than others, and the evidence suggests that those which can forage profitably over long distances and cope with fragmented patches of habitat, such as *B. lucorum* and *B. terrestris*, survive relatively well. Crops, too, may provide some nutritional benefit, as studies by Osborne *et al.* (1999), Saville *et al.* (1997) and others show. However, as we have seen, all social bumblebees require a succession of appropriate forage sources for the whole colony cycle. Crops may provide a superabundance of rewards, but for a short period only. For all bumblebee species, but for those with long colony cycles especially, agricultural crops must be supplemented by other forage sources. Studies by Osborne *et al.* (1999) and Fussell & Corbet (1992*b*) both suggested that bees were foraging beyond the boundaries of the agricultural mosaic, in the former case visiting garden flowers.

Even within intensively farmed landscapes, there are residual habitat-fragments that supply nesting sites and foraging resources for populations of at least some species. These include remaining hedgerows, field margins, the edges of ditches and streams, verges of farm tracks, lanes and roads and farm woodlands (Fig. 215). In their study of bumblebee foraging in Cambridge University farm, Fussell & Corbet (1992*b*) identified these features, and evaluated them as bumblebee habitat. Their study revealed the importance of biennial and perennial plants in permanent grassland, as opposed to the annuals that colonise disturbed areas and recently cultivated ground. The former were, generally, richer in rewards for foragers, and most frequently used by bumblebees. The study indicates the importance for bumblebee conservation on farmland of maintaining areas of permanent grassland, ungrazed, but subject to occasional cutting to prevent secondary succession. Farm woodland could also be of value, especially if maintained with wide, flowery rides and open glades. Small patches of old

FIG 215. An agricultural landscape, with intensive arable, old hedgerows, a lane, permanent grassland and a field of rape in the distance.

woodland may also have a spring-flowering ground flora that provides forage when other sources are scarce (Fig. 216). In their view, hedgerows were more important for the herbaceous plants growing in the hedge-bottom than for the hedgerow shrubs themselves. However, my own observations in Essex indicate the value of early flowering hedgerow shrubs such as blackthorn and, a little later, hawthorn, for overwintered queens of short-tongued species where few other sources are available (Benton, 2000).

In Fussell & Corbet's study, shorter- and longer-tongued bumblebees showed different but overlapping preferences, with the latter dependent on a seasonal succession of Lamiaceae: white deadnettle, hedge woundwort and black horehound. The shorter-tongued bumblebees, together with the honey bee, favoured brambles, spear thistle, hairy willowherb, hogweed and oil-seed rape (Fig. 217). However, both groups visited a much wider range of flowers less frequently. The dependence of the longer-tongued species on a relatively small group of plant species is significant in view of Corbet's comments on the conservation importance of the long-tongued bee/deep flower compartment (Figs 218 & 219) (Corbet, 2000, and see Chapter 7).

An instructive comparison is provided by Bäckman & Tiainen's study of bumblebee foraging on farmland in southern Finland (2002). They identified

FIG 216. Bluebells at the edge of farm woodland, adjacent to a field of oil-seed rape.

FIG 217. *Bombus lucorum*, a short-tongued species, foraging from bramble flowers in a hedgerow.

FIG 218. *Bombus ruderatus*, a scarce long-tongued bumblebee, foraging from deep flowers of marsh woundwort.

FIG 219. View of the face and extended tongue of *Bombus ruderatus* foraging on large-flowered hemp-nettle.

15 *Bombus* and *Psithyrus* species in their study, as against five in the study by Fussell & Corbet (16 and six species respectively if *B. lucorum* and *B. terrestris* are separated). Bäckman and Tiainen found that the density of bees was, as expected, greater where field margins were wider, but this was due to the greater numbers of one species, *B. lucorum*, which totalled 47 per cent of all sightings. In general the diversity of bumblebee species was not increased with wider margins, but bumblebee diversity was most strongly associated with the presence and abundance of a small range of flower species: field scabious, harebell, clustered bellflower, goldenrod, silverweed, large-flowered hemp-nettle and bifid hemp-nettle. The longer-tongued bumblebees were associated with the final three of the above list of flowers. Interestingly, silverweed would not be expected on the basis of blossom morphology, but the other two plant species mirror the association of long-tongued bumblebees with related Lamiaceae in the English studies. However, both these species are high- to late-summer flowering, and the Finnish study did not cover forage sources earlier in the season. Overall, zigzag clover was judged the most important forage plant for bumblebees (in terms of numbers of foragers, rather than species diversity).

As expected, field margins dominated by herbaceous dicotyledonous flowering plants, rather than by shrubs and trees or rank grasses were more favourable to bumblebees, but field margins in two areas were richer in bumblebees than expected on this criterion. Though they were less flowery, these margins had greater abundance of particular flowers, such as clovers, which are attractive to bumblebees, and in one case it was thought that closeness to the forest edge was significant. This parallels the evidence from UK studies that bumblebees often draw resources from adjacent non-agricultural habitat. It could also be that the setting of the farmland in the Finnish study in large tracts of semi-natural forest habitat goes some way to explain the striking disparity in bumblebee diversity. Valuable as this study is (including identification of cuckoo bumblebees, and discrimination between sexes and castes, often beyond the scope of observational studies of this sort), it can give only a very incomplete impression of the overall suitability of farmland for bumblebees. Foraging was observed at one time of year only, and no distinction was made between foraging for pollen and for nectar. More recent work suggests that preferences for pollen sources are a limiting factor for at least some bumblebee species, and that merely recording flower visits may be quite misleading. In addition, habitat shown to be important for foraging may not have been suitable for nesting or hibernating.

However, these and other studies (for example, Williams, 1985a; Dramstad & Fry, 1995; Svensson *et al.*, 2000) do illustrate the way intensification has affected the species composition of the bumblebee assemblages in farmland. In the British studies the assemblages included only 'mainland ubiquitous' species. Although the Finnish researchers were able to record more species, there were very striking differences in observed abundance, with five species recorded fewer than ten times each (compared with 900 sightings of *B. lucorum*). Two of these, *B. distinguendus* and *B. ruderarius* are species that have undergone severe declines in Britain. Ominously, of the species generally considered still common, the long-tongued *B. hortorum* was the least frequently recorded in both the British and Finnish studies. In the study by Svensson *et al.* of nest-searching queens in southern Sweden, *B. pratorum* and *B. hortorum* were the least frequently seen species in farmland, but both *B. subterraneus* and *B. sylvarum* were seen relatively frequently in open areas.

Both set-aside and the Countryside Stewardship schemes offer opportunities for landowners and managers to enter into agreements that combine conservation objectives with productive farming outside the ESA designation. Enough time has elapsed for some provisional assessment of the success of the Stewardship schemes to be attempted. One valuable review is provided by Critchley *et al.* (2003), covering a wide range of agri-environmental schemes in relation to semi-natural grasslands. Their findings are moderately optimistic, suggesting that the schemes have been successful in maintaining the quality of grasslands – mainly in upland and western areas – that were already of high conservation value. In the main, this had been achieved by supporting traditional management systems. Attempts to rehabilitate semi-natural grasslands that had been allowed to deteriorate (for example, through abandonment of grazing, or inappropriate grazing pressures) had proved more successful than attempts to restore or recreate grassland from previously 'improved' or arable land. Key problems included continuing high levels of soil fertility, changes in moisture content, and the availability of sources of suitable wild flower species. Better results were achieved where prescriptions regarding grazing levels were flexible enough to be adapted to local conditions and objectives. As well as the adoption of suitable grazing regimes, cessation or reduction of applications of inorganic fertiliser was a significant factor in the enhancement of grassland biodiversity. A comparative study of the herbaceous vegetation of hedgerows on conventional and organic farms in Denmark found that the species composition of the latter was more diverse and closer to semi-natural communities (Aude *et al.*, 2004). Given the importance of hedgerows for both foraging and nesting sites for bumblebees in agricultural landscapes, this finding suggests that the increasing popularity of organic produce may benefit bumblebee conservation. The use of agricultural legumes in crop rotations on arable farms is also likely to benefit bumblebees.

In the context of intensive arable farming, the main opportunities have been provided by conservation management of set-aside, as well as provision of field-edge habitat. This has included maintaining grassy strips along hedgerows, grant-aided restoration of hedgerows themselves, and 'conservation headlands', which involve reduction or cessation of pesticide spraying around field edges. A shift in favour of biological pest-control is also represented by the construction of 'beetle banks': strips of land sown with tussock-forming grasses across the middle of fields. These are designed to provide habitat for beetle species that prey on aphids and other pests. Longer-term set-aside schemes are now available, and these are likely to be of particular value for bumblebees in view of the greater foraging resources generally provided by perennial plant species, and the nesting habitat created by later successional stages (Corbet, 1995). Since the late 1990s the Bumblebee Working Group together with a variety of other voluntary groups and agencies has been sponsoring experimental work to foster bumblebee conservation by adapting these techniques. Also directly bearing on bumblebee conservation in the farmed landscape, but with a much wider remit, are the experimental studies now being carried out under the auspices of the 'Buzz Project' jointly run by the Farmed Environment Company and the Centre for Ecology and Hydrology (see Meek *et al.*, 2004). This project includes a study of the value of different methods of conservation management of field margins in six farmland sites. Whilst it is too early to provide definitive prescriptions, the initial results are very promising from the point of view of bumblebee conservation.

As we have seen, key causes of bumblebee decline include disruption of continuity of food sources throughout the colony cycle, reduction and fragmentation of habitat, and loss, or reduced abundance, of key plant species for pollen collection. Deep flowers of a small number of families – Fabaceae, Lamiaceae and Scrophulariaceae, together with some species in the Asteraceae – have been shown to be especially important for the threatened long-tongued species of bumblebee. Various techniques have been used to reintroduce legumes such as red clover, bird's-foot trefoil and meadow vetchling into modern agricultural systems. One method, used for 'improved' permanent grassland, is to spread wild flower seed harvested from a local flower-rich meadow onto it, and monitor in successive seasons for signs of germination. Another approach, in the context of arable cultivation, is to plant set-aside as strips comprising a mix of grasses and agricultural legumes such as red clover and bird's-foot trefoil (Fig. 220). As noted by Critchley *et al.* (2003), one problem that has been encountered is limited availability of seed of appropriate plant species or strains. The most widely available modified strains of red clover turn out to be relatively short-lived, and so are less suitable if the objective is to create a permanent grass

FIG 220. Cereal field margin sown with a mix of legumes (in its first year), which has attracted *Bombus ruderatus*. This is recommended as the 'pollen and nectar' mix for a forthcoming UK agri-environmental stewardship scheme (photograph by Claire Carvell).

sward that remains rich in red clover. The more suitable wild strains are less readily available so far (Edwards, pers. comm.). Agricultural mixes seem to be successful in set-aside strips, but resowing within the ten-year period of the stewardship schemes is necessary. Further experimentation has been directed at finding out what methods of subsequent management favour maintenance of abundant forage for the bumblebees in the longer term, as well as providing habitat for small mammals and associated nesting sites for the bees.

Efforts to enhance the quality of permanent grassland in the Dungeness area and elsewhere by a combination of enhancing the presence of legumes in the sward and adjusting the grazing regime, produced abundant bumblebee forage surprisingly quickly in some sites, and generally increased the numbers of foraging bees recorded. Agricultural legumes planted as strips in arable land on Romney Marsh also succeeded in enhancing numbers of foraging bees, including several queens of *B. muscorum*. Workers of another BAP species, *B. ruderatus*, were observed foraging at a strip of agricultural red clover in arable land in Warwickshire, along with large numbers of the commoner species (Edwards, 2002). A carefully controlled study of the effects of different field-margin treatments on bumblebee foraging was carried out over three years at a farm in North Yorkshire (Carvell *et al.*, 2003). This compared a mix sown with perennial wild flowers, another with tussocky grass, and another with a mix of the two, with natural regeneration and cereal cropping to the field boundary. The study illustrated the value of the annually cut wild flower mix in all three years in providing forage from May to August. The same was true of the mixed planting, but the margin with natural regeneration produced uneven results over the years of the study. In this study only the six 'mainland ubiquitous' species were recorded (as expected), and no distinction between nectar and pollen collection was made.

This and other evidence of increased numbers of foraging bumblebees in suitably planted conservation strips suggests that these methods are of conservation value where (as in most lowland arable landscapes) forage sources are an important limiting factor for bumblebees. However, it is important to bear in mind that several of the scarce and declining species seem to have a narrower range of preferred sources for pollen than for nectar, so evaluation of agri-environmental schemes needs to take into account specific flower preferences of the target bee species. In addition, for some species and in some areas it may be that other partial habitats limit bumblebee populations: for example, several of the common species seek out nest sites in tussocky grassland, so lack of foraging records in this treatment does not imply that it is of no value to the bees. Finally, as Carvell *et al.* point out, bumblebee foraging ranges and nesting densities are such that conservation measures should be conducted at the landscape scale, and enhanced foraging patches need to be designed and located with this in mind. Williams (2005) cites some anecdotal evidence to the effect that some of the scarcer species may be poor colonisers of newly established habitat-patches.

A further implication of this is that for the scarce and declining bees of large-scale grassland habitats, such as the four threatened carder bumblebees, and possibly *B. soroeensis*, attempts to recreate suitable habitat should be concentrated on the periphery of their few remaining strongholds, to extend the area of the total habitat mosaic utilised by the remaining metapopulations. As more reliable evidence becomes available on the relative foraging ranges and dispersal abilities of the different species it should better inform conservation measures such as provision of suitably located nesting and foraging habitat and 'corridors' for movement between partial habitats. It seems likely that these and other declining species may benefit significantly in the short term from suitably located agri-environmental schemes designed to increase availability of suitable forage through the colony cycle. However, in the longer term the recovery of such species as *B. sylvarum*, *B. muscorum* and *B. humilis* will depend on rehabilitation and recreation of extensively managed, flower-rich grassland over large areas of the countryside. Several of the existing lowland ESAs could form the nuclei for any such transition. But this would presuppose a fairly deep-level shift of agricultural policy and the pattern of incentives for landowners.

However, the species regarded as still common, and which retain populations in agricultural habitats, could be expected to benefit significantly from even small-scale shifts within an agricultural practice still predominantly production-oriented. Evidence so far from monitoring field-edge schemes has, naturally enough, concentrated on these species (they are the only ones left!), and suggests that their numbers are boosted. Since this group includes two members (*B. pascuorum* and *B. hortorum*) of the threatened 'long-tongued bee/deep flower' compartment (Corbet, 2000) this may have a conservation importance beyond our concern with the bumblebees themselves, in sustaining pollination services for a range of wild and cultivated plants. There is some evidence (Carvell, pers. comm.; Edwards, 2002), consistent with our discussion above (Chapter 10), that *B. ruderatus*, another long-tongued bee of great conservation concern, may benefit particularly from plantings of agricultural legumes in arable landscapes (Fig. 221).

FIG 221. *Bombus ruderatus* foraging from red clover.

THE URBAN LANDSCAPE: PARKS, GARDENS AND
THE INDUSTRIAL LEGACY

Finally, however, it is important to recognise that in the face of an inclement agricultural environment, urban and suburban spaces now play an important, and perhaps in some cases decisive, role in the survival of our bumblebee fauna, as well as much of the rest of our wildlife (Wheater, 1999). Chapman's recent study of sites across London illustrated the extent to which large populations of the common species thrive even in the capital city. More than this, however, as many as 12 sites in East London provided forage for the BAP species *B. humilis*, and small populations of *B. sylvarum* and *B. ruderarius* were also discovered (Chapman, 2004). This study also offered important insights into the diversity of habitats used by bumblebees in the urban context, with significant differences between the species both in their forage plant preferences and in the habitats they were able to exploit. Perhaps the most obvious of these urban habitats is the domestic garden. Gardens provide forage for all the common species and, according to Chapman's findings, are the preferred foraging habitat for some species, notably the least secure of the still-common species, *B. hortorum*.

It may be that in some areas some species are entirely dependent on gardens for forage at critical times of year. In my Essex survey, flowering shrubs in parks and gardens were intensively used by overwintered queens of all the common species at a time when few other sources were available (Benton, 2000). Gardens also provide forage late in the season, and may be important for late-maturing colonies, as well as for species, such as *B. pratorum*, which are multi-brooded. In Scotland, where the flowering season for wild flowers is relatively short, recent range expansions of *B. terrestris* and *B. lapidarius* have been dependent on use of early and late forage sources in gardens (Macdonald, 2001). Observations in a Leicester garden over a three-year period included sightings of all the 'ubiquitous' species (*terrestris* and *lucorum* counted as a single taxon) plus two cuckoo bumblebee species, with foraging activity through from early March to the end of October (Frankum, 2003). The national survey co-ordinated by Fussell & Corbet (1992c, 1993) revealed very extensive use by all the common bumblebee species of garden flowers – both herbaceous and woody.

But, as we have seen, bumblebees forage at the landscape scale. In an urban setting, individual gardens may feature as foraging patches, and possibly also offer nesting, overwintering or mating partial habitats. There is now clear evidence that bumblebees in urban areas forage very widely, and that workers from any single colony will be dispersed across a number of different foraging sites and patches (Darvill *et al.* 2004; Chapman *et al.*, 2003). In terms of bumblebee ecology, an urban area forms a fragmented mosaic of habitat patches just as does the agricultural landscape. As well as gardens, these patches are found in urban parks, informal green spaces, allotments, derelict industrial sites, roadside verges, railway cuttings and embankments, cemeteries and churchyards, the margins of rivers and canals, waste tips, worked-out quarries, golf courses and many other places. Typically, open spaces close to town centres are more intensively managed, and high land values tend to eliminate the more lightly managed spaces that favour bumblebees and most other wildlife. However, towards the urban fringe, suburban domestic gardens may form a more-or-less continuous mix of nesting and foraging habitat, phasing out into 'edgeland' features such as business parks, disused mineral workings, long-term development land, garden centres, golf courses, derelict industrial complexes and waste disposal units. In some urban areas planning policy has provided for connectivity between open amenity and wildlife sites, whereas elsewhere railway tracks, roadside verges and canals or rivers provide a degree of connection as a result of their chance location (Fig. 222).

We are at an early stage in our understanding of the ways bumblebees move

FIG 222. Linkage between habitat patches for bumblebees is provided by this railway line, with abundant purple toadflax.

between and variously exploit these landscapes, but exciting new discoveries are already being made by using modern genetic analysis. A recent study of foraging workers of *B. terrestris* and *B. pascuorum* at several sites in London used genetic evidence of kinship among samples collected to estimate how many colonies were represented at each site (Chapman *et al.*, 2003). The astonishing result was that an average of 96 colonies of *B. terrestris* and 66 colonies of *B. pascuorum* were represented at each urban site (including cemeteries and public parks) of approximately one hectare. Even at the level of foraging patches within each site, several colonies were represented. A study using a slightly different method (Darvill *et al.*, 2004), and conducted in an agricultural landscape, also yielded evidence of surprisingly large numbers of colonies represented at an average foraging site: 20.4 colonies of *B. terrestris* and 54.7 of *B. pascuorum*.

Allowing for differences in what counts as a site, and evidence that at least some bumblebee species nest at higher densities in urban areas (for example, Goulson *et al.*, 2002), these results are closely comparable. Inferences from these findings about foraging range depend to some extent on estimates of average nesting densities in the habitats from which the foraging workers were drawn. Chapman *et al.* (2003) give very high estimates for foraging distances: for *B. terrestris* from 0.6–2.8 kilometres, and for *B. pascuorum* 0.51–2.3 kilometres. Darvill *et al.* estimated rather higher nesting densities (13 per square kilometre for *B. terrestris* and 193 per square kilometre for *B. pascuorum*) and consequently smaller foraging ranges: up to 312 metres for *B. pascuorum* and 625 metres for *B. terrestris*. Chapman *et al.* also studied the extent of genetic differentiation across the various sites and found none in the case of *B. terrestris*, and very little in the case of *B. pascuorum*. Even on the rather lower estimates of foraging range made by Darvill *et al.*, these are still considerable, and illustrate the ability of these species to cope effectively with fragmented foraging habitat. Both studies also indicate much greater nesting densities for these species than often supposed. The high degree of genetic uniformity over large geographical areas also suggests that fertilised queens regularly disperse long distances from their nest of origin, maintaining gene flow through large metapopulations. As indicated in other studies, *B. pascuorum* may have a somewhat smaller foraging range and weaker powers of dispersal than *B. terrestris*. Comparison with other species, including our scarcer species, would be of great interest in estimating the importance of these characteristics in explaining patterns of decline, as well as contributing to designing suitable conservation strategies.

Urban parks and gardens

Although individual gardens may be quite small, they collectively account for some 3 per cent of the total land area of England and Wales (Owen, 1991) and offer a wide range of wildlife habitat. The wildlife potential of any garden will clearly be limited by its size and physical relationship to other gardens, green spaces and the linkages between them. In general, species richness of gardens declines towards urban centres, and is enhanced by closeness to larger areas of green open spaces or other gardens. There are three broad approaches to wildlife gardening (Gibbons & Gibbons, 1988; Good, 2000). Conventional gardening without pesticides and avoiding disturbance of hedges and compost heaps during breeding seasons is the least demanding. A more positive approach combines conventional gardening with provision of resources for wildlife. This might include bird nest boxes, feeders and the like, but for bumblebees would focus on providing a sequence through the season of suitable forage plants.

The third approach to gardening for wildlife involves transformation of the garden to mimic or recreate semi-natural habitat types. In many ways, gardens figure as woodland edge habitats from the point of view of bumblebees, and much can be done to enhance their potential for bumblebees beyond the provision of suitable forage.

As some species do nest in gardens, features such as compost heaps or stands of long tussocky grass (replacing the lawn) might provide suitable habitat. An alternative is to deploy purpose-built bumblebee nest boxes in the hope of attracting the attentions of visiting queens in the spring. With long experience, some gardeners have been very successful in this. Manfred Intenthron is regularly successful in persuading queens of all the common species to establish nests in a variety of containers of his own design, placed strategically in his medium-sized suburban garden in Kidderminster. However, beginners should be warned that this is no easy feat, and many disappointments lie ahead! (Advice is given in Intenthron & Gerrard, 2003, as well as Sladen, 1912, and Prŷs-Jones & Corbet, 1991. Commercially produced nest boxes can be obtained from Oxford Bee Company (see Appendix 2)). Finally, bumblebees often hibernate in gardens, and so disturbance of their hibernating places should be avoided: the problem is that we have very little information about what they are!

For most gardeners, the option of providing more suitable forage sources for bumblebees within a broadly conventional framework will be the one most readily adopted. The same is true for managers of urban parks, who face conflicting de-mands from public users. That this approach can still provide important resources for a great diversity of species is illustrated by the astonishing list recorded in her Leicester garden by Dr Jennifer Owen over a 14-year period (Owen, 1991). Both urban parks and domestic gardens offer particularly rewarding forage for bumble-bees, and, for the species that can access the more exotic flower varieties, gardens are an important fall-back when wild flowers are scarce, especially early and late in the season (Else, 1995).

However, gardens will vary in the resources they can provide for bumblebees, and a series of studies by Corbet, Comba and others have evaluated the relative merits of a range of different species and varieties for pollinating insects. In a study of experimental plots in Cambridge University Botanic Garden, Comba *et al.* (1999*a*) compared a series of more and less horticulturally modified varieties for their attractiveness to insect visitors. The species studied were nasturtium, larkspur, snapdragon, violas and pansies, French marigold and hollyhock. Horticultural modification may involve a range of different alterations, including loss of a spur, multiplication of petals, colour changes and increased size of the blossom. Spurless cultivars of larkspur and nasturtium offered no nectar reward, but this form of nasturtium was still visited for pollen. The less modified varieties of both species provided nectar in the long spurs that was accessible to (non-robbing) long-tongued bees only, thus acting as a 'trophic refuge' for them. Double larkspur did not secrete nectar, and the added flower parts obstructed access. In the case of snapdragon, the less modified form required large-bodied bees to gain access, but the modified form allowed access to a wider spectrum of visitors. The larger flowered cultivars of pansy were seldom visited, despite greatly increased nectar secretion. Apparently these were inaccessible either because the spur was too deep, or because (in the case of bumblebees) the changed floral structure did not provide an adequate platform. In the case of double French marigold, the greater number of florets on each capitulum resulted in more insect visits per plot. In general, the study showed that the less modified varieties were preferred to the more modified cultivars, but with some exceptions. The presence of a functioning spur, and a floral morphology appropriate for the 'target' group of pollinators, seem to be the most significant considerations for conservation-minded gardeners.

In a second study, Comba *et al.* (1999*b*) studied insect visitors to a selection of 24 native or naturalised flower species, focusing on their value as nectar sources. All species chosen had high nectar rewards, but differed in the timing and rates of secretion, and in their accessibility to different groups of insects. Butterflies, flies, solitary bees and the different bumblebee species demonstrated differing patterns of preference. Added interest was provided by the interference between territorial males of the solitary bee *Anthidium manicatum* and bumblebees foraging on woundworts. In yet another study, Corbet *et al.* (2001) compared a selection of native and exotic flowers, and of single and 'double' varieties from the point of view of their status as forage for nectaring insect visitors. The native species studied all had high rates of nectar secretion and high standing crops of nectar. They were also accessible to various assemblages of insect visitors, depending on floral morphology, tongue lengths and so on. By contrast, most of the exotics, having evolved in the context of quite different assemblages of pollinators, proved inaccessible to the local insect fauna. In some cases, this was despite their much greater secretion of nectar. In the case of 'double' cultivars, as in the earlier experiment, little or no nectar was secreted and few insect visits were recorded, though the pot marigold proved to be an exception to this.

These studies are valuable in drawing attention to the ways the interest of a garden can be enhanced by planting flowers that are attractive to insect visitors, and particularly in informing the choice of plant species of interest to bumblebees. Recent studies have emphasised the importance of flowers as pollen sources, and comparable research on bumblebee queen- and worker-preferences in their foraging for pollen would be of particular conservation interest, as would studies of the sequential use of garden flowers through the colony cycle of each species. Frankum's study illustrates interesting differences in foraging preferences shown by the common species, with *B. pratorum*, *B. pascuorum* and *B. hortorum* including more deep flowers in their 'top ten' than *B. terrestris/lucorum* and *B. lapidarius*. The ability of *pratorum*, a relatively short-tongued species, to forage from deep flowers is a reminder that caution is needed in relating insect morphology to flower type. Small *pratorum* workers can probe deep flowers such as comfrey by pushing their heads into the mouth of the flower. They also use the holes in the corolla made by other bees to rob nectar.

Garden flowers, including both herbaceous species and shrubs, can provide valuable forage for bumblebees, especially for overwintered queens early in the year, and for species whose colonies continue into late summer and autumn, when suitable wild flowers are often in short supply (Figs 223–232). Garden flowers used by overwintered queens in my area of Essex include japonica, rosemary, *Erica* species, flowering currant, *Viburnum*, *Berberis*, *Escallonia*, *Ceanothus*, *Aubrieta*, green alkanet, bluebell, crocus and daffodil. In late summer and autumn *Hebe*, *Buddleia*, jasmine, *Fuchsia*, *Tricyrtis*, *Caryopteris*, snowberry, *Sedum*, Michaelmas daisy and *Verbena* are commonly visited garden flowers. The giant viper's bugloss provides ample pollen and nectar from early May to August (Gibson & Gibson, 2001).

Surveys organised by Fussell & Corbet (1992a) and more recently by Osborne *et al.* (pers. comm.) have shown that gardens are frequently used by bumblebees for nesting as well as foraging. *Bombus terrestris/lucorum* are reported as nesting under garden sheds and outhouses, and *B. pascuorum* often nests in undisturbed corners of gardens, in compost heaps and other sheltered spots. *Bombus pratorum* is very

FIG 223. An urban garden with *Verbena, Perovskia, Sedum,* Michaelmas daisy and other valuable late summer forage plants for bumblebees.

FIG 224. An overwintered queen *Bombus pratorum*, foraging from *Erica carnea* in an urban park, mid-March.

FIG 225. A queen *Bombus jonellus* foraging from *Rhododendron*, early summer.

FIG 226. A *Bombus terrestris* worker foraging from *Escallonia* in an urban garden, early summer.

FIG 227. A male *Bombus lucorum* foraging from *Astrantia* in a suburban garden, early summer.

FIG 228. A male *Bombus hortorum* foraging from *Philadelphus*, mid-summer.

FIG 229. A *Bombus pascuorum* worker foraging from a summer-flowering *Geranium* (*himalayense*) in a suburban garden.

FIG 230. A *Bombus lucorum* daughter queen foraging from a *Salvia* cultivar, late summer.

FIG 231. A *Bombus terrestris* daughter queen foraging from *Echinacea*, late summer.

FIG 232. A *Bombus lapidarius* daughter queen foraging from *Caryopteris* in a garden centre, early autumn.

adaptable in its choice of nesting sites and has been reported as nesting in roof spaces, in bird boxes and in trees and shrubs. However, it is unclear how important gardens are as nesting habitat for urban bumblebees. Overwintered queens of *B. lapidarius*, *B. pascuorum*, *B. terrestris*, *B. lucorum* and *B. hortorum* can often be observed prospecting for nest sites in unmanaged tussocky grassland in urban wasteland such as river banks, abandoned allotment sites and edges of sports fields. *Bombus lapidarius* is also often seen investigating potential nesting holes in short-mown turf, unlike the other species. *Bombus pratorum* is more cryptic in its nest-site prospecting, possibly reflecting its preference for more concealed above-ground locations under cover. Hibernating sites for bumblebees are occasionally discovered by chance, but there is evidence that loose soil or leaf litter in gardens is frequently used. There is ample room here for conservation-oriented local studies by amateurs to refine our understanding of how best to garden with bumblebees in mind (as has already been done in many places for birds and butterflies).

Urban sites and the industrial legacy

There is little evidence that the scarcer and more vulnerable species of bumble-bees make extensive use of gardens, except where these are close to suitable nesting habitat. But this certainly does not mean that the scarce and declining species have no urban presence. My own study in Colchester revealed the presence of foragers of 12 species (seven socials and five of our six cuckoo bumblebees) on an area of lightly managed public open space adjacent to the town centre. Significantly, this site is bounded on two sides by suburban gardens, and on a third by a series of riverside grazing meadows, a small wetland and a busy road (Figs 233–236) (Benton, 2000). Another site close to the centre of nearby Chelmsford has the six 'ubiquitous' species, together with *B. ruderarius* and *B. ruderatus*.

FIG 233. Bluebells in urban woodland, Colchester. Valuable spring forage for bumblebees.

FIG 234. A grazing meadow (recently converted from arable) with a heath and scrub-covered hillside in the background, close to the centre of Colchester.

FIG 235. An unmanaged 'brownfield' site close to Colchester town centre.

FIG 236. A *Bombus pascuorum* worker collecting pollen from ivy, a valuable late forage plant in many urban sites, early autumn.

FIG 237. *Fuchsia* in an urban park, a valuable late forage plant, favoured by *Bombus pascuorum*.

This is a complex comprising an old grazing meadow and a larger area of former arable land purchased by a developer but as yet undeveloped, and with extensive stands of deadnettles, clovers and black horehound. This site is bounded on one side by a river, on two sides by suburban gardens and on the fourth by more intensively managed grasslands and arable fields (own obs.).

Neither of these sites compares with the astonishing invertebrate assemblages that have become established in the East Thames corridor, in south Essex and north Kent (see Harvey, 2000). On both sides of the Thames, extending westwards into east London, and eastwards towards Southend and the Isle of Grain, lies a vast area of residential, industrial and post-industrial, retail, waste disposal, port, storage, and transport facilities. Urban districts include Barking, Dagenham, Dartford, Gravesend, Tilbury, Rainham, Grays, Thurrock, Swanscombe, Basildon, Pitsea, Canvey and Benfleet. Scattered among the built-up areas is an exceptional mosaic of sites of great wildlife value: relict expanses of old, unimproved grazing marshes, sea walls and ditches, disused chalk quarries and sand-and-gravel pits, abandoned industrial sites, roadside verges, silt lagoons and areas formerly spread with power-station waste, and lightly managed public open spaces (Figs 238–246). A combination of the warm, dry climate, and nutrient-poor, well-drained soil has made possible the establishment of extensive areas of flower-rich grassland. Succession to scrubland has been retarded in many sites by the dry climate and nutrient-poor substrates, and in others by low-level grazing, recurrent fires, and occasional cutting. Small-scale disturbance by motorcycle scramblers and other occasional vehicle use has increased the habitat diversity, and encouraged the colonisation of plants such as narrow-leaved bird's-foot trefoil and red bartsia, both important late forage for several of the rare bumblebees.

Recent surveys have established the national – perhaps international – importance of the associated invertebrate assemblage of the east Thames corridor. The bees, wasps and ants are the most thoroughly surveyed groups, with 74 per cent of the national aculeate fauna present. Just one 10-kilometre square in Thurrock has 55 per cent of the national aculeate list (Payne & Harvey, 1996; Harvey, 1999a, 2000). Numerous sites within the area have many red data book and nationally notable species, including at least four of the BAP bumblebee species: *B. sylvarum*, *B. humilis*, *B. muscorum* and *B. ruderarius*. In the case of *B. sylvarum* and *B. humilis* the metapopulation sustained by the network of habitat on both sides of the Thames may be as large as in any other part of Britain.

Unfortunately, the extent of ex-industrial wasteland in the area has long been seen by planners as a blight on the area, and both national government and local authorities strongly support a massive regeneration project, the 'Thames Gateway'. Already many of the richest sites have been destroyed for housing estates or

FIG 238. A Thames estuary 'brownfield' site with industrial backdrop, Canvey Island. The site offers nesting habitat for three scarce carder bumblebee species, as well as many other scarce invertebrates.

FIG 239. Bumblebee habitat in a Thames estuary 'brownfield' site: Pulverised Fuel Ash lagoon, West Thurrock (photograph by Peter Harvey).

FIG 240. Another rich wildlife site on the lower Thames estuary, Wouldham's Quarry, being cleared for development (photograph by Peter Harvey).

FIG 241. A 'brownfield' site at Canvey Island, with fodder vetch, a valuable forage plant for overwintered *Bombus sylvarum* queens in late spring.

FIG 242. A queen *Bombus sylvarum* foraging from fodder vetch, Canvey Island.

FIG 243. Late summer foraging habitat for *Bombus sylvarum* and *B. humilis*, Canvey Island. Note the abundant narrow-leaved bird's-foot trefoil.

FIG 244. Late summer foraging habitat of *Bombus sylvarum* and *B. humilis*, with red bartsia, red clover and knapweed, Wat Tyler Country Park, Pitsea. This former waste tip forms part of the outstanding mosaic of habitats along the lower Thames estuary.

FIG 245. A *Bombus sylvarum* male foraging from red bartsia in late summer, Pitsea.

FIG 246. A *Bombus humilis* male foraging from red clover in late summer, Pitsea.

massive retail developments, and others are the subject of existing planning permissions for development. Permissions have been given despite clear knowledge of the conservation importance of the sites, and there is continuing evidence that the planning system offers little protection to BAP habitats and species where powerful development pressures are at work (Edwards, 2002). Sustained efforts by English Nature to save one of the richest remaining wildlife sites in the complex – with perhaps the densest nesting populations of both *B. humilis* and *B. sylvarum* – have been largely successful, but the prospects for the area as a whole look poor.

There are several important implications here. One is that for invertebrate conservation in particular, urban areas may be of great value. This is particularly true of the central and southern lowland areas of Britain that have been most affected by agricultural change. The widely assumed association of wildlife and 'nature' with the countryside no longer holds good, and urban areas, especially large derelict and ex-industrial zones, can act as vital refuges for species virtually eliminated from the agricultural landscape. Despite acknowledged difficulties involved in maintaining semi-natural habitats such as lowland heath in urban areas (see, for example, Haskins, 2000), the simple fact of exclusion from the intensive cultivation, nutrient enrichment and pesticide application suffered by agricultural land is more than compensation. For bees, wasps and ants, too, some of the informal pressures such as disturbance caused by motorcycle scrambling and even occasional burning have a positive role.

Another implication is directly political. The immense expenditure of time, energy and goodwill that has gone into researching and drawing up BAPs will have no discernable effect on conservation unless the planning system is radically reformed to give legal powers capable of contesting the huge political and economic pressures for development. There is currently no sign of this happening. Only if the environmental movement as a whole is able to mobilise public opinion in favour of a quite different understanding of 'quality of life', which puts our aspirations for development within a wider environmental setting, will the necessary political will emerge. A clear majority of our human population lives out most of its life in an urban context. More distant rural locales are beyond the reach of many urban dwellers, some of whom may lack resources, while others have limited mobility. There is good evidence that health and well-being are enhanced by contacts and engagements with non-human nature, so there are powerful arguments from social justice and inclusion, as well as environmental conservation, to give high priority to defending and extending existing wildlife habitats in our towns and cities. The current presumption in favour of developing so-called 'brownfield' sites is a relic of the pre-Second World War identification of the countryside with tranquillity, aesthetic beauty and moral virtue, and should be resisted, especially where threatened sites provide wildlife habitat, as well as amenity and educational value for town-dwellers.

But, as we have seen, just preventing development of a site is not enough. Much then depends on how it is managed, and how it is linked to other neighbouring patches of habitat. Urban conservation, like conservation in the agricultural context, has to be conceived and implemented at the landscape scale. This is at least as important for bumblebees as for any other groups of organisms.

CONCLUSIONS AND SUGGESTIONS FOR FURTHER RESEARCH

Although we are still a long way from full understanding of the diverse habitat requirements of the British bumblebee species, the greatly increased research effort of the past decade or so has provided some valuable new insights. Some provisional conclusions can be drawn, with appropriate caution:

1. Whilst most species will take nectar from a wide variety of flowers, some, including several of the scarce and declining species, are much more

specialised in their choice of pollen sources. This dimension of foraging behaviour was much less thoroughly researched in the past, and has important implications for conservation.

2. Perhaps because of prior habitat specialisation (for example, to open grassland or to woodland edge) some species may have been more able than others to colonise urban parks and gardens and other green spaces as substitutes for habitats lost to agricultural intensification or development. Even scarce species of open grassland may use urban areas as refuges, highlighting the conservation importance of so-called 'brownfield' sites.

3. It is not established that the earlier focus on foraging efficiency of the workers is always and for all species the only or the main determinant of the reproductive success of colonies. For some species, and in some areas, other partial habitats may be critical: availability of suitable nesting or hibernation sites, availability of nesting materials, and so on. The broad distinction between surface and underground nesting species is significant here. The surface nesters tend to be species of open, flower-rich grasslands, and would be most likely to be harmed by 'improvement' or conversion of grasslands to arable, as well as by early cutting of hay meadows.

4. Workers of at least some species travel much further from their nests to foraging patches than used to be assumed. Foraging range and the dispersal abilities of fertilised daughter queens probably vary considerably among species. Those adapted for long-distance foraging and with good dispersal powers would be likely to cope better with habitat fragmentation, in either urban or agricultural landscapes.

5. Since the reproductive unit for social bumblebees is the colony, numbers of individuals observed foraging may give a misleading impression of abundance, as most will be infertile workers, or males. This, combined with estimated low nesting densities (of the order of one or two successful nests per hectare per species) means that viable metapopulations require large areas of suitable habitat: for some species a mosaic of habitat at least 10 square kilometres in extent (Edwards, 2002). Conservation efforts, therefore, need to be implemented on the landscape scale.

6. Several declining species are late to establish their colonies and correspondingly late to produce their daughter queens and males. Availability of suitable forage throughout the colony cycle is vital for all species, and for late-season bumblebees, shortage of forage resources late in the season may be critical.

7. Management of grassland sites for bumblebees has to take into account the requirement for 'partial habitats'. In particular, grazing or cutting regimes that

produce good foraging habitat may be inconsistent with formation of the vegetation structure and build-up of small mammal populations that are important for nesting. Where it is practically feasible, a rotational system that provides a mosaic of habitat at different successional stages is desirable. Winter grazing by cattle or sheep often produces good spring and summer foraging habitat, but summer grazing, especially by sheep, as well as cutting during the colony cycle, eliminates forage plants and may also damage surface nests.

Much remains to be discovered. Of particular conservation importance, given impending development pressures, is evidence about the dispersal abilities and foraging ranges of our more threatened species. To what extent will species such as *B. sylvarum* and *B. humilis* be able to sustain metapopulations along the East Thames corridor in the face of increasing habitat fragmentation and loss of important nesting sites? Can attempts at mitigation by providing linkage between remaining habitat patches, and by habitat re-creation, have any hope of success? In less immediately threatened areas, such as the ESAs, what density and size of new habitat patches on the periphery of existing habitat mosaics can be colonised by the scarce species?

Within the agricultural landscape, continuing research is needed both to find suitable seed mixes for bumblebee forage and to investigate the value of alternative grassland management regimes for different bumblebee species. In particular, studies are needed that take into account the distribution of resources on a landscape scale, record both pollen and nectar foraging by sex, caste and species, and cover the succession of forage plants used through the full colony cycle. This is a very tall order, but anything less will miss crucial information.

Although there is now a good deal of information about the habitats chosen by most species for their nests, some important questions remain. It is, for example, generally believed that most, if not all, social bumblebee species make use of disused nests of small mammals. However, little is known about how constraining this is. Are some species able to construct their nests independently of the start given by a mammal nest: that is, are some 'nest builders', as distinct from 'nest adapters' (von Hagen & Aichhorn, 2003)? Further, are some species of bumblebees particularly associated with the nests of particular mammal species? If so, bumblebee conservation would need to be linked closely with conservation of the relevant species of small mammals.

Apart from a small number of common and well-studied species, there is little detailed knowledge of the processes of colony development, and how they vary from species to species. Some valuable information has come from discoveries of naturally established nests, but finding nests of most species is difficult and relies to a considerable extent on luck. Attempts to breed some of the scarce species in captivity might well give valuable insights for conservation, as well as adding to our understanding of such challenging aspects of bumblebee social life as queen dominance, internal conflict, and the timing and determination of the switch to production of males and daughter queens.

Finally, as we saw in Chapters 4 and 5, bumblebees are susceptible to a large number of parasites, parasitoids and predators. Relatively little quantitative research has been done in the UK on the relative incidence and impacts of these on populations of the different bumblebee species, although there are strong theoretical grounds for expecting the species composition of local bumblebee populations to be significantly affected (see Chapter 5).

It is one thing to have worked towards a better understanding of the bumblebees and their needs, quite another to have the conservation measures in place to put this understanding to practical effect. Valuable 'brownfield' sites are under threat as never before by pressures of development. Despite increasing concern about the health and environmental implications of industrialised agriculture, it remains the dominant system, only marginally moderated by the growing organic movement and by agri-environmental schemes. Conservation, including the conservation of our threatened bumblebees, is up against immensely powerful economic and political forces. Some provisional successes can be achieved by working through existing planning arrangements, and by drawing attention to the economic value of bumblebees as pollinators, but in the longer term more fundamental changes will be needed. The achievements of the Bumblebee Working Group, English Nature and some academic specialists in stimulating wider public awareness of and affection for bumblebees has been of great value. Strong and broadly based support is indispensable if powerful vested interests are to be restrained. But even this will not be enough. It seems probable that the conservation of bumblebees – all our fauna, and not just those singled out as currently at risk – will happen only as a by-product of deeper and broader changes to the way we as a society respect and value the rest of nature.

Species Considered Extinct in Britain

Subgenus *Cullumanobombus* Vogt
***Bombus cullumanus* (Kirby)**
The queen is black with a red tail, superficially similar to *B. lapidarius*. However, there are usually some yellow hairs mixed with the black on the collar and scutellum. The hind metatarsi appear black and shiny, in contrast to those of *B. lapidarius*, which are densely covered with short hairs and look yellowish. The workers are similar but smaller. The males are similar in appearance to *B. sylvarum* males, but the genitalia are distinctive (volsella long and curved, sagitta inwardly hooked).

This species was known from a few chalk grassland sites in the nineteenth century. It was subsequently rediscovered by Sladen in 1911, and then recorded from several other sites up to 1926. There have been no subsequent British records.

Like other grassland species, queens are late to emerge from hibernation and establish their nests. Most British records have been of males in August and September. *B. cullumanus* is reported to be in decline elsewhere in Europe.

Alford, 1975; Banaszak (Ed.) 1995; Sladen, 1912, Yarrow, 1954.

Subgenus *Rhodobombus* Dalla Torre
***Bombus pomorum* (Panzer)**
The queen is black with a red tail. The red is more extensive on the abdomen than in either *B. lapidarius* or *B. ruderarius*, and the black shades more gradually into red. The corbicular hairs are black. The head is more elongate than either *B. lapidarius* or *B. ruderarius*. The male has a similar colour pattern to males of *B. rupestris*, but the genital capsule is quite different.

The only known British specimens of *B. pomorum* are a female and three males collected on sand hills at Deal, Kent by Frederick Smith and his son. In different accounts Smith confusingly gives 1837, 1863 and 1857 as the year in which the three males were captured. It remains doubtful whether *B. pomorum* was ever an established species in Britain. It occurs in northern France and central Europe, but is apparently declining.

Alford, 1975; Amiet, 1996; Banaszak, 1995; Sladen, 1912.

Organisations and Useful Addresses

Amateur Entomologists' Society
P.O. Box 8774
London
SW7 5ZG

Bees, Wasps and Ants Recording Society
http://www.BWARS.com/
Membership Secretary
D. Baldock
Nightingales
Haslemere Road
Milford
Surrey
GU8 5BN

British Entomological and Natural History Society
http://www.BENHS.org.uk
Secretary
J. Muggleton
30 Penton Road
Staines
Middlesex
TW18 2LD

International Bee Research Association
http://www.cardiff.ac.uk
18 North Road
Cardiff
CF1 3DY

The Natural History Museum
Cromwell Road
London
SW7 5BD

Dr Paul Williams maintains a valuable and informative website devoted to bumblebees. The current address is:
http://www.nhm.ac.uk/research-curation/projects/bombus/
For bumblebee identification add: bumblebeeid.html

Oxford Bee Company Ltd.
Ark Business Centre
Gordon Road
Loughborough
LE11 1JP
info@oxbeeco.com

Vernacular and Scientific Names of Flowering Plants Mentioned in the Book

Apple,	*Malus domestica*
crab	*Malus sylvestris*
Aubretia	*Aubrieta deltoidea*
Barberry	*Berberis* species
Basil, wild	*Clinopodium vulgare*
Bay	*Laurus nobilis*
Bean, field	*Vicia faba*
Bellflower,	
clustered	*Campanula glomerata*
Bell heather	*Erica cinerea*
Bilberry	*Vaccinium myrtillus*
Bindweed, greater	*Calystegia silvatica*
Bird's-foot trefoil,	
common	*Lotus corniculatus*
greater	*Lotus pedunculatus*
narrow-leaved	*Lotus glaber*
Bistort	*Polygonum bistorta*
Bittersweet	*Solanum dulcamara*
Black horehound	*Ballota nigra*
Blackthorn	*Prunus spinosa*
Bladder senna	*Colutea arborescens*
Bleeding-heart	*Dicentra* species
Bluebell	*Hyacinthoides non-scripta*

Borage	*Borago officinalis*
Box	*Buxus* species
Bramble	*Rubus fruticosus agg.*
Bristly oxtongue	*Picris echioides*
Broad-leaved everlasting pea	*Lathyrus latifolius*
Broom	*Cytisus scoparius*
Burdock,	
greater	*Arctium lappa*
lesser	*Arctium minus*
Busy lizzie	*Impatiens* species
Buttercup, creeping	*Ranunculus repens*
Calamint, lesser	*Clinopodium calamintha*
Campion, red	*Silene dioica*
Catchfly, sticky	*Lychnis viscaria*
Catmint	*Nepeta* species
Celandine, lesser	*Ranunculus ficaria*
Cherry	*Prunus avium*
Chestnut, horse	*Aesculus hippocastanum*
Chickweed	*Stellaria media*
Chive	*Allium schoenoprasum*
Christmas rose	*Heleborus niger*
Cinquefoil,	
shrubby	*Potentilla fruticosa*
marsh	*Potentilla palustris*
creeping	*Potentilla reptans*
Clary	*Salvia* species
Clover,	
hare's-foot	*Trifolium arvense*
red	*Trifolium pratense*
sea	*Trifolium squamosum*
strawberry	*Trifolium fragiferum*
sulphur	*Trifolium ochroleucon*
white	*Trifolium repens*
zig-zag	*Trifolium medium*
Columbine	*Aquilegia* species
Comfrey	*Symphytum* species
Coneflower	*Echinacea purpurea*
Corncockle	*Agrostemma githago*

Cornflower,	*Centaurea cyanus*
perrennial	*Centaurea montana*
Cowberry	*Vaccinium vitis-idaea*
Cranesbill,	*Geranium* species
dove's-foot	*Geranium molle*
Cross-leaved heath	*Erica tetralix*
Daffodil	*Narcissus pseudonarcissus*
Daisy,	*Bellis perennis*
Michaelmas	*Aster × salignus*
ox-eye	*Leucanthemum vulgare*
Dandelion	*Taraxacum* species
Deadnettle,	
red	*Lamium purpureum*
white	*Lamium album*
Dewberry	*Rubus caesius*
Dogwood	*Cornus* species
Dyer's greenweed	*Genista tinctoria*
Elephant-ears	*Bergenia crassifolia*
Eryngo	*Eryngium* species
Eyebright	*Euphrasia* species
Figwort,	
common	*Scrophularia nodosa*
water	*Scropularia auriculata*
Flowering currant	*Ribes sanguineum*
Foxglove	*Digitalis purpurea*
Germander speedwell	*Veronica chamaedrys*
Globe-thistle	*Echinops exaltatus*
Goat's-rue	*Galega officinalis*
Goldenrod	*Solidago virgaurea*
Gorse,	
common	*Ulex europaeus*
western	*Ulex gallii*
Grape-hyacinth	*Muscari* species
Green alkanet	*Pentaglottis sempervirens*
Ground ivy	*Glechoma hederacea*

Harebell	*Campanula rotundifolia*
Hawkbit,	
autumn	*Leontodon autumnalis*
Heathers	Ericaceae
Hemp-nettle,	
bifid	*Galeopsis bifida*
large-flowered	*Galeopsis speciosa*
Himalayan (Indian) balsam	*Impatiens glandulifera*
Hoary plantain	*Plantago media*
Hogweed	*Heracleum sphondylium*
Hollyhock	*Alcea rosea*
Honeysuckle	*Lonicera periclymenum*
Hound's-tongue	*Cynoglossum officinale*
Iris,	
yellow	*Iris pseudacorus*
Ivy *Hedera helix*	
Japonica	*Chaenomeles speciosa*
Knapweed	
common	*Centaurea nigra*
greater	*Centaurea scabiosa*
Larkspur	*Consolida ajacis*
Lamb's ear	*Stachys byzantina*
Laurel, cherry	*Prunus laurocerasus*
Lavender	*Lavandula* species
Lilac	*Syringa vulgaris*
Ling	*Calluna vulgaris*
Loosestrife, purple	*Lythrum salicaria*
Lucerne	*Medicago sativa*
Lungwort	*Pulmonaria officinalis*
Lupin,	
tree-	*Lupinus arboreus*
Mallow	*Malva sylvestris*

Marigold,	
French	*Tagetes patula*
pot	*Calendula officinalis*
Marjoram	*Origanum vulgare*
Masterwort	*Peucedanum ostruthium*
Meadowsweet	*Filipendula ulmaria*
Melilot	*Melilotus* species
Mignonette	*Reseda* species
Mint, water	*Mentha aquatica*
Monk's-hood	*Aconitum napellus*
Myrtles	Myrtaceae
Nasturtium	*Tropaeolum majus*
Oil-seed rape	*Brassica napus*
Perennial sow-thistle	*Sonchus arvensis*
Periwinkle	*Vinca* species
Poppy,	
common	*Papaver rhoeas*
Prickly oxtongue	*Picris echioides*
Privet	*Ligustrum* species
Purple milk-vetch	*Astragalus danicus*
Rampion,	*Phyteuma* species
black	*Phyteuma nigrum*
Raspberry	*Rubus idaeus*
Red bartsia	*Odontites vernus*
Ragwort,	*Senecio* species
hoary	*Senecio erucifolius*
Restharrow,	
common	*Ononis repens*
spiny	*Ononis spinosa*
Rosemary	*Rosemarinus officinalis*
Sage,	*Phlomis* species
Russian	*Perovskia atriplicifolia*
Sainfoin	*Onobrychis viciifolia*
St John's wort	*Hypericum* species

Sallow	*Salix* species
Scabious,	
devil's-bit	*Succisa pratensis*
field	*Knautia arvensis*
small	*Scabiosa columbaria*
Sea aster	*Aster tripolium*
Sea holly	*Eryngium maritimum*
Self-heal	*Prunella vulgaris*
Silverweed	*Potentilla anserine*
Snowberry	*Symphoricarpos* species
Stinking hellebore	*Helleborus foetidus*
Stonecrop,	*Sedum* species
caucasian	*Sedum spurium*
Sycamore	*Acer pseudoplatanus*
Tamarisk	*Tamarix gallica*
Teasel	*Dipsacus fullonum*
Thistles,	
carline	*Carlina vulgaris*
cotton	*Onopordum acanthium*
creeping	*Cirsium arvense*
marsh	*Cirsium palustre*
musk	*Carduus nutans*
slender	*Carduus tenuiflorus*
sow-	*Sonchus* species
spear	*Cirsium vulgare*
Thyme	*Thymus* species
Toadflax,	
common	*Linaria vulgaris*
purple	*Linaria purpurea*
Toad lilly	*Tricyrtis* species
Vervain	*Verbena* species
Vetch,	
bush	*Vicia sepium*
common	*Vicia sativa*
fodder	*Vicia villosa*
horseshoe	*Hippocrepis comosa*

kidney	*Anthyllis vulneraria*
tufted	*Vicia cracca*
Vetchling,	
grass	*Lathyrus nissolia*
meadow	*Lathyrus pratensis*
Viper's bugloss	*Echium vulgare*
giant	*Echium pininana*
Wallflower	*Erysimum cheiri*
Willowherb,	
hairy	*Epilobium hirsutum*
rosebay	*Chamerion angustifolium*
Wood sage	*Teucrium scorodonia*
Woundwort,	
hedge	*Stachys sylvatica*
marsh	*Stachys palustris*
Yellow archangel	*Lamiastrum galeobdolon*
Yellow-rattle	*Rhinanthus minor*

Some Other Books on Bumblebees

Alford, D. V. (1975). *Bumblebees.* **London: Davis-Poynter.**
A classic work, with detailed information of the life history, behaviour and classification of bumblebees, with identification keys and brief accounts of the British species. Particularly valuable for its expert coverage of parasites and nest associates.

Alford, D. V. (1978). *The Life of the Bumblebee.* **London: Davis-Poynter.**
A brief but very informative introduction to the natural history of bumblebees for the non-specialist reader.

Benton, T. (2000). *The Bumblebees of Essex.* **Wimbish: Lopinga.**
Includes a brief account of the natural history of bumblebees, and detailed information about behaviour and distribution of all the Essex species, together with a key to most of the southern British species.

Edwards, M. & Jenner, M. (2005). *Field Guide to the Bumblebees of Great Britain & Ireland.* **Eastbourne: Ocelli.**
An excellent portable field guide covering bumblebee natural history, ecology and conservation, and with expert and up-to-date information on all British species. Includes colour photos of the British species and a unique colour-pattern guide to identification.

Free, J. B. & Butler, C. G. (1959). *New Naturalist Bumblebees.* **London: Collins.**
A landmark classic work by two pioneering researchers, focusing on the life

histories of bumblebees and their foraging behaviour. An inspiration for the present book.

Goulson, D. (2003). *Bumblebees: Behaviour and Ecology.* **Oxford: Oxford University**
A highly readable and informative account of the natural history and biology of bumblebees by a leading UK academic researcher, with a particularly useful chapter on conservation.

Macdonald, M. (2003). *Naturally Scottish: Bumblebees* **Perth: Scottish Natural Heritage.**
A colourful guide to Scottish bumblebees, with much information of more general relevance, and an emphasis on habitats and conservation, by a leading Scottish expert.

O'Toole, C. (2002). *Bumblebees.* **Banbury: Osmia.**
A readable and informative introduction to bumblebee natural history, with an emphasis on conservation and encouraging bumblebees in the garden.

Pinchen, B. J. (2004). *A Pocket Guide to the Bumblebees of Britain and Ireland.* **Lymington: Forficula.**
Genuinely as concise and portable as indicated by the title, this booklet includes succinct accounts of the appearance, distribution and natural history of the British species.

Prŷs-Jones, O. E. & Corbet, S. A. (1991). *Bumblebees.* **Cambridge: Cambridge University.**
An excellent, concise account of the behaviour and life history of bumblebees and their cuckoos, with an illustrated key to the British species, and encouragement for further research. Includes fine paintings of the British species by Tony Hopkins.

Sladen, F. W. L. (1912/ 1989). *The Humble-bee, its Life-history and How to Domesticate it.* **Originally published by Macmillan, and reprinted by Logaston. Currently out of print.**
The classic English-language book on bumblebees, by a pioneer of their study. Full of fascinating first-hand observations and a 'must' for all students of bumblebees.

Von Hagen, E. & Aichhorn, A. (2003). *Hummeln.* **Nottuln: Fauna Verlag.**
A superb field guide, covering central European species as well as species that also occur in Britain. Excellent colour illustrations make this a worthwhile purchase even for non-German readers.

Westrich, P. (1989). *Die Wildbienen Baden-Wurtemburgs.* **Stuttgart: Eugen Ulmer.**
Ostensibly a local study, this is an outstanding work on bees, including bumblebees. Fast becoming a classic work. Text in German.

References

Aigner, P. A. (2001). Optimality modelling and fitness trade-offs: when should plants become pollinator specialists? *Oikos* **95(1):** 177–84.

Alford, D. V. (1975). *Bumblebees.* London: Davis-Poynter.

Allander, K. & Schmid-Hempel, P. (2000). Immune defence reaction in bumble-bee workers after a previous challenge and parasitic coinfection. *Functional Ecology* **14:** 711–7.

Allen-Wardell, G., Bernhardt, P., Burquez, A., Buchman, S., Cane, J. Cox, P. A., Dalton, V., Feinsinger, P., Ingram, M., Inouye, D., Jones, C. E., Kennedy, K, Kevan, P., Koopowitz, H., Medellin, R., Medellin-Morales, S. & Nabhan, G. P. (1998). The potential consequences of pollinator declines on the conservation of biodiversity and stability of food crop yields. *Conservation Biology* **12:** 8–17.

Amiet, F. (1996). *Insecta Helvetica 12: Hymenoptera Apidae, 1. Tiel.* Neuchatel: Schweizerschen Entomologischen Gesellschaft.

Archer, M. E. (1998). Status and quality coding of species of aculeate Hymenoptera – Part 5: the social wasps and bees. *BWARS Newsletter.* Autumn: 13–14.

Aude, E., Tybirk, K., Michelsen, A., Ejrnaes, R., Hald, A. B. & Mark, S. (2004). Conservation value of the herbaceous vegetation in hedgerows – does organic farming make a difference? *Biological Conservation* **118:** 467–78.

Awram, W. J. (1970). *Flight Route Behaviour of Bumblebees.* Ph.D. dissertation: London: London University.

Awram, W. J. & Free, J. B. (1987a). Reactions of male bumblebees (*Bombus* spp.) to queens on their flight routes. *In:* Free, J. B., op. cit.

Awram, W. J. & Free, J. B. (1987b). Observations on the flight routes of bumblebee males and the development of a bioassay for site marking pheromones. *In:* Free, J.B., op. cit.

Bäckman, J-P. & Tiainen, J. (2002). Habitat quality in a Finnish farmland area for bumblebees (Hymenoptera: *Bombus* and *Psithyrus*). *Agriculture, Ecosystems and Environment* **89:** 53–68.

Baer, B., Morgan, E. D. & Schmid-Hempel, P. (2001). A non-specific fatty acid within the bumblebee mating plug prevents females from remating. *Proceedings of the National Academy of Science* **98**: 3926–8.

Baer, B. & Schmid-Hempel, P. (1999). Experimental variation in polyandry affects parasite loads and fitness in a bumblebee. *Nature* **397**: 151–4.

Baer, B. & Schmid-Hempel, P. (2000). The artificial insemination of bumblebee queens. *Insectes Sociaux* **47**: 183–7.

Baer, B. & Schmid-Hempel, P. (2001). Unexpected consequences of polyandry for parasitism and fitness in the bumble bee *Bombus terrestris*. *Evolution* **55(8)**: 1639–43.

Baker, D. B. (1996). On a collection of *Bombus* and *Psithyrus* principally from Sutherland, with notes on the nomenclatures or status of three species (Hymenoptera, Apoidea). *British Journal of Entomology and Natural History* **9**: 7–19.

Banaszak, J. (Ed.) (1995). *Changes in Fauna of Wild Bees in Europe*. Bydgoszcz: Pedagogical University.

Beattie, A. J. (1976). Plant dispersal, pollination and gene flow in *Viola*. *Oecologia* **25**: 291–300.

Beirne, B. P. (1952). *British Pyralid and Plume Moths*. London & New York: Frederick Warne.

Bellamy, P. A., Shore, R. F., Ardeshir, D., Treweek, J. R. & Sparks, T. H. (2000). Road verges as habitat for small mammals in Britain. *Mammal Review* **30**: 131–9.

Benton, T. (2000). *The Bumblebees of Essex*. Saffron Walden: Lopinga.

Bergman, P., Bergsrtröm, G. & Appelgren, M. (1996). Labial gland marking secretion in males of two Scandinavian cuckoo bumblebees (genus *Psithyrus*). *Chemoecology* **7**: 140–5.

Bergström, G. & Svensson, B. G. (1973). Characteristic marking secretions of the forms *lapponicus* and *scandinavicus* of *Bombus lapponicus* Fabr. (Hymenoptera, Apidae). *Chemica Scripta* **4**: 231–8.

Bergström, B. G., Svensson, M., Appelgren, M. & Groth, I. (1981). Complexity of bumble bee marking pheromones: biochemical, ecological and systematical interpretations. *In*: Howse P.E. & Clement J.-L., *op. cit.*: 175–83.

Bertsch, A. (1997). Abgrenzung der hummelarten *Bombus cryptarum* und *B. lucorum* mittels mannlicher labialdrusen-secrete und morphologischer merkmale (Hymenoptera, Apidae). *Entomologia Generalis* **22**: 129–45.

Best, L. S. & Bierzychudek, P. (1982). Pollinator foraging on foxglove (*Digitalis purpurea*): a test of a new model. *Evolution* **36**: 70–9.

Biernaski, J. M., Cartar, R. V. & Hurley, T. A. (2002). Risk-averse inflorescence departure in humming-birds and bumblebees: could plants benefit from variable nectar volumes? *Oikos* **98**: 98–104.

Bignel, E., Jones, G. & McCracken, D. (2001). Comment: future directions in agriculture policy and nature conservation. *British Wildlife* **13(1)**: 16–20.

Billen, J. & Morgan, E. D. (1998). Pheromone communication in social insects: sources and secretions. *In*: Vander Meer, R. K. *et al.*, *op. cit.*

Bloch, G. (1999). Regulation of queen-worker conflict in bumble-bee (*Bombus terrestris*) colonies. *Proceedings of the Royal Society of London B* **266**: 2465–9.

Bloch, G. & Hefetz, A. (1999a). Regulation of reproduction by dominant workers in bumblebee (*Bombus terrestris*) queenright colonies. *Behavioral Ecology and Sociobiology* **45**: 125–35.

Bloch, G. & Hefetz, A. (1999b). Re-evaluation of the role of mandibular glands in regulation of reproduction in bumblebee colonies. *Journal of Chemical Ecology* **25(4)**: 881–96.

Bloch, G., Borst, D. W., Huang, Z.-Y., Robinson, G. E. & Hefetz, A. (1996). Effects of social conditions on juvenile Hormone mediated reproductive development in *Bombus terrestris* workers. *Physiological Entomology* **21**: 257–67.

Blum, M. S. (1981). Sex pheromones in social insects: chemotaxonomic potential. *In*: Howse P. E. & Clement J.-L., *op. cit.*: 163–83.

Blunden, J. & Curry, N. (1985). *The Changing Countryside*. London: Croom Helm.

Blunden, J. & Curry, N. (1988). *A Future for our Countryside*. Oxford: Blackwell.

Boatman, N. & Stoate, C. (1999). Arable farming and wildlife – can they co-exist? *British Wildlife* **10(4)**: 260–7.

Borlotti, L., Duchateau, M. J. & Sbrenna, G. (2001). Effect of juvenile hormone on caste determination and colony processes in the bumblebee *Bombus terrestris*. *Entomologia Experimentalis et Applicata* **101**: 143–58.

Bourke, A. F. G. (1994). Worker matricide in social bees and wasps. *Journal of Theoretical Biology* **167**: 283–92.

Bourke, A. F. G. (2001). Social insects and selfish genes. *Biologist* **48(5)**: 205–8.

Bourke, A. F. G. & Ratnieks, F. L. W. (2001). Kin-selected conflict in the bumble-bee *Bombus terrestris* (Hymenoptera: Apidae). *Proceedings of the Royal Society of London B* **268**: 347–55.

Boyd, J. (1999). Bombus sylvarum *Survey 1999*. W.E.B.S. Report.

Boyd, J. & Boyd J. (2000). Bombus sylvarum *Survey 2000*. W.E.B.S. Report.

Boyd, J. & Boyd, J. (2001*a*). Bombus sylvarum *Survey 2001*. W.E.B.S. Report.

Boyd, J. & Boyd, J. (2001*b*). Bombus muscorum *Report 2001*. W.E.B.S. Report.

Boyd, J. & Boyd, J. (2002). *Somerset Bumblebees Report 2002*. W.E.B.S. Report.

Brian, A. D. (1951). The pollen collected by bumble-bees. *Journal of Animal Ecology* **20**: 191–4.

Brian, A. D. (1952). Division of labour and foraging in *Bombus agrorum* Fabricius. *Journal of Animal Ecology* **21**: 223–40.

Brian, M. V. (1980). Social control over sex and caste in bees, wasps and ants. *Biological Reviews* **55**: 379–415.

Bronstein, J. L. (1995). The plant-pollinator landscape. *In*: Hansson, L. *et al.*, *op. cit.*

Brown, M. J. F., Loosli, R. & Schmid-Hempel, P. (2000). Condition-dependent expression of virulence in a trypanosome infecting bumblebees. *Oikos* **91**: 421–7.

Buchmann, S. L. & Nabhan, G. P. (1996). *The Forgotten Pollinators*. Washington D. C. & Covelo, California: Island & Shearwater.

Buckingham, H., Chapman, J. & Newman, R. (1999). The future for hay meadows in the Peak District National Park. *British Wildlife* **10(5)**: 311–8.

Cartar, R. V. (1992). Adjustment of foraging effort and task switching in energy manipulated wild bumblebee colonies. *Animal Behaviour* **44**: 75–87.

Cartar, R. V. & Dill, L. M. (1991). Costs of energy shortfall for bumble bee colonies: predation, social parasitism, and brood development. *The Canadian Entomologist* **123(2)**: 283–93.

Carvell, C. (2000). *Studies of the distribution and habitat requirements of* Bombus sylvarum *(the shrill carder bee) and other bumblebees at Castlemartin Range, Pembrokeshire and Kenfig National Nature Reserve, Glamorgan and surrounding areas. Unpublished Report.*

Carvell, C. (2002). Habitat use and conservation of bumblebees (*Bombus* spp.) under different grassland management regimes. *Biological Conservation* **103**: 33–49.

Carvell, C., Meek, W. R., Pywell, R. F., Nowakowski, M. & Westrich, P. (2003). *Providing Nectar and Pollen sources for Bumblebees on Farmland*. Report to English

Nature. Monks Wood: Centre for Ecology and Hydrology.

Cederberg, B. (1977). Evidence for trail marking in Bombus terrestris workers (Hymenoptera, Apidae). Zoon 5: 143–6.

Cederberg, B. (1983). The role of trail pheromones in host selection by Psithyrus rupestris (Hymenoptera, Apidae). Annales Entomologici Fennici 49(1): 11–16.

Cederberg, B., Svensson, B. G., Bergstrøm, G., Appelgren, M. & Groth, I. (1984). Male marking pheromones in North European cuckoo bumble bees, Psithyrus (Hymenoptera, Apidae). Nova Acta Regiae Societatis Scientiarum Upsaliensis. V: C, 3: 161–6.

Cham, S. (2004). Dragonfly predation by European Hornets Vespa crabro (L.) (Hymenoptera, Vespidae). Journal of the British Dragonfly Society 20(1): 1–3.

Chapman, R. E. (2004). Conservation and Foraging Ecology of Bumble Bees in Urban Environments. London: Ph. D. Thesis.

Chapman, R. E. & Bourke, A. F. G. (2001). The influence of sociality on the conservation biology of social insects. Ecological Letters 4: 650–62.

Chapman, R. E., Wang, J. & Bourke, A. F. G. (2003). Genetic analysis of spatial foraging patterns and resource sharing in bumble bee pollinators. Molecular Ecology 12: 2801–8.

Charnov, E. (1976). Optimal foraging: the marginal value theorem. Theoretical Population Biology 9: 129–36.

Chittka, L., Shmida, A., Troje, N. & Menzel, R. (1994). Ultraviolet as a component of flower reflections, and the colour perception of Hymenoptera. Vision Research 34(11): 1489–1508.

Chittka, L., Spaethe, J., Schmidt, A. & Hickelsberger, A. (2001). Adaptation, constraint, and chance in the evolution of flower color and pollinator color

vision. In: Chittka, L. & Thomson, J. D., op. cit.

Chittka, L. & Thomson, J. D. (1997). Sensory-motor learning and its relevance for task specialization in bumble bees. Behavioral Ecology and Sociobiology 41: 385–98.

Chittka, L. & Thomson, J. D. (Eds) (2001). Cognitive Ecology of Pollination: Animal Behaviour and Floral Evolution. Cambridge: Cambridge University.

Chittka, L., Thomson, J. D. & Waser, N. M. (1999). Flower constancy, insect psychology, and plant evolution. Naturwissenschaften 86: 361–77.

Chittka, L. & Waser, N. M. (1997). Why red flowers are not invisible to bees. Israel Journal of Plant Sciences 45(2–3): 169–83.

Clements, D. K. (1997). The enemy within: conopid flies as parasitoids of bees and wasps in Britain. British Wildlife 8(5): 310–15.

Cnaani, J., Borst, D. W., Huang, Z.-Y., Robinson, G. E. & Hefetz, A. (1997). Caste determination in Bombus terrestris: differences in development rates of JH biosynthesis between queen and worker larvae. Journal of Insect Physiology 43(4): 373–81.

Cnaani, J., Robinson, G. E., Bloch, G., Borst, D. & Hefetz, A. (2000). The effect of queen-worker conflict on caste determination in the bumblebee Bombus terrestris. Behavioral Ecology and Sociobiology 47: 346–52.

Colyer, C. N. & Hammond, C. O. (1968). Flies of the British Isles. London: Frederick Warne.

Comba, L. Corbet, S. A., Barron, A., Bird, A., Collinge, S., Miyazaki, N. & Powell, M. (1999a). Garden flowers: insect visits and the floral reward of horticulturally modified variants. Annals of Botany 83: 73–86.

Comba, L., Corbet, S. A., Hunt, L. &

Warren, B. (1999b). Flowers, nectar and insect visits: evaluating British plant species for pollinator-friendly gardens. *Annals of Botany* **83:** 369–83.

Conway, G. R. & Pretty, J. N. (1991). *Unwelcome Harvest: Agriculture and Pollution.* London: Earthscan.

Coppock, J. T. (1971). *An Agricultural Geography of Great Britain.* London: Bell.

Corbet, S. A. (1978). Bee visits and the nectar of *Echium vulgare* L. and *Sinapis alba* L. *Ecological Entomology* **3:** 25–37.

Corbet, S. A. (1991). Applied pollination ecology. *Trends in Ecology and Evolution* **6(1):** 3–4.

Corbet, S. A. (1995). Insects, plants and succession: advantages of long-term set-aside. *Agriculture, Ecosystems and Environment* **53:** 201–17.

Corbet, S. A. (1996). Which bees do plants need? Ch. 8 in Matheson, A. *et al.*, op. cit.

Corbet, S. A. (1997). Role of pollinators in species preservation, conservation, ecosystem stability and genetic diversity. *Acta Horticulturae* **437:** 219–29.

Corbet, S. A. (1998). Fruit and seed production in relation to pollination and resources in bluebell, *Hyacinthoides non-scripta. Oecologia* **114:** 349–60.

Corbet, S. A. (2000). Conserving compartments in pollination webs. *Conservation Biology* **14(5):** 1229–31.

Corbet, S. A., Bee, J., Dasmahapatra, K., Gale, S., Gorringe, E., La Ferla, B., Moorhouse, T., Trevail, A., van Bergen, Y. & Vorontsova, M. (2001). Native or exotic? Double or single? Evaluating plants for pollinator-friendly gardens. *Annals of Botany* **87:** 219–32.

Corbet, S. A., Cuthill, I., Fallows, M., Harrison, T, & Hartley, G. (1981). Why do nectar-foraging bees and wasps work upwards on inflorescences? *Oecologia* **51:** 79–83.

Corbet, S. A., Fussell, M., Ake, R., Fraser, A., Gunson, C., Savage, A. & Smith, K. (1993). Temperature and the pollinating behaviour of social bees. *Ecological Entomology* **18:** 17–30.

Corbet, S. A., Kerslake, C. J. C., Brown, D. & Morland, N. E. (1984). Can bees select nectar-rich flowers in a patch? *Journal of Apidological Research* **23:** 234–42.

Corbet, S. A. & Morris, R. J. (1999). Mites on bumblebees and bluebells. *The Entomologist's Monthly Magazine* **135:** 77–83.

Corbet, S. A., Saville, N. M., Fussell, M., Prŷs-Jones, O. E. & Unwin, D. M. (1995). The competition box: a graphical aid to forecasting pollinator performance. *Journal of Applied Ecology* **32:** 707–19.

Corbet, S. A. & Tiley C. F. (2000). Insect visitors to the flowers of bluebell (*Hyacinthoides non-scripta*). *The Entomologist's Monthly Magazine* **136:** 133–41.

Corbet, S., Unwin, D. M. & Prŷs-Jones, O. (1979). Humidity, nectar and insect visits to flowers, with special reference to *Crataegus, Tilia* and *Echium. Ecological Entomology* **4:** 9–22.

Corbet, S. A., Williams, I. H. & Osborne, J. L. (1991). Bees and the pollination of crops and wild flowers in the European Community. *Bee World.* **72:** 47–51.

Crespi, B. J. (1992). Cannibalism and trophic eggs in subsocial and eusocial insects. *In:* Elgar, M. & Crespi, B. J. (Eds) *Cannibalism: Ecology and Evolution among Diverse Taxa.* Oxford: Oxford University.

Cresswell, J. E. (1997). Spatial heterogeneity, pollinator behaviour and pollinator-mediated gene-flow. *Oikos* **78:** 546–56.

Cresswell, J. E., Osborne J. L. & Goulson, D. (2000). An economic model of the limits to foraging range in central place foragers with numerical solutions for bumblebees. *Ecological Entomology* **25:** 249–55.

Critchley, C. N. R., Burke, M. J. W. &
Stevens, D. P. (2003). Conservation of
lowland semi-natural grasslands in the UK:
a review of botanical monitoring results
from agri-environmental schemes.
Biological Conservation **115**: 263–78.

Croxton, P. J., Carvell, C., Mountford, J. O.
& Sparks, T. H. (2002). A comparison of
green lanes and field margins as
bumblebee habitat in an arable landscape.
Biological Conservation **107**: 365–74.

Crozier, R. H. & Page, R. E. (1985). On being
the right size: male contributions and
multiple mating in social Hymenoptera.
Behavioral Ecology and Sociobiology **18**:
105–16.

Crozier, R. H. & Pamilo, P. (1996). *Evolution
of Social Insect Colonies: Sex Allocation and
Kin Selection.* Oxford: Oxford University.

Cumber, R. A. (1949). Humble-bee
parasites and commensals found within a
thirty mile radius of London. *Proceedings
of the Royal Society of London, A.*
24: 119–27.

Cumber, R. A. (1953). Some aspects of the
biology and ecology of humble-bees
bearing upon the yields of red clover seed
in New Zealand. *New Zealand Journal of
Science and Technology B.* **34**: 227–40.

Dafni, A. (1992). *Pollination Ecology: A Practical
Approach.* Oxford: Oxford University.

Darvill, B., Knight, M. E. & Goulson, D.
(2004). Use of genetic markers to quantify
bumblebee foraging range and nest
density. *Oikos* **107**: 471–8.

Darwin, C. (1854, 1965). On the flight paths
of male humble bees (translated from
German by R. B. Freeman). *The Works of
Charles Darwin: An Annotated Bibliographical
Handlist.* Appendix. London: Dawson's of
Pall Mall.

Day, M. C. (1979). The species of
Hymenoptera described by Linnaeus in
the genera *Sphex, Vespa, Apis* and *Mutilla.*

Biological Journal of the Linnaean Society
12: 45–84.

Department of the Environment (1994).
Biodiversity: The UK Action Plan. London:
HMSO.

Dicks, L. V., Corbet, S. A. & Pywell, R. F.
(2002). Compartmentalisation in plant-
insect flower visitor webs. *Journal of Animal
Ecology* **71**: 32–43.

Disney, R. L. H. (2002). Phoridae (Dipt.)
reared from dead bumblebees (Hym.,
Apid.). *The Entomologist's Monthly Magazine*
138: 138.

Doums, C. & Schmid-Hempel, P. (2000).
Immunocompetence in workers of a social
insect, *Bombus terrestris* L., in relation to
foraging activity and parasitic infection.
Canadian Journal of Zoology **78**:1060–6.

Dornhaus, A. & Chittka, L. (2001). Food alert
in bumblebees (*Bombus terrestris*): possible
mechanisms and evolutionary
implications. *Behavioral Ecology and
Sociobiology* **50**: 570–6.

Dramstad, W. E. (1996). Do bumblebees
(Hymenoptera: Apidae) really forage close
to their nests? *Journal of Insect Behaviour*
9(2): 163–82.

Dramstad, W. & Fry, G. (1995). Foraging
activity of bumblebees (*Bombus*) in relation
to flower resources in arable land.
Agriculture, Ecosystems and Environment
53: 123–35.

Duchateau, M. J. & Velthuis, H. H. W.
(1988). Development and reproductive
strategies in *Bombus terrestris* colonies.
Behaviour **107**: 186–207.

Duchateau, M. J., Velthuis, H. H. W. &
Boomsma, J. J. (2004). Sex ratio variation in
the bumble bee *Bombus terrestris. Behavioral
Ecology* **15**: 71–82.

Dukas, R. (1995). Transfer and interference
learning in bumble bees. *Animal Behaviour*
49: 1481–90.

Dukas, R. & Edelstein-Keshet, L. (1998).

The spatial distribution of colonial food provisioners. *Journal of Theoretical Biology* **190:** 121–34.

Durrer, S. & Schmid-Hempel, P. (1994). Shared use of flowers leads to horizontal pathogen transmission. *Proceedings of the Royal Society of London, B.* **258:** 299–302.

Durrer, S. & Schmid-Hempel, P. (1995). Parasites and the regional distribution of bumblebee species. *Ecography* **18:** 114–22.

Eder, J. & Rembold, H. (Eds) (1987). *Chemistry and Biology of Social Insects.* Munchen: Verlag J. Peterny.

Edwards, M. (1991). Hibernating *B. terrestris* queens. *The Entomologist's Monthly Magazine* **127:** 108.

Edwards, M. (1997). *Survey of* Bombus distinguendus *Morawitz (Hymenoptera: Apidae) on the Outer Hebrides, August 1997.* Unpublished Report.

Edwards, M. (1998). *UK BAP Bumblebee Working Group Report, 1998.*

Edwards, M. (1999). *UK BAP Bumblebee Working Group Report, 1999.*

Edwards, M. (2000a). Species profile: *Bombus humilis* Illiger, 1806 [Apidae, Apinae]. *BWARS Newsletter*, Autumn: 23–4.

Edwards, M. (2000b). *UK BAP Bumblebee Working Group Report, 2000.*

Edwards, M. (2001a). *UK BAP Bumblebee Working Group Report, 2001.*

Edwards, M. (2001b). Species profile of *Bombus distinguendus* Morawitz, F. 1869 [Apidae: Apinae]. *In*: Edwards, R. & Telfer, M. G. (Eds), *op. cit.*

Edwards, M. (2002). *UK BAP Bumblebee Working Group Report, 2002.*

Edwards, M. (2004). Separation of *Bombus hortorum* and *Bombus ruderatus*. *BWARS Newsletter*. Autumn: 27–9.

Edwards, M. & Jenner, M. (2004) *Field Guide to the Bumblebees of Great Britain and Ireland.* Eastbourne: Ocelli.

Edwards, M. & Philp, E. G. (1999). Species

Profile: *Bombus ruderarius* (Muller, 1776) [Apidae: Apinae]. *BWARS Newsletter.* Autumn: 20.

Edwards, M. & Williams, P. H. (2004). Where have all the bumblebees gone, and could they ever return? *British Wildlife* **15(5):** 305–12.

Edwards, R. (Ed.) (1997). *Provisional Atlas of the Aculeate Hymenoptera of Britain and Ireland Pt. 1.* Bees, Wasps and Ants Recording Society. Huntingdon: Biological Records Centre.

Edwards, R. (Ed.) (1998). *Provisional Atlas of the Aculeate Hymenoptera of Britain and Ireland. Pt. 2.* Bees, Wasps and Ants Recording Society. Huntingdon: Biological Records Centre.

Edwards, R. & Telfer, M. G. (Eds) (2001). *Provisional Atlas of the Aculeate Hymenoptera of Britain and Ireland. Part 3.* Huntingdon: Biological Records Centre.

Edwards, R. & Telfer, M. G. (Eds) (2002). *Provisional Atlas of the Aculeate Hymentoptera of Britain and Ireland. Part 4.* Huntingdon: Biological Records Centre.

Eldredge, N. (1995). *Reinventing Darwin.* London: Weidenfeld & Nicolson.

Ellis, J. S., Knight, M. E. & Goulson , D. (2005) Delineating species for conservation using mitochondrial sequence data: the taxonomic status of two problematic *Bombus* species (Hymenoptera: Apidae). *Journal of Insect Conservation* **9:** 75–83.

Else, G. R. (1995). Wildlife Reports: Bees and Wasps. *British Wildlife* **6(4):** 260.

Else, G. R. (2000). Observations on *Bombus soroeensis* (F.) *B. humilis* Illiger and *B. muscorum* (L.) on Salisbury Plain, Wiltshire in 1998–2000. *BWARS Newsletter* Autumn: 5–6.

Else, G. R. (2002). An introduction to the bumblebees of the Orkney islands. *BWARS Newsletter.* Autumn: 15–17.

Else, G. R. (2003). An introduction to the

bumblebees of the Shetland islands. *BWARS Newsletter*. Autumn: 10–12.

Engels, W. (Ed.) (1990). *Social Insects: an Evolutionary Approach to Castes and Reproduction*. Berlin, etc.: Springer-Verlag.

English Nature (2003). *England's Best Wildlife and Geological Sites: The Condition of Sites of Special Scientific Interest in England in 2003*. Peterborough: EN.

Estoup, A., Scholl, A., Pouvreau, A. & Solignac, M. (1995). Monandry and polyandry in bumble bees (Hymenoptera; Bombinae) as evidenced by highly variable microsatellites. *Molecular Ecology* **4**: 84–93.

Everett, S. (2004). The quality of nature in England. *British Wildlife* **15**(3): 168–73.

Faegri, K & van der Pijl, L. (1979). *The Principles of Pollination Ecology*. Oxford etc.: Pergamon.

Falk, S. (1991). *A Review of the Scarce and Threatened Bees, Wasps and Ants of Britain*. Research and Survey in Nature Conservation 35. Peterborough: N.C.C.

Falk, S. (2004). Some notes on the separation of *Bombus ruderatus* (Fab.) from *B. hortorum* (L.) and some possible ecological distinctions between the two species. *BWARS Newsletter*. Autumn: 24–6.

Ferry, C. & Corbet, S. A. (1996). Water collection by bumble bees. *Journal of Apicultural Research* **35**(3/4): 120–2.

Fisher, R. M. (1983a). Recognition of host nest odour by the bumblebee social parasite *Psithyrus ashtoni* (Hymenoptera: Apidae). *New York Entomological Society* **91**(4): 503–7.

Fisher, R. M. (1983b). Behavioural interactions between a social parasite, *Psithyrus citrinus* (Hymenoptera: Apidae), and its bumble bee hosts. *Proceedings of the Entomological Society of Ontario* **114**: 55–60.

Fisher, R. M. (1985). Evolution and host-specificity: dichotomous invasion success of *Psithyrus citrinus* (Hymenoptera: Apidae),

a bumblebee social parasite in colonies of its two hosts. *Canadian Journal of Zoology* **63**: 977–81.

Fisher, R. M. (1987). Social parasitism in bumble bees (Hymenoptera: Apidae): hosts often succeed in reproducing. In: Eder, J. & Rembold, H. (Eds) *Chemistry and Biology of Social Insects*. Munchen: Verlag J. Peperny.

Fisher, R. M. (1988). Observation on the behaviours of three European bumble bee species (*Psithyrus*). *Insectes Sociaux* **35**(4): 341–54.

Fisher, R. M. & Sampson, B. J. (1992). Morphological specialisations of the bumble bee social parasite *Psithyrus ashtoni* (Cresson) (Hymenoptera: Apidae). *The Canadian Entomologist* **124**(1): 69–77.

Fonseca, C. R. & Ganade, G. (1996). Asymmetries, compartments and null interactions in an Amazonian ant-plant community. *Journal of Animal Ecology* **65**: 339–47.

Forster Johnson, A. P. (2002). Bird predation on bumblebee queens. *Entomologist's Monthly Magazine* **138**: 138.

Frankum, M. (2003). *Foraging Behaviour of Bumblebees and Cuckoo Bumblebees in a Suburban Garden in Knighton, Leicester 1998–2001*. Leicestershire Entomological Society.

Fraser, F. C. (1947). *Bombus jonellus* (Kirby) (Hym.) nesting in a discarded bird's nest. *The Entomologist's Monthly Magazine* **83**: 280.

Free, J. B. (1955a). The division of labour within bumblebee colonies. *Insectes Sociaux* **2**: 195–212.

Free, J. B. (1955b). The collection of food by bumblebees. *Insectes Sociaux* **2**: 303–11.

Free, J. B. (1971). Stimuli eliciting mating behaviour of bumble-bee (*Bombus pratorum* L.) males. *Behaviour* 40:55–61.

Free, J. B. (1987). *Pheromones of Social Bees*. London: Chapman & Hall.

Free, J. B. (1993). *Insect Pollination of Crops.* London: Academic.

Free, J. B. & Butler, C. G. (1959). *Bumblebees.* New Naturalist. London: Collins.

Free, J. B. & Williams, I. H. (1976). Pollination as a factor limiting the yield of field bean (*Vicia faba* L.) *Journal of Agricultural Science* **87:** 395–9.

Frehn, E. & Schwammberger, K.-H. (2001). Social parasitism of *Psithyrus vestalis* in free-foraging colonies of *Bombus terrestris* (Hymenoptera: Apidae). *Entomologia Generalis* **25:** 103–5.

Fuller, R. M. (1987). The changing extent and conservation interest of lowland grasslands in England and Wales: a review of grassland surveys 1930–84. *Biological Conservation* **40:** 281–300.

Fussell, M. & Corbet, S. A. (1991). Forage for bumblebees and honey bees in farmland: a case study. *Journal of Apicultural Research.* **30(2):** 87–97.

Fussell, M. & Corbet, S. A. (1992*a*). The nesting places of some British bumblebees. *Journal of Apicultural Research* **30(2):** 87–97.

Fussell, M. & Corbet, S. A. (1992*b*). Flower usage by bumblebees: a basis for plant management. *Journal of Applied Ecology* **29:** 451–65.

Fussell, M. & Corbet, S. A. (1992*c*). Observations on the patrolling behaviour of male bumblebees (Hym.). *The Entomologist's Monthly Magazine* **128:** 229–35.

Fussell, M. & Corbet, S. A. (1993). Bumblebee (Hym., Apidae) forage plants in the United Kingdom. *The Entomologist's Monthly Magazine* **129:** 1–14.

Gegear, R. J. & Laverty, T. M. (2001). The effect of variation among floral traits on the flower constancy of pollinators. *In:* Chittka L. & Thomson, J. D., op. cit.

Gibbons, B. & Gibbons, L. (1988). *Creating a Wildlife Garden.* London: Hamlyn.

Gibson, C. (2004) Canvey Wick – a model of sustainable development? *Talk of the Thames.* Autumn/ Winter.

Gibson, C. & Gibson, M. (2001). A bumblebee restaurant. *Essex Field Club Newsletter* **34:** 10.

Good, R. (2000). The value of gardening for wildlife – what contribution does it make to conservation? *British Wildlife* **12(2):** 77–84.

Goodman, L. (2003). *Form and Function in the Honey Bee.* Cardiff: IBRA.

Goodwin, B. (1994). *How the Leopard Changed its Spots.* London: Weidenfeld & Nicolson.

Gould, S. J. (1990). *Wonderful Life.* London etc.: Hutchinson Radius.

Gould, S. J. & Lewontin, R. C. (1979). The spandrels of San Marco and the Panglossian paradigm: a critique of the adaptationist programme. *Proceedings of the Royal Society* **205:** 581–98.

Goulson, D. (1999). Foraging strategies of insects for gathering nectar and pollen, and implications for plant ecology and evolution. *Perspectives in Pant Ecology, Evolution and Systematics* **2:** 185–209.

Goulson, D. (2000*a*). Are insects flower constant because they use search images to find flowers? *Oikos* **88:** 547–52.

Goulson, D. (2000*b*). Why do bumblebees visit proportionately fewer flowers in large patches? *Oikos* **91:** 485–92.

Goulson, D. (2003). *Bumblebees: Behaviour and Ecology.* Oxford: Oxford University.

Goulson, D., Chapman, J. W. & Hughes, W. O. H. (2001). Discrimination of unrewarding flowers by bees; direct detection of rewards and use of repellent scent marks. *Journal of Insect Behaviour* **14(5):** 669–78.

Goulson, D. & Darvill, B. (2003). Distribution and floral preferences of the rare bumblebees *Bombus humilis* and

B. soroeensis (Hymenoptera: Apidae) on Salisbury Plain. *British Journal of Entomology and Natural History* **16(2)**: 95–102.

Goulson, D. & Darvill, B. (2004). Niche overlap and dietary breadth in bumblebees; are rare species more specialized in their choice of flowers? *Apidologie* **35**: 55–63.

Goulson, D. & Hanley, M. E. (2004). Distribution and forage use of exotic bumblebees in South Island, New Zealand. *New Zealand Journal of Ecology* **28(2)**: 225–32.

Goulson, D., Hanley, M. E., Darvill, B., Ellis, J. S. & Knight, M. E. (2005). Causes of rarity in bumblebees. *Biological Conservation* **122**: 1–8.

Goulson, D., Hawson, S. A. & Stout, J. C. (1998). Foraging bumblebees avoid flowers already visited by conspecifics or by other bumblebee species. *Animal Behaviour* **55**: 199–206.

Goulson, D., Hughes, W. O. H., Derwent, L. C. & Stout, J. C. (2002). Colony growth of the bumblebee, *Bombus terrestris*, in improved and conventional agricultural and suburban habitats. *Oecologia* **130**: 267–73.

Goulson, D. & Stout, J. C. (2001). Homing ability of the bumblebee *Bombus terrestris*. *Apidologie* **32**: 105–12.

Goulson, D., Stout, J. C., Langley, J. & Hughes, W. O. (2000). The identity and function of scent marks deposited by foraging bumblebees. *Journal of Chemical Ecology* **26**: 2897–911.

Griffiths, D. & Robberts, E. J. (1996). Bumblebees as pollinators of glasshouse crops. *In*: Matheson, A., *op. cit.*

Hall, S. J. & Raffaelli, D. G. (1993). Food-webs: theory and reality. *Advances in Ecological Research* **24**: 187–239.

Hamilton, W. D. (1964). The genetical evolution of social behaviour, I, II. *Journal of Theoretical Biology* **7**: 1–52.

Hansson, L., Fahrig, L. & Merriam, G. (Eds) (1995). *Mosaic Landscapes and Ecological Processes*. London etc.: Chapman & Hall.

Harder, L. D. (1983). Flower handling efficiency of bumble bees: morphological aspects of probing time. *Oecologia* **57**: 274–80.

Harder, L. D., Williams, N. M., Jordan, C. Y. & Nelson, W. A. (2001). The effects of floral design and display on pollinator economics and pollen dispersal. *In*: Chittka, L. & Thomson, J. D., *op. cit.*

Hartfelder, K., Cnaani, J. & Hefetz, A. (2000). Caste-specific differences in ecdysteroid titers in early larval stages of the bumblebee *Bombus terrestris*. *Journal of Insect Physiology* **46**: 1433–9.

Harvey, G. (1997). *The Killing of the Countryside*. London: Jonathan Cape.

Harvey, P. R. (1999*a*). South Essex and the East Thames Corridor. *Essex Naturalist (New Series)* **16**: 41–5.

Harvey, P. R. (1999*b*). A report on the status of the shrill carder bee *Bombus sylvarum* in Essex. *Essex Naturalist (New Series)* **16**: 79–82.

Harvey, P. R. (2000). The East Thames Corridor: a nationally important invertebrate fauna under threat. *British Wildlife* **12(2)**: 91–8.

Haskins, L. (2000). Heathlands in an urban setting – effects of urban development on heathlands of south-east Dorset. *British Wildlife* **11(4)**: 229–37.

Hefetz, A. (1990). Individual badges and specific messages in multicomponent pheromones of bees (Hymenoptera, Apidae). *Entomologia Generalis* **15**: 103–13.

Hefetz, A., Taghizadeh, T. & Francke, W. (1996). The exocrinology of the queen bumble bee *Bombus terrestris* (Hymenoptera: Apidae, Bombini). *Zeitschrift für Naturforschung* **51**: 409–22.

Hefetz, A, Tengo, J., Lubke, G. & Francke, W. (1993). Inter-colonial and intra-colonial variation in dufour's gland secretion in the bumble bee species *Bombus hypnorum* (Hymenoptera: Apidae). *In*: Weise, K. *et al., op. cit.*

Heinrich, B. (1975). Energetics of pollination. *Annual Review of Ecology and Systematics* **6:** 139–70.

Heinrich, B. (1976). Foraging specialisations of individual bumblebees. *Ecological Monographs* **46:** 105–28.

Heinrich, B. (1979). *Bumblebee Economics.* Cambridge, Mass. & London: Harvard University.

Heinrich, B. (1993). *The Hot-Blooded Insects: Strategies and Mechanisms of Thermoregulation.* Berlin etc.: Springer-Verlag.

Herrera, C. M. (1990). Daily patterns of pollinator activity, differential pollinating effectiveness, and floral resource availability, in a summer-flowering Mediterranean shrub. *Oikos* **58:** 277–88.

Herrera, J. (1988). Pollination relationships in southern Spanish Mediterranean shrublands. *Journal of Ecology* **76:** 274–87.

Hoffer, E. (1889). *Die Schmarotzerhummeln Steiermarks.* Graz. Nat. Ver.

Hopkins, J. (2003). How is the countryside changing? *British Wildlife* **14(5):** 305–10.

Howse, P. E. & Clement, J.-L. (Eds) (1981). *Biosystematics of Social Insects.* London: Academic.

Hughes, L. (1998). *The Great Yellow Bumblebee,* Bombus distinguendus (Morawitz): *Aspects of Habitat Use, Phenology and Conservation on the Machair of the Outer Hebrides.* M.Sc. Thesis, University College, London.

IBRA/ITE (International Bee Research Association and Institute of Terrestrial Ecology) (1980). *Atlas of the Bumblebees of the British Isles.* Cambridge: ITE.

Imhoof, B. & Schmid-Hempel, P. (1998). Patterns of local adaptation of a protozoan parasite to its bumblebee host. *Oikos* **82:** 59–65.

Imhoof, B. & Schmid-Hempel, P. (1999). Colony success of the bumble bee, *Bombus terrestris* in relation to infections by two protozoan parasites, *Crithidia bombi* and *Nosema bombi. Insectes Sociaux* **46:** 233–8.

Intenthron, M. & Gerrard, J. (2003). *Making Nests for Bumblebees.* Cardiff: International Bee Research Association.

Janzen, D. H. (1980). When is it coevolution? *Evolution* **34(3):** 611–2.

Johnson, S. D. & Steiner, K. E. (2000). Generalisation versus specialisation in plant pollination systems. *Trends in Ecology and Evolution* **15(4):** 140–3.

Jones, D. (1983). *The Country Life Guide to Spiders of Britain and Northern Europe.* Hamlyn.

Jordano, P. (1987). Patterns of mutualistic interactions in pollination and seed dispersal: connectance, dependence asymmetries, and coevolution. *The American Naturalist* **129(5):** 657–77.

Kay, A. (2002). Applying optimal foraging theory to assess nutrient availability ratios for ants. *Ecology* **83(7):** 1935–44.

Kearns, C. A., Inouye, D. W. & Waser, N. M. (1998). Endangered mutualisms: the conservation of plant-pollinator interactions. *Annual Review of Ecology and Systematics.* **29:** 83–112.

Keller, L. & Nonacs, P. (1993). The role of queen pheromones in social insects: queen control or queen signal? *Animal Behaviour* **45:** 787–94.

Kells, A. R., Holland, J. & Goulson, D. (2001). The value of uncropped field margins for foraging bumblebees. *Journal of Insect Conservation* **5:** 283–91.

King, M. J. (1993). Buzz foraging mechanism

of bumblebees. *Journal of Apicultural Research* **32:** 41–9.

Konig, C. & Schmid-Hempel, P. (1995). Foraging activity and immunocompetence in workers of the bumble bee *Bombus terrestris* L. *Proceedings of the Royal Society of London, B* **260:** 225–7.

Kosiov, A. (1995). Changes in the fauna of bumble-bees (*Bombus* Latr.) and cuckoo-bees (*Psithyrus* Lep.) in selected regions of southern Poland. *In:* Banaszak, J., *op. cit.*

Koulianos, S. & Schmid-Hempel, P. (2000). Phylogenetic relationships among bumble bees (*Bombus,* Latreille) inferred from mitochondrial cytochrome *b* and cytochrome oxidase 1 sequences. *Molecular Phylogenetics and Evolution* **14(3):** 335–41.

Krüger, E. (1917). Zur systematic der mitteleuropaischen hummeln (Hym.). *Entomologische Mitteilungen* **6:** 55–66.

Kukuk, P. F. (1992). Cannibalism in social bees. *In:* Elgar M. A. & Crespi B. J. (Eds) *Cannibalism: Ecology and Evolution among Diverse Taxa.* Oxford: Oxford University.

Kullenberg, B. (1973). Field experiments with sexual attractants on Aculeate males. II. *Zoon Suppl.* **1:** 31–42.

Kullenberg, B., Bergstrom, G., Bringer, B., Carlberg, B. & Cederberg, B. (1973). Observations on scent marking by *Bombus* Latr. and *Psithyrus* Lep. males (Hym., Apidae) and localization of the site of production of the secretion. *Zoon Suppl.* **1:** 23–9.

Kullenberg, B., Bergstrom, G., & Stallberg-Stenhagen, S. (1970). Volatile components of the cephalic marking secretion of male bumblebees. *Acta Chemica Scandinavica* **24:** 1481–3.

Kunin, W. E. (1997). Population biology and rarity: on the complexity of density-dependence in insect-plant interactions. *In:* Kunin, W. E. & Gason, K. J. (Eds) *The Biology of Rarity.* London: Chapman & Hall: 150–73.

Küpper, G. & Schwammberger, K. H. (1995). Parasitism in bumble bees (Hymenoptera, Apidae): observations on *Psithyrus sylvestris* in *Bombus pratorum* nests. *Apidologie* **26(3):** 245–54.

Kwak, M. M., van den Brand, C., Kremer, P., & Boerrigter, E. (1991). Visitation, flight distances and seed set in populations of the rare species *Phyteuma nigrum* (Campanulaceae). *In:* van Heemert, C. & de Ruijter, A. (Eds) *Sixth International Symposium on Pollination.* Tilburg: Research Centre for Insect Pollination & International Society for Horticultural Science: 303–7.

La Ferla, B. (2000). Bee-flower interactions: a field test of an optimal foraging hypothesis. *Journal of Biological Education* **34(3):** 147–51.

Larson, B. M. H. & Barrett, S. C. H. (1999). The ecology of pollen limitation in buzz-pollinated *Rhexia virginica* (Melastomataceae) *Journal of Ecology* **87:** 371–81.

Larson, B. M. H. & Barrett, S. C. H. (2000). A comparative analysis of pollen limitation in flowering plants. *Biological Journal of the Linnean Society* **69:** 503–20.

Laverty, T. M. (1994). Bumblebee learning and floral morphology. *Animal Behaviour* **47:** 531–45.

Laverty, T. M. & Plowright, R. C. (1988). Bumblebee learning and flower morphology. *Animal Behaviour* **36:** 733–40.

Lepeletier de Saint-Fargeau, A. L. M. (1832). Observations sur l'ouvrage intitule: 'bombi scandinaviae monographice tractato, etc. a Gustav. Dahlbohm.'. *Annales de la Societe Entomologique de France* **1:** 366–82.

Liersch, S. & Schmid-Hempel, P. (1998). Genetic variation within social insect colonies reduces parasite load. *Proceedings of the Royal Society of London, B* **265:** 221–5.

Løken, A. (1973). Studies on Scandinavian Bumble bees (Hymenoptera, Apidae). *Norsk Entomologisk Tidsskrift* **20:** 1–218.

Løken, A. (1984). Scandinavian Species of the Genus Psithyrus Lepeletier (Hymenoptera: Apidae). *Entomologia Scandinavica,* Supplement 23. Stockholm.

Lopez-Vaamonde, C., Koning, J. W., Jordan, W. C. & Bourke, A. F. G. (2003). No evidence that reproductive bumblebee workers reduce the production of new queens. *Animal Behaviour* **66:** 577–84.

Lopez-Vaamonde, C., Koning, J. W., Brown, R. M., Jordan, W. C. & Bourke, A. F. G. (2004a). Social parasitism by male-producing reproductive workers in a eusocial insect. *Nature* **430:** 557–60.

Lopez-Vaamonde, C., Koning, J. W., Jordan, W. C. & Bourke, A. F. G. (2004b). A test of information use by reproductive bumblebee workers. *Animal Behaviour* **68:** 611–18.

Lundberg, H. & Svensson, Bo G. (1975). Studies on the behaviour of *Bombus* Latr. species (Hym., Apidae) parasitized by *Sphaerularia bombi* Dufour (Nematoda) in an alpine area. *Norwegian Journal of Entomology* **22:** 129–34.

Mabey, R. (1973). *The Unofficial Countryside.* London: Collins.

Maccagnani, B., Velthuis, H. H. W. & Duchateau, M. J. (1994). Mating behaviour in *Bombus terrestris* L. (Hymenoptera, Apidae). *Les Insectes Sociaux* (abstract cited in Vander Meer, R. K. *et al.* (1998), *op. cit.*)

McCall, C. & Primack, R. B. (1992). Influence of flower characteristics, weather, time of day and season on insect visitation rates in three plant communities. *American Journal of Botany* **79:** 434–42.

Macdonald, M. A. (1998a). The status and distribution of *Bombus* and *Psithyrus* bees in north and west Scotland. *Highland Biological Recording Group Newsletter* **11:** 29–33.

Macdonald, M. A. (1998b). The feeding ecology of some *Bombus* and *Psithyrus* bumble-bees (Hym., Apidae) in northern Scotland. *The Scottish Naturalist* **110:** 51–104.

Macdonald, M. A. (1999). A contribution to the *Bombus magnus/lucorum* debate. BWARS Newsletter. Autumn: 9.

Macdonald, M. A. (2000a). Observations on *Bombus soroeensis* (Fabr.) (Hym., Apidae) in northern Scotland. *The Scottish Naturalist* **112:** 45–53.

Macdonald, M. A. (2000b). Ecological observations on *Bombus jonellus* (Kirby) (Hym., Apidae) in Northern Scotland. *The Scottish Naturalist* **112:** 3–14.

Macdonald, M. A. (2001). The colonisation of northern Scotland by *Bombus terrestris* (L.) and *B. lapidarius* (L.) (Hym. Apidae), and the possible role of climate change. *The Entomologists' Monthly Magazine* **137:** 1–13.

MAFF/ DEFRA various dates *Farming* UK. HMSO.

Mangel, M. & Clark, C. W. (1986). Towards a unified foraging theory. *Ecology* **67(5):** 1127–38.

Marshall, E. J. P. & Smith, B. D. (1987). Field margin flora and fauna: interactions with agriculture. *In*: Way J. M. & Grieg-Smith P. W. (Eds) *Field Margins.* Thornton Heath: British Crop Protection Council.

Matheson, A. (Ed.) (1996). *Bumblebees for Pleasure and Profit.* Cardiff: International Bee Research Association.

Matheson, A., Buchmann, S. L., O'Toole, C., Westrich, P. & Williams, I. (Eds) (1996). *The Conservation of Bees.* London etc.: Academic.

Mayfield, M. M., Waser, N. M. & Price, M. V. (2001). Exploring the 'most effective pollinator principle' with complex flowers:

bumblebees and *Ipomopsis* aggregate. *Annals of Botany* **88**: 591–6.

Meek, W. R., Carvell, C., Pywell, R., Nowakowski, M., Sparks, T., Loxton, D., Skidmore, P., Bell, D., Croxton, P., Warman, E., Lobel, S. & Walker, K. (2004). *The BUZZ Project Technical Report 2003.* Report to The Farmed Environment Company/ Syngenta Ltd./ Unilever/ Defra.

Menzel, R. (1999). Memory dynamics in the honeybee. *Journal of Comparative Physiology A* **185**: 323–40.

Menzel, R. (2001). Behavioural and neural mechanisms of learning and memory as determinants of flower constancy. Ch. 2 in Chittka, L. & Thomson, J. D., *op. cit.*

Menzel, R. & Erber, J. (1978). Learning and memory in bees. *Scientific American* **239**(1): 102–8.

Michener, C. D. (1974). *The Social behaviour of the Bees.* Cambridge, Mass.: Harvard University.

Moret, Y. & Schmid-Hempel, P. (2000). Survival for immunity: the price of immune system activation for bumblebee workers. *Science* **290**: 1166–8.

Morley, C. (1899). *The Hymenoptera of Suffolk. Part 1: Aculeata.* Plymouth: J. H. Keys.

Morris, W. F. (1996). Mutualism denied? Nectar-robbing bumblebees do not reduce female or male success of bluebells. *Ecology* **77**: 145162.

Morse, D. H. (1982). Behaviour and ecology of bumble bees. *In:* Hermann, H. R. (Ed.) *Social Insects.* Vol. 3. New York: Academic Press.

Morse, D. H. (1986). Predatory risk to insects foraging at flowers. *Oikos* **46**: 223–8.

Mortimer, C. H. (1922). A new British *Bombus, nigrescens* (Perez), from Sussex. *The Entomologist's Monthly Magazine* **58**: 16–17.

Müller, C. B. (1993). *The Impact of Conopid Parasites on Life History Variation and Behavioural Ecology of Bumblebees.* Basel: Ph. D. Thesis.

Müller, C. B. (1994). Parasitoid-induced digging behaviour in bumblebee workers. *Animal Behaviour* **48**: 961–6.

Müller, C. B. & Schmid-Hempel, P. (1992*a*). Correlates of reproductive success among field colonies of *Bombus lucorum*: the importance of growth and parasites. *Ecological Entomology* **17**: 343–53.

Müller, C. B. & Schmid-Hempel, P. (1992*b*). Variation in life-history pattern in relation to worker mortality in the bumble-bee *Bombus lucorum. Functional Ecology* **6**: 48–56.

Müller, C. B. & Schmid-Hempel, R. (1992). To die for host or parasite? *Animal Behaviour* **44**: 177–9.

Müller, C. B. & Schmid-Hempel, P. (1993) Exploitation of cold temperature as defence against parasitoids in bumblebees. *Nature* **363**: 65–6.

Müller, C. B., Shykoff, J. A. & Sutcliffe, G. H. (1992). Life history patterns and opportunities for queen-worker conflict in bumblebees (Hymenoptera: Apidae). *Oikos* **65**: 242–8.

Mustajärvie, K, Siikamäki, P., Rytkönen, S. & Lammi, A. (2001). Consequences of plant population size and density for plant-pollinator interactions and plant performance. *Journal of Ecology* **89**: 80–7.

Nature Conservancy Council (1987). *13th Report.* Peterborough: NCC.

Newsholm, E. A., Crabtree, B., Higgins, S. J., Thornton, S. D. & Start, C. (1972). The activities of fructose diphosphatase in flight muscles from the bumble-bee and the role of this enzyme in heat generation. *Biochemical Journal* **128**: 89–97.

Ney-Nifle, M., Kaesar, T. & Shmida, A. (2001). Location and color learning in bumblebee in a two-phase conditioning experiment. *Journal of Insect Behaviour* **14**(5): 697–711.

Nisbet, G. E. (2004a). The ecology of the bumblebee *Bombus jonellus* (Kirby) (Hym., Apidae), in the Central Highlands of Scotland. *The Entomologist's Monthly Magazine* **140**: 69–88.

Nisbet, G. E. (2004b). The ecology of the bumblebee *Bombus monticola* Smith (Hym., Apidae) in the Central Highlands of Scotland. *The Entomologist's Monthly Magazine* **140**: 193–214.

Nisbet, G. E. (2005) A Comparison of the Phenology and Ecology of Bumblebees, *Bombus* spp. (Hym. Apidae) in the Central Highlands of Scotland. *The Entomologist's Monthly Magazine* **141**.

O'Donnell, S., Reichardt, M. & Foster, R. (2000). Individual and colony factors in bumble bee division of labour (*Bombus bifarius nearcticus* Handl; Hymenoptera, Apidae). *Insectes Sociaux* **47**: 164–70.

Ohashi, K. & Yahara, T. (1999). How long to stay on, and how often to visit a flowering plant? *Oikos* **86**: 386–92.

Oleson, J. M. (1994). A fatal growth pattern and ways suspected of postponing death: corm dynamics of the perennial herb *Corydalis cava*. *Botanical Journal of the Linnean Society* **115**: 95–113.

Osborne, J. L., Clark, S. J., Morris, R. J., Williams, I. H., Riley, J. R., Smith, A. D., Reynolds, D. R. & Edwards, A. S. (1999). A landscape-scale study of bumble bee foraging range and constancy, using harmonic radar. *Journal of Applied Ecology* **36**: 519–33.

Osborne, J. L. & Williams, I. H. (1996). Bumblebees as pollinators of crops and wild flowers. *In*: Matheson, A., op. cit.

Owen, J. (1991). *The Ecology of a Garden.* Cambridge: Cambridge University.

Pamilo, P., Pekkarinen, A. & Varvio, S.-L. (1987). Clustering of bumblebee subgenera based on interspecific genetic relationships (Hymenoptera, Apidae:

Bombus and *Psithyrus*). *Annales Zoologici Fennici* **24**: 19–27.

Pamilo, P. Tengo, J., Rasmont, P., Pirhonen, K., Pekkarinen, A. & Kaarnama, E. (1997). Pheromonal and enzyme genetic characteristics of the *Bombus lucorum* species complex in northern Europe. *Entomologica Fennica* **7**: 187–94.

Parker, G. A. & Maynard-Smith, J. (1990). Optimality theory in evolutionary biology. *Nature* **348**: 27–33.

Payne, R. G. & Harvey, P. R. (1996). The natural history of the Thames Terraces at West Tilbury. *The Essex Naturalist (New Series)* **13**: 121–130.

Pedersen, B. V. (1996). A phylogenetic analysis of cuckoo bumblebees (*Psithyrus*, Lepeletier) and bumblebees (*Bombus*, Latreille) inferred from sequences of the mitochondrial gene cytochrome oxidase 1. *Molecular Phylogenetics and Evolution* **5(2)**: 289–97.

Pedersen, B .V. (2002). European bumblebees (Hymenoptera: Bombini) – phylogenetic relationships inferred from DNA sequences. *Insect Systematics and Evolution* **33(4)**: 361–86.

Pereboom, J. J. M. (2000). The composition of larval food and the significance of exocrine secretions in the bumblebee *Bombus terrestris*. *Insectes Sociaux* **47**: 11–20.

Philp, E. G. (1997). Species account: *Bombus rupestris* (Fabricius, 1793) [Apidae: Apinae]. BWARS Newsletter. Autumn: 21.

Philp, E. G. (1998). Species Profile: *Bombus sylvarum* (Linnaeus, 1761) [Apidae: apinae]. BWARS Newsletter. Spring: 28.

Philp, E. G. & Edwards, M. (2001). *Bombus sylvarum* (Linnaeus, 1761). *In*: Edwards, R. & Telfer, M. G., op. cit.

Pierce, G. J. & Ollason, J. G. (1987). Eight reasons why optimal foraging theory is a complete waste of time. *Oikos* **49(1)**: 111–8.

Pinchen, B. J. (2003). *Bumblebees on Ex-arable and Gravel Extraction Land.* Unpublished report.

Pinchen, B. J. (2004). *Martin Down National Nature Reserve: Bumblebee Forage Plant Use and Pollen Studies.* Report for English Nature.

Pinchen, B. J. & Edwards, M. (2000). *Pre-Recovery Project:* Bombus monticola *Smith. Survey Work and Report.* Unpublished Report.

Pinchen, B. J. & Wright, A. (2001). *Pre-Recovery Project* Bombus monticola *Smith. Survey Work and Report.* Unpublished report.

Plant, C. W. & Harvey, P. R. (1997). *Biodiversity Action Plan. Invertebrates of the South Essex Thames Terrace Gravels – Phase 1: Characterisation of the Existing Resource.* Report. Peterborough: English Nature.

Plath, O. E. (1934). *Bumblebees and their Ways.* New York: Macmillan.

Plowright, R. C. & Laverty, T. M. (1984). The ecology and sociobiology of bumblebees. *Annual Review of Entomology* **29:** 175–9.

Plowright, R. C., Thomson, J. D., Leftkovitch, L.P. & Plowright, C. M. S. (1993). An experimental study of the effect of colony resource level manipulation on foraging for pollen by worker bumble bees (Hymenoptera: Apidae). *Canadian Journal of Zoology* **71:** 1393–6.

Poinar, G. O. & van der Laan, P. A. (1972). Morphology and life history of *Sphaerularia bombi. Nematologica* **18:** 239–52.

Poulin, R. (1992). Altered behaviour in parasitized bumblebees: parasite manipulation or adaptive suicide? *Animal Behaviour* **44:** 174–6.

Pretty, J. N. (2002). *Agri-Culture: Reconnecting People, Land and Nature.* London: Earthscan.

Proctor, M., Yeo, P. & Lack, A. (1996). *The Natural History of Pollination.* New Naturalist. London: HarperCollins.

Prŷs-Jones, O. E. (1986). Foraging behaviour and the activity of substrate cycle enzymes in bumblebees. *Animal Behaviour* **34:** 609–11.

Prŷs-Jones, O. E. & Corbet, S. A. (1991). *Bumblebees.* Slough: Richmond Publishing.

Pyke, G. H. (1979). Optimal foraging in bumblebees: rule of movement between flowers in inflorescences. *Animal Behaviour* **27:** 1167–81.

Pyke, G. H. (1980). Optimal foraging in bumblebees: calculation of net rate of energy intake and optimal patch choice. *Theoretical Population Biology* **17:** 232–46.

Rackham, O. (1986). *The History of the Countryside.* London & Melbourne: Dent.

Raguso, R. A. (2001) Floral scent, olfaction, and scent-driven behaviour. Ch. 5 in Chittka, L. & Thomson, J. D., *op. cit.*

Rasheed, S. A. & Harder, L. D. (1997*a*). Economic motivation for plant-species preferences of pollen-collecting bumble bees (Apidae, Hymenoptera, *Bombus*). *Ecological Entomology* **22:** 209–19.

Rasheed, S. A. & Harder, L. D. (1997*b*). Foraging currencies for non-energetic resources: pollen collection by bumblebees. *Animal Behaviour* **54:** 911–26.

Rasmont, P. (1995). How to restore Apoid diversity in Belgium and France? Right and wrong ways, or the end of protection paradigm. *In:* Banaszak, J., *op. cit.*

Rasmont, P. & Mersch, P. (1988). Premiere estimation de la derive faunique chez les bourdons de la Belgique (Hymenoptera, Apidae). *Annales de la Societe Royale Zoologique de Belgique* **118(2):** 141–7.

Ratnieks, F. L. W. (1988). Reproductive harmony via mutual policing by workers in eusocial Hymenoptera. *American Naturalist* **132:** 217–36.

Real, L. (Ed.) (1983). *Pollination Biology.* Orlando etc.: Academic.

Ribiero, M. F., Velthuis, H. H. W., Duchateau, M. J. & van der Tweel, I. (1999). Feeding frequency and caste differentiation in *Bombus terrestris* larvae. *Insectes Sociaux* **46:** 306–14.

Richards, A. J. (1997). *Plant Breeding Systems.* London: Chapman & Hall.

Richards, A. J. (2001). Does low biodiversity resulting from modern agricultural practice affect crop pollination and yield? *Annals of Botany* **88:** 165–72.

Richards, K. W. (1973). Biology of *Bombus polaris* Curtis and *B. hyperboreus* Schoenherr at Lake Hazen, Northwest Territories (Hymenoptera: Bombini). *Quaestiones Entomologicae* **9:** 115–57.

Richards, L. A. & Richards, K. W. (1976). Parasitid mites associated with bumblebees in Alberta, Canada (Acarina: parasitidae; Hymenoptera: Apidae). II. Biology, *Kansas University Scientific Bulletin* **51:** 1–18.

Richards, O. W. (1968). The subgeneric divisions of the genus *Bombus* Latreille (Hymenoptera: Apidae). *Bulletin of the British Museum (Natural History): Entomology Series* **22:** 209–76.

Rose, S. (1997). *Lifelines.* Harmondsworth: Allen Lane/Penguin.

Röseler, P.-F. & Röseler, I. (1977). Dominance in bumblebees. *Proceedings of 8th International Congress of I U S S I*: 232–5.

Röseler, P.-F., Röseler, I. & van Honk, C. G. J. (1981). Evidence for inhibition of corpora allata activity in workers of *Bombus terrestris* by a pheromone from the queen's mandibular glands. *Experientia* **37:** 348–51.

Röseler, P.-F. & van Honk, C. G. J. (1990). Castes and reproduction in bumblebees. *In*: Engels, W., *op. cit.*: 147–66.

Saunders, E. (1896). *The Hymenoptera Aculeata of the British Islands.* London: L. Reeve & Co.

Saville, N. M., Dramstad, W. E., Fry, G. L. A., & Corbet, S. A. (1997). Bumblebee movement in a fragmented agricultural landscape. *Agriculture, Ecosystems and Environment* **61:** 145–54.

Schmid-Hempel, P. (1998). *Parasites in Social Insects.* Princeton, NJ: Princeton University.

Schmid-Hempel, P. (2001). On the evolutionary ecology of host-parasite interactions: addressing the question with regard to bumblebees and their parasites. *Naturwissenschaften* **88:** 147–58.

Schmid-Hempel, P. & Durrer, S. (1991). Parasites, floral resources and reproduction in natural populations of bumblebees. *Oikos* **62:** 342–50.

Schmid-Hempel, P. & Loosli, R. (1998). A contribution to the knowledge of *Nosema* infections in bumble bees (*Bombus* spp.). *Apidologie* **29:** 525–35.

Schmid-Hempel, P., Müller, C. B., Schmid-Hempel, R. & Shykoff, J. A. (1990). Frequency and ecological correlates of parasitism by conopid flies (Conopidae, Diptera) in populations of bumblebees. *Insectes Sociaux* **37(1):** 14–30.

Schmid-Hempel, P., Puhr, K., Krüger, N., Reber, C. & Schmid-Hempel, R. (1999). Dynamic and genetic consequences of variation in horizontal transmission for a microparasitic infection. *Evolution* **53(2):** 426–34.

Schmid-Hempel, P. & Schmid-Hempel, R. (1993). Transmission of a pathogen in *Bombus terrestris*, with a note on division of labour in social insects. *Behavioral Ecology and Sociobiology* **33:** 319–27.

Schmid-Hempel, P. & Wolf, T. (1988). Foraging effort and life span of workers in a social insect. *Journal of Animal Ecology* **57:** 500–21.

Schmid-Hempel R. & Müller, C. B. (1991). Do parasitised bumblebee forage for their colony? *Animal Behaviour* **41:** 910–12.

Schmid-Hempel, R. & Schmid-Hempel, P. (1989). Superparasitism and larval competition in conopid flies (Dipt., Conopidae), parasitizing bumblebees

(Hym., Apidae). *Mitteilungen Schweizerischen Entomologischen Gesellschaft* **62:** 279–89.

Schmid-Hempel, R. & Schmid-Hempel, P. (1996*a*). Host choice and fitness correlates for conopid flies parasitising bumblebees. *Oecologia* **107:** 71–8.

Schmid-Hempel, R. & Schmid-Hempel, P. (1996*b*). Larval development of two parasitic flies (Conopidae) in the common host, *Bombus pascuorum*. *Ecological Entomology* **21:** 63–70.

Schmid-Hempel, R. & Schmid-Hempel, P. (1998). Colony performance and immunocompetence of a social insect, *Bombus terrestris*, in poor and variable environments. *Functional Ecology* **12:** 22–30.

Schoener, T. W. (1979). generality of the size-distance relation in models of optimal foraging. *American Naturalist* **114:** 902–14.

Schousboe, C. (1987). Deutonymphs of *Parasitellus* phoretic on Danish bumblebees (Parasitidae, Mesostigmata; Apidae, Hymenoptera). *Acarologia* XXVIII, **1:** 37–41.

Schulke, B. & Waser, N. M. (2001). Long-distance pollinator flights and pollen dispersal between populations of *Delphinium nuttallianum*. *Oecologia* **127:** 239–45.

Schwarz, H. & Huck, K. (1997). Phoretic mites use flowers to transfer between foraging bumblebees. *Insectes Sociaux* **44:** 303–10.

Schwarz, H. H., Huck, K. & Schmid-Hempel, P. (1996). Prevalence and host preferences of mesostigmatic mites (Acari: Anactinochaeta) phoretic on Swiss bumble bees (Hymenoptera: Apidae). *Journal of the Kansas Entomological Society* **69(4):** 35–42.

Sherman, P. W., Seeley, T. D. & Reeve, H. K. (1988). Parasites, pathogens, and polyandry in social Hymenoptera. *The American Naturalist* **131(4):** 602–10.

Shoard, M. (2002). Edgelands. *In:* J. Jenkins (Ed.) *Remaking the Landscape*. London: Profile.

Shuckard, W. E. (1866). *British Bees*. London: Lovell & Reeve.

Shykoff, J. A. & Schmid-Hempel, P. (1991*a*). Genetic relatedness and eusociality: parasite-mediated selection on the genetic composition of groups. *Behavioral Ecology and Sociobiology* **28:** 371–6.

Shykoff, J. A. & Schmid-Hempel, P. (1991*b*). Parasites delay worker reproduction in bumblebees: consequences for eusociality. *Behavioral Ecology* **2(3):** 242–7.

Skovgaard, O. S. (1936). *Rødkløverens Bestøvning Humlebier og Humelboer*. Copenhagen: Levin & Munksgaard.

Sladen, F. W. L. (1989) [1912]. *The Humble-bee: its life history and how to domesticate it*. Little Logaston: Logaston.

Soper, M. H. R. & Carter, E. S. (1991). *Farming and the Countryside*. Ipswich: Farming Press.

Sowig, P. (1989). Effects of flowering plant's patch size on species composition of pollinator communities, foraging strategies, and resource partitioning in bumblebees (Hymenoptera: Apidae). *Oecologia* **78:** 550–8.

Spaethe, J., Tautz, J. & Chittka, L. (2001). Visual constraints in foraging bumblebees: flower size and color affect search time and flight behavior. *Proceedings of the National Academy of Science, USA* **98:** 3898–903.

Stearns, S. C. & Schmid-Hempel, P. (1987). Evolutionary insights should not be wasted. *Oikos* **49(1):** 118–25.

Stebbins, G. L. (1970). Adaptive radiation of reproductive characteristics in angiosperms. 1. Pollination mechanisms. *Annual Review of Ecology and Systematics* **1:** 307–26.

Steffan-Dewenter, I. & Tscharntke, T. (1999). Effects of habitat isolation on pollinator communities and seed set. *Oecologia* **121:** 432–40.

Steffan-Dewenter, I. & Tscharntke, T. (2002). Insect communities and biotic interactions on fragmented calcareous grasslands – a mini review. *Biological Conservation* **104:** 275–84.

Step, E. (1932). *Bees, Wasps, Ants and Allied Insects of the British Isles.* London & New York: Warne.

Stephens, D. W. & Krebs, J. R. (1986). *Foraging Theory.* Princeton, N. J.: Princeton University.

Stoate, C. (1996). The changing face of lowland farming and wildlife Part 2: 1945–1995. *British Wildlife* **7(3):** 162–72.

Stout, J. C., Allen, J. A. & Goulson, D. (1998). The influence of relative plant density and floral morphological complexity on the behaviour of bumblebees. *Oecologia* **117:** 543–550.

Stout, J. C., Allen, J. A. & Goulson, D. (2000). Nectar robbing and seed set: Bumblebees foraging on the self incompatible plant *Linaria vulgaris* (Scrophulariaceae). *Acta Oecologica* **(4–5):** 277–83.

Stout, J. C. & Goulson, D. (2001). The use of conspecific and interspecific scent marks by foraging bumblebees and honeybees. *Animal Behaviour* **62:** 183–9.

Stout, J. C., Goulson, D. & Allen, J. A. (1998). Repellent scent marking of flowers by a guild of foraging bumblebees (*Bombus spp.*). *Behavioral Ecology and Sociobiology* **43:** 317–26.

Svensson, B., Lagerlof, J. & Svensson, Bo G. (2000). Habitat preferences of nest-seeking bumble bees (Hymenoptera: Apidae) in an agricultural landscape. *Agriculture, Ecosystems and Environment* **77:** 247–55.

Svensson, Bo G. (1979a). *Pyrobombus lapponicus* auct., in Europe recognised as two species: *P. lapponicus* (Fabricius, 1793) and *P. monticola* (Smith, 1849)

(Hymenoptera, Apoidea, Bombinae). *Entomologica Scandinavica* **10:** 279–96.

Svensson, Bo G. (1979b). Patrolling behaviour of bumble bee males (Hymenoptera, Apidae) in a subalpine/alpine area, Swedish Lapland. *Zoon* **7:** 67–94.

Svensson, Bo G. & Lundberg, H. (1977). Distribution of bumble bee nests in a subalpine/ alpine area in relation to altitude and habitat (Hymenoptera, Apidae). *Zoon* **5:** 63–72.

Taylor, K. (2000). Machair – a land with a flower-sweet taste. *British Wildlife* **11(6):** 414–22.

Thomas, C. D. (2000). Dispersal and extinction in fragmented landscapes. *Proceedings of the Royal Society of London. Series B* **267:** 139–45.

Thomson & Chittka (2001) TO COME

Thompson, H. M. (2001). Assessing the exposure and toxicity of pesticides to bumblebees (Bombus sp.). *Apidologie* **32:** 305–21.

Toynton, P. & Ash, D. (2002). Salisbury Plain training area – the British steppes? *British Wildlife* **13(5):** 335–43.

Trivers, R. L. & Hare, H. (1976). Haplodiploidy and the evolution of the social insects. *Science* **191:** 349–63.

Tucker, G. (2004). The burning of uplands and its effect on wildlife. *British Wildlife* **15(4):** 251–7.

UK Biodiversity Steering Group (1995). *Biodiversity: The UK Steering Group Report: Vol. 2 Action Plans.* London: HMSO.

UK Biodiversity Steering Group (1999). *Tranche 2 Action Plans Vol. IV Invertebrates.* Peterborough: English Nature.

Van der Blom, J. (1986). reproductive dominance within colonies of *Bombus terrestris* (L.) *Behaviour* **97:** 37–49.

Vander Meer, R. K., Breed, M. D., Espelie, K. E. & Winston, M. L. (Eds) (1998). *Pheromone*

Communication in Social Insects. Boulder, Colorado and Oxford, UK: Westview.

Van Doorn, A. (1987). Investigation into the regulation of dominance behaviour and of the division of labour in bumblebee colonies (*Bombus terrestris*). *Netherlands Journal of Zoology* **37**(3–4): 255–76.

van Honk, C, G. J., Röseler, P.-F., Velthuis, H. H. W. & Hoogeveen, J. C. (1981a). Factors influencing the egg-laying of workers in a captive *Bombus terrestris* colony. *Behavioral Ecology and Sociobiology* **9**: 9–14.

van Honk. C. G. J., Röseler, P. F., Velthuis, H. H. W. & Malataux, M. E. (1981b). The conquest of a *Bombus terrestris* colony by a *Psithyrus vestalis* female. *Apidologie* **12**: 57–67.

van Honk, C. G. J., Velthuis, H. & Röseler, P. F. (1978). A sex pheromone from the mandibular glands in bumblebee queens. *Experientia* **34**: 838.

von Frisch, K. (1967). *The Dance Language and Orientation of Bees* (tr. L. E. Chadwick). Cambridge Mass.: Harvard University.

von Hagen, E. & Aichorn, A. (2003). *Hummeln.* Nottuln: Fauna Verlag.

Waddington, K. D. (2001). Subjective evaluation and choice behaviour by nectar- and pollen-collecting bees. Ch. 3 in Chittka, L. & Thomson, J. D., *op. cit.*

Waddington, K. D. & Heinrich, B. (1979). The foraging movements of bumblebees on vertical inflorescences: an experimental analysis. *Journal of Comparative Physiology* **134**: 113–17.

Walther-Hellwig, K. & Frankl, R. (2000). Foraging distances of *Bombus muscorum, Bombus lapidarius,* and *Bombus terrestris* (Hymenoptera, Apidae). *Journal of Insect Behaviour.* **13**(2): 239–46.

Waser, N. M., Chittka, L., Price, M., Williams, N. M. & Ollerton, J. (1996). Generalisation in pollination systems, and why it matters. *Ecology* **77**(4): 1043–60.

Wcislo, W. T. (1987). The roles of seasonality, host synchrony, and behaviour in the evolutions and distributions of nest parasites in Hymenoptera (Insecta), with special reference to bees (Apoidea). *Biological Reviews* **62**: 515–43.

Webster, G. & Goodwin, B. (1996). *Form and Transformation.* Cambridge: Cambridge University.

Weise, K., Gribakin, F. G., Popov, A. V. & Renninger, G. (Eds) (1993). *Sensory Systems of Arthropods.* Basel, etc.: Birkhauser.

West, E. I. & Laverty, T. M. (1998). Effect of floral symmetry on flower choice and foraging behaviour of bumble bees. *Canadian Journal of Zoology* **76**: 730–9.

Westrich, P. (1989). *Die Wildbienen Baden-Wurtenbergs.* Stuttgart: Eugen Ulmer.

Westrich, P. (1996). Habitat requirements of central European bees and the problems of partial habitats. *In:* Matheson, A. *et al.,* op. cit.: 1–15.

Wheater, C. P. (1999). *Urban Habitats.* London & New York: Routledge.

Williams, C. S. (1997). Bumblebees in non-natal nests. *Entomologist's Monthly Magazine* **133**: 233–41.

Williams, G. & Hall, M. (1987). The loss of coastal grazing marshes in south and east England, with special reference to east Essex, England. *Biological Conservation* **39**: 243–53.

Williams, I. H. (1996). Aspects of bee diversity and crop pollination in the European Union. *In:* Matheson, A. *et al., op. cit.*

Williams, I. H., Martin, A. P. & White, R. P. (1987). The effect of insect pollination on plant development and seed production in winter oilseed rape (*Brassica napus* L.) *Journal of Agricultural Science* **109**: 135–9.

Williams, P. H. (1982). The distribution and decline of British bumblebees (*Bombus*

Latr.) *Journal of Apicultural Research*
21(4): 236–45.

Williams, P. H. (1985a). *On the Distribution of
Bumble Bees (Hymenoptera, Apidae) with
Particular Regard to Patterns Within the
British Isles.* Cambridge: Ph. D. thesis.

Williams, P. H. (1985b). A preliminary
cladistic investigation of relationships
among the bumble bees (Hymenoptera,
Apidae). *Systematic Entomology* **10:** 239–55.

Williams, P. H. (1986). Environmental
change and the distributions of British
bumble bees (*Bombus* Latr.). *Bee World*
67: 50–61.

Williams, P. H. (1988). Habitat use by
bumble bees (*Bombus* spp.) *Ecological
Entomology* **13:** 223–37.

Williams, P. H. (1989a). Why are there so
many species of bumblebees at
Dungeness? *Botanical Journal of the
Linnaean Society* **101:** 31–44.

Williams, P. H. (1989b). *Bumble Bees and their
Decline in Britain.* Ilford: Central
Association of Beekeepers.

Williams, P. H. (1991). The bumble bees of
the Kahmir Himalaya (Hymenoptera:
Apidae, Bombini). *Bulletin of the British
Museum (Natural History): Entomology Series*
60: 1–204.

Williams, P. H. (1994). Phylogenetic
relationships among bumble bees (*Bombus*
Latr.): a reappraisal of morphological
evidence. *Systematic Entomology* **19:** 327–44.

Williams, P. H. (1998). An annotated
checklist of bumble bees with an analysis
of patterns of description (Hymenoptera:
Apidae, Bombini). *Bulletin of the Natural
History Museum: Entomology Series*
67(1): 79–152.

Williams, P. H. (2000). Are *Bombus lucorum*
and *Bombus magnus* separate species?
BWARS Newsletter. Spring: 15–17.

Williams, P. H. (2005) Does specialization
explain rarity and decline among
bumblebees? A response to Goulson *et al.*
Biological Conservation, **122(1):** 33–43.

Willmer, P. G. (1986). Foraging patterns and
water balance: problems of optimization
for a zerophilic bee, *Chalicodoma sicula.*
Journal of Animal Ecology **55:** 941–62.

Yalden, P. E. (1982). Pollen collected by the
bumblebee *Bombus monticola* Smith in the
Peak District, England. *Journal of Natural
History* **16:** 823–32.

Yarrow, I. H. H. (1954). Some observations
on the genus Bombus, with special
reference to Bombus cullumanus (Kirby)
(Hym. Apidae). *Journal of the Society for
British Entomology* **5:** 34–9.

Yarrow, I. H. H. (1970). Is *Bombus
inexspectatus* (Tkalcu) a workerless obligate
parasite? (Hym. Apidae). *Insectes Sociaux*
17: 95–112.

**Ydenberg, R. C., Welham, C. V. J., Schmid-
Hempel, R., Schmid-Hempel, P. &
Beauchamp, G.** (1994). Time and energy
constraints and the relationships between
currencies in foraging theory. *Behavioral
Ecology* **5:** 28–34.

Zimmerman, M. (1988). Nectar production,
flowering phenology, and strategies for
pollination. *In*: Lovett Doust, J. & Lovett
Doust, L. (Eds) *Plant Reproductive Ecology.*
Oxford: Oxford University.

Index